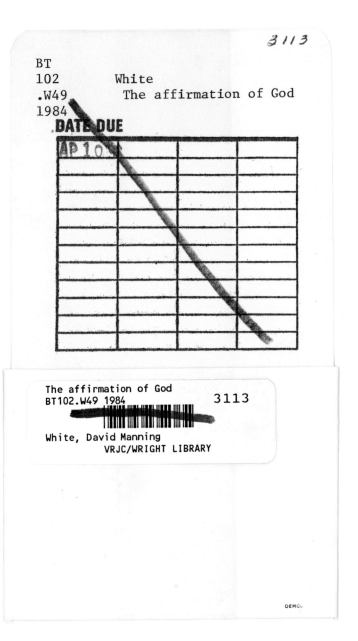

THE AFFIRMATION OF GOD

THE
AFFIRMATION OF
GOD

·

David Manning White

MACMILLAN PUBLISHING COMPANY

New York

COLLIER MACMILLAN PUBLISHERS

London

Macmillan Publishing Company
866 Third Avenue, New York, N.Y. 10022
Collier Macmillan Canada, Inc.

Library of Congress Cataloging in Publication Data
White, David Manning.
The affirmation of God.
Bibliography: p.
Includes indexes.
1. God—Meditations.   I. Title.
BT102.W49 1984   291.2'11   84-9715
ISBN 0-02-626590-7

Macmillan books are available at special discounts
for bulk purchases for sales promotions, premiums, fund-raising,
or educational use.

For details, contact:
Special Sales Director
Macmillan Publishing Company
866 Third Avenue
New York, New York 10022

10 9 8 7 6 5 4 3 2 1

Designed by Jack Meserole

Printed in the United States of America

Ich finde dich in allen diesen Dingen,
denen ich gut und wie ein Bruder bin;
als Samen sonnst du dich in den geringen
und in den grossen giebst du gross dich hin.

Das Stunden-Buch
(Erstes Buch: *Das Buch vom mönchischen Leben,* 1899)
RAINER MARIA RILKE

Contents

Acknowledgments

In preparing a book of this kind, one is dependent upon the goodwill of the publishers and copyright holders of many books. I wish therefore to express my gratitude to the following distinguished publishing houses and acknowledge their gracious permission to reprint material from their books. In some instances it has proved impossible to get in touch with any individual holding proprietary rights. Moreover, if in my attempt to clear permissions I have inadvertently overlooked any matters of this kind, I wish to express my regrets and to assure any concerned parties of my readiness to rectify this in any subsequent edition.

Abingdon Press: *Prayer* by George Arthur Buttrick © *So We Believe, So We Pray* by George Arthur Buttrick; © *Religious Values* by Edgar Brightman © 1925; *Nature and Values* by Edgar Brightman © 1945; *Prayer and the Common Life* by Georgia Harkness © 1948; *The Dark Night of the Soul* by Georgia Harkness © 1945; *The Doctrine of God* by Albert C. Knudson © 1930; *Recoveries in Religion* by Ralph W. Sockman © 1938; *The Highway of God* by Ralph W. Sockman © 1942.

Allen and Unwin, Ltd., London: *Appearance and Reality* by Frances Herbert Bradley © (1916); *Brahma-Sutra* by Sarvepalli Radhakrishnan © (1960); *An Idealist View of Life* by Sarvepalli Radhakrishnan © (1933).

Andrews and McMeel, Inc.: *Dostoevski* by Nicolai Berdyaev © (1934); *The End of Our Time* by Nicolai Berdyaev © (1933).

Moses Asch: For permission to reprint passages from Sholem Asch, *One Destiny* © (1945) and Sholem Asch, *What I Believe* © (1941).

Dr. Peter A. Bertocci for permission to quote from his book, *Introduction to the Philosophy of Religion,* published by Prentice-Hall © (1951).

Geoffrey Bles, Ltd., London: *The Heart of Man* by Gerald Vann © (1944).

Cambridge University Press: *Philosophical Theology* by F. R. Tennant © (1928).

Wm. Collins, Ltd., London: *The Divine Pity* by Gerald Vann © (1972); *Stones or Bread* by Gerald Vann © (1957).

Columbia University Press: *Christianity and the Encounter of the World's Religions* by Paul Tillich © (1963).

Cornell University Press: *Faith and Knowledge* by John Hick © 1957.

Crossroad Publishing Company: From *Meditations on the Sacraments* by Karl Rahner, copyright 1975 by Dimension Books, Inc. This edition and arrangement © 1977 by the Crossroad Publishing Co. From *Foundations of Christian Faith* by Karl Rahner, English translation copyright © 1978 by the Crossroad Publishing Company. Used by permission.

Doubleday and Co. Inc.: *The Roots of Religion in the Human Soul* by John Baillie © (1926); *Under Western Eyes* by Joseph Conrad © (1921); *Notes on Life and Letters* by Joseph Conrad © (1922); *Social Life in the Spiritual World* by Rufus Jones © (1923); *Collected Poems* by Rudyard Kipling; *The Open Door* by Helen Keller © (1957); *On Being a Christian* by Hans Küng © (1976); *Seven Pillars of Wisdom* by T. E. Lawrence © (1936); *The Shoes of Happiness* by Edwin Markham © (1922); *Contemplative Prayer* by Thomas Merton © (1971); *Contemplation in a World of Action* by Thomas Merton © (1971); *Christianity and the Religions of the World* by Albert Schweitzer © (1923).

E. P. Dutton and Co. Inc.: *The Thread of God* by Arthur Christopher Benson, copyright 1907.

William B. Eerdmans Publishing Co.: *The Silence of God* by Helmut Thielicke © (1962).

Epworth Press, London: *The Living God of Nowhere and Nothing* by Nels Ferré © (1966).

Fortress Press: Reprinted from *Life Can Begin Again* by Helmut Thielicke, copyright 1963; *How to Believe Again* by Helmut Thielicke, copyright 1972, by permission of Fortress Press.

Harcourt Brace Jovanovich, Inc.: *Till We Have Faces* by C. S. Lewis © (1952); *No Man Is an Island* by Thomas Merton © (1955); *The Conduct of Life* by Lewis Mumford © (1951); *Flight to Arras* by Antoine de Saint-Exupéry © (1943); *The Little Prince* by Antoine de Saint-Exupéry.

Hollis & Carter, London: *Collected Poems* by Alice Meynell, copyright 1947.

Holt, Rinehart & Winston: *The Two Sources of Morality and Religion* by Henri Bergson © 1935; *The Resources of Religion* by Georgia Harkness © 1936; *The Presidential Papers* by Norman Mailer © 1963; *Life, Mind and Spirit* by Conway Lloyd Morgan © 1926; *The Star of Redemption* by Franz Rosenzweig, translated by William W. Hallo © 1970.

Horizon Press: Reprinted from *Hasidism and Modern Man* by Martin Buber, copyright 1958, by permission of the publisher. Horizon Press, New York.

Judson Press: *God's Revolution and Man's Responsibility* by Harvey Cox © (1965). Used by permission of Judson Press.

Alfred Knopf, Inc.: *The Fall* by Albert Camus © (1958); *The Myth of Sisyphus and Other Essays* by Albert Camus © (1955); *The Plague* by Albert Camus © (1948); *Joseph and His Brothers* by Thomas Mann, translated by H. T. Lowe-Porter © (1943); *Dr. Faustus* by Thomas Mann, translated by H. T. Lowe-Porter © (1948); *Essays and Soliloquies* by Miguel de Unamuno, translated by J. E. Crawford Flitch.

Longman Group Limited, London: *Personal Religion and the Life of Devotion* by William R. Inge © (1924); *Freedom, Love and Truth* by William R. Inge © (1936); *Outspoken Essays* by William R. Inge © (1921); *Things Old and New* by William R. Inge © (1933); *God and the Astronomers* by William R. Inge © (1934); *The Mount of Purification* by Evelyn Underhill © (1946); *The Fruits of the Spirit* by Evelyn Underhill © (1952).

Macmillan Publishing Company: *Letters and Papers from Prison* by Dietrich Bonhoeffer, rev. enlarged ed., Copyright ©

Emerson Fosdick, Copyright 1921. By Permission of New Century Publishers, Inc., Piscataway, N.J.

New Directions: *New Seeds of Contemplation* by Thomas Merton © 1961.

Northwestern University Press: Gabriel Marcel, *Tragic Wisdom and Beyond: Including Conversations between Paul Ricoeur and Gabriel Marcel*. Translated by Stephen Jolin and Peter McCormick. Northwestern University Press, Evanston, Ill. Copyright © 1973.

Ohio University Press: *Potestas Clavium* by Lev Shestov, Copyright © 1969; *Athens and Jerusalem*, Copyright © 1966; *In Job's Balances*, Copyright © 1975.

Open Court Publishing Co.: Reprinted from *The Logic of Perfection and Other Essays in Neoclassical Metaphysics* by Charles Hartshorne, by permission of the Open Court Publishing Company, La Salle, Ill. © 1962; reprinted from *The Point of View* by Paul Carus © 1927.

Paulist Press: Reprinted from Abraham Isaac Kook—*The Lights of Penitence, Lights of Holiness, The Moral Principles, Essays, Letters and Poems*, translated by Ben Zion Bokser, Copyright © 1978 by Ben Zion Bokser. Used by permission of Paulist Press.

Penguin Books, Ltd.: *Christianity and the Social Order* by William Temple, Penguin Special, Copyright 1942 by William Temple.

Philosophic Library, Inc.: *Religion of Tomorrow* by John Elof Boodin © 1943; *The Word of God and the Word of Man* by Karl Barth © 1949; *Dogmatics in Outline* by Karl Barth © 1949; *Hasidism* by Martin Buber © 1948; *The Perennial Scope of Philosophy* by Karl Jaspers © 1949; *Words of Faith* by

François Mauriac © 1955; *Perplexities and Paradoxes* by Miguel de Unamuno © 1945; *Intellectual Foundation of Faith* by Henry Nelson Wieman © 1961.

Princeton University Press: Diasetz T. Suzuki, *Zen and Japanese Culture*, Bollingen Series 64. Copyright © 1959 by Princeton University Press. Excerpt reprinted by permission of Princeton University Press.

Fleming H. Revell Company: *Christianity and Progress* by Harry Emerson Fosdick © 1922; *Sermons* by George Herbert Morrison © 1929.

Routledge & Kegan Paul Ltd., London: *Two Types of Faith* by Martin Buber © 1951; *Man in the Modern Age* by Karl Jaspers © 1951; *Answer to Job* by Carl Jung © 1954; *Notebooks* by Simone Weil © 1956; *Waiting for God* by Simone Weil © 1951.

Schocken Books, Inc.: *Israel and the World* by Martin Buber, Copyright © 1948 by Schocken Books, Inc.; *On Judaism* by Martin Buber, Copyright © 1967 by Schocken Books, Inc.; *Parables* by Franz Kafka, Copyright © 1971 by Schocken Books, Inc.

Charles Scribner's Sons: William Adams Brown, *The Life of Prayer in a World of Science* ©1927; William Adams Brown, *Beliefs That Matter* © 1928; William Adams Brown, *God at Work* © 1933; Emil Brunner, *Our Faith* © 1936; Emil Brunner, *The Theology of Crisis* © 1929; Emil Brunner, *The Word and the World* © 1931; Emil Brunner, *Man in Revolt* © 1939; John Baillie, *The Interpretation of Religion* © 1928; John Baillie, *Our Knowledge of God* © 1939; Martin Buber, *Good and Evil* © 1953; Martin Buber, *I and Thou* © 1958; Nicholas Berdyaev, *the Meaning of History* © 1936; Nicholas Berdyaev, *The Destiny of Man* © 1937; Nicholas Berdyaev, *Freedom and Spirit* ©

1935; Nicholas Berdyaev, *Solitude and Society* © 1938; Henry Sloane Coffin, *Joy in Believing* © 1956; Henry Sloane Coffin, *The Meaning of the Cross* © 1931; William R. Inge, *Faith and Its Psychology* © 1910; Jacques Maritain, *The Range of Reason* © 1952; Jacques Maritain, *Freedom in the Modern World* © 1936; Jacques Maritain, *Ransoming the Time* © 1941; Jacques Maritain, *The Degrees of Knowledge* © 1959; Jacques Maritain, *True Humanism* © 1938; Reinhold Niebuhr, *The Nature and Destiny of Man* © 1941; Reinhold Niebuhr, *Discerning the Signs of the Times* © 1946; Reinhold Niebuhr, *Beyond Tragedy* © 1937; James A. Pike, *Beyond Anxiety* © 1953; Josiah Royce, *Sources of Religious Insight* © 1914; George Santayana, *The Life of Reason* © 1922; George Santayana, *Reason in Religion* © 1926; George Santayana, *Soliloquies in England* © 1923; Paul Tillich, *The New Being* © 1955; Paul Tillich, *The Shaking of the Foundations* © 1948; Henry Van Dyke, *The Builders* © 1897.

Seabury Press, Inc.: From *He Who Lets Us Be* by Geddes MacGregor, Copyright © 1975 by Seabury Press, Inc. Used by permission of the publisher.

Simon & Schuster, Inc.: *Peace of Mind* by Joshua Loth Liebman © 1948.

Stanford University Press: *Exploration into God* by John A. T. Robinson © 1967.

Taplinger Publishing Company, Inc.: From *Reality and Man: An Essay in the Metaphysics of Human Nature* by S. L. Frank, translated by Natalie Duddington (Taplinger Publishing Co., Inc. 1966). Copyright © 1965 by Tatiana Frank. Reprinted by permission.

University of Chicaco Press: Reprinted from *Systematic Theology* by Paul Tillich by permission of the University of Chicago Press © 1951; reprinted from *Biblical Religion and the Search for Ultimate Reality* by Paul Tillich by permisison of the University of Chicago Press © 1952.

Westminster Press: *The Christian Doctrine of God* by Emil Brunner © 1950; *Truth as Encounter* by Emil Brunner © 1964; *Eternal Hope* by Emil Brunner © 1954; *Revelation and Reason* by Emil Brunner © 1946; *The Divine-Human Encounter* by Emil Brunner © 1943; *Christian Freedom in a Permissive Society* by John A. T. Robinson © 1970.

Yale University Press: *The Meaning of God in Human Experience* by William E. Hocking © 1919; *The Courage to Be* by Paul Tillich © 1952.

YMCA Press: *The Meaning of the Creative Act* by Nicolai Berdyaev, Copyright 1955 by YMCA Press, Paris, France.

Introduction

In this anthology's companion volume, *The Search for God,* my wish was to gather a lasting bouquet of the spiritual flowering of seven hundred memorable God Seekers. Their collective quest for Eternal Reality has given the world a repository of religious wisdom that far transcends the credal differences which too often divide humanity. My synthesis of their unceasing exploration of divinity began with the very earliest expressions of the omnipresence of the One God in the Hindu scriptures, where He was called Brahman.

Thus, from the ancient authors of the Rig-Vedas to religious philosophers like Martin Buber and Simone Weil in our day, men and women of great spiritual sensibility have pondered the implications of one universal truth: God is the immanent ground of all that is permanently real. In the words of Sebastian Franck, a little-known sixteenth-century God Seeker, "Man must seek, find, and know God through an interrelation—he must find God in himself and himself in God."

Striving continuously to interpret their lives vis-à-vis God, although often scorned, reviled, and persecuted for their words, the God Seekers have been the perennial conscience of humanity. From Egypt's Ikhnaton and the Hebrew patriarch Abraham, and throughout history, their uncompromising faith has given us, their spiritual heirs, a heritage of immeasurable dimensions.

This second collection of the God Seekers' wisdom may at first seem to have a different point of convergence from its predecessor; but, actually, the two volumes constitute one organic whole. Whereas *The Search for God* might be likened to the first movements of a divine symphony, *The Affirmation of God* is the final resounding movement, a mighty chorus extolling the presence of God as the absolute core of our existence. Seeking, finding, and joyously acknowledging— this is the road each God Seeker must travel in looking for and finally encountering the Ultimate Reality.

Franz Kafka said in one of his parables that man cannot truly live without an enduring belief in something that is indestructible within him. Yet all our life we may be unaware of that indestructible thing and of our trust in it. To follow implicitly the love, compassion, and unlimited power of the indestructible God within us is the leitmotiv of this volume.

C. S. Lewis, in "The Moment of Prayer," pointed out that the door in God that opens is the door that man knocks at. Yet he also recognized that all our talk of "knowing" God is at best an anthropomorphic metaphor, one that has to be balanced by many variants of metaphysical and theological abstractions.

We should, then, recognize the inadequacy of any gender-related symbol such as He or Him to describe the Primal Spirit of all creation. God is totally beyond describing as He or She, or a similarly ungrounded It. So we must inevitably return to the germinal wisdom found in the third chapter of the Book of Exodus in which God answers Moses' fervent plea to reveal his name with the inscrutable "I am that I am."

This passage from the Torah reveals how very clearly the early Hebrews perceived the eternal creativity of God. Their symbolic interpretation of the Divine Name was always written with the Hebrew letters YHWH. These four letters —called the Tetragrammaton—come from the same Hebrew root word meaning "to be." The God they sought *was, is,* and *always will be,* the I AM whose magnitude was beyond their summation.

Indeed, no configuration of words or symbols could ever sum up, describe, or define the Indivisible Unity. Yet, as Paul Tillich reminds us, even when we address God in symbolic terms, every true symbol participates in the reality it symbolizes. So whatever name we give to God, He never forsakes us or any of his creations, for all are equally conceived from the fountainhead of his divine law.

To me, it is inconceivable that the Ultimate Reality underlying all races could ever reject the affirmation of any man or woman, regardless of the form in which it is offered. Does it matter that an Eskimo shaman uses his magic to achieve an underwater journey to the Mother of Animals to assure the abundance of game or to help a barren woman? Or that a Sufi dervish achieves *dhikr* in the paroxysm of a ritual dance? Or that a Hindu yogi seeks the absorption of his individual soul into the All through deep meditation? Whatever road they take, the Eternal Source of Reality is in the heart of each of them.

For most of my life I kept asking myself whether thinking that I am *known* to God wasn't just a presumptuous, self-deceiving illusion? I often asked myself how I dared even consider that the Lord of the Universe, Creator of galaxies beyond counting, could know or care that I existed? In my impatient, pseudoagnostic frustration to "know" and define God, I had concluded that He couldn't possibly have the time or the inclination to "know" me. Enmeshed in my myopic vision, I perceived God as some kind of super-Manager, an overtaxed executive endlessly engaged in cosmic time-and-motion deals.

Many times during the years when I was grappling to discover my own spiritual roots I would look at the vast array of stars in the nightly sky and feel completely insignificant, a zero sum in the universe. Since I couldn't or didn't want even to begin to assimilate the magnitude of God's creativity, I continued to live each day completely immersed in the ways, the problems, and the contradictions of the little planet on which I existed.

Fettered with so dim an overview, it is small wonder that I was overlooking one irrefutable fact. In all of eternity there had never been an entity exactly like me, and there would never be again, once my earthly sojourn was over. I was a unique entity living among countless numbers of other unique beings on a mere dot moving among billions of stars. *Yet each of us was a singular representation of divine will.*

One day I stopped to consider the implications of that fact. As I contemplated the immeasurable architectonic of God's creativity in just the tiny speck of his universe in which I lived, I knew that from that moment on I would never again doubt that *anything* is possible to the Creator of all possibilities.

In the deepest recess of my heart, in that place within myself where all subterfuge and worldly rhetoric cannot hide, I had finally begun to see that God's universe and every single creature existing within it are interrelated and form one interdependent whole. At last I had begun to understand that everything that has ever or will ever exist—whether it be the atoms in an earthworm, the cells in my body, or entire galaxies—was conceptualized by the same Creative Reality. Then, and only then, was I able to finally realize that God could "know" me, even if I were only a miniscule particle in the totality of his creativity.

Thomas R. Kelly, the Quaker mystic, urges us to understand that the nexus between man and God is never, in any sense, one-directional. As he said in his *Testament of Devotion,* "Life is meant to be lived from a Center, a Divine Center. There is a divine abyss within us all, a holy Infinite Center, a Heart, a Life which speaks in us and through us to the world."

We cannot know the Master of all creation's reason for totally encompassing our world in a time-space continuum, but surely we must realize that the magnitude of God transcends all vestiges of time and space.

Once I intuited in the sacred grove of my own soul that God seeks me, even as I seek Him, I began to realize that my temporal bonds are merely one segment of a journey to an Eternal Now. Thus, imbued with a sense of his presence, my fears and anxieties receded and I began to perceive my time-bound life in its true perspective.

One of my deepest wishes in compiling this anthology is to familiarize the general reader with the profound insights, not only of the greatest, but also of some of the lesser-known, religious figures. As I studied the lives of such diverse God Seekers as Mahomed Iqbal, Swami Vivekananda, Sri Ramakrishna, Sri Aurobindo, Abraham Isaac Kook, Leo Baeck, Reinhold Niebuhr, Karl Barth, Jacques Maritain, Simone Weil, and Baha'U'llah I began to empathize deeply with their search for the Ultimate Reality. I recognized how much they shared in common, whether Sufi, Hindu, Jew, Catholic, Protestant, or Bahai. What emerged clearly from each of their voices were thoughts I had long yearned to express in my own personal search.

Drawing upon their own great reservoirs of natural endowment and personality, each of these religious geniuses tried to understand as much as humanly possible of the mystery of God. But they also understood that this mystery had not been formulated by any human. Therefore, not even the greatest of the God Seekers can do more than speculate on the answer to what Jacob Boehme called the *Mysterium Magnum*. God will solve us, not we him.

Throughout this anthology you will find passages from God Seekers of every faith and every era who express exaltation in the mystery of God's universe. From al-Ghazzali and Ibn Arabi to Jalal-ud-din Rumi in the Sufi tradition, from Moses Cordervero and the Baal Shem Tov to Martin Buber among Jewish inquirers, from Dionysius the Areopagite and François Fénelon to Evelyn Underhill in the Christian consuetude, the God Seekers collectively have told us that this mystery defies expression. It suffices for them that God is the Ultimate Reality, the Thou of their existence beyond which nothing can be known or imagined.

In one of his luminous sermons, Meister Eckhart, truly one of the most enlightened God Seekers, opened the door of this mystery a small crack. He said that the great prophets, such as Isaiah, "walking in the light were moved sometimes to return to this world and speak of things they knew, thinking to teach us to know God." Yet when they tried to do this, three things caused them to become tongue-tied, if not virtually mute.

First, Eckhart said, the "good they knew by sight in God was too immense and too mysterious to take definite shape in their understanding." Further, what they perceived in God "revealed God's very self in its immensity and sublimity, and yielded no idea nor any form for them to express." They thus became dumbfounded "because the hidden truth they saw in God, the mystery they found there, was ineffable."

Two hundred fifty years after Eckhart's death, Jacob Boehme became another major voice in the God Seekers' mystic tradition. But where Eckhart graduated as a learned Master of Theology from a famous seminary in Paris, Boehme had virtually no formal schooling. Eckhart, an ordained priest of the Dominican Order, became well known as the vicar-general of all Catholics in Bohemia; Boehme, a Lutheran, spent most of his life as an obscure cobbler. Yet these two extraordinary God Seekers were in the deepest sense spiritual brothers.

Both Eckhart and Boehme, like the prophet Jeremiah in biblical days, were attacked during their lifetimes by their more orthodox coreligionists. Boehme, in fact, was driven away from his home in Görlitz by his detractors, prompting him to comment that "life is a strange bath of thorns and thistles."

Though reviled, laughed at, and spit upon by his fellow townsmen, Boehme, in many ways, is the quintessential God Seeker. Confused and wearied by the endless controversies and scholastic wranglings about religion, Boehme set out to define himself vis-à-vis God. In *Aurora* he describes his poignant, dramatic search this way: "While I was in affliction and trouble, I elevated my spirit and earnestly raised it up unto God, as with a great stress and onset, lifting up my whole heart and mind and will and resolution to wrestle with the love and mercy of God and not to give over unless He blessed me—*then the Spirit did breathe through.*"

Boehme intuitively knew that he must discover *for* himself and *in* himself "the Temple of the Holy Spirit where God's living Word is taught." As he wrote near the end of his life, "What would it profit me if I were continually quoting the Bible and knew the whole book by heart but did not know the Spirit that inspired the holy men who wrote that book, nor the source from which they received their knowledge? How can I expect to understand them in truth, if I have not the same Spirit they had?" Jacob Boehme's arduously honest search for God became the kind of moral fabric from which true affirmation is woven.

We live in a world where American nuclear missiles in West Germany face similar Russian missiles in Czechoslovakia, each with their encoded *dies irae* by which all of civilization may crumble. With this kind of international anxiety, it is small wonder that we are pervaded by "the energy of despair." We appear to be at a crossroad, albeit one where we cannot stop and wait because we are being pushed in every direction.

As I read and reread the perennial wisdom of the God Seekers I am certain that they are nothing less than ambassadors from the Court of Creation, endowed with words that bespeak God's care and compassion for this world. This being so, and with the spectre of nuclear annihilation hovering above us, some responsible, caring leader in this world should quickly convene a global conference based on the Unity of Humanity, an affirmation of the One Master of all creation. The cost of one B-24 bomber or its Soviet counterpart would more than underwrite such a conference.

The delegates would be the clerical leaders and other chosen representatives of every religion in the world. Bretton Woods in New Hampshire or perhaps some locale in England's Lake District could provide an idyllic setting for such a parliament of religions. It should take place in an environment where, for example, the chief rabbi of Israel and his Islamic peer from Saudi Arabia or Pakistan could examine how much they shared in common rather than voicing their areas of disagreement. And both could listen to the views of a Jain leader from India and broaden their understanding of how God is found by all peoples.

They might hear a Sikh read from the divinely inspired poetry of Guru Nanak in his affirmation of the Ultimate Mystery:

> Let knowledge of God be thy food,
> Let mercy keep thy store,
> And listen to the Divine Music
> That beats in every heart.

In one of the informal sessions they might join a small group listening to a grandson of Rabindranath Tagore reciting a portion of the Bhagavad Gita: "I am equal toward all beings; nor is any hated or favored by Me; but they who love Me with dear love, they are in Me and I am in them."

The chief rabbi might tell the assemblage that at the heart of their theology Jews turn to chapter 6 of the Book of Deuteronomy. There, after proclaiming the unity of God in the traditional Shema, they read: "And thou shalt love the Lord thy God with all thy heart, and with all thy soul, and with all thy might."

A Catholic prelate attending the session might turn to a Methodist bishop sitting next to him and say, "Why this is just what Jesus preached! When a lawyer came up to him after one of his great public gatherings and asked which is the greatest commandment in the Torah, Jesus also recited the same verse from Deuteronomy."

"Yes, that's very true," the Methodist bishop would agree with the prelate, "but Jesus also added, 'This is the greatest and first commandment. And a second is like it: "You shall love your neighbor as yourself." On these two commandments depend all the law and the prophets.'"

In this great meeting dedicated to the Affirmation of the Creator, whether sought as Allah, Adonai, Brahman, Ahurah Mazda, Lord God of the Universe, or the Tao, there would be time for long, reflective walks in the burgeoning woods. The beauty of the blooming tulip trees would speak without words of the Creator's manifold gifts to all of his children.

The agenda of the conference would be formulated on the *sine qua non* premise that *all* the peoples of this earth are equally loved by God. Its goal would be to affirm the interdependence of *all* nations under God's law so that we can learn to live together in the full meaning of the word *ecumenical.*

We have drifted too far away from the original sense of this Greek word *oikoumenikos,* i.e., "of the whole world." The power brokers who think they rule this world should also look further into the etymology of *ecumenical.* For its root *oikein* means "to inhabit," and it in turn goes back to *oikos* or "house." It signifies that all humans share the one *oikos* of earth, which they inhabit by the grace of their Eternal Creator.

Theodore Parker, were he still living, would be an ideal keynoter at this Conclave of Unity I envision. He dreamed, as I do, that the peoples of this earth, without needing to forsake any particular form of religious faith, would someday acknowledge that One God of all creation is the Author of all humanity's religious sensibility. This, in Parker's words, is the core of essential religion, "which, like sunshine, goes everywhere; its temple, all space; its shrine, the good heart; its creed, all truth; its ritual, works of love; its profession of faith, divine living."

Let me turn yet one more time to some lines by Rainer Maria Rilke, whose religious poems literally inspired me to begin this anthology:

> You must not wait until God comes to you and says: I am.
> A god who confesses his strength has no meaning.
> You must know that God breathes through you from the beginning of time,
> And when your heart secretly reveals Him to you, then He creates inside it.

In this volume, the God Seekers, after their long search for the divine rationale, now are able to voice their acceptance of the Ultimate Mystery on God's terms. This, then, is my collection of their religious explorations in which they proclaim with a resounding yes their affirmation of God and his universal rule.

I · Finding God

There where the creature ends, God begins to be. God does not ask anything of
you other than you go out of yourself according to your mode as creature and that
you let God be God in you.

—MEISTER ECKHART

Having explored in the companion volume, *The Search for God,* the God Seekers' joyous rationale for the eternal quest, we now will turn to the ways they tell us we can *find* God. For only when the *seeking* and the *finding* combine into a spiritual nexus is the quest truly joined.

It appears that at the precise moment of earth's history that coincides with his eternal plan (and we must always remember that time is a human concept and as irrelevant to him as space or matter), God sends his prophets to the world to teach us the awareness of his presence. If it had been his will these prophets could have appeared three million years ago among the first humans instead of a mere three to four thousand years ago.

It is intriguing to consider the metaphors by which God has revealed himself to the great prophets and sages during various periods of history. Since only God can perceive the incalculable magnitude of himself, can "see" himself, on those occasions when He feels that direct communication with one of his human creatures is in order He appears in a metaphorical form, such as an intensely bright and shining light.

Consider the great religious figures who have "found" God through dramatic theophanies in the wilderness—Moses and the burning bush; Zoroaster and the bright angel of Ahura Mazda on the banks of the river Daiti; Paul, dazed and momentarily blinded on the Damascus Road; or Jesus of Nazareth's baptism in the river Jordan.

Moses did not ask whether he was hallucinating or make a mental note to see his psychiatrist the next day when he saw a burst of flame with an angel in the midst of it, while leading his flock near Mount Horeb. Even when the flame came from a bush that kept burning yet never was consumed, and God's voice emerged from it, Moses did not cry out in disbelief. God, as in his divine call to every prophet, was telling Moses that there was a task that must be done, that he had been chosen to lead his enslaved compatriots in Egypt to freedom, and that this challenge could not be shifted to someone else's shoulders.

The God Seekers, especially the prophets, find the Living God in many symbolic ways. Jeremiah, for example, who had become filled with despair by the dissolute religious practices of his age, found God in an almond tree. During a melancholy walk one winter day Jeremiah saw that a branch of the tree was blossoming. Suddenly God spoke to him, promising that just as that blossoming branch foretold that the coming of spring would bring new life to the earth, so He would soon awaken a seemingly dead faith among the Israelites.

Some of the principal God Seekers, Zoroaster, for example, like Moses before him, questioned their fitness to lead their people. Yet once they were certain and able to forego all doubts that God had spoken to them these master God Finders accepted the divine call to service.

How fiercely Zoroaster must have wrestled with his own doubts as he stood in the door of his cave and watched the transcending fire that filled the mountain. Just as Gautama Buddha would have to grapple with the problem of human suffering a century later, so, too, Zoroaster must have felt the agony of this enigma. The theophany on the banks of the Daiti River, during which the archangel Vohu Manah bade Zoroaster to lay aside his body and follow him into the presence of Ahura Mazda, the God of Light, was similar to the calls that came to many prophets, an overwhelming perception of a great, shining light and a command to go forth and preach.

It is almost as if God had devised a link between those great religious figures under the metaphor of a great light or flame. Moses, Zoroaster, Gautama Buddha, and Paul, were they not all spiritual brothers who found the same Father of the Universe?

Although only a select few have experienced the kind of theophany in which He appears before them, it surely cannot mean that God wishes to be inaccessible to the rest of humankind. Then why, as Bishop Fulton Sheen observed in *Peace of Soul*, have people been hiding from their Creator ever since the days of Adam? Even while we are peeking out from our hiding place we mutter that God is hard to find. To Dr. Sheen, however, the truth is "that in each heart there is a secret garden which God made uniquely for Himself." The garden is locked, like a safety-deposit box, with two keys. If God has one key we cannot let anyone else in but God. Since the human heart has the only other key, not even God can get in without our consent.

We seem to be afraid of the immensity, the complexity, the awesome beauty of God. Rather than face up to our fears we fuel them with bitter frustration when He does not heed our *demands* that He forthwith share all the secrets of his creativity with us.

We throw away the key and fix our sights on a limited God who will conform to the narrow vision of just one species of his limitless acts of creation in the universe. Were it not for his love and compassion for every thing He has created, the heavens might reverberate with God's laughter at the temerity of his children. We have taken his earth-world, itself a mere dot which may not constitute even one trillion-trillionth of God's immensity, and tried to use it as a hiding place from the Master of Creation.

Few poets have experienced deeper concern with exploring the boundaries of our spiritual dimension than Robert Browning. In poem after poem in his voluminous works, Browning returns to the theme of finding God, as in these lines from his *Christmas Eve:*

> What is left for us, save, in growth
> of soul? To rise up, for past both,
> From the gift looking to the giver,
> And from the cistern to the river,
> And from finite to infinity,
> And from man's dust to God's divinity!

In one of his most remarkable essays, "The Over-Soul," Emerson recalled a proverb that stated, "God comes to see us without bell." He interpreted this to mean that just as there is no screen or ceiling separating us from the infinite heavens above us, so there can be no impediments, no walls or bars in the soul "where man, the effect, ceases, and God, the cause, begins."

The God Seekers keep reminding us that God, far from putting roadblocks in our path, never fails to help us find him, nor does He place restrictions on where He can be found. As Meister Eckhart noted in one of his sermons, surely we may find rapport with God in a religious retreat or a solitary prison, but it is also true that He may be found as we gaze into a fireplace. But Eckhart offers this caveat: if you think you can find God by merely reciting some ritual or by some show of devotion in a cathedral or synagogue or mosque, "then you might just as well think you could seize God and wrap a mantle around his head and stick him under the table!"

There is a story about Henry David Thoreau said to have taken place in the weeks shortly before his death at age forty-five from tuberculosis. One of his self-righteous neighbors in Concord, a widow who had always considered Thoreau a bit of an eccentric but who felt it her Christian duty to call upon the dying man, asked him, "Well, Henry, have you made your peace with God?" And Thoreau, although pale and weak, looked right into her eyes and said, "Don't recall that I ever had a quarrel with him."

Far from contending with God, Thoreau found him in every leaf and flower he beheld during the daily hikes that brought so much contentment to his life.

He would have gladly agreed with what the nineteenth-century American preacher Thomas De Witt Talmage said in one of his sermons:

You may take your telescope and sway it across the heavens in order to behold the glory of God; but I will take the leaf holding the spider and the spider's web, and I will bring the microscope to my eyes, and while I gaze and look and study, and am confounded, I will kneel down in the grass and cry, "Great and marvellous are thy works, Lord God Almighty."

There are some who believe that God could not possibly have been "found" before Ikhnaton's short-lived attempt to establish a monotheistic theocracy in Egypt some thirty-five hundred years ago, or Moses' more profound contributions a century or so later. This chauvinistic attitude denies that all the men and women who lived in the previous three or four million years were as much God's children as any of us living today.

Who are we to say that a primitive family of ten or twenty thousand years ago, kneeling before some totem, perhaps a sacred tree or boulder, did not thrill with the thought that somewhere a force, a power beyond their ken, existed? If God's plan for the world involved a physical evolution that saw the emergence of humankind from single-celled beginnings, why shouldn't a spiritual evolution also have been part of his plan?

If we believe in the reality of the Master of the Universe, that He exists as the central core of every single thing He has ever created or ever will create, we must understand that, in some measure or another, God cannot be "lost" to us, and that every human who ever lived has "found" him in his or her individual way.

Even if we choose to evade God in self-destructive negation He is the alpha and omega of our lives, and we cannot run away from him. Through the precepts of love and peace He has sent to us by the greatest of God Seekers, those to whom he dramatically appeared, we know, in our deepest selves, what God desires from us. Although we cannot even begin to speculate how He is perceived by his countless megaquintillions of "other" children who probably exist on the millions of his other planetary manifestations, we can rejoice in the knowledge that *we* can find and affirm him.

· FINDING THE ETERNAL NOW ·

God, always interior to man, and un-yielding, He, the true conscience to the false; a prohibition to the spark to extin-guish itself; an order to the ray to remember the sun; an injunction to the soul to recognize the real absolute when it is con-

fronted with the fictitious absolute; humanity imperishable; the human heart inadmissible; that splendid phenomenon, the most beautiful perhaps of our interior wonders.   VICTOR HUGO (1802–1885)
Les Misérables

Thus saith the Lord, Stand ye in the ways, and see, and ask for the old paths where is the good way, and walk therein, and ye shall find rest for your souls.
The Old Testament
Jeremiah 6:16

It has always been a two-way road. It is a Double Search. God is forever seeking us with the Love that comes down from Above. And man is forever striving for eternal reality and the Beauty of the Lord, our God.   RUFUS JONES (1863–1948)
Sermons

Let any true man go into silence: strip himself of all pretense, and selfishness, and sensuality, and sluggishness of soul; lift off thought after thought, passion after passion, till he reaches the inmost depth of all; remember how short a time and he was not at all; how short a time again, and he will not be here; open his window and look upon the night, how still its breath, how solemn its march, how deep its perspective, how ancient its forms of light; and think how little he knows except the perpetuity of God, and the mysteriousness of life:—and it will be strange if he does not feel the Eternal Presence as close upon his soul as the breeze upon his brow; if he does not say, "O Lord, art thou ever near as this, and have I not known thee?"
JAMES MARTINEAU (1805–1900)
Endeavors After the Christian Life

When you say to God, "O God, take me, for the highest thing that I can do with myself is to give myself to Thee," when you say that to God, humbly, but with all your heart, kneeling all apart in your chamber, where no one can see you, it is bewildering to me to think into what company you are taken instantly by that prayer of devotion. You sweep into the current of the best, the holiest, and the most richly human of our humanity, which in every age has dedicated itself to God. The worshippers of all the world—the Jew, the Greek, the Hindu, the Christian in all his various cultures, take you for their brother.   PHILLIPS BROOKS (1835–1893)
The Battle of Life

The hand of our God is upon all them for good that seek him.
The Old Testament
Ezra 8:22

No man should ever grope outside of his best self to find God. He should always seek the God who is speaking to him in his best self.
HARRY EMERSON FOSDICK (1878–1969)
Sermons

Man without God is a bubble in the sea, a single grain of sand on an infinite beach. Without God, our entire human adventure appears as a side show on a ridiculous star.   PINCUS GOODBLATT (1927–1983)
A Bargain with God

I find the great thing in this world is not so much where we stand, as in what direction we are moving: To reach the port of heaven, we must sail sometimes with the wind and sometimes against it—but we must sail, and not drift, nor lie at anchor.
OLIVER WENDELL HOLMES (1809–1894)
The Autocrat of the Breakfast-Table

Within! within, oh turn
Thy spirit's eyes, and learn
Thy wandering senses gently to control;
Thy dearest Friend dwells deep within
     thy soul,

And asks thyself of thee,
That heart, and mind, and sense, He may
    make whole
In perfect harmony.
                GERHARD TERSTEEGEN (1697–1769)
                                        Hymns

He who sees the Infinite in all things
sees God. He who sees the Ratio only sees
himself only.
                WILLIAM BLAKE (1757–1827)
                There Is No Natural Religion

As he that fears God, fears nothing else,
so he that sees God sees everything else:
when we shall see God as he is we shall see
all things as they are, for that is their essence as they conduce to his glory. We
shall be no more deluded with outward
appearances, for when this sight comes
there will be no delusory thing to be seen.
All that we have made as though we saw,
in this world, will be vanished, and I shall
see nothing but God and what is in him,
and him I shall see.
                JOHN DONNE (1572–1631)
                                    Sermons

The Kingdom is inside you, and it is outside of you. When you come to know yourselves, then you will be known, and you
will realize that you are the sons of the
living Father. But if you will not know
yourselves, then you dwell in poverty, and
it is you who are that poverty.
                Gospel of Thomas (2nd century)

Whoever perceives the infinite universe
as an edifice of truth to which our momentary feeling and thinking are instantly responding has been cured of the illusion of
vastness, for he has touched, as directly as
sensation itself, the garment of the living
God.   WILLIAM E. HOCKING (1873–1966)
                Science and the Idea of God

The creation we behold is the real and
ever-existing word of God, in which we

cannot be deceived. It proclaims his
power, it demonstrates his wisdom, it manifests his goodness and beneficence.
                THOMAS PAINE (1737–1809)
                                The Age of Reason

I tell thee, believer, if thou canst go back
to the years of eternity; if thou canst in thy
mind run back to that period, or ere the
everlasting hills were fashioned, or the
fountains of the great deep scooped out,
and if thou canst see thy God inscribing
thy name in His eternal book; if thou canst
see in His loving heart eternal thoughts of
love to thee, thou wilt find this a charming
means of giving thee songs in the night.
                CHARLES HADDON SPURGEON (1834–1892)
                                            Sermons

There can be no cultivation of the mind,
no opening of the heart to the flow of the
living spirit of the living God, no raw lac-
eration of the nervous system created by
the agony of human suffering, pain, or
tragedy; there can be no thing that does
not have within it the signature of God, the
Creator of life, the living substance out of
which all particular manifestations of life
arise; there is nothing that does not have
within it as part of its essence, the impri-
matur of God, the Creator of all, the Bot-
tomer of existence.
                HOWARD THURMAN (1899–1981)
                                With Head and Heart

Nothing should alienate us from one another but that which alienates us from
God.
                BENJAMIN WHICHCOTE (1609–1683)
                                        Aphorisms

I call that mind free which is not pas-
sively framed by outward circumstance
and is not the creature of accidental impulse, and which discovers everywhere the
radiant signatures of the Infinite Spirit,

and in them finds help to its own spiritual enlargement.

WILLIAM ELLERY CHANNING (1780–1842)
Sermons

Go where he will, the wise man is at
    home,
His hearth the earth—his hall the azure
    dome;
Where his clear spirit leads him, there's
    the road,
By God's own light illumined and
    foreshadowed.

RALPH WALDO EMERSON (1803–1882)
Wood Notes

The Stoics say, "Retire within yourselves; it is there you will find your rest." But that is not true.

Others say, "Go out of yourselves; seek happiness in amusement." And that is not true. Illness comes.

Happiness is neither without us nor within us. It is in God, both without us and within us.

BLAISE PASCAL (1623–1662)
Pensées

Only when his heart becomes purified through the practice of spiritual disciplines does a man attain to wisdom. He then becomes convinced of the existence of God through realizing Him in his own soul. There is, however, something greater than this attainment. To become convinced that fire lies hidden in the wood is one thing, but greater is it to light the fire, cook food, and satisfy one's hunger.

SRI RAMAKRISHNA (1834–1886)
Gospel

If man is not one with the Eternal in the unity of intuition and feeling which is immediate, he remains, in the unity of consciousness which is derived, for ever apart.

FRIEDRICH SCHLEIERMACHER (1768–1835)
On Religion

As rivers flow and disappear at last
In ocean's waters, name and form
    renouncing,
So too the sage from name and form
Is merged in the divine and ultimate
    existence.

The Upanishads

The very best and utmost of attainment in this life is to remain still and let God act and speak in thee.

MEISTER ECKHART (1260–1327)
Works

To get at the transcendent within oneself, one must break through one's normal self. We must impose silence on our familiar self, if the spirit of God is to become manifest in us. The divine is more deeply in us than we are ourselves.

SARVEPALLI RADHAKRISHNAN (1888–1975)
Fragments of a Confession

I feel like the deluge. The waters of the great deep are broken up, and the windows of heaven are opened.

GEORGE ELIOT (1819–1880)
Daniel Deronda

Rising above physical consciousness, knowing the Self as distinct from the sense-organs and the mind, knowing Him in his true light, one rejoices and one is free. *The Upanishads*

The world is full of Thee and thou art
    not in the world,
All are lost in Thee and Thou art not in
    the midst,

Thy silence is from Thy speech;
Thine hiding from Thine appearing,
I see the way to Thee by means of the
  smallest atom.
    FARID UD-DIN ATTAR (12th century)
        Pandnama

The superficial reasoner believes that there exists no faculty of seeing except by the exterior eye, and that if that sight has departed there will be an end of seeing. It is very unfortunate if the soul can only see through the external mirror of the eye. What will such a soul see if that mirror is broken?   JACOB BOEHME (1575–1624)
        Mysterium Magnum

Piety is unity, and the final proof that we have really found God is that all the discordant elements in our life fall into place and we are at peace.
    WILLIAM ADAMS BROWN (1865–1943)
        The Life of Prayer in a World of Science

There may be some souls who cannot dwell upon nor engage their minds with any mystery; they are drawn to a certain gentle simplicity before God, and held in this simplicity, without other consideration save to know that they are before God.
    SAINT FRANCIS OF SALES (1567–1622)
        Letters

The prophet says: "God leads the righteous through a narrow way out onto a broad street, so that they may come into his wide and open spaces"—which is to say, into the true freedom of the spirit which has become one spirit with God.
    MEISTER ECKHART (1260–1327)
        Works

No man can build a bridge to God. But God never forces man to cross the bridge he builds for him. God never drags man across unwillingly to a relationship of love and communion. Even man's obedience, in order to be real, must be from the heart; it must be willed by man.
    NELS F. S. FERRE (1908–1971)
        The Finality of Faith

Those who live in God have not only got their priorities straight; they have learned that to live with God is to live always in the present, with him who is the eternal Now.
    JOHN A. T. ROBINSON (1919–1984)
        Christian Freedom in a Permissive Society

The necessity of an inward stillness has appeared clearly to my mind. In true silence strength is renewed, the mind is weaned from all things, save as they may be enjoyed in the divine Will.
    JOHN WOOLMAN (1720–1772)
        Journal

The "sound of gentle stillness" (1 Kings 19:12) wherein the prophet Elijah heard God's voice was no sound at all, but the stillness of a believing heart, discerning God as only faith can discern him, in and through and beneath all sense impressions.
    WALTER MARSHALL HORTON (1895–1966)
        Christian Theology

The first stage for that one who has found the knowledge of the unity of God and the realization of that, is that there passes from his heart the remembrance of all things and he becomes alone with God Most High.
    ABU SAID AL-KHARRAZ (died 899)
        Kitab al-luma

Whatever is God to a man, that is his heart and soul; and conversely, God is manifested inward nature, the expressed self of a man—religion the solemn unveil-

ing of a man's hidden treasures, the revelation of his intimate thoughts, the open
confessions of his love-secrets.

LUDWIG FEUERBACH (1804–1872)
The Essence of Christianity

You must ask yourself first, what God is.
You must see how at the very bottom of
His existence, as you conceive of it, lie
these two thoughts—purpose and righteousness; how absolutely impossible it is
to give God any personality except as the
fulfillment of these two qualities—the intelligence that plans in love, and the righteousness that lives in duty.

PHILLIPS BROOKS (1835–1893)
Sermons

All spiritual strength for ourselves, all
noble ties to one another, have their real
source in that inner sanctuary where God
denies His lonely audience to none. Its secrets are holy; its asylum, inviolate; its con-
solations, sure; and all are open to the
simple heart-word, "Thou art my hiding
place."   JAMES MARTINEAU (1805–1900)
Sermons

Make body the field, the mind the
    ploughman, honest labor the irrigating
    water.
Sow the seed of the Lord's Name.
Let contentment be the leveller, and
    humility the fence.
With deeds of love the seed will fertilize.

GURU NANAK (1469–1539)
The Adi Granth

I saw the Lord with the eye of my heart.
He said, "Who are you?" I said, I am You.
You are He Who fills all place, but place
does not know where You are. In my sub-
sistence is my annihilation; I remain
You.

AL-HALLAJ (857–922)
Akbar-al-Hallaj

When we consider the visible world with
its essence and consider the life of the
creatures, then we find therein the likeness of the invisible, spiritual world, which
is hidden in the visible world as the soul in
the body; and we see thereby that the hidden God is nigh unto all and through all,
and yet wholly hidden to the visible essence.   JACOB BOEHME (1575–1624)
Mysterium Magnum

Our entering into an inward revolution
of human existence—this is the great miracle in which the presence of a new world
manifests itself with great clearness. He
who does not find the miracle here is not
likely to find it anywhere else, and will seek
in vain for it in the "far, far away," for the
words of Paracelsus hold valid in this respect: "You are long-sighted, you see in
the distance, but you do not see close at
hand."   RUDOLF EUCKEN (1846–1926)
The Truth of Religion

Those people who, rising above mere
material good, have placed their affections
on the true good; who, to obtain that true
good, have spared no labor, no fatigue, no
sacrifice, shall hear this word: "For those
who have a soul, there is the recom-
pense of souls. Because thou hast loved
justice and liberty before all things, come
and   possess   forever   liberty   and
justice."

F. R. DE LAMENNAIS (1782–1854)
Words of a Believer

A constant increase in spirituality is possible for each one until he dies, and for
successive generations until the end of the
world, if there is an Uncreated Spirit, sub-
sisting Love, to whom each can be more
and more united by advancing more and
more towards sanctity.

JACQUES MARITAIN (1882–1973)
Freedom in the Modern World

The love of beauty which exalts the poet; that devotion to the One and that ascent of science which makes the ambition of the philosopher, and that love and those prayers by which some devout and ardent soul tends in its moral purity towards perfection: these are the great highways conducting to that height above the actual and the particular, where we stand in the immediate presence of the Infinite, who shines out as from the deeps of the soul.   PLOTINUS (205–270)
Enneads

When, to a man who understands, the Self has become all things, what sorrow, what trouble can there be to him who once beheld that unity?   *The Upanishads*

If any human being were ever to respond to God in harmony with His Word, and upon the basis of His Word, in believing love, he would truly be human. He would know what human existence means, and he alone would express and represent this knowledge in his life.
EMIL BRUNNER (1889–1966)
Man in Revolt

When a man's prime object is not his soul, but the Kingdom of God, he has set his hands to a task that will never end and will always expand. It will make ever larger demands on his intellect, his sympathy, and his practical efficiency. It will work him to the last ounce of his strength. But it will keep him growing.
WALTER RAUSCHENBUSCH (1861–1918)
Christianizing the Social Order

The motion of every atom is toward its origin;
A man comes to be the thing on which he is bent.
By the attraction of fondness and yearning, the soul and the heart

Assume the qualities of the Beloved, who is the Soul of souls.
JALAL-UD-DIN RUMI (1207–1273)
The Masnawi

The nearest way to God
Leads through love's open door;
The path of knowledge is
Too slow for evermore.
ANGELUS SILESIUS (1624–1677)
The Cherubic Wanderer

That we may arrive at an understanding of the First Principle, which is most spiritual and eternal and above us, we ought to proceed through the traces which are corporeal and *outside us;* and this is to be led into the way of God. We ought next to enter *into our minds,* which are the eternal image of God, spiritual and internal; and this is to walk in the truth of God. We ought finally to pass over into that which is eternal, most spiritual, and *above us,* looking to the First Principle; and this is to rejoice in the knowledge of God and in the reverence of His majesty.
SAINT BONAVENTURE (1221–1274)
The Mind's Road to God

Him Whom I thought without me I now find within me.
When I found this secret, I recognized the Lord of the World.
KABIR (1440–1518)
Hymns

One person who has mastered life is better than a thousand persons who have mastered only the contents of books, but no one can get anything out of life without God.   MEISTER ECKHART (1260–1327)
Works

God is so great in his vastness that we can think of Him only in symbolic terms, but He has a near range. I believe we come close to God wherever there is beauty, love, integrity, truth. Often if you ask people where God is, their thoughts go shooting off among the stars; but it is deep down within human life that we find God.

HARRY EMERSON FOSDICK (1878–1969)
Sermons

Through love to light! Through light, O
  God, to Thee,
Who art the love of love, the eternal light
  of light!

RICHARD WATSON GILDER (1844–1909)
Collected Poems

It is because the spirit of God is resisting the pressure, the true man is struggling to dethrone the false man. When through some chink or momentary pause, the spirit within sees the face of God, when the hand of God reaches and grasps the hand of the man within, then there comes such a reinforcement to the soul that it can throw off the incubus of years and the misery of countless deeds, and can stand erect above all the ruins.

JOHN A. HUTTON (1868–1947)
The Soul's Leap to God

I am sought of *them that* asked not *for me;*
I am found of *them that* sought me not.

The Old Testament
Isaiah 65:1

Like a flock of homesick cranes flying night and day back to their mountain nests, let all my life take its voyage to its eternal home in one salutation to thee.

RABINDRANATH TAGORE (1861–1941)
Gitanjali

Bathe me, O God, in thee—mounting to
  thee,
I and my soul to range in range of thee.

WALT WHITMAN (1819–1892)
Passage to India

How can I know what it will mean to posterity that I now listen to Mozart for an hour? Perhaps nothing of any significance. And this applies to much of my life. But there is One to whom it may mean something. For while God is already familiar with Mozart He is not already familiar with the experience I may now have of Mozart, which is bound to be a variation on the theme, human experiences of Mozart— how significant a variation depends on my alertness, sensitivity, and imagination. All of one's life can be a "reasonable, holy, and living sacrifice" to deity, a sacrifice whose value depends on the quality of the life, and this depends on the depth of the devotion to all good things, to all life's possibilities, neither as mine nor as not mine but as belonging to God's creatures and thus to God.

CHARLES HARTSHORNE (1897–)
The Logic of Perfection

The kingdom of heaven is within us. That which is the substance of the religion, its hopes and consolation, its intermixture with the thoughts by day and night, the devotion of the heart, the control of appetite, the steady direction of the will to the commands of God, is necessarily invisible. Yet upon these depend the virtue and the happiness of millions.

WILLIAM PALEY (1743–1805)
View of the Evidences of Christianity

The Light, Life and Love of God— which are all the same thing really—are aspects of His Being, His Living Presence, and will be disclosed in the silence to each soul according to its capacity and need.

EVELYN UNDERHILL (1875–1941)
The Fruits of the Spirit

The great difference between religion and metaphysics is that religion looks for God at the top of life and metaphysics at the bottom; a fact which explains why metaphysics has such difficulty in finding God, while religion has never lost him.

GEORGE SANTAYANA (1863–1952)
Reason in Religion

The essence of life is not man's separate being, but God contained in man.

LEO TOLSTOY (1828–1910)
Diary

It is not the way a man talks about God, but the way he talks about things of the world that best shows whether his soul has passed through the fire of the love of God. In this matter no deception is possible. There are false imitations of the love of God, but not of the transformation it effects in the soul, because one has no idea of this transformation except by passing through it oneself.

SIMONE WEIL (1909–1943)
First and Last Notebooks

But thou canst not behold Me with this eye of yours; I will bestow on thee the supernatural eye. Behold my divine power.

The Bhagavad Gita

For all our penny-wisdom, for all our soul-destroying slavery to habit, it is not to be doubted that all men have sublime thoughts; that all men value the few real hours of life; they love to be heard; they love to be caught up in the vision of principles.

RALPH WALDO EMERSON (1803–1882)
Collected Essays

The place where man vitally finds God, deals with God, discovers the qualities of God, and learns to think religiously about God, is not primarily among the stars but within his own experience of goodness, truth, and beauty, and the truest images of God are therefore to be found in man's spiritual life.

HARRY EMERSON FOSDICK (1878–1969)
Adventurous Religion

From the moment that I heard the divine sentence, "I have breathed into man a portion of my Spirit," I was assured that we were His and He ours.

HAFIZ (14th century)
The Diwan

One of the most famous of Sören Kierkegaard's parables is his story of the King, who, falling in love with a simple peasant girl, must in some way win her love without dazzling and overwhelming her by the magnificence of his royal state. This is God's problem with man. To reveal Himself in the nakedness of His glory would destroy man's significance and autonomy. How shall He make Himself "visible to those who seek Him and not to those who seek Him not," as Pascal put it? The dark and hidden character of the way of faith is a continual reminder that God will have us on no other terms than as freely-loving sons. He will never batter down the doors of any skeptic's heart, but He is faithful to His promise—"Seek and ye will find."

JAMES A. PIKE (1913–1969)
Roadblocks to Faith

The soul sees God suddenly appearing within it, because there is nothing between: they are no longer two, but one; while the presence lasts, you cannot distinguish them. When in this state the soul would exchange its present condition for nothing in this world, though it were offered the kingdom of all the heavens: for this is the Good, and there is nothing better.

PLOTINUS (205–270)
Enneads

Your feeling is piety, in so far as it expresses the being and life common to you
and to the All. Your feeling is piety in so
far as it is the result of the operation of
God in you by means of the operation of
the world upon you.

FRIEDRICH SCHLEIERMACHER (1768–1834)
On Religion

He whose joy is within, whose delight is
  within,
He whose light likewise is within—
That devotee, becoming one with
  Brahma,
Attains unto the bliss of Brahma.

The Bhagavad Gita

Fools alone do not perceive Him, manifest within everything! Who is the Lord,
worthy of being worshipped? His form
cannot be seen by the eye. Those who follow pure lives see him.   *The Mahabarata*

Thee, God, I come from, to thee go,
All day long I like fountain flow
From thy hand out, swayed about
Mote-like in thy mighty glow.

GERARD MANLEY HOPKINS (1844–1889)
Thee, God, I Come From, to Thee go

Till your spirit filleth the whole world,
and the stars are your jewels; till you are
familiar with the ways of God in all ages as
with your walk and table; till you are intimately acquainted with that shady nothing
out of which the world was made; till you
love men so as to desire their happiness
with a thirst equal to the zeal of your own;
till you delight in God for being good to
all: you never enjoy the world.

THOMAS TRAHERNE (1637–1674)
Centuries of Meditations

Be still and cool in thy own mind and
spirit, from thy own thoughts, and then

thou wilt feel the principle of God to turn
the mind to the Lord from whence comes
life.   GEORGE FOX (1624–1691)
Journal

He is a personal God to those who need
His personal presence. He is embodied to
those who need His touch. He is the purest
essence. He simply *is* to those who have
faith.

MOHANDAS K. GANDHI (1869–1948)
Young India

When one has attained union with God
he has no need of intermediaries. Prophets and apostles are needed as links to con-
nect ordinary men with God, but he who
hears the "inner voice" within him has no
need to listen to outward words, even of
apostles.

JALAL-UD-DIN RUMI (1207–1273)
The Masnawi

What do you worship? To what do you
bring the most precious increments of
your spirit, your mind and your possessions? The need is ever present. Whatever
it is that holds so central a place in your
reaction to living, that is your God!

HOWARD THURMAN (1899–1981)
Meditations of the Heart

When we feel that we serve God, we feel
reverence for Him; if we feel that we serve
God, we feel love towards Him, we feel
that we attach ourselves to God, that we
bind ourselves to Him. Our whole individuality and independence are manifested in
this love; not only a part of our being, but
our complete self, our personality and
freedom, "all our heart, all our soul, and
all our might."   LEO BAECK (1873–1956)
The Essence of Judaism

Exultation is the going
Of an inland soul to sea,

Past the houses—past the headlands—
Into deep Eternity.

EMILY DICKINSON (1830–1886)
Collected Verse

What more can a man in the street want to learn than this, that the one God and Creator and Master of all that lives pervades the Universe? If you believe that God pervades everything that He has created you must believe that you cannot enjoy anything that is not given by Him, and seeing that He is the Creator of His numberless children, it follows that you cannot covet anybody's possessions.

MOHANDAS K. GANDHI (1869–1948)
Teachings

Religion is the consequence of the estrangement of man from the ground of his being and of his attempts to return to it. This return has taken place in Eternal Life, and God is everything in and to everything. The gap between the secular and the religious is overcome.

PAUL TILLICH (1886–1965)
Systematic Theology

If a person believes that the only approach to truth is the approach of the laboratory, he will never be able to be able to find a spiritual God. God is a property of the universe as a whole, and not of its observable parts.

EDGAR S. BRIGHTMAN (1884–1953)
Is God a Person?

God would be an inexperienced and too-hazardous archer if he directed our desires like arrows toward Himself as a target and did not add wings to the arrows by which they could reach the target some time. He would be unfortunate if His attempt to attract us toward Himself reached its end.

MARSILIO FICINO (1433–1499)
Theologia Platonica

Man's responsibility to God is the scaffold on which he stands as daily he goes on building life. His every deed, every incident of mind, takes place on this scaffold, so that unremittingly man is at work either building up or tearing down his life, his home, his hope of God.

ABRAHAM JOSHUA HESCHEL (1907–1972)
The Wisdom of Heschel

Drawn nigh to God, and he will draw nigh to you.   *The New Testament*
James 4:8

Seers can reach him because he is visible;
Worshippers too can see him, if they
    possess love for him;
Hara who is the first cause of the ancient
    universe will manifest himself to their
    mind as light.

KARAIKKALAMMAIYAR (6th century)
Poem of the Admirable

As the moonshine during the day remains united with the sunshine, so do souls, the sacred feet of the Lord Siva reaching, in eternal bliss remain united with him.

KATANTAR (13th century)
Unmaivilakkam

When by means of the Self as it really is, as with a lamp, an integrated man sees the true nature of *Brahman*, the unborn, undying God, the Pure beyond every essence as it really exists, and knowing him, he will be released from all fetters.

The Upanishads

The biblical God's hiddenness stands at the very center of the doctrine of God. It is so commanding that Pascal was echoing its intention when he said, "Every religion which does not affirm that God is hidden is not true." It means that God discloses himself at those places and in those ways he chooses and not as man would want. And he always discloses himself as one who is at once different *from* man, unconditionally *for* man, and entirely unavailable for coercion and manipulation *by* man.

HARVEY COX (1929–)
The Secular City

It is only by the exercise of reason that man can discover God. Take away that reason, and he would be incapable of understanding any thing; and, in this case it would be as consistent to read even the book called the Bible to a horse as to a man. THOMAS PAINE (1737–1809)
The Age of Reason

The courage to be is rooted in the God who appears when God has disappeared in the anxiety of doubt.

PAUL TILLICH (1886–1965)
The Courage to Be

God is seen God
In the star, in the stone, in the flesh, in the soul and the clod.

ROBERT BROWNING (1812–1889)
Saul

The human mind racks itself over the never-to-be known answer to the great riddle, and all that is clearly revealed is the fact that man must continue to hope and struggle on; that each day, if he would not be lost, he must with renewed courage take a fresh hold on life and face with fortitude the turns of circumstances. To do this, he needs to be able to touch God; let the idea of God mean to him whatever it may.

JAMES WELDON JOHNSON (1871–1938)
Along This Way

Within himself he found the law of right,
He walked by faith and not the letter's
  light,
And read his Bible by the Inward Light.

JOHN GREENLEAF WHITTIER (1807–1892)
Of the Pennsylvania Pilgrim

If in carnal wealth, how much more in spiritual does God love a cheerful giver?

SAINT AUGUSTINE (354–430)
Of the Catechizing of the Unlearned

God cannot be used as a stop-gap. We must not wait until we are at the end of our tether; he must be found at the center of life; in life, and not only in death; in health and vigor, and not only in suffering; in activity, and not only in sin.

DIETRICH BONHOEFFER (1906–1945)
Letters and Papers from Prison

If you explore the life of things and of conditioned being you come to the unfathomable, if you deny the life of things and of conditioned being you stand before nothingness, if you hallow this life you meet the living God.

MARTIN BUBER (1878–1965)
I and Thou

Those who believe that they are nonbelievers may, in their practical lives, by choosing as the aim of their activity the authentic moral good, choose God, and may do so by virtue of God's grace, without their knowing God in a consciously and conceptually formulated manner.

JACQUES MARITAIN (1882–1973)
Ransoming the Time

God will not ask man of what race he is. He will ask what he has done.

The Adi Granth

If for one moment God's name dwell in the heart, it is as bathing at the sixty-eight places of Hindu pilgrimage.

GURU AMAR DAS (1479–1574)
Mohan Pothi

Let not the wise man glory in his wisdom, neither let the mighty man glory in his might, let not the rich man glory in his riches: But let him that glorieth glory in this, that he understandeth and knoweth me, that I am the Lord which exercise loving-kindness, judgment, and righteousness in the earth: for in these things I delight, saith the Lord.

The Old Testament
Jeremiah 9:24

Thou who hast given me eyes to see
    And love this world so fair,
Give me a heart to find out Thee
    And read Thee everywhere.

JOHN KEBLE (1792–1866)
The Christian Year

In relation to God it can easily become the ruin of man, who is able to speak, that he is too willing to speak. God is in heaven, man upon the earth; therefore they can not well talk together.

SÖREN KIERKEGAARD (1813–1855)
Journals

I ended my first book with the words No Answer. I know now, Lord, why you utter no answer. You are yourself the answer. Before your face questions die away. What other answers would suffice? Only words, words; to be led out to battle against other words.   C. S. LEWIS (1898–1963)
Till We Have Faces

Make divine knowledge thy food, compassion thy store-keeper, and the voice which is in every heart the pipe to call to repast.   GURU NANAK (1469–1539)
The Japji

God sits effulgent in heaven, not for a favored few, but for the universe of life, and there is no creature so poor, or so low, that he may not look up with childlike confidence, and say, "My Father, Thou art mine."

HENRY WARD BEECHER (1813–1887)
Sermons

A man does not become a Brahmana by his plaited hair, by his family, or by both; he is blessed in whom there is truth and righteousness; he is a Brahmana.

GAUTAMA BUDDHA (563–483 B.C.)
The Dhammapada

He to whom all things are one and who draweth all things to one and seeth all things in one may be stable in heart and peaceably abide in God.

THOMAS À KEMPIS (1380–1471)
The Imitation of Christ

To find God is but the beginning of wisdom, because then for all our days we have to learn his purpose with us and to live our lives with him.

H. G. WELLS (1866–1946)
God the Invisible King

Not for anything in the world would I be free from God; I wish to be free *in* God and *for* God. It is needful that my passion for a freedom without bounds should involve a conflict with the world, but not with God.   NIKOLAI BERDYAEV (1874–1948)
The End of Our Time

At fifteen my mind was bent on learning; at thirty, I stood firm; at forty, I was free from delusions; at fifty, I understood the will of God; at sixty, my ears were receptive to the truth; at seventy, I could follow the promptings of my heart without overstepping the boundaries of right.

CONFUCIUS (551–479 B.C.)
Analects

There is one approach to an infinite realm where God *might be*. There is one door that opens into a holy of holies. The truth path is through personality. The search must *begin* in our bosom: Who am I? What do I live by? What does personality involve? How am I related to my fellows

and to nature? What does my sense of
worth imply? What do I mean by goodness? Can I draw any finite circle about
"myself"? Do I have any dealings with "a
Beyond"? These are questions which take
us into regions where microscope and telescope do not avail, but the full answers to
them would bring us to *that which is*.

RUFUS JONES (1863–1948)
Social Law in the Spiritual World

If God can be found by worshiping a
stone, I will worship a mountain.

KABIR (1450–1518)
The Adi Granth

As the lotus lives in water detached,
As the duck floats without drenching,
So does one cross the ocean of life.
If one's mind is attuned to the word
One lives in detachment, enshrines the
    Lord in his mind,
And sees the unperceivable and
    unfathomable.

GURU NANAK (1469–1539)
Ramkali

The God-seeing man can always enter,
naked and unencumbered with images,
into the inmost part of his spirit. There he
finds revealed an Eternal Light.

JAN VAN RUYSBROECK (1293–1381)
The Sparkling Stone

God's holiness will always be something
external and alien to a man whose freedom of moral self-determination is par-
alysed, who is incapable of spiritual initia-
tive, of moral heroism, and of attaining
holiness; such a man will never be a friend
of God.

VLADIMIR SOLOVIËV (1853–1900)
The Church of Christ

Far, far above all earthly things,
    Triumphantly you rode;

You soared to heaven on eagles' wings,
    And found, and talked with God.

JOHN WESLEY (1703–1791)
Hymns and Sacred Poems

To lose one's life that one may gain it, to
offer it that one may receive it, to possess
nothing that one may conquer all, to renounce self that God may give Himself to
us—how impossible a problem, and how
sublime a reality!

HENRI FRÉDÉRIC AMIEL (1821–1881)
Journal Intime

Examine your heart diligently and inquire of it, and you will surely find
whether or not it cleaves to God alone. Do
you possess a heart that expects from him
nothing but good, especially when in need
and distress, and that renounces and forsakes all that is not God? Then you have
the only true God. On the contrary, does
your heart cleave to something from which
it expects more good and more aid than it
does from God, and does it flee, not to
him, but from him? Then you have another god, an idol.

MARTIN LUTHER (1483–1546)
Large Catechism

We say that God, who must be at least as
high as the highest thoughts He has implanted in the best of men, will withhold
His smile from those who have desired but
to please Him; and that they only who
have done good for the sake of good and
as though He existed not, they only who
have loved virtue more than they loved
God Himself, shall be allowed to stand by
His side.

MAURICE MAETERLINCK (1862–1949)
Wisdom and Destiny

The Yogin puts himself into direct relation with that which is omniscient and omnipotent within man and without him. He

is in tune with the infinite, he becomes a channel for the strength of God to pour itself out upon the world whether through calm benevolence or active beneficence.

SRI AUROBINDO (1872–1950)
Works

The book of nature lies open to every eye. It is from this sublime and wonderful volume that I learn to serve and adore its Divine Author. No person is excusable for neglecting to read this book, as it is written in an universal language, intelligible to all mankind.

JEAN JACQUES ROUSSEAU (1712–1778)
Emile

Make continence thy furnace, resignation thy goldsmith, understanding thine anvil, divine knowledge thy tools, the fear of God thy bellows, austerities thy fire, divine love thy crucible, and melt God's name therein.

GURU NANAK (1469–1539)
The Japji

God is for man the commonplace book where he registers his highest feelings and thoughts, the genealogical album into which he enters the names of things most dear and sacred to him.

LUDWIG FEUERBACH (1804–1872)
The Essence of Christianity

And what is the way that will lead to the love of Him and the fear of Him? When a person contemplates His great and wondrous works and creatures and from them obtains a glimpse of His wisdom which is incomparable and infinite, he will straightaway love Him, praise Him, glorify Him, and long with an exceeding longing to know His great Name; even as David said

"My soul thirsted for God, for the living God" (Psalms 42:3).

MAIMONIDES (1135–1204)
Mishneh Torah

Yet, if he would, man cannot live all to this world. If not religious, he will be superstitious. If he worship not the true God, he will have his idols.

THEODORE PARKER (1810–1860)
A Lesson for the Day

I have just told the story of a missed vocation; I needed God; He was given to me, and I received him without understanding what I was looking for. Unable to take root in my heart, he vegetated in me for a while and then died. Today, when he is mentioned, I say with the amusement and lack of regret of some aging beau who meets an old flame: "Fifty years ago, without that misunderstanding, without that mistake, without the accident which separated us, there might have been something between us."

JEAN-PAUL SARTRE (1905–1980)
The Words

Do not imagine that God is like a carpenter who works or not, just as he pleases, suiting his own convenience. It is not so with God, for when he finds you ready he must act, and pour into you, just as when the air is clear and pure the sun must pour into it and may not hold back. Surely, it would be a very great defect in God if he did not do a great work, and anoint you with great good, once he found you empty and innocent.

MEISTER ECKHART (1260–1327)
Sermons

The end of creation is that all things may return to the Creator and be united with Him.

EMANUEL SWEDENBORG (1688–1772)
Divine Love and Wisdom

Is this not the Vision of visions, the Vision in which all other visions are enfolded? Man shall find God; the imperfect shall come to perfection; the part shall rest itself in the whole; the child shall come to the Father's house. In many forms, in many colors, that is the vision which keeps the world's fainting heart alive, and makes the earth, through all its years of sorrow, rich with an under-treasure of perpetual joy.   PHILLIPS BROOKS (1835–1893)
Sermons

To be attached to God is the most natural aspiration of a person. What is throughout all existence in a state of dumbness and deafness, in a form of potentiality, is developed in man in a conceptual and experiental form. There can be no substitute in existence for the longing to be absolutely linked with the living God, with the infinite light.

ABRAHAM ISAAC KOOK (1865–1935)
Essays

Turning to the light and Spirit of God within thee is thy only true turning unto God; there is no other way of finding Him but in that place where he dwelleth in thee. For though God be everywhere present, yet He is only present to thee in the deepest and most central part of thy soul.

WILLIAM LAW (1686–1761)
The Spirit of Prayer

God is the ground of all our good; and all that we adequately call our *ideals,* the inner experience that looks at us through the symbols of the universe, the better possibilities that seem ever to struggle through the material conditions of life, the contrite longing to be free from self and at peace with God—these, while they are in us, yet are not of us; they are not ours, but his; nay, they are his very self; first, standing at the door to knock, and then, if the latch be lifted by a hospitable hand, entering to abide and dwell, and turning the bread and wine of life into a sacrament.

JAMES MARTINEAU (1805–1900)
Hours of Thought on Sacred Things

Consider the immeasurable distance from us of what we know as God's dwelling-place, the heavens; yet how near He is to us when we call upon Him.

The Midrash

Many teachers praise Love as the highest virtue; I, however, place seclusion higher than love. First: the best about love is that it forces me to love God. But it is much more important that I force God down to me than that I force myself up to God. For God is more able to penetrate into me and to become united with me, than I with Him.

That seclusion forces God down to me, I can prove in the following way: Every creature likes to be in its natural abode, the abode that is appropriate for it is the most natural, the most appropriate abode of God, unity and purity. Both rest upon seclusion. That is why God cannot help abandoning himself to a secluded heart.

MEISTER ECKHART (1260–1327)
Sermons

Though the eyes of our soul are closed because we do not desire to see, or cannot do so, still do thou uphold us and help us and not cease to anoint us until thou hast initiated us into the hidden meaning of the sacred utterances and revealed those locked beauties that are invisible to the uninitiated. This is meet for thee to do.

PHILO JUDAEUS (30 B.C.–A.D. 40)
On Virtues

It is a great misery for man not to be with Him without whom he cannot exist. For there is no doubt that without Him, in whom he has his being, he does not exist.

And yet, if he does not remember Him, if he does not understand Him or love Him, he is not with Him.

SAINT AUGUSTINE (354–430)
On the Trinity

The wise man lives after the image of God and is not guided by the ways of the world. And he who imitates the images of God will conquer the stars.

PARACELSUS (1493–1541)
Works

Everything finite is more or less obscure, dark, doubtful. Only the Infinite Self, the problem-solver, the complete thinker, the one who knows what we mean even when we are most confused and ignorant, the one who includes us, who has the world present to himself in unity, before whom all past and future truth, all distant and dark truth is clear in one external moment, to whom far and forgot is near, who thinks the whole of nature, and in whom are all things, the Logos, the world-possessor—only his existence, I say, is perfectly sure.

JOSIAH ROYCE (1855–1916)
The Spirit of Modern Philosophy

The Lord taketh not joy in a multitude of words, but rather in a fervent spirit.

GIROLAMO SAVONAROLA (1452–1498)
Sermons

Religion is what the individual does with his own solitariness. It runs through three stages, if it evolves to its final satisfaction. It is the transition from God the void to God the enemy, and from God the enemy to God the companion.

ALFRED NORTH WHITEHEAD (1861–1947)
Religion in the Making

In every age and in every clime men of every race and of every tongue have felt that the good man could be at home in the Universe only if at the heart of it there be a living Spirit.

JOHN BAILLIE (1886–1960)
The Roots of Religion in the Human Soul

This choice of ours, the choice between an alliance with God or a conflict, is not made once for all and in a moment. It is a choice that we have to be making always; it is never finally achieved either one way or the other. We are always growing and changing because we live; and the adventure of life is never determined for us one way or the other; because there is always the grace of God pouring out for all men, and always in them the power to accept or refuse it.

ARTHUR CLUTTON-BROCK (1868–1924)
Studies in Christianity

How dear, how soothing to man, arises the idea of God, peopling the lonely place, effacing the scars of our mistakes and disappointments! When we have broken our god of tradition and ceased from our god of rhetoric, then may God fire the heart with his presence.

RALPH WALDO EMERSON (1803–1882)
The Over-Soul

If you learn to see God in all things you will learn to love them according to His will, not your own self-will. If you see things as in eternity you are less a prey to the pain of their passing, and so you can learn the more easily not to clutch at them as they pass. GERALD VANN (1906–1963)
The Divine Pity

Those whose sins have perished, whose doubts are destroyed, who are self-restrained and are intent on the welfare of all other beings, those obtain God's everlasting joy. *The Bhagavad Gita*

Go not to seek Him out of thyself, for that will be but distraction and weariness, and thou shalt not find Him; because there is no fruition of Him more certain, more ready, more intimate than that which is within.

SAINT JOHN OF THE CROSS (1542–1591)
The Spiritual Canticle

There is a Divine Center into which your life can slip, a new and absolute orientation in God, a Center where you live with Him and out of which you see all of life, through new and radiant vision, tinged with new sorrows and pangs, new joys unspeakable and full of glory.

THOMAS R. KELLY (1893–1941)
The Eternal Promise

Do not scrupulously confine yourself to fixed rules, or particular forms of devotion, but act with faith in God, with love or humility.

BROTHER LAWRENCE (1605–1691)
The Practice of the Presence of God

Whom have I in heaven but thee? and there is none upon earth that I desire beside thee. My flesh and my heart faileth: but God is the strength of my heart, and my portion for ever.   *The Old Testament*
Psalms 73:25–26

My path hitherto has been like a road through a diversified country, now climbing high mountains, then descending into the lowest vales. From the summits I saw the heavens; from the vales I looked up to the heights again. In prosperity I remember God, or memory is one with consciousness; in adversity I remember my own elevations, and only hope to see God again.

HENRY DAVID THOREAU (1817–1862)
Journals

Intelligence of the intelligent, eternal among the transient, he, though one, makes possible the desires of many. To him who sees the Self revealed in his own heart belongs eternal peace—to none else!
The Upanishads

This is the living knowledge of God, which is found in the heart and lives in it. Psalm 84:2 speaks of "My heart and flesh sing for joy in the living God," and Psalm 63:3 "Your steadfast love is better than life." In these Psalms the joy and sweetness of God in the faithful heart is described. Thus, a man lives in God and God in him; he knows God in truth and is known by him.   JOHANN ARNDT (1555–1621)
True Christianity

I have not so far left the coasts of life
To travel inland, that I cannot hear
The murmur of the Outer Infinite.

ELIZABETH BARRETT BROWNING
(1806–1861)
Aurora Leigh

It is but right that our hearts should be on God, when the heart of God is so much on us.   RICHARD BAXTER (1615–1691)
The Saints' Everlasting Rest

Follow you the star that lights a desert
   highway, yours and mine,
Forward, till you learn the highest
   Human Nature is divine.

ALFRED LORD TENNYSON (1809–1892)
Collected Poems

In the faculty of sight there are two eyes forever trembling with the natural tension of looking to the light which is God: love and reason. When one makes the attempt without the other, it does not get very far. When they help each other, they can do a great deal, just as when one eye helps the other, so reason teaches love and love illumines reason.

WILLIAM OF SAINT THIERRY (1070–1148)
On the Nature and Dignity of Love

Paul said that we exist in God and move in him, for we are wayfarers. The wayfarer takes his name and his existence from the way. The wayfarer who walks or moves in the Infinite Way, if he is asked where he is, says, "On the way"; if asked, where he moves, replies, "In the way"; if asked why he moves, says, "Because of the way"; and if asked whither he goes, says, "From the way to the way." Accordingly, the Infinite Way is called the place of the wayfarer, and this is God.

NICHOLAS OF CUSA (1401–1464)
Sermons

If thou knewest the whole Bible by heart, and the sayings of all the philosophers, what would it profit thee without the love of God and without grace?

THOMAS À KEMPIS (1380–1471)
The Imitation of Christ

We do not clamber to God by the steps of logic; we reach him by the feelings of the heart. And it is just because, when the heart is moved profoundly, there falls upon it a silence and a stillness, that we are bidden to be still, and know that he is God.

GEORGE HERBERT MORRISON (1866–1928)
Sermons

The miracle of miracles is this—"A new heart will I give you, and a new spirit will I put within you." To put the law in the inward parts, and to write it on the heart, is more than to fill the firmament with stars.   JOSEPH PARKER (1830–1902)
Sermons

Until a man has found God and been found by God, he begins at no beginning, he works to no end. He may have his friendships, his partial loyalties, his scraps of honour. But all these things fall into place, and life falls into place only with God. Only with God. God who fights through man against Blind Force and Night and Non-Existence; who is the end, who is the meaning.

H. G. WELLS (1866–1946)
Mr. Britling Sees It Through

Man will at length attain that awfully triumphant epoch when he shall recognize his existence as that of Jehovah. In the meantime bear in mind that all is Life—Life—Life within Life—the less within the greater, and all within the *spirit divine*.

EDGAR ALLAN POE (1809–1849)
Eureka

When God, who inhabits the innermost recess of everything, displays Himself in your conscience, one with Himself, inhabiting as He does your inmost recess, you will be lost in the immense sea, without temporal consciousness of your own, living in Him within your own sight.

MIGUEL DE UNAMUNO (1864–1936)
Nicodemus the Pharisee

Those are the enlightened great souls of this world who happen to be firmly fixed in eternal unborn Calmness. The world can not even dream of it.   *The Upanishads*

Ah! somehow life is bigger after all
Than any painted angel could we see
The God that is within us!

OSCAR WILDE (1854–1900)
Humanitad

By aspiring to a similitude of God in goodness, or love, neither man nor angel ever transgressed, or shall transgress.

FRANCIS BACON (1561–1626)
Advancement of Learning

My being known by God is my reality, and I become real in the measure that my life and action are in harmony with the knowledge of God.

ROMANO GUARDINI (1885–1968)
The Word of God

Man is an individual, but he is not self-sufficing. The law of his nature is love, a harmonious relation of life to life in obedience to the divine center and source of his life. This law is violated when man seeks to make himself the center and source of his own life.

REINHOLD NIEBUHR (1892–1971)
The Nature and Destiny of Man

Men may tire themselves in a labyrinth of search and talk of God; but if we would know him indeed, it must be from the impressions we receive of him; and the softer our hearts are, the deeper and livelier those will be upon us.

WILLIAM PENN (1644–1718)
Some Fruits of Solitude

How are we to explain that moral miracle which occurs when a man whose inner spirit has been drab and slattern is converted to God? Now a victim of his own crass presumption, and now a dupe of his own deluded conscience, such a man has ceased to know himself; and suddenly an Angel has placed a fiery sword in his hand, and the light and sweetness of God have taken possession of him.

KARL RAHNER (1904–)
Happiness Through Prayer

Little ought you to care who you are; the urgent thing is what you will be. The being that you are is but an unstable, perishable being, which eats of the earth and which the earth some day will eat; what you will to be is the idea of you in God, the Consciousness of the universe; it is the divine idea of which you are the manifestation in time and space. And your longing impulse toward the one you will to be is only homesickness drawing you toward your divine home.

MIGUEL DE UNAMUNO (1864–1936)
The Life of Don Quixote and Sancho

God can be denied only on the surface; but he cannot be denied where human ex-

perience reaches down beneath the surface of flat, vapid, commonplace existence.

NIKOLAI BERDYAEV (1874–1948)
Dream and Reality

Somehow, somewhere, in beginning, middle, or end of autobiography, or in all three, as in life, your life and mine, we are bound to meet with God.

GAMALIEL BRADFORD (1863–1932)
Biography and the Human Heart

From the primitive savage, kneeling before some supposedly sacred tree or holy stone, thrilled with the thought that somewhere at the back of created matter lies and vibrates a Force, a Power beyond his knowing, into contact with which he must somehow come, down to the great faiths of today, men have understood that God is the reality behind and beyond and within the shifting panorama of nature and history.

SARVEPALLI RADHAKRISHNAN (1888–1975)
Addresses

It is only in solitude, when it has broken the thick crust of shame that separates us from one another and separates us all from God, that we have no secrets from God; only in solitude do we raise our hearts to the Heart of the Universe; only in solitude does the redeeming hymn of supreme confession issue from our soul.

MIGUEL DE UNAMUNO (1864–1936)
Essays and Soliloquies

And I smiled to think God's greatness
   flowed around our incompleteness—
Round our restlessness, his rest.

ELIZABETH BARRETT BROWNING
(1806–1861)
Round Our Restlessness

On the roaring billows of Time, thou art not engulfed, but borne aloft into the azure of Eternity. Love not Pleasure; love God. This is the Everlasting Yea, wherein all contradiction is solved: wherein whoso walks and works, it is well with him.

THOMAS CARLYLE (1795–1881)
Sartor Resartus

The good mariner, when he draws near the port, furls his sails, and enters it softly; so ought we to lower the sails of our worldly operations, and turn to God with all our heart and understanding.

DANTE (1265–1321)
Il Convito

Only in the sacredness of inward silence does the soul truly meet the secret, hiding God. The strength of resolve, which afterwards shapes life and mixes itself with action, is the fruit of those sacred, solitary moments. There is a divine depth in silence. We meet God alone.

FREDERICK WILLIAM ROBERTSON
(1816–1853)
Sermons

For this I think charity, to love God for himself, and our neighbor for God.

SIR THOMAS BROWNE (1605–1682)
Religio Medici

A touch divine—
And the scaled eyeball owns the mystic
rod;
Visibly through his garden walketh God.

ROBERT BROWNING (1812–1889)
Sordello

When you have built up the interior of your heart in piety, at that the veils between you and your Lord will be removed, the light of mystic knowledge will be revealed to you, there will burst forth from your heart the springs of wisdom, and the secrets of the supernal realm will be made clear to you.

ABU-HAMID MUHAMMAD AL-GHAZZALI
(1058–1111)
The Beginning of Guidance

God is in some measure to a man as that man is to God. The door in God that opens is the door he knocks at.

C. S. LEWIS (1898–1963)
The Joyful Christian

In order to find God, whom we can only find in and through the depths of our own soul, we must therefore first find ourselves. To use common figures of speech, we must "return to ourselves," we must "come to ourselves."

THOMAS MERTON (1915–1968)
The New Man

I rest not from my great task!
To open the Eternal Worlds, to open the
immortal Eyes
Of man inwards into the Worlds of
Thought, into Eternity
Ever expanding in the Bosom of God, the
Human Imagination.

WILLIAM BLAKE (1757–1827)
Jerusalem

God says to man as he said to Moses: "Put off shoes from off thy feet"—put off the habitual which encloses your foot and you will recognize that the place on which you happen to be standing at this moment is holy ground. For there is no rung of being on which we cannot find the holiness of God everywhere and at all times.

MARTIN BUBER (1878–1965)
Tales of the Hasidim

To find or know God in reality by any outward proofs, or by anything but by God Himself made manifest and self-evident in you, will never be your case, here or hereafter.

WILLIAM LAW (1686–1761)
The Spirit of Love

Be comforted. You would not be seeking Me, if you had not found Me.

BLAISE PASCAL (1623–1662)
Pensées

Where there is something to be seen,
God has an eye for it; where man calls,
God lends an ear; where man extends his
hands in supplication, God's hands can
clasp them.

FRANZ ROSENZWEIG (1886–1929)
Kleinere Schriften

There is in God (some say)
A deep, but dazzling darkness; As men
    here
Say it is late and dusky, because they
    See not all clear;
  O for that night! where I in him
  Might live invisible and dim.

HENRY VAUGHAN (1621–1695)
The Night

Who worship God, shall find him.
    Humble love
And not proud reason, keep the doors of
    heaven;
Love finds admission, where proud
    science fails.

EDWARD YOUNG (1683–1765)
Night Thoughts

God will see to it that the man who finds
him in his earthly happiness and thanks
him for it does not lack reminder that
earthly things are transient, that it is good
for him to attune his heart to what is eternal, and that sooner or later there will be
times when he can say in all sincerity, "I
wish I were home."

DIETRICH BONHOEFFER (1906–1945)
Letters and Papers from Prison

If there is a reason for the existence of
the novelist on earth it is this: to show the
element which holds out against God in
the highest and noblest characters—the
innermost evils and dissimulations; and
also to light up the secret source of purity
in creatures who seem irreparably fallen.

FRANÇOIS MAURIAC (1885–1970)
Dieu et Mammon

God's discoveries of himself to us are
some small part of his great excellencies,
and when we have said all that we can to
set him forth, how little will it be in comparison of himself! It will not bear the proportion that one drop doth to the sea.

SAMUEL WILLARD (1640–1707)
Compleat Body of Divinity

He who does My work, who is given over
to Me, who is devoted to Me, void of attachment, without hatred to any born
being, comes to Me.   *The Bhagavad Gita*

All Friends, mind that which is Eternal,
which gathers your Hearts together up to
the Lord, and lets you see that ye are written in one another's Heart.

GEORGE FOX (1624–1691)
Epistles

Whosoever walks toward God one cubit,
God runs toward him twain.

Hebrew Proverb

If an Arab in the desert were suddenly
to discover a spring in his tent, and so
would always be able to have water in
abundance, how fortunate he would consider himself—so too, when a man qua
physical being is always turned towards
the outside, thinking that his happiness
lies outside him, finally turns inward and
discovers that the source is within him; not
to mention his discovering that the source
is his relation to God.

SÖREN KIERKEGAARD (1813–1855)
Journals

Man is able to cry "Here am I," for the
echo of these words come back to him
from God's mouth.

FRANZ ROSENZWEIG (1886–1929)
Judah Halevi

Earth's crammed with heaven,
And every common bush afire with God;
But only he who sees takes off his shoes—

The rest sit around and pluck
   blackberries.

ELIZABETH BARRETT BROWNING
(1806–1861)
Aurora Leigh

Man cannot approach the divine by reaching beyond the human; he can approach Him by becoming human. To become human is why he, this individual man, has been created.

MARTIN BUBER (1878–1965)
Hasidism and Modern Man

And then—when you find your own manhood—your womanhood . . . then you know it is not your own to do as you like with. You don't have it of your own will. It comes from—from the middle—from the God. Beyond me, at the middle, is the God.

D. H. LAWRENCE (1885–1930)
The Plumed Serpent

I found Him in the shining of the
   stars,
I mark'd Him in the flowering of His
   fields,
But in His ways with men I find Him
   not.

ALFRED LORD TENNYSON (1809–1892)
Idylls of the King

Hast thou not known? hast thou not heard, that the everlasting God, the Lord, the Creator of the ends of the earth, fainteth not, neither is weary? there is no searching of his understanding. He giveth power to the faint; and to them that have no might he increaseth strength. Even the youths shall faint, and be weary, and the young men shall utterly fall; but they that wait upon the Lord shall renew their strength; they shall mount up with wings as eagles; they shall run, and not be weary; and they shall walk, and not faint.

Old Testament
Isaiah 40:28–31

At the heart of the cyclone tearing the
   sky
And flinging the clouds and Towers by,
   Is a place of central calm;
So here in the roar of mortal things,
I have a place where my spirit sings,
   In the hollow of God's Palm.

EDWIN MARKHAM (1852–1940)
The Shoes of Happiness

So great is the force of memory, so great the force of life, even in the mortal life of man. What shall I do then, O thou my true life, my God? I will pass even beyond this power of mine which is called memory; yea I will pass beyond it, that I may approach unto Thee, O sweet Light.

SAINT AUGUSTINE (354–430)
Confessions

Then dawns the Invisible; the Unseen its
   truth reveals;
My outward sense is gone, my inward
   essence feels;
Its wings are almost free—its home, its
   harbour found,
Measuring the gulf, it stoops and dares
   the final bound.

CHARLOTTE BRONTË (1816–1855)
The Prisoner

Hate Man, and O, thou hatest, losest
   God;
Keep faith in Man, and rest with God
   indeed.
And what if, after all, the God thou
   seekest
Were here, not yonder—God in act to be,
To find and know Himself for evermore.

ROBERT WILLIAMS BUCHANAN (1841–1901)
The Last Faith

When you have closed your doors and darkened your room, remember never to say that you are alone; God is within, and your genius is within—and what need

have they of light to see what you are
doing?

> EPICTETUS (1st century)
> *Discourses*

'Tis hard to find God, but to comprehend
Him, as He is, is labour without end.

> ROBERT HERRICK (1591–1674)
> *God Not to Be Comprehended*

I could not say I believe. I know! I have
had the experience of being gripped by
something that is stronger than myself,
something people call God.

> CARL JUNG (1875–1961)
> *Quoted in* Time, *February 14, 1955*

> The works of God, above, below,
>   Within us and around,
> Are pages in that book to show
>   How God Himself is found.

> JOHN KEBLE (1792–1866)
> *Christian Year*

> Because the road was steep and long
>   And through a dark and lonely
>   land,
> God set upon my lips a song
>   And put a lantern in my hand.

> JOYCE KILMER (1886–1918)
> *Love's Lantern*

God is alpha and omega in the great
world: endeavor to make Him so in the
little world; make Him thy evening epi-
logue and thy morning prologue, so shall
thy rest be peaceful, thy labours prosper-
ous, thy life pious, and thy death
glorious.

> FRANCIS QUARLES (1592–1644)
> *Enchiridion*

Whoever has, in his inward exercise, an
imageless and free ascent with God, and
means nought else but the glory of God,
must taste of the goodness of God; and

must feel from within a true union with
God.   JAN VAN RUYSBROECK (1293–1381)

> *The Mirror of Eternal Salvation*

Consider what Saint Augustine said—
that he sought God within himself. Settle
yourself in solitude, and you will come
upon Him in yourself.

> SAINT TERESA (1515–1582)
> *El Castillo Interior*

As flowing rivers disappear into the sea,
losing their name and form, thus a wise
man, freed from name and form, goes to
the Divine Person who is beyond all.

> *The Upanishads*

There is but one thing needful—to possess God. All our senses, all our powers of
mind and soul, are just so many ways of
approaching The Divine, so many modes
of tasting and adoring God.

> HENRI FRÉDÉRIC AMIEL (1821–1881)
> *Journal Intime*

God, to be God, must rule the heart to
transform it. He must express Himself in
every smallest act of His votary. This can
only be done through a definite realization
more real than the five senses can ever
produce. Where there is realization outside the senses it is infallible. It is proved,
not by extraneous evidence, but in the
transformed conduct and character of
those who have felt the real presence of
God within.

> MOHANDAS K. GANDHI (1869–1948)
> *The Choice Is Always Ours*

> And this I know: whether the one True
>   Light
> Kindle to Love, or Wrath consume me
>   quite,
> One flash of It within the Tavern caught
> Better than in the Temple lost outright.

> OMAR KHAYYÁM (died c. 1123)
> *Rubáiyát*

He who thinks to reach God by running away from the world, when and where does he expect to meet him? How far can he fly—can he fly and fly, till he flies into nothingness itself? No, the coward who would fly can nowhere find him. We must be brave enough to be able to say: We are reaching him here in this very spot, now at this very moment.

RABINDRANATH TAGORE (1861–1941)
Sadhana

How glorious, how divine, how great, how good
May we become! How like the Deity
In managing our Thoughts aright! A Piety
More grateful to our God than building Walls
Of Churches. . . .

THOMAS TRAHERNE (1637–1674)
The Inference

· TO EXPERIENCE THE LIVING GOD ·

When thou art quiet or silent, then thou art that which God was before nature and creature, and whereof he made thy nature and creature. Then thou hearest and seest with that wherewith God saw and heard in thee before thy own willing, seeing and hearing began.

JACOB BOEHME (1575–1624)
The Way to Christ

Wretch, you are carrying about a god with you, and you know it not. Do you think I mean some god of silver or of gold, and external? You carry him within yourself, and you perceive not that you are polluting him by impure thoughts and dirty deeds. And if an image of God were present, you would not dare to do any of the things which you are doing: but when God himself is present within and sees all and hears all, you are ashamed of thinking such things, ignorant as you are of your own nature and subject to the anger of God.

EPICTETUS (1st century)
Enchiridion

The Infinite Power and Love that has grounded a new spontaneous nature in man over against a dark and hostile world, will conserve such a new nature and its spiritual nucleus, and shelter it against all perils and assaults, so that life as the bearer of Life Eternal can never be wholly lost in the stream of time.

RUDOLF EUCKEN (1846–1926)
The Truth of Religion

Truth, not in distinct and clear-cut definitions but in the limpid obscurity of a single intuition that unites all dogmas in one simple Light, shining into the soul directly from God's eternity, without the medium of created concept, without the intervention of symbols or of language or the likeness of material things. Here the Truth is One Whom we not only know and possess but by Whom we are known and possessed. Here theology ceases to be a body of abstractions and becomes a Living Reality Who is God Himself.

THOMAS MERTON (1915–1968)
New Seeds of Contemplation

I saw into that which was without end, things which cannot be uttered, and of the greatness and infinitude of the love of God which cannot be expressed by words.

GEORGE FOX (1624–1691)
Autobiography

When we feel within ourselves that we desire God, then God has touched the mainspring of power, and through this touch it swings beyond itself and towards God.   *Theologia Germanica*

God is that within me which I consciously experience in my higher moments as a greater-than-myself and which urges me to try again when I default.

GEORGIA HARKNESS (1891–1974)
The Resources of Religion

If the Real is God, it is with God that we have to do from moment to moment of daily living. For each action the world concentrates itself into a point of resistance and support; and that point is a Thou, not an It.

WILLIAM ERNEST HOCKING (1873–1966)
The Mystical Spirit

In the world He appears to me as the mysterious, marvellous creative Force; within me He reveals Himself as ethical Will. In the world He is impersonal Force; within me He reveals Himself as Personality. The God who is known through philosophy and the God whom I experience as ethical Will do not coincide. They are one; but how they are one I do not understand.

ALBERT SCHWEITZER (1875–1965)
Christianity and the Religions of the World

O world invisible, I see thee;
O world intangible, I touch thee;
O world unknowable, I know thee;
Inapprehensible, I clutch thee.

FRANCIS THOMPSON (1859–1907)
In No Strange Land

Never was there a more troubled seeker after God than Pascal, but his comfort came to him when he heard God say, "Thou wouldst not be seeking me, hadst thou not already found me. Be not therefore disquieted." All we can say will be an expansion of that.

JOHN BAILLIE (1886–1960)
Our Knowledge of God

If the chosen soul could never be alone
In deep mid-silence, open-doored to God,
No greatness ever had been dreamed or
   done.

JAMES RUSSELL LOWELL (1819–1891)
Columbus

God does not so speak to us through the occurrences of life, that you can persuade others that He speaks. He does not act upon such explicit laws, that you can speak of them with certainty. He gives us sufficient tokens of Himself to raise our minds in awe towards Him; but He seems so frequently to undo what He has done, and to suffer counterfeits of His tokens, that a conviction of His wonder-working presence can but exist in the individual himself.

JOHN CARDINAL NEWMAN (1801–1890)
Sermons

Experiences are fleeting. Sometimes one has a strong awareness of the ultimate mystery of the divine, and sometimes one is troubled by what mystics call periods of dryness. For me the main point is that the experience of faith is a total attitude toward the mystery of God and life which includes commitment, love, and hope.

REINHOLD NIEBUHR (1892–1971)
Gifford Lectures

To believe in God, not far off but here; to understand prayer, not as a form of words but as an inner opening of the life to the Divine resources, and so to experience what the prophet said, "They that wait upon the Lord shall renew their strength"; to go out into life, in consequence, not afraid of being overborne, because you know you are not a closed reservoir that can be exhausted but a channel in touch with inexhaustible resources, and that therefore as your day is so shall your strength be—that is vital, personal religion.

HARRY EMERSON FOSDICK (1878–1969)
Riverside Sermons

Let no man that does not hear God speaking to him despair that he shall never hear him, but hearken still and in one language or other, perchance a sickness, perchance a sin, he shall hear him. For these are several dialects in God's language, several instruments in God's concert.

JOHN DONNE (1572–1631)
Sermons

I am as certain as that I live that nothing is so near to me as God.

MEISTER ECKHART (1260–1327)
Works

I see plainly that my love of God must be as special as God's love of me. I must love Him out of my special place, love Him through my special work; and what is that place, what is that work? Is not this precisely the question of questions?

FREDERICK WILLIAM FABER (1814–1863)
Spiritual Conferences

Father in Heaven, when the thought of Thee wakes in our hearts, let it not awaken like a frightened bird that flies about in dismay, but like a child waking from its sleep with a heavenly smile.

SÖREN KIERKEGAARD (1813–1855)
Journals

As a cataract from the mountain's side,
Or roar of winds upon a wooded steep.
So comes to us at times, from the
  unknown
And inaccessible solitudes of being,

The rushing of the sea-tides of the soul;
And inspirations, that we deem our own,
Are some divine foreshadowing and
  foreseeing
Of things beyond our reason or control.

JOHN GREENLEAF WHITTIER (1807–1892)
Collected Poems

Pure of heart the pure of heart find God, kindly the kind see him, affectionate the affectionate find him, and to the merciful he shows mercy.

SAINT FRANCIS OF SALES (1567–1622)
The Love of God

I am sure that if a soul knew the very least of all that Being means, it would never turn away from it.

MEISTER ECKHART (1260–1327)
Mystical Writings

When a man lives with God, his voice shall be as sweet as the murmur of the brook and the rustle of the corn.

RALPH WALDO EMERSON (1803–1882)
Self-Reliance

If the whole is ever to gladden thee,
That whole in the smallest thing thou
  must see.

JOHANN WOLFGANG VON GOETHE
(1749–1832)
God, Soul, and the World

Man is born with the religious capacity along with every other. If only his sense for the profoundest depths of his own nature is not crushed out, if only all fellowship between himself and the Primal Source is not quite shut off, religion would, after its own fashion, infallibly be developed. But in our time, alas! that is exactly what, in very large measure, does happen. With pain I see daily how the rage for calculating and explaining suppresses the sense. I see how all things unite to bind man to the finite, and to a very small portion of the finite, that the infinite may as far as possible vanish from his eyes.

FRIEDRICH SCHLEIERMACHER (1768–1834)
On Religion

A man who really and truly enters, feels as though he had been here through all eternity.

JOHANNES TAULER (1300–1361)
Sermons on the Inner Way

Once a man has fallen in love with the divine milieu, he cannot bear the darkness, tepidity, and emptiness he sees on every side in what ought to be filled with God and pulsating in him.

PIERRE TEILHARD DE CHARDIN (1881–1955)
The Divine Milieu

Say, Lord, when is a man in mere "understanding"? I say to you: "When a man sees one thing separated from another." And when is a man above mere understanding? That I can tell you: "When he sees all in all, then a man stands beyond mere understanding."

MEISTER ECKHART (1260–1327)
Works

Touch His feet, who is one and indivisible, immutable and peaceful; who fills all vessels to the brim with joy, and whose form is love.   KABIR (1440–1518)
The Adi Granth

I felt the sentiment of Being spread
O'er all that moves and all that seemeth
    still;
O'er all that, lost beyond the reach of
    thought
And human knowledge, to the human
    eye
Invisible, yet liveth to the heart
        WILLIAM WORDSWORTH (1770–1850)
The Prelude

In the depth of the night, on your lonely bed, when you sink into the bottomless darkness, you feel faith near to your heart, like a beloved wife; her arms are about you, more boundless, eternally brimming joy than the passionate arms of your beloved.   SHOLEM ASCH (1880–1957)
What I Believe

At the very moment when we seem to touch God by a stroke of thought, he escapes if we do not keep him, if we do not seek him through action.

MAURICE BLONDEL (1861–1949)
L'Action

To sense the living God is to sense infinite goodness, infinite wisdom, infinite beauty. The world may be dismal; the wrath may turn the gardens into a desert; yet the prophet "will rejoice in the Lord."

ABRAHAM JOSHUA HESCHEL (1907–1972)
The Prophets

There is an experience of the love of God which, when it comes upon us, and enfolds us, and bathes us, and warms us, is so utterly new that we can hardly identify it with the old phrase, God is love. Can this be the love of God, this burning, tender, wooing, wounding pain of love that pierces the marrow of my bones and burns out old loves and ambitions? God experienced is a vast surprise.

THOMAS R. KELLY (1893–1941)
A Testament of Devotion

Still, still with thee, when purple morning
    breaketh,
    When the bird waketh, and the
        shadows flee;
Fairer than morning, lovelier than the
    daylight,
    Dawns the sweet consciousness, I am
        with Thee.

HARRIET BEECHER STOWE (1811–1896)
Hymns

The divine voice says to every man: "Hampered and sore hindered as you are, you are yet My dearly beloved son and child; only turn to Me, open your heart to Me; only struggle, however faintly, to be what you can desire to be, and I will guide and lead you to myself; all that is needed is that your heart should be on My side in the battle.

ARTHUR CHRISTOPHER BENSON
(1865–1922)
The Altar Fire

The little that we know of God seems so precious that we grasp it as if it were the whole. We set up our narrow standards and build our protecting bulwarks to guard what we have won against the mutations of the years. And we forget that God is the living God, everywhere present, in the changing as in the permanent; in the future as in the past and in the present.

WILLIAM ADAMS BROWN (1865–1943)
The Life of Prayer in a World of Science

Every moment we live through is like an ambassador who declares the will of God, and our hearts always utter their acceptance.

JEAN-PIERRE DE CAUSSADE (1675–1751)
Abandonment to Divine Providence

The work of God in the heart, as upon the body, is invisible; it is by a train of almost insensible events. He not only produces these effects gradually, but by ways that seem so simple, and so calculated to succeed, that human wisdom attributes the success to these natural causes, and thus the finger of God is overlooked.

FRANÇOIS FÉNELON (1651–1715)
Meditations

By opening up to God's presence beyond understanding, and beyond even personal power of will, man finds that the strange haunting within him, although he still continues to think and act, is nevertheless stilled by a peculiar power that grasps him as he reaches out for it. He knows a deep inner peace. Satisfaction settles over the hubbub and he knows the healing touch of eternity on his life.

NELS F. S. FERRE (1908–1971)
The Finality of Faith

All living knowledge of God rests upon this foundation: that we experience Him in our lives as Will-to-Love.

ALBERT SCHWEITZER (1875–1965)
Out of My Life and Thought

Swiftly arose and spread around me the peace and knowledge that pass all the argument of the earth,
And I know that the hand of God is the promise of my own,
And I know that the spirit of God is the brother of my own,
And that all men ever born are also my brothers, and the women my sisters and lovers,
And that a kelson of the creation is love.

WALT WHITMAN (1819–1892)
Song of Myself

In Godmanhood human freedom unites with the divine freedom, the human image with the divine image. By inward experience and inward living of freedom the light of that Truth is attained.

NIKOLAI BERDYAEV (1874–1948)
Dostoevski

I know Thee, who hast kept my path, and made
Light for me in the darkness, tempering sorrow
So that it reached me like a solemn joy;
It were too strange that I should doubt thy love.

ROBERT BROWNING (1812–1889)
Paracelsus

God is known as that of which I am primarily certain; and being certain, am certain of self and of my world of men and men's objects. I shall always be more certain *that* God is, than *what* he is: it is the age-long problem of religion to bring to light the deeper characters of this fundamental experience.

WILLIAM ERNEST HOCKING (1873–1966)
The Meaning of God in Human Experience

We feel God present in nature, whether in its awe or its beauty; and in human history, whether in its justice or its weird mysteriousness; and in the life of a good man, or the circumstances of a generous or noble act. Most of all we feel Him near when conscience, His inward messenger, speaks plainly and decisively to us.

HENRY PARRY LIDDON (1829–1890)
Sermons

For many years I have preached, "There is a peace of God which passeth all understanding." Convince me that this word has fallen to the ground; that in all these years none have attained this peace; that there is no living witness of it at this day; and I will preach it no more.

JOHN WESLEY (1703–1791)
Christian Perfection

It is not a question of knowing God when the veil be lifted, but of knowing Him in the veil itself.

AL-ALAWI (1869–1934)
Aphorisms

To place the central point of existence outside God, who is the true Center, in the "I" and the world, is madness; for it cannot be a real center; the world cannot provide any resting place for the Self; it only makes it oscillate hither and thither.

EMIL BRUNNER (1889–1966)
Man in Revolt

Thy Spirit is mingled in my spirit even as wine is mingled with pure water,
When anything touches Thee, it touches me. Lo, in every case Thou art I.

AL-HALLAJ (857–922)
Kitab al-Tawasin

A living experience of God is the crowning knowledge attainable to a human mind.

WALTER RAUSCHENBUSCH (1861–1918)
Christianizing the Social Order

As soon as God touches you, you shall burn with a light so truly your own that you shall reverence your own mysterious life, and yet so truly His that pride shall be impossible.

PHILLIPS BROOKS (1835–1893)
Perennials

The universe's mighty Keeper, wise,
Hath entered into me the simple.

The Rig-Veda

To say Thou art God, without knowing what the Thou means—of what use is it? God is a name only, except we know God.

GEORGE MACDONALD (1824–1905)
Unspoken Sermons

The happiness of a mind which by deep meditation hath been purged from all impurity and hath entered within the Self, cannot be told in words; it can be felt by the inward power only.   *The Upanishads*

He who is able to stand here on earth, before casting off his body, the urges of desire and anger, he is a Yogi; he enjoys fellowship with God and is a happy man.

The Bhagavad Gita

When the sun rises, do you not see a round disk of fire something like a gold piece? O no, no, I see an innumerable company of the Heavenly host crying "Holy, Holy, Holy, is the Lord God Al-

mighty." I do not question my bodily eye any more than I would question a window concerning sight. I look through it and not with it.   WILLIAM BLAKE (1757–1827)
Works

Every new experience is a new opportunity of knowing God. Every new experience is like a jewel set into the texture of our life, on which God shines and makes interpretation and revelation of Himself.
                    PHILLIPS BROOKS (1835–1893)
Sermons

To get at the core of God at his greatest, one must first get into the core of himself at his least, for no one can know God who has not first known himself. Go to the depths of the soul, the secret place of the Most High, to the roots, to the heights; for all that God can do is focused there.
                    MEISTER ECKHART (1260–1327)
Works

As people who do not know the country walk again and again over a gold treasure that has been hidden somewhere in the earth and do not discover it, thus do all those who day after day live in the spirit world and yet do not discover it; because they are carried away by untruth, they do not discover the true Self in Brahman.
                    The Upanishads

Although no man on earth can explain the particular manner wherein the Spirit of God works on the soul, yet whosoever has these fruits, cannot but know and *feel* that God has wrought them in his heart.
                    JOHN WESLEY (1703–1791)
A Further Appeal to Men of Reason and Religion

Be not curious about God,
For I who am curious about each am not curious about God,

No array of terms can say how much I am at peace about God.
                    WALT WHITMAN (1819–1892)
Song of Myself

The kingdom of God cometh not with outward observation, neither shall they say, lo, here, or lo, there it is; for behold, the kingdom of God is within you.
                    JACOB BOEHME 1575–1624)
The Way to Christ

And He said unto me:
"Son of man, stand upon thy feet, and I will speak with thee."
And the spirit entered into me
when He spoke unto me, and set me upon my feet;
and I heard Him that spoke unto me.
                    The Old Testament
Ezekiel 2:1–2

The only surer ground is direct experience of God, which many persons claim to have. Arguments lead to the base of the mountain, experience alone scales it. He who has climbed the peak gets an evidence —and a thrill—of summit-vision which the dwellers in the valley-hotels can never have.   RUFUS JONES (1863–1948)
Religious Foundations

It is the heart which experiences God, and not the reason. This, then, is faith: God felt by the heart, not by the reason.
                    BLAISE PASCAL (1623–1662)
Pensées

See where you do not see, hear where no sound comes through,
Go where you cannot go, and God will speak to you.
                    ANGELUS SILESIUS (1624–1677)
The Cherubic Wanderer

When thou beholdest God with a new eye, thou seest everything in Him, as in a mirror; everything has always been in Him, but thou has never seen it before.

GREGORY SAVVICH SKOVORODA
(1722–1794)
Works

Two prisoners whose cells adjoin communicate with each other by knocking on the wall. The wall is the thing which separates them but it is also their means of communication. It is the same with us and God. Every separation is a link.

SIMONE WEIL (1909–1943)
Gravity and Grace

When one sees Eternity in things that pass away and Infinity in finite things then one has pure knowledge.

The Bhagavad Gita

Great things did the Lord lead me unto, and wonderful depths were opened unto me, beyond what can by words be declared; but as people come into subjection to the Spirit of God, and grow up in the image and power of the Almighty, they may receive the Word of wisdom that opens all things, and come to know the hidden unity in the Eternal Being.

GEORGE FOX (1624–1691)
Journal

At its best and truest, worship seems to me to be a direct, vital, joyous, personal experience and practice of the presence of God.   RUFUS JONES (1863–1948)
The Inner Life

God is the fire in me, I am the glow in Him.   ANGELUS SILESIUS (1624–1677)
The Cherubic Wanderer

But it is with man's Soul as it is with Nature; the beginning of Creation is— Light. Till the eye have vision, the whole members are in bonds.

THOMAS CARLYLE (1795–1881)
Sartor Resartus

Let it be said to thee: to be empty of everything created, that is to be full of God.   MEISTER ECKHART (1260–1327)
Works

To be drunk, not with liquor, but with God. To feast to one's heart's content, not on food, but on God. In dreaming and in waking hours, in sorrow and in laughter, to walk in a world flooded with light, this is a phenomenon experienced only by those who truly know the soul's art.

TOYOHIKO KAGAWA (1888–1960)
Meditations

O Lord, open our inner eye that we may see thee as thou art, touch thou our soul with thine own inspiration that we may know thee, that we may love thee, that we may serve thee with our daily life.

THEODORE PARKER (1810–1860)
Sermons

Today is our day of rejoicing; today we are very happy. Our anxieties have departed, since we have met God. Today Spring is in our hearts.

GURU ARJAN (1563–1606)
Hymns

I have known, beyond all darkness, that great Person of golden effulgence. Only by knowing him does one conquer death. There is no other way of escaping the wheel of birth, death, and rebirth.

The Upanishads

I cannot know whether God is something else in himself or for himself than he is for me; what he is to me is to me all that he is. For me, there lies in these predicates under which he exists for me, what he is in himself, his very nature, he is for me what he can alone ever be for me.

LUDWIG FEUERBACH (1804–1872)
The Essence of Christianity

My firm belief is that He reveals Himself daily to every human being, but we shut our eyes to the "still small voice." We shut our eyes to the "Pillar of Fire" in front of us. I realize his omnipresence.

MOHANDAS K. GANDHI (1869–1948)
Young India

Lord, I want to be more holy in my mind. My thoughts tend ever to be divisive and scattered. In so many ways, my mind is a house divided; and the conflicts rage up and down all my corridors. I need wholeness. O that my mind may be stilled by thy holy hush! Lord, I want to be more holy in my mind.

HOWARD THURMAN (1899–1981)
Meditations of the Heart

Whenever the hidden, the unfathomable, is experienced whenever the meaning of all things is felt and grasped, then it is either the devoutness of silence, that most intimate feeling of the living God, that deepest force of religious intuition and emotion, which takes hold of man, or, again, it is the uplift to imagery which is stirred up within him, the poetry which sings in prayer of the ineffable.

LEO BAECK (1873–1956)
The Essence of Judaism

Thou art but the glass,
And He the face confronting it, which casts
Its image on the mirror. He alone
Is manifest, and thou in truth art hid.

JAMI (1414–1492)
Yusuf and Zulaikhah

It is not the image we create of God which proves God. It is the effort we make to create this image.

PIERRE LECOMTE DU NOUY (1883–1947)
Human Destiny

Why should we not believe that that which is highest in ourselves is a reflection of that which is deepest in the universe— that we are children of a Power who makes possible the growing achievement of relatedness, fulfillment, goodness?

JOSHUA LOTH LIEBMAN (1907–1948)
Peace of Mind

Man, in experiencing himself as man, is conscious of being determined in his nature by spirit as a dimension of his life. This immediate experience makes it possible to speak symbolically of God as Spirit, as of the divine Spirit.

PAUL TILLICH (1886–1965)
Systematic Theology

It seems to be a general pretense of the unthinking herd that they cannot see God. Could we but see him, say they, as we see a man, we should believe that he is, and believing, obey his commands. But alas, we need only open our eyes to see the sovereign Lord of all things, with a more full and clear view than we do any one of our fellow creatures.

GEORGE BERKELEY (1685–1753)
Of the Principles of Human Understanding

God is felt in us as a divine restlessness which spurs us on so long as we truly live. When it deserts us, we are really dead. Be productive and be productive for the common good—that is the eternal commandment.

JOHN ELOF BOODIN (1869–1950)
The Religion of Tomorrow

Standing on the bare ground—my head bathed by the blithe air, and uplifted into infinite space—all mean egotism vanishes. I become a transparent eyeball; I am nothing; I see all; the currents of the Universal Being circulate through me. I am part or parcel of God.

RALPH WALDO EMERSON (1803–1882)
Nature

No one can be a *person* in the full meaning of the word and not partake of God, the Complete Spirit, any more than a river can be a river without partaking of the ocean, or than an atom can be an atom without partaking of electrical energy.

RUFUS JONES (1863–1948)
New Studies in Mystical Religion

All the mystery which surrounds life and pervades life is really one mystery. It is God. Called by His name, taken up into His being, it is filled with graciousness. It is no longer cold and hard; it is all warm and soft and palpitating. It is love. And of this personal mystery of love—of God—it is supremely true that only by reverence, only by the hiding of the eyes, can He be seen.   PHILLIPS BROOKS (1835–1893)
Selected Sermons

Acquaint thyself with God, if thou
  would'st taste
His works. Admitted once to his embrace,
Thou shalt perceive that thou wast blind
  before:
Thine eye shall be instructed; and thine
  heart
Made pure shall relish with divine delight
Till then unfelt, what hands divine have
  wrought.
WILLIAM COWPER (1731–1800)
The Task

Let not the wise man glory in his wisdom, neither let the mighty man glory in his might, let not the rich man glory in his riches. But let him that glorieth, glory in this, that he understandeth and knoweth Me, that I am the Lord which exercise loving-kindness, judgment, and righteousness in the earth: for in these things I delight.   *The Old Testament*
Jeremiah 9:23–24

I have gone the whole round of creation:
  I saw and I spoke:

I, a work of God's hand for that purpose,
  received in my brain
And pronounced on the rest of his
  handiwork—returned him again
His creation's approval or censure: I
  spoke as I saw:
I report, as a man may of God's work.
ROBERT BROWNING (1812–1889)
Saul

Nowhere is it said that the Lord reveals his mysteries to those before all others who are most advanced in many languages and in the sciences and who think themselves a light to the world and the leaders of the blind. Rather Scripture testifies that it is to the little ones that God gives understanding and that it is the Holy Spirit who teaches all truth, applies all healing balm and admonishes all of us.

SEBASTIAN FRANCK (1499–1542)
Chronicles

When one's mind is religiously awakened, one feels as though in every blade of wild fern and solid stone there is something really transcending all human feelings, something which lifts one to be a real equal to that of heaven. He plunges himself into the very source of creativity and there drinks from life all that life has to give. He not only sees by taking a look, but he enters into the source of things and knows them at the point where life receives its existence.

D. T. SUZUKI (1870–1966)
Zen Buddhism and Psychoanalysis

Lord, what a change within us one short
  hour
Spent in Thy presence will avail to make!
RICHARD CHENEVIX TRENCH (1807–1886)
Prayer

The way by which a man can reach God is revealed to him only through the knowledge of his own being, the knowledge of

his essential quality and inclination. Everyone has in him something precious, that is in no one else! But this precious something in man is revealed to him only if he truly perceives his strongest feeling, his central wish, that in him which stirs his inmost being.   MARTIN BUBER (1878–1965)
Two Types of Faith

Each one of us can, at certain moments in his existence, descend into the innermost depths of the Ego, to make there some eternal pledge or gift of himself, or face some irrefutable judgment of his conscience; and each one of us, on such occasions, alone with himself, feels that he is a universe unto himself, immersed in, but not dominated by, the great star-studded universe.

JACQUES MARITAIN (1882–1973)
The Range of Reason

Moreover, something is or seems,
That touches me with mystic gleams,
Like glimpses of forgotten dreams—

Of something felt, like something here;
Of something done, I know not where;
Such as no language may declare.
        ALFRED LORD TENNYSON (1809–1892)
The Two Voices

In order to make himself known to men, God can and need use neither words, nor miracles, nor any other created thing, but only Himself.

BENEDICT SPINOZA (1632–1677)
God

That light guided me
More surely than the noonday sun
To the place where He was waiting for
    me,
Whom I knew well,
And where none but He appeared.
    SAINT JOHN OF THE CROSS (1542–1591)
The Ascent of Mount Carmel

It is not rational necessity, but vital anguish that impels us to believe in God. And to believe in God is, before all and above all, to feel a hunger for God, to wish that God may exist, to wish to save the human finality of the Universe.

MIGUEL DE UNAMUNO (1864–1936)
The Tragic Sense of Life

No one who once the glorious sun has
    seen,
And all the clouds, and felt his bosom
    clean
For his great Maker's presence, but must
    know
What 'tis I mean, and feel his being glow.
        JOHN KEATS (1795–1821)
Sleep and Poetry

God, the root, has brought forth fruit;
Go and dash the bell to pieces;
We are come to the quieter days
in which the hours stand ripe.
God, the root, has brought forth fruit.
Be serious and see.
    RAINER MARIA RILKE (1875–1926)
Book of Hours

The problem of God is a human problem which concerns the rapport between men. It is a total problem to which each man brings a solution by his entire life, and the solution one brings to it reflects the attitude one has chosen towards other men and towards oneself.

JEAN-PAUL SARTRE (1905–1980)
Situations

When at last the individual breaks through the limiting darkness to him, the irradiation of that moment, the smile and soul clasp, is in God as well as man. He has won us from his enemy. We come staggering through into the golden light of his kingdom henceforth, until at last we are altogether taken up in his being.

H. G. WELLS (1866–1946)
God the Invisible King

Then I became a bird, whose body was of Oneness, and whose wings were Everlastingness, and I continued to fly in the air of the Absolute until I passed into the sphere of Purification, and gazed upon the field of Eternity, and beheld there the tree of Oneness.

ABU YAZID OF BISTAM (died 875)
The Diwan

We always live beyond our margins. We leap beyond anything that *is*—the here and now—and we are by the necessity of our being concerned with a more yet that ought to be. A God who is immanent, if He is to be thought of as Spirit, is just as certainly transcendent. A God who is the foundational Life of our lives must be the eternal guarantor of all that can be or that ought to be, as well as of all that is.

RUFUS JONES (1863–1948)
Pathways to the Reality of God

If a man has experienced the presence of God, not only has he no need of proofs, he may even go so far as to consider the idea of a demonstration as a slur on what is for him a sacred evidence.

GABRIEL MARCEL (1889–1973)
The Mystery of Being

To come from a gaze at the stars is to catch a glance at the inscrutable face of him that hurries us on, as on a wheel, from dust to dust. I saw beyond good and evil, to a great stillness.

GEORGE MEREDITH (1828–1909)
Letters

We find ourselves to be more truly human when we are raised to the level of the divine. We transcend ourselves, we see ourselves in a new light, by losing sight of ourselves and no longer seeing ourselves, but God.   THOMAS MERTON (1915–1968)
The New Man

The highest and most divine things which it is given us to see and to know are but the symbolic language of things subordinate to Him who transcends all: through which things His incomprehensible Presence is shown, walking on those heights of Holy Places which are perceived by the mind.

DIONYSIUS THE AREOPAGITE (5th century)
Mystical Theology

Now therefore, I pray thee, if I have found grace in thy sight, show me now thy way, that I may know thee, that I may find grace in thy sight.   *The Old Testament*
Exodus 33:13

God, says Plato, is not far from every one of us, but is near to all without their knowing it. It is they themselves who flee away from Him, or rather they flee away from their own true selves.

PLOTINUS (205–270)
Enneads

And when thou sendest thy free soul
    thro' heaven,
Nor understandest bound or
    boundlessness,
Thou seest the Nameless of the hundred
    names,
And if the Nameless should withdraw
    from all
Thy frailty counts most real, all thy world
Might vanish like thy shadow in the dark.
ALFRED LORD TENNYSON (1809–1892)
The Ancient Sage

In mystical experience the soul is aware of God as a reality into which it flows or which flows into it and lives in it, and at the same time is conscious that this indissoluble unity is a union of two—of itself and of God who transcends it.

SIMON L. FRANK (1877–1950)
Reality and Man

The most humane doctrine about what it means to be a man is that every individual is capable of a God-relationship, in which consists his essential humanity, and for the sake of which every earthly establishment and order may and must at times be opposed.

SÖREN KIERKEGAARD (1813–1855)
Training in Christianity

One thing is certain: we must always live close to the presence of God, for that is newness of life; and then nothing is impossible, for all things are possible with God; no earthly power can touch us without his will, and danger can only drive us closer to him.

DIETRICH BONHOEFFER (1906–1945)
Letters and Papers from Prison

How my mind and will, which are not God, can yet cognize and leap to meet him, how I ever came to be separate from him, and how God himself came to be at all, are problems that for the theist can remain unsolved and insoluble forever. It is sufficient for him to know that he himself simply is, and needs God; and that behind this universe God simply is and will be forever, and will in some way hear his call.

WILLIAM JAMES (1842–1910)
Essays on Faith and Morals

God is felt only is so far as he is lived; and man does not live by bread alone, but by every word that proceedeth out of the mouth of God (Matthew 4:4; Deuteronomy 8:3).

MIGUEL DE UNAMUNO (1864–1936)
The Tragic Sense of Life

In this Light, my spirit suddenly saw through all, and in all created things, even in herbs and grass, I knew God—who He is, how He is, and what His will is—and suddenly in that Light my will was set upon by a mighty impulse to describe the being of God.

JACOB BOEHME (1575–1624)
Aurora

They who are free and untrammelled enter into the true Mystical Darkness of Unknowing, whence all perception of understanding is excluded, and abide in that which is intangible and invisible, being wholly absorbed in Him Who is beyond all, and are united in their higher part to Him Who is wholly unknowable and Whom, by understanding nothing, they understand above all intelligence.

DIONYSIUS THE AREOPAGITE (5th century)
Mystical Theology

Seeing's believing, but feeling is God's own truth. *Irish Proverb*

The righteous man may say: I will that there be a God, that my existence in this world be also an existence outside the chain of physical causes and in a pure world of the understanding, and lastly that my duration be endless; I firmly abide by this, and will not let this faith be taken from me; for in this instance alone my interest, because I must not relax anything of it, inevitably determines my judgment.

IMMANUEL KANT (1724–1804)
Critique of Pure Reason

I am roused from the body to my true self, and emerge from all else and enter Himself, and behold a marvelous Being. He who has beheld this Beloved knows the truth of what I say. It is possible for us, even while here in the body, to behold Him and ourselves in such wise as it is lawful for us to see. We see ourselves as made, nay, as being God himself.

PLOTINUS (205–270)
Enneads

What is that which gleams through me and smites my heart without wounding it?

I am both a-shudder, and a-glow. A-shudder insofar as I am unlike it; a-glow insofar as I am like it.

SAINT AUGUSTINE (354–430)
Confessions

I never saw anything without seeing God therein; I have stilled my restless mind, and my heart is radiant; for in Thatness I have seen beyond Thatness, in company I have seen the Comrade Himself.

KABIR (1440–1518)
Granthali

Life from the Center is a life of unhurried peace and power. It is simple. It is serene. It is amazing. It is triumphant. It is radiant. It takes no time, but it occupies all our time.

THOMAS R. KELLY (1893–1941)
A Testament of Devotion

Thy natural senses cannot possess God or unite thee to Him; nay, thy inward faculties of understanding, will, and memory can only reach after God, but cannot be the place of His habitation in thee. But there is a root or depth in thee from whence all these faculties come forth, as lines from a centre or as branches from the body of the tree. This depth is called the centre, the *fund* or bottom of the soul. This depth is the unity, the eternity, I almost said the infinity, of thy soul; for it is so infinite that nothing can satisfy it or give it any rest but the infinity of God.

WILLIAM LAW (1686–1761)
The Spirit of Prayer

These are the pentecostal hours of our existence, when the Spirit comes as a mighty rushing wind, in cloven tongues of fire, filling the soul with God.

FREDERICK WILLIAM ROBERTSON
(1816–1853)
Sermons

All those men who are raised up above their created being into a contemplative life are one with the divine brightness and are that brightness itself.

JAN VAN RUYSBROECK (1293–1381)
The Adornment of Spiritual Marriage

Not by words can we attain unto it, not by the heart, not by the eye. He alone attains unto it, who exclaims: It is! It is! Thus may it be perceived, and apprehended in its essence. The Essence appears, when one has perceived it as It is!

The Upanishads

The pursuit of the will of God is an ardent desire for blessedness; its attainment is blessedness itself. We pursue Him by loving Him but we attain Him when, illumined and captivated in the depths of our being by His truth and holiness, we grasp Him in a wondrous and rational fashion.

SAINT AUGUSTINE (354–430)
De Moribus Ecclesiae

An old French sentence says, "God works in moments"—"En peu d'heure Dieu labeure." We ask for long life, but 'tis deep life, or grand moments, that signify. Let the measure of time be spiritual, not mechanical. Moments of insight, of fine personal relation, a smile, a glance—what ample borrowers of eternity they are!

RALPH WALDO EMERSON (1803–1882)
Works and Days

As people come into subjection to the Spirit of God, and grow up in the image and power of the Almighty, they may receive the Word of Wisdom that opens all things, and come to know the hidden unity in the Eternal Being

GEORGE FOX (1624–1691)
Journal

No matter how true an idea of God religion may hand on, the true idea may constitute a wall which keeps God out, if it is adopted as an idea simply—that is to say, as a repetition of other men's insights, as a universal idea. God, who is truly said to explain man to himself, must explain *me to myself.*

WILLIAM ERNEST HOCKING (1873–1966)
The Meaning of God in Human Experience

The truly religious man is always more concerned about what God will do *in* him than what He will do *to* him; in his intense desire for the purification of his motives he almost wishes that heaven and hell were blotted out, that he might serve God for Himself alone.

WILLIAM RALPH INGE (1860–1954)
Light, Life and Love

The most fundamental and primordial of all religious experiences, and perhaps in a sense the only experience that is as such religious, is just the experience of believing, the experience of faith in God, the experience of casting oneself in utter trust upon His love.

JOHN BAILLIE (1886–1960)
The Roots of Religion in the Human Soul

God screens us evermore from premature ideas. Our eyes are holden that we cannot see things that stare us in the face, until the hour arrives when the mind is ripened; then we behold them, and the time when we saw them not is like a dream.

RALPH WALDO EMERSON (1803–1882)
Spiritual Laws

We should not deny the word that is in the heart, but should diligently and earnestly listen to what God in us wants to say.

JOHANNES DENCK (1495–1527)
Works

With You, my heart is a mosque; without You, it is but a fire-temple:

Without You, my heart is hell itself: with You, it becomes paradise!

SHARAFUDDIN MANERI (14th century)
The Hundred Letters

Thrice stirred below my conscious self, I have felt
That perfect disenthralment which is God.

JAMES RUSSELL LOWELL (1819–1891)
The Cathedral

God-haunted our lives are until they give themselves to God, as the brain of a sleeper is haunted by the daylight until he opens his eyes and gives himself a willing servant to the morning.

PHILLIPS BROOKS (1835–1893)
Sermons

If I stoop
Into a dark tremendous sea of cloud,
It is but for a time; I press God's lamp
Close to my breast; its splendour, soon or late,
Will pierce the gloom: I shall emerge one day.

ROBERT BROWNING (1812–1889)
Paracelsus

God outside of us is an hypothesis; God inside of us is an experience.

HARRY EMERSON FOSDICK (1878–1969)
Sermons

It is eternity now. I am in the midst of it. It is about me in the sunshine; I am in it, as the butterfly floats in the light-laden air. Nothing has to come; it is now. Now is the eternity; now is the immortal life. Here this moment, by this tumulus, on earth, now; I exist in it.

RICHARD JEFFERIES (1848–1887)
The Story of My Heart

There is a difference between having an opinion that God is holy and gracious, and having a sense of the loveliness and beauty of that holiness and grace.

JONATHAN EDWARDS (1703–1758)
A Divine and Supernatural Light

When he can read God directly, the hour is too precious to be wasted on other men's transcripts of their readings.

RALPH WALDO EMERSON (1803–1882)
The American Scholar

There is a growth from inside out, a growth which proceeds from God, who lives within us; and there is another growth, from outside inward, which proceeds from those layers of alluvium the world deposits around our eternal nucleus in an attempt to drown it in time.

MIGUEL DE UNAMUNO (1864–1936)
Nicodemus the Pharisee

He who knows Him who has no beginning and no end, in the midst of chaos, creating all things, having many forms, alone enveloping everything, is freed from all fetters.   *The Upanishads*

The ears were made, not for such trivial uses as men are wont to suppose, but to hear celestial sounds. The eyes were not made for such groveling uses as they are now put to and worn out by, but to behold beauty now invisible. May we not *see* God?

HENRY DAVID THOREAU (1817–1862)
A Week on the Concord and Merrimack Rivers

I see Thy light, I feel Thy wind; the
    world, it is Thy word;
Whatever wakes my heart and mind Thy
    presence is, my Lord.

GEORGE MACDONALD (1824–1905)
My Morning Song

I see Thee in the distant blue;
But in the violet's dell of dew,
Behold, I *breathe* and *touch*
Thee too.

JOHN BANNISTER TABB (1845–1909)
Collected Verse

Open your eyes and the whole world is full of God.

JACOB BOEHME (1575–1624)
The Threefold Life of Man

Passing away, saith my God, passing
    away:
Winter passeth after the long delay:
New grapes on the vine, new figs on the
    tender spray,
Turtle calleth turtle in Heaven's May.

CHRISTINA ROSSETTI (1830–1894)
Passing Away

My God, my God, Thou art a direct God, may I not say a literal God, a God that wouldest be understood literally, and according to the plain sense of all that thou sayest? But thou art also a figurative, a metaphorical God too; a God in whose words there is such a height of figures, such voyages, such peregrinations to fetch remote and precious metaphors, such extensions, such spreadings, such Curtains of Allegories, such third Heavens of Hyperboles, such harmonious elocutions. O, what words but thine can express the inexpressible texture, and composition of thy word.   JOHN DONNE (1572–1631)
Devotions Upon Emergent Occasions

I call God to witness that if we confined ourselves to the rational arguments of philosophy, which, though they enable us to know the divine Essence, do so in a negative way, no creature would ever have experienced the love of God. Positive religion teaches us that He is that and that; the exoteric appearances of these attributes are absurd to philosophical reason, and yet it is because of these positive attributes that we love Him.

IBN ARABI (1165–1240)
Kitab-al-Futuhat

I heard it all, I heard the whole
Harmonious hymn of being roll

Up through the chapel of my soul
And at the altar die.
And in the awful quiet then
Myself I heard, Amen, Amen,
Amen I heard me cry.

RALPH HODGSON (1871–1962)
The Song of Honour

The great beacon-light God sets in all,
The conscience of each bosom.

ROBERT BROWNING (1812–1889)
Strafford

As salt resolved in the ocean
I was swallowed in God's sea,
Past faith, past unbelieving,
Past doubt, past certainty.

Suddenly in my bosom
A sun shone clear and
    bright;
All the suns of heaven
Vanished in that star's light.

JALAL-UD-DIN RUMI (1207–1273)
The Masnawi

True and substantial wisdom principally consists of two parts, the knowledge of God and the knowledge of ourselves. But, while these two branches of knowledge are so intimately connected, which of them precedes the other, is not easy to discover.

JOHN CALVIN (1509–1564)
Institutes of the Christian Religion

Our awareness of God is a syntax of the silence, in which our souls mingle with the divine, in which the ineffable in us communes with the ineffable beyond us.

ABRAHAM JOSHUA HESCHEL (1907–1972)
Man Is Not Alone

For God can only be found after everything that is in the way has been cleared away, every finitude and above all, the individual himself in his finitude and his disputatiousness in the face of God.

SÖREN KIERKEGAARD (1813–1855)
Fear and Trembling

· ACCEPTING GOD'S PLAN FOR US ·

As you do not know how life enters an embryo in the womb of a pregnant woman, so you cannot know the work of God who does everything. Therefore, in the morning sow your seed and in the evening do not be idle, for you cannot tell which will prosper or whether both shall have equal success.   *The Old Testament
Ecclesiastes 11:5–6*

Observe the work of God, for who can straighten out what He has made crooked? In the day of good fortune, enjoy it, and in the day of trouble consider that God has set the one against the other, so that man may not discover anything that happens after he is gone.

*The Old Testament
Ecclesiastes 7:13–14*

People often think that for our will to find rest in God's means a fatalistic resignation to the will of God. But frequently the passive will of such people finds this impossible, because their active will has not found its way into God's will. How can they find the way by night if they haven't looked for it by day?

ALBERT SCHWEITZER (1875–1965)
Reverence for Life

If a man accepts everything that happens to him in this world with love, then he will have both this physical world and also the higher world of the soul.

BAAL SHEM TOV (1700–1760)
Sayings

It is permissible to take life's blessings with both hands provided thou dost know thyself prepared in the opposite event to leave them just as gladly.

MEISTER ECKHART (1260–1327)
Sermons

Why art thou so weary, O my soul! No malice of men can antedate my end by a minute, while my Maker hath any work for me to do. And when all my daily task is ended, why should I grudge then to go to bed.   THOMAS FULLER (1608–1661)
Good Thoughts in Bad Times

If we knew how much God loves us, we should always be ready to receive equally and with indifference from His hand the sweet and the bitter.

BROTHER LAWRENCE (1605–1691)
The Practice of the Presence of God

He who is satisfied with the portion alloted to him by his Creator may properly be deemed the richest of all mankind.

Arab Proverb

It is not by regretting what is irreparable that true work is to be done, but by making the best of what we are. It is not by complaining that we have not the right tools, but by using well the tools we have. What we are, and where we are, is God's providential arrangement—God's doing, though it may be man's undoing; and the wise way is to look your disadvantages in the face, and see what can be made of them.   FREDERICK WILLIAM ROBERTSON
(1816–1853)
Sermons

All as God wills, who wisely heeds
    To give or to withhold,
And knoweth more of all my needs
    Than all my prayers have told!

JOHN GREENLEAF WHITTIER (1807–1892)
My Psalm

Death, life, and sleep, reality and thought
Assist me, God, their boundaries to know,
O teach me calm submission to thy will.

WILLIAM WORDSWORTH (1770–1850)
Maternal Grief

O God, I have made an ill use of thy mercies, if I have not learned to be content with thy corrections.

JOSEPH HALL (1574–1656)
Contemplations

A true lover of God loveth him or the Eternal Goodness alike, in having, and in not having, in sweetness and bitterness, in good or evil report, and the like, for he seeketh alone the honour of God, and not his own, either in spiritual or natural things. And therefore he standeth alike unshaken in all things, at all seasons.

Theologia Germanica

The superior man is quiet and calm, waiting for the appointments of Heaven, while the mean man walks in dangerous paths, looking for lucky occurrences.

CONFUCIUS (551–479 B.C.)
Analects

God is the source and goal of ideals by which to live triumphantly in the face of starkest grief. The sufferer who finds God as the strength and mainstay of his life does not merely acquiesce before the inevitable with stoic fortitude. He looks the tragedy in the face, and looks up to new heights of spiritual beauty to which he may mount by using his grief as a stairway to God's glory.

GEORGIA HARKNESS (1891–1974)
The Recovery of Ideals

Have courage for the great sorrows of life and patience for the small ones; when you have laboriously accomplished your daily tasks, go to sleep in peace. God is awake. VICTOR HUGO (1802–1885)
Autobiography

Whatever is, is right. Though purblind man
Sees but a part o' the chain, the nearest link:
His eyes not carrying to the equal beam
That poises all above.
JOHN DRYDEN (1631–1700)
Collected Verse

He who unreservedly accepts whatever God may give him in this world—humiliation, trouble, and trial from within or from without—has made a great step towards self-victory; he will not dread praise or censure, he will not be sensitive; or if he finds himself wincing, he will deal so cavalierly with his sensitiveness that it will soon die away. Such full resignation and unfeigned acquiescence is true liberty, and hence arises perfect simplicity.
FRANÇOIS FÉNELON (1651–1715)
Letters to Women

To face God and eternal life aright, each person must accept reality. Flight from God is the flight of fear. Acceptance of God is the acceptance of the love that involves the acceptance of self and others. It is the acceptance of life.
NELS F. S. FERRE (1908–1971)
Know Your Faith

According to St. Paul, those who do not have the key to the mystery of life and of God are tempted either to sleep or be drunken, to be either complacent or hysterical when confronted with the evils of history. But those who have the key are enabled to watch and be sober.
REINHOLD NIEBUHR (1892–1971)
The Christian Idea of Education

I must endure the Will of God in whatever form it is laid upon me—in joy or in pain, in contentment or sick despair. Why am I at one with the Will of God when it gives me strength, and hope, and delight? Why am I so averse to it when it brings me languor, and sorrow, and despair?
ARTHUR CHRISTOPHER BENSON
(1862–1925)
The Thread of Gold

Let him not exult when he meets happiness, let him not grieve when he meets sorrow; firm in Soul-Vision, undeluded, knowing the Eternal, he stands firm in the Eternal. *The Bhagavad Gita*

He to whom sorrow is the same as joy,
And joy the same as sorrow,
May thank God for his equanimity.
JACOB BOEHME (1575–1624)
Aurora

"I am part of all that I have met," says the poet. God can say: I am part of all that admits me, all that is not shrunken by prejudice, hardened by habit, or dead through sin—part of all that have ever realized my presence in a new birth of insight. There He leaves, if not His image, something of his creative energy and inspiration, as the true teacher lives again in a new way in the souls of his pupils.
JOHN ELOF BOODIN (1869–1950)
Religion of Tomorrow

The highest knowledge which man can attain is the longing for peace, that our will becomes one with the infinite Will, our human will with the Will of God.
ALBERT SCHWEITZER (1875–1965)
Religion in Modern Civilization

I have no control over what may be helpful or hurtful to me, but as God wills. Had I the knowledge of his secrets I should revel in the good, and evil should not touch me.　　　　*The Koran*

One lesson which it costs us all much trouble to learn, but which we all must learn if we are to prosper and do good to others, is to desire to be nothing more and nothing different, in regard to an individual personality, from that which God has really given us capacity to become.

RICHARD ROTHE (1799–1867)
Still Hours

I have seen a man whom the world called a fearful sufferer living delightful days in his high study of the ways of God. Day by day his Maker took some strength out of his life, unstrung some nerve, put some pain in; but the suffering of a decaying body was so far surpassed by the rare joy of feeling his Maker's hands busy on the body and the spirit he had made, and of studying his wondrous ways of working, that his hours of sickness were the happiest that he had ever lived. He saw God glorifying himself, and was abundantly content; that was the well of which he drank.　　　PHILLIPS BROOKS (1835–1893)
The Battle of Life

It is possible, when the future is dim, when our depressed faculties can form no bright ideas of the perfection and happiness of a better world—it is possible still to cling to the conviction of God's merciful purpose towards His creatures, of His parental goodness even in suffering; still to feel that the path of duty, though trodden with a heavy heart, leads to peace; still to be true to conscience; still to do our work, to resist temptation, to be useful, though with diminished energy, to give up our wills when we cannot rejoice under God's

mysterious providence. In this patient, though uncheered obedience, we become prepared for light. The soul gathers force.

WILLIAM ELLERY CHANNING (1780–1842)
Sermons

Devotion is really neither more or less than a general inclination and readiness to do that which we know to be acceptable to God. To be truly devout, we must not only do God's will, but we must do it cheerfully.

SAINT FRANCIS OF SALES (1567–1622)
Introduction to a Devout Life

It is a vain thought to flee from the work that God appoints us, for the sake of finding a greater blessing to our own souls; as if we could choose for ourselves where we shall find the fullness of the Divine Presence, instead of seeking it where alone it is to be found, in loving obedience.

GEORGE ELIOT (1819–1880)
Letters

Accustom yourself to unreasonableness and injustice. Abide in peace in the presence of God, who sees all these evils more clearly than you do, and who permits them. Be content with doing with calmness the little which depends upon yourself, and let all else be to you as if it were not.

FRANÇOIS FÉNELON (1651–1715)
Works

Yet I argue not
Against Heaven's hand or will, nor bate a
　jot
Of heart or hope; but still bear up and
　steer
Right onward.

JOHN MILTON (1608–1674)
Paradise Lost

Enjoy the blessings of this day, if God send them; and the evils of it bear patiently and sweetly: for this day only is ours, we are dead to yesterday, and we are not born to the morrow.

JEREMY TAYLOR (1613–1667)
The Rule of Holy Living

In stormy times, when the foundation of existence is shaken, when the moment trembles in fearful expectation of what may happen, when every explanation is silent at the sight of the wild uproar, when a man's heart groans in despair, and "in bitterness of soul" he cries to heaven, then Job still walks at the side of the race and guarantees that there is a victory, guarantees that even if the individual loses in the strife, there is still a God, who, as with every human temptation, even if a man fails to endure it, will still make its outcome such that we may be able to bear it; yea, more glorious than any human expectation. SÖREN KIERKEGAARD (1813–1855)
Edifying Discourses

He knew not God and worshipped not,
Who displayed not contentment with his
  fortune and daily food.

SAADI (1184–1291)
Bustan

Yet spake yon purple mountain,
Yet said yon ancient wood,
That Night or Day, that Love or Crime,
Lead all souls to the Good.

RALPH WALDO EMERSON (1803–1882)
The Park

Go to now, ye that say, Today or tomorrow we will go into such a city, and continue there for a year, and buy and sell, and get gain: Whereas ye know not what shall be on the morrow. For what is your life? It is even a vapour, that appeareth for a little time, and then vanisheth away. For that ye ought to say, If the Lord will, we shall live, and do this, or that.

*The New Testament
James 4:13–15*

Submit: in this, or any other sphere,
Secure to be as blessed as thou canst bear
Safe in the hand of one disposing Pow'r,
Or in the natal, or the mortal hour.
All nature is but art unknown to thee,
All chance, direction which thou canst not
  see;
All discord, harmony not understood;
All partial evil, universal good;
And spite of pride, in erring reason's
  spite,
One truth is clear, Whatever is, is right.

ALEXANDER POPE (1688–1744)
Essay on Man

We stand on a mountain pass in the midst of whirling snow and blinding mist, through which we get glimpses now and then of paths which may be deceptive. If we stand still we shall be frozen to death. If we take the wrong road we shall be dashed to pieces. We do not certainly know whether there is any right one. What must we do? "Be strong and of a good courage." Act for the best, hope for the best, and take what comes.

WILLIAM JAMES (1842–1910)
The Will to Believe

If there be good in that I wrought,
Thy hand compelled it, Master, Thine—
Where I have failed to meet Thy
  Thought
I know, through Thee, the blame was
  mine.

RUDYARD KIPLING (1865–1936)
Collected Poems

Pursue thy secret path, everlasting Providence, only let me not, because thou art hidden, despair of thee. Let me not despair of thee even if thy steps appear to me to retreat. It is not true that the shortest line is always straight.

GOTTHOLD EPHRAIM LESSING (1729–1781)
The Education of the Human Race

Judge not the Lord by feeble sense,
But trust him for his grace;
Behind a frowning providence
He hides a smiling face.

WILLIAM COWPER (1731–1800)
Olney Hymns

We cannot have only the blessings that come with mind and conscience and that distinguish us from the lifeless rock and expect God to be our heavy insurance policy against all of the dangers and the failures of life.

JOSHUA LOTH LIEBMAN (1907–1948)
Peace of Mind

O man of God, follow the way of God,
Unlucky is he who turns his head
Away from this door, for he will find no
other door.   SAADI (1184–1291)
Gulistan

It is better to fight for the good, than to
rail at the ill;
I have felt with my native land, I am one
with my kind,
I embrace the purpose of God, and the
doom assign'd.

ALFRED LORD TENNYSON (1809–1892)
Maud

As if you took the chisel which had been trying to carve by itself and put it into the hand of Michelangelo, so only infinitely higher is it when you teach your soul to say "O Lord, not my will but thy will be done." It is no cry of a defeated man. It is the soul seizing on the privilege and the right of having itself completed after God's pattern.

PHILLIPS BROOKS (1835–1893)
Sermons

Fret not thyself because of evil-doers. Trust in the Lord: and do good. Commit thy way unto the Lord; trust also in Him.

And He shall bring it to pass. Rest in the Lord; and wait patiently for Him.

The Old Testament
Psalms 37:1–7

Pass through this tiny span of time in accordance with Nature, and come to thy journey's end with a good grace, just as an olive falls when it is fully ripe, praising the earth that bare it and grateful to the tree that gave it growth.

MARCUS AURELIUS (121–180)
Fragments

Better is poverty in the hand of God
Than riches in the storehouse;
And better are loaves where the heart is
joyous,
Than riches in unhappiness.

AMENOPE (10th century B.C.)
Egyptian Book of Wisdom

Do not be conformed to this world, but be transformed by the renewal of your mind, that you may prove what is the will of God, what is good and acceptable and perfect.   *The New Testament*
Romans 12:2

The superior man does not murmur against Heaven, nor grudge against men.

CONFUCIUS (551–479 B.C.)
Analects

In the foothills of the Himalayas, among the Khonds of North India, one hears the prayer: "Oh Lord, we know not what is good for us. Thou knowest what it is. For it we pray."

HARRY EMERSON FOSDICK (1878–1969)
The Meaning of Prayer

What God takes away is His own, and not ours, and who shall say: Why hast Thou done this?

FRANÇOIS FÉNELON (1651–1715)
Spiritual Letters

God is the master of the scenes; we must not choose which part we shall act; it concerns us only to be careful that we do it well.　　JEREMY TAYLOR (1613–1667)
Holy Living

Deem life a blessing with its numerous
　　woes,
Nor spurn away a gift a God bestows.
　　WILLIAM COWPER (1731–1800)
Hope

Who is honorable in the sight of the Creator? He who has met with adversity but bravely endures whatever befalls him.
　　SOLOMON IBN GABIROL (1021–1058)
The Choice of Pearls

If we murmur here, we may at the next melancholy be troubled that God did not make us to be angels or stars.
　　JEREMY TAYLOR (1613–1667)
The Rule and Exercises of Holy Living

Let us humbly accept from God even our own nature, and treat it charitably, firmly, intelligently. Not that we are called upon to accept the evil and the disease in us, but let us accept *ourselves* in spite of the evil and the disease.
　　HENRI FRÉDÉRIC AMIEL (1821–1881)
Journal Intime

Never say about anything, "I have lost it," but only "I have given it back." Is your child dead? It has been given back. "I had my farm taken away." Very well, this too has been given back. "Yet it was a rascal who took it away." But what concern is it of yours by whose instrumentality the Giver called for its return? So long as He gives it to you, take care of it as a thing that is not your own, as travellers treat their inn.　　EPICTETUS (1st century)
Enchiridion

If Thou pour Thy light upon me, and turn my night into day, blessed be Thy name; and if Thou leave me in darkness, blessed be Thy name. I will take alike from Thee sweet and bitter, joy and sorrow, good and evil: for all that befalls me I will thank the love that prompts the gift.
　　THOMAS À KEMPIS (1380–1471)
The Imitation of Christ

All is best, though we oft doubt
What the unsearchable dispose
Of Highest Wisdom brings about.
　　JOHN MILTON (1608–1674)
Samson Agonistes

A true lover of God loveth Him alike in having or in not having, in sweetness or in bitterness, in good report or in evil report. And therefore he standeth alike unshaken in all things, at all seasons.
　　Theologia Germanica

It is God's doing: sometimes sunshine, sometimes shadow.　　*Hindu Proverb*

The Wanderer said:—One adequate
　　support
For the calamities of mortal life
Exists—one only; an assured belief
That the procession of our fate, howe'er
Sad or disturbed, is ordered by a Being
Of infinite benevolence and power;
Whose everlasting purposes embrace
All accidents, converting them to good.
　　WILLIAM WORDSWORTH (1770–1850)
The Excursion

Though God take the sun out of the Heaven, yet we must have patience.
　　GEORGE HERBERT (1593–1633)
Outlandish Proverbs

· THE REALIZATION OF GOD ·

It is less terrible to fall to the ground when the mountains tremble at the Voice of God than it is to sit at the table with him as an equal; and yet it is God's concern precisely to have it so.

SÖREN KIERKEGAARD (1813–1855)
The Divine Incognito

God is for ever becoming incarnate in the world. This is the meaning of the historical process that God becomes man so that man may one day become God.

VLADIMIR SOLOVIËV (1853–1900)
The Justification of the Good

I am not a God afar off,
I am your brother and friend.
Within your bosom I reside,
And you reside in me.

WILLIAM BLAKE (1757–1827)
Collected Poems

The whole world is an omen and sign. Why look so wistfully in a corner? Man is the image of God. Why run after a ghost or a dream?

RALPH WALDO EMERSON (1803–1882)
Nature

God finds His complete Life in and through us as we find ours in and through Him and through each other in love and joy and cooperation.

RUFUS JONES (1863–1948)
Pathways

Everyone has in the eyes of God a specific importance in the fulfillment of which none can compare with him.

MARTIN BUBER (1878–1965)
Hasidism

The art of life is to live in the present moment, and to make that moment as per-

fect as we can by the realization that we are the instruments and expression of God Himself.   EMMET FOX (1886–1951)
Power Through Constructive Thinking

The ritual acts of man are an answer and reaction to the action of God upon man. That man feels capable of formulating valid replies to the over-powering influence of God, and that he can render back something which is essential even to God, induces pride, for it raises the human individual to the dignity of a metaphysical factor.

CARL JUNG (1875–1961)
Memories, Dreams, Reflections

With all the strength which God has given us, let us be fulfillers. Let us try to make the life of the world more complete. What can we do? First, each of us can put one more healthy and holy life into the world, and so directly increase the aggregation of righteousness. That is much. To fasten one more link, however small, in the growing chain that is ultimately to bind humanity to God beyond all fear of separation, is very much indeed.

PHILLIPS BROOKS (1835–1893)
Visions and Tasks

God does not look at us merely in the mass and multitude. As we shall stand single and alone before His judgment-seat, so do we stand, so have we always stood, single and alone before His boundless love. This is what each man has to believe of himself. From all eternity, God determined to create me, not simply a fresh man, not simply the son of my parents, a new inhabitant of my native country, an additional soul to the work of the century.

But He resolved to create me such as I am, the me by which I am myself, the me by which other people know me, a different me from any that will be created hereafter.

FREDERICK WILLIAM FABER (1814–1863)
Spiritual Conferences

Let each man think himself an act of God,
His mind a thought, his life a breath of
  God;
And let each try, by great thoughts and
  good deeds,
To show the most of heaven he hath in
  him.

PHILIP JAMES BAILEY (1816–1902)
Festus

It is not men in the mass who can and will save Man. It is Man himself, created in the image of God so that he shall have the power and the will to choose right from wrong, and so be able to save himself because he is worth saving; Man, the individual, men and women, who will refuse always to be tricked or frightened or bribed into surrendering, not just the right but the duty too, to choose between justice and injustice, courage and cowardice, sacrifice and greed, pity and self.

WILLIAM FAULKNER (1897–1962)
Essays

The Kingdom of God cannot be built by man alone from below up, nor, we may reverently say, can it be built by God without us, entirely and solely from Above down. "We are fellow-laborers with God" in this supreme creative task of the ages.

RUFUS JONES (1863–1948)
The Eternal Gospel

Human progress never rolls in on wheels of inevitability; it comes through the tireless efforts of men willing to be co-workers with God, and without this hard work, time itself becomes an ally of the forces of social stagnation.

MARTIN LUTHER KING, JR. (1929–1968)
Why We Can't Wait

So far as we live and strive at all, our lives are various, are needed for the whole, and are unique. No one of our lives can be substituted for another; no one of us finite beings can take another's place. And all of this is true just because the Universe is one significant whole.

JOSIAH ROYCE (1855–1916)
The Conception of Immortality

'Tis the sublime of man,
Our noontide majesty, to know ourselves
Part and proportion of one wondrous
  whole.

SAMUEL TAYLOR COLERIDGE (1772–1834)
Religious Musings

If we would be co-workers with God in the process of redemption, we must be prepared to meet obloquy and defeat, economic jeopardy, loneliness, perhaps even physical death. With a clear vision of the sin and weakness and also the goodness and greatness of human nature, we must labor to remove those barriers which separate men from God and from their own best selves.

GEORGIA HARKNESS (1891–1974)
The Recovery of Ideals

There is no doubt that God wants us to overcome our inner split, and to undo the errors of the past, individual as well as collective. He wants us to share in the task of creation, to become creative peacemakers in the outer world, and therefore in our inner life, too; he wants us, as the Beatitude says, to be "ranked sons of God."

FRITZ KUNKEL (1889–1956)
Creation Continues

We are part of the Universe, and the Universe is a part of God. We, therefore, have a Divine Nature and may truly be called sons and co-workers with God. The consciousness of this constitutes our highest privilege, and likewise our gravest responsibility.

SIR OLIVER LODGE (1851–1940)
The Substance of Faith

Each single human life in the world amounts to nothing less than a private revelation of God, a revelation which would be enough for the whole world, if an inspired pen recorded it.

FREDERICK WILLIAM FABER (1814–1863)
Bethlehem

God comes to each man with a pattern for him, his own image, that can be realized only through a process of understanding, acceptance and growth, in both encounter and indwelling.

NELS F. S. FERRE (1908–1971)
The Living God of Nowhere and Nothing

If man is a dependent being, his relationship to God is that which gives him existence. Can a wave continue to be if it leaves the water? Can a thought exist apart from the person who thinks it?

CHARLES EDWARD GARMAN (1850–1907)
Lectures

With God you may cross the sea; without him, do not cross the doorstep.

Russian Proverb

Man does possess the power, insofar as he works in obedience to God as His instrument, to bring the earth, which is now under the curse, under the blessing, and out of the anguish of death to create a kingdom of the highest joy. Yet he cannot do this himself, but his will must cooperate with the Divine intelligence to this end, bringing together that which belongs together, and so reducing all things to unity.

JACOB BOEHME (1575–1624)
Aurora

The more man becomes irradiated with Divinity, the more, not the less, truly he is man. To enter into it therefore is no wise strange. The wonder and the unnaturalness is that any child of God should live outside of it, and so in all his life should never be himself.

PHILLIPS BROOKS (1835–1893)
Sermons

The sun meets not the springing bud that stretches toward him with half that certainty with which God, the Source of all good, communicates Himself to the Soul that longs to partake of Him.

WILLIAM LAW (1686–1761)
The Spirit of Prayer

Man is man's A.B.C. There is none that can
Read God aright, unless he first spell Man.

FRANCIS QUARLES (1592–1644)
Hieroglyphics

God longs for His other self, His friend: He wants him to answer the call to enter the fullness of the divine life and participate in God's creative work of conquering non-Being.

NIKOLAI BERDYAEV (1874–1948)
The Destiny of Man

Why, God, did you include me in your great scheme?
Will you not make me a partner at last?

HENRY DAVID THOREAU (1817–1862)
Journals

When a man begins the Amidah and says the opening verse: "O Lord, open Thou my lips!" the Shekinah immediately enters within his voice, and speaks with his voice. Remember this, and you will have no fear.   BAAL SHEM TOV (1700–1760)
Sayings

As man is of the world, the heart of man
Is an epitome of God's great book
Of creatures, and men need no farther
  look.
          SAMUEL TAYLOR COLERIDGE (1772–1834)
                                      Eclogue

Acting and becoming are one. God and
I are one in this work: he acts and I become. Fire transforms all things it touches
into its own nature. The wood does not
change the fire itself, but the fire changes
the wood into itself. In the same way we
are transformed into God so that we may
know him as he is.
               MEISTER ECKHART (1260–1327)
                                      Sermons

We and God have business with each
other; and in opening ourselves to his influence our deepest destiny is fulfilled.
               WILLIAM JAMES (1842–1910)
               The Varieties of Religious Experience

God has planted many marvellous secrets in man, so that they lie in him like
seeds in the earth. And just as the seeds
burgeon from the earth in spring, so the
flowers and fruits that God has put in men
will come to light at the appointed time.
                    PARACELSUS (1493–1541)
                                      Works

When man does what he can, and can
go no further because of his weakness, it is
the infinite goodness of God which must
finish this work.
               JAN VAN RUYSBROECK (1293–1381)
                                On the Active Life

Ah, little recks the labourer
  How near his work is holding him to
     God,
The loving Labourer through space and
    time.
                  WALT WHITMAN (1819–1892)
                                Leaves of Grass

There is not in the world a kind of life
more sweet and delightful than that of a
continual walk with God. Those only can
comprehend it who practise and experience it.
               BROTHER LAWRENCE (1605–1691)
               The Practice of the Presence of God

The voice of the people is the kettle-
drum of God.   *Hindu Proverb*

All true religion is divine-human. Something of God comes into our world with
every child that is born. There is here with
the newborn child a divine spark, a light
within, something potential, that raises the
child out of the animal class, and intro-
duces a unique spiritual element.
                    RUFUS JONES (1863–1948)
                            A Call to What Is Vital

Man is a rudiment and embryon of God:
eternity shall develop in him the divine
image.   BRONSON ALCOTT (1799–1888)
                                Orphic Sayings

If you remember that God stands by to
behold and visit all that you do, whether
in the body or in the soul, you surely will
not err in any prayer or deed, and you
shall have God to dwell with you.
                    EPICTETUS (1st century)
                                    Discourses

Each man himself, as an individual,
should render his account to God. No
third person dares venture to intrude
upon this accounting between God and the
individual.
               SÖREN KIERKEGAARD (1813–1855)
                                Purity of Heart

God plants a secret in the soul of each
man, the deeper the more He loves the
man; that is, the more of a man He makes
him. In order to plant the mystery in us

He works our soul with the sharp spade of tribulation.

MIGUEL DE UNAMUNO (1864–1936)
The Secret of Life

God is He who knows man as he really is. Not man in general, but each individual according to the particular qualities of his nature and the uniqueness of his acts. And not with mere knowledge, but with personal love. From this knowledge and love He leads man towards that goal which, as Paul says, is "far beyond what we ask or conceive."

ROMANO GUARDINI (1885–1968)
Faith and the Modern Man

As sure as God ever puts his children in the furnace, he will be in the furnace with them.

CHARLES HADDON SPURGEON (1834–1892)
Privileges of Trial

O the nobility of Divine Friendship! Are not all His treasures yours, and yours His? Is not your very Soul and Body His: is not His life and felicity yours: is not His desire yours? Is not His will yours? And if His will be yours, the accomplishment of it is yours, and the end of all is your perfection. You are infinitely rich as He is: being pleased in everything as He is. And if His will be yours, yours is His.

THOMAS TRAHERNE (1637–1674)
Centuries of Meditations

Man is God's courier through time and eternity, and nothing that concerns him can be considered as little.

HENRY WARD BEECHER (1813–1887)
Sermons

Remarkable it is, truly, how everywhere the eternal fact begins again to be recognized, that there is a Godlike in human affairs; that God not only made us and beholds us, but is in us and around us; that the Age of Miracles, as it ever was, now is.

THOMAS CARLYLE (1795–1881)
Characteristics

If what philosophers say of the kindred between God and man be true, what has anyone to do, but, like Socrates, when he is asked of what country he is, never to say he is a citizen of Athens, or of Corinth, but of the world?   EPICTETUS (1st century)
Discourses

Liberality contemplates a harvest of usefulness. God has made us treasurers of His bounty. He has not given, only entrusted to us for special purposes what we have.

JOSEPH PARKER (1830–1902)
Sermons

Use me, God, in Thy great harvest field,
Which stretcheth far and wide like a wide sea;
The gatherers are so few; I fear the precious yield
Will suffer loss. Oh, find a place for me!

CHRISTINA ROSSETTI (1830–1894)
Send Me

The unconsciousness of man is the consciousness of God.

HENRY DAVID THOREAU (1817–1862)
A Week on the Concord and Merrimack Rivers

Who is man? A being in travail with God's dreams and designs, with God's dream of a world redeemed, of reconciliation of heaven and earth, of a mankind which is truly His image, reflecting His image, reflecting his wisdom, justice, and compassion. God's dream is not to be alone, to have mankind as a partner in the drama of continuous creation.

ABRAHAM JOSHUA HESCHEL (1907–1972)
Who Is Man?

True religion is man's relation to the infinite life about him, as established by him, a relation which is concordant with reason and human knowledge and binds his life up with this infinity and governs his acts.

LEO TOLSTOY (1828–1910)
Works

In the world of our moral consciousness God must wait upon our decisions. Our choices alter the constitution of the universe; they are not the rehearsal of an old tale. And while God, like a master chess player, can foresee our possible moves, he must wait for the outcome and make his own moves accordingly.

JOHN ELOF BOODIN (1869–1950)
Religion of Tomorrow

Man is God-conditioned, God divided from himself in order to look backward upon himself. He that doth not believe himself a God hath lost all sense, all remembrance of his Father. He is an outcast from the paternal mansion, an orphan and forlorn.

BRONSON ALCOTT (1799–1888)
Journals

· THE AFFIRMATION OF GOD ·

It is absolutely necessary to conclude that God exists: for though the idea of substance be in my mind owing to this, that I myself am a substance, I should not, however, have the idea of an infinite substance, seeing I am a finite being, unless it were given me by some substance in reality infinite. RENÉ DESCARTES (1596–1650)
Principles of Philosophy

God is really all in all to me. I hold of him, derive from him, live by him, enjoy myself under him, hope in him, expect from him. There is nothing more written in my heart than the sense of my dependency upon him.

BENJAMIN WHICHCOTE (1609–1683)
Letters

God is not imprisoned in His own Transcendence.

SRI AUROBINDO (1872–1950)
Studies in the Gita

If we cannot believe in God as a noun, maybe we can still believe in God as a verb. And the verb that God is, is transitive, it takes an object, and the object of the verb that God is, is the world.

FREDERICK BUECHNER (1926–)
The Hungering Dark

"How do you know," a Bedouin was asked, "that there is a God?" "In the same way," he replied, "that I know, on looking at the sand, when a man or a beast has crossed the desert—by His footprints in the world around me."

HENRY PARRY LIDDON (1829–1890)
Sermons

Stand fast in the Unchangeable Life and Seed of God which was before all changings and alterings were, and which will remain when all that is gone.

GEORGE FOX (1624–1691)
Epistles

The hope of the world is in the ever-richer naturalness of the highest life. "The earth shall be full of the knowledge of God as the waters cover the sea."

PHILLIPS BROOKS (1835–1893)
Sermons

Faith can be only the affirmation of God's action upon us, the answer to his Word directed to us. For if the realization of our own existence is involved in faith and if our existence is grounded in God and is non-existent outside God, then to apprehend our existence means to apprehend God.

RUDOLF BULTMANN (1884–1976)
Faith and Understanding

The fundamental symbol of our ultimate concern is God. It is always present in any act of faith, even if the act of faith includes the denial of God. Where there is ultimate concern, God can be denied only in the name of God. One God can deny the other one; ultimate concern cannot deny its own character as ultimate. Therefore, it affirms what is meant by the word "God."

PAUL TILLICH (1886–1965)
Dynamics of Faith

The king was seated in a garden, and one of his counselors was speaking of the wonderful works of God. "Show me a sign," said the king, "and I will believe." "Here are four acorns," said the counselor; "will your majesty plant them in the ground, and then stoop down for a moment and look into this clear pool of water?" The king did so. "Now," said the other, "look up." The king looked up and saw four oak-trees where he had planted the acorns. "Wonderful!" he exclaimed; "this is indeed a work of God." "How long were you looking into the water?" asked the counselor. "Only a second," said the king. "Eighty years have passed as a second," said the other. The king looked at his garments; they were threadbare. He looked at his reflection in the water; he had become an old man. "There is no miracle here, then," he said angrily. "Yes," said the other; "it is God's work,

whether he do it in one second or in eighty years."

BORDEN P. BOWNE (1847–1910)
The Immanence of God

The older I grow—and I now stand on the brink of eternity—the more comes back to me the sentence in the Catechism which I learned when a child, and the fuller and deeper its meaning becomes:— "What is the chief end of man? To glorify God, and to enjoy him forever."

THOMAS CARLYLE (1795–1881)
Autobiography

There is a Spirit which beareth witness with our spirits; there is a God who "is not far from any of us"; there is a "light which lighteth every man which cometh into the world." Do not be unnaturally humble. The thought of your mind, perchance, is the thought of God. To refuse to follow that may be to disown God. To take the judgment and conscience of other men to live by, where is the humility of that?

FREDERICK WILLIAM ROBERTSON
(1816–1853)
Sermons

The whole force of the argument of which I have availed myself to establish the existence of God consists in this, that I perceive I could not possibly be of such a nature as I am, and yet have in my mind the idea of a God, if God did not really exist.

RENÉ DESCARTES (1596–1650)
Principles of Philosophy

The most flawless proof of the existence of God is no substitute for it; and if we have that relationship, the most convincing disproof is turned harmlessly aside. If I may say it with reverence, the soul and God laugh together over so odd a conclusion.   SIR ARTHUR STANLEY EDDINGTON
(1882–1944)
Science and the Unseen World

If man has a higher nature and is called to a higher end, it is because God exists, and man must believe in Him; but if there be no God, then neither is there a higher nature in man, and he must fall back into the social ant-heap whose principle is compulsion.

NIKOLAI BERDYAEV (1874–1948)
Dostoevski

If you say that God is good, great, blessed, wise, or any such thing, the starting point is this: God is.

SAINT BERNARD OF CLAIRVAUX (1091–1153)
De Consideratione

Idealism sees the world in God. It beholds the whole circle of persons and things, of actions and events, of country and religion, not as painfully accumulated, atom after atom, act after act, in an aged creeping Past, but as one vast picture which God painted on the instant eternity for the contemplation of the soul.

RALPH WALDO EMERSON (1803–1882)
Nature

In one verse I shall tell you what has been taught in thousands of volumes: Brahman is true, the world is false; the soul is Brahman and nothing else.

SANKARACHARYA (780–820)
Sayings

There is a savage phrase attributed to Voltaire, the one which goes: "If God did not exist, it would be necessary to invent Him." A God thus invented, a deceit for oneself and others, would not even be a non-God, but would be an anti-God, an absolute Devil. And that Devil is the only one that exists: the God invented by those who do not in their hearts believe in Him.

MIGUEL DE UNAMUNO (1864–1936)
Essays on Faith

Walk with thy fellow-creatures: note the hush

And whispers among them. There is not a spring
Or leaf but hath his morning hymn; each bush
And oak doth know I AM. Canst thou not sing?

HENRY VAUGHAN (1622–1695)
Collected Verse

God is the binding element in the world. The consciousness which is individual in us, is universal in him: the love which is partial in us is all-embracing in him.

ALFRED NORTH WHITEHEAD (1861–1947)
Religion in the Making

My religion is founded on the love of God and my neighbor; on the hope of pardon for my offences; upon contrition; upon the duty as well as the necessity of supporting with patience the inevitable evils of life; in the duty of doing no wrong, but all the good I can, to the creation, of which I am but an infinitesimal part.

JOHN ADAMS (1735–1826)
Letter to F. A. Van der Kemp

The fact that God Himself preserves the Divine alive within us and protects man from himself has been the stand upon which all hope of an ultimate conquest of the Yea over the Nay within the soul of man rests.

RUDOLF EUCKEN (1846–1926)
The Truth of Religion

There is a God. The plants of the valley and the cedars of the mountain bless his name; the insect hums his praise; the elephant salutes him with the rising day; the bird glorifies him among the foliage; the lightning bespeaks his power, and the ocean declares his immensity. Man alone has said, "There is no God."

FRANÇOIS RENÉ DE CHATEAUBRIAND
(1768–1848)
The Genius of Christianity

Sometimes the great world and the human life which it contains grow wonderfully simple. Its mixed confusion disappears. Its one or two great certainties stand out to view. It all seems for one bright moment to come just to this—if there is a God, everything is right; if there is no God, everything is wrong. And there is a God. There is a God. Into the world all full of God comes man, and God is there before him. He finds God there. God takes him as he comes. Sometimes he talks as if he made God, and could make God over again to be what he would. But God made him. And it is to the God who made him that he comes. "Of Him and through Him and to Him are all things."

PHILLIPS BROOKS (1835–1893)
The Light of the World

May we meditate on the effulgent light of
Him
Who is worshipful, and who has given
birth to all worlds.
May He direct the rays of our intelligence
towards
The Path of Good.

The Rig-Veda

Whoso hath felt the Spirit of the Highest
Cannot confound, nor doubt Him, nor
deny:
Yea with one voice, O world, tho' thou
deniest,
Stand thou on that side, for on this am
I.

FREDERIC WILLIAM HENRY MYERS
(1843–1901)
Saint Paul

From eternity without beginning, to their
ear comes: "Am I not your God?"
With clamor, in a shout, they utter, "Yes!"
SAADI (1184–1291)
Bustan

The infinite God, the great one life, than whom is no other—only shadows, lovely shadows of Him.

GEORGE MACDONALD (1824–1905)
Unspoken Sermons

Who has a better religion than he who resigns his face to God, and does good?

The Koran

"For God saw all things which he made and they were very good." (Genesis 1:12) Why not? They are from a good artisan, who impressed his likeness upon all things that are from him. Therefore, in the being of things, we can admire the power of God working; in truth, we can venerate the wisdom of the artisan

GIOVANNI PICO DELLA MIRANDOLA
(1463–1494)
On the Dignity of Man

I know I did not make myself and yet, I have existence, and by searching into the nature of things I find no other thing can make itself; and yet millions of other things exist; therefore it is that I know by positive conclusions resulting from this search that there is a power superior to all those things, and that power is God.

THOMAS PAINE (1737–1809)
The Age of Reason

O friend, never strike sail to a fear! Come into port greatly, or sail with God the seas.

RALPH WALDO EMERSON (1803–1882)
Heroism

Delight—top-gallant delight—is to him who acknowledges no law or lord but the Lord his God, and is only patriot to heaven.

HERMAN MELVILLE (1819–1891)
Moby Dick

O Adorable and Eternal God! Hast Thou made me a free agent? And enabled

me if I please to offend Thee infinitely? What other end couldst Thou intend by this, but that I might please Thee infinitely? That having the power of pleasing or displeasing, I might be the friend of God! THOMAS TRAHERNE (1637–1674)
Centuries of Meditations

Even the enlightened person is never more than his own limited self before the One who dwells within him, whose form has no knowable boundaries, who encompasses him on all sides, fathomless as the abysms of the earth and vast as the sky.
CARL JUNG (1875–1961)
Answer to Job

I believe in God, the first, unknown, unique, omnipotent source of all creation. I feel within me that spark, that atom, emanation of the Divine Spirit, which gives life and movement to the universe and which we call the soul.
GIUSEPPE VERDI (1813–1901)
Letters

I have not hid thy righteousness within
  my heart;
I have declared thy faithfulness and thy
  salvation:
I have not concealed thy lovingkindness
  and thy truth from the great
  congregation.
The Old Testament
Psalms 40:9

Tell them I am, Jehovah said
To Moses; while earth heard in dread,
  And smitten to the heart,
At once above, beneath, around,
All nature, without voice or sound,
  Replied, O Lord, Thou art.
CHRISTOPHER SMART (1722–1771)
A Song to David

How can I doubt of God, who is my being? To doubt of God is to doubt of myself. Only when God is thought of abstractly, when his predicates are the result of philosophic abstraction, arises the distinction or separation between subject and predicate, existence and nature—arises the fiction that the existence or the subject is something else than the predicate, something immediate, indubitable, in distinction from the predicate, which is held to be doubtful. But this is only a fiction. A God who has abstract predicates has also an abstract existence.
LUDWIG FEUERBACH (1804–1872)
The Essence of Christianity

I believe in one God, and no more; and I hope for happiness beyond this life. I believe in the equality of man; and I believe that religious duties consist in doing justice, loving mercy, and endeavoring to make our fellow-creatures happy.
THOMAS PAINE (1737–1809)
The Age of Reason

When nothing here exists without Thee,
Then wherefore all this tumult, O Lord?
ASADULLAH KHAN GHALIB (1797–1869)
Works

I am aware of the sacred, of the mystery in man. And I do not see why I should not confess the emotion I experience before Christ and his teaching. I fear, unfortunately, that in certain quarters, especially in Europe, the avowal of an ignorance or limit to man's knowledge would only appear as a weakness. If these admissions are weaknesses, then I accept them with strength. ALBERT CAMUS (1913–1960)
Interview in Stockholm, December 1957

There is one God, one Love, one
  everlasting
Mystery of Incarnation, one creative
Passion behind the many-colored veil.
ALFRED NOYES (1880–1958)
Michael Oaktree

It is perhaps not important in the end that men either admit or deny God. This neither adds nor takes away anything from His existence. Even if one admitted that among the hundreds of millions of men who have confessed God in words, only a few have truly felt His presence, there would be nothing terrible in this: the *concensus omnium* plays no role here. That God exists is the chief thing, even if no one had ever heard anything of him. And, conversely, if all men on earth believed in God but He did not exist, it would be necessary to curse this faith, no matter how sweet and consoling it may be.

LEV SHESTOV (1866–1938)
Potestas Clavium

· OPENING THE DOORS OF PERCEPTION ·

If the eye were not made to receive the rays of the sun it couldn't behold it; if the singular power of God lay not in us, how could he reach us?

JOHANN WOLFGANG VON GOETHE
(1749–1832)
Essex

Keep your feet upon the top of the mountains and sound deep to the witness of God in every man.

GEORGE FOX (1624–1691)
Epistles

Man's ultimate aim is the realization of God, and all his activities—social, religious—have to be guided by the ultimate aim of the vision of God. The immediate service of all human beings becomes a necessary part of the endeavor simply because the only way to God is to see Him in His creation and be one with it.

MOHANDAS K. GANDHI (1869–1948)
Harijan

If He had refused thee a heart, truth-hearing,
Truth would have appeared to thy eye the essence of falsehood.

SAADI (1184–1291)
Bustan

Is it not our blindness, our hastiness, and our lack of charity, that sees only black and white, when God sees many shades of grey?

JOHN BAILLIE (1886–1960)
Our Knowledge of God

If you have power to see with the eyes of the mind, then, my son, He will manifest Himself to you. For the Lord manifests Himself ungrudgingly through all the universe; and you can behold God's image with your eyes, and lay hold on it with your hands.

Corpus Hermeticum (1st century)

Those who know beyond this the High Brahman, the vast, hidden in the bodies of all creatures, and alone enveloping everything, as the Lord, they become immortal.

The Upanishads

The walls are taken away. We lie open on one side to the deeps of spiritual nature, to all the attributes of God. Justice we see and know, Love, Freedom, Power. These natures no man ever got above, but always they tower over us, and most in the moment when our interests tempt us to wound them.

RALPH WALDO EMERSON (1803–1882)
The Over-Soul

It pleases God that we should achieve knowledge of His works, and that we should not with sound eyes grope in the darkness as though totally blind.

PARACELSUS (1493–1541)
Works

All things that are, are equally removed from being nothing; and whatsoever hath any being is by that very being a glass in which we see God, who is the root and the fountain of all being.

JOHN DONNE (1572–1631)
Sermons

The concept "God" is not a grasp of God by which a person masters the mystery, but it is letting oneself be grasped by the mystery which is present and yet ever distant.

KARL RAHNER (1904–)
Foundations of Christian Faith

We must perceive by our senses, before we can reflect with the mind. Our sensorium is that essential medium between the divine and human mind, through which God reveals to man the knowledge of nature, and is our only door of correspondence with God or with man.

ETHAN ALLEN (1738–1789)
Reason, the Only Oracle of Man

Some wise men, deluded, speak of Nature, and others of Time, as the cause of everything; but it is the greatness of God by which this Brahma-wheel is made to turn.
The Upanishads

Once my understanding was let down into the bottom of the sea, and there I saw green hills and valleys, with the appearance of moss strewn with seaweed and gravel. Then I understood in this way: that if a man or woman were there under the wide waters, if they could see God, as God is continually with man, they would be safe in soul and body, and come to no harm.

JULIAN OF NORWICH (1343–1416)
Showings

It is upon the inward condition that the outward reality depends. The visible universe is to us what our invisible souls choose to make it. Here we have a reason for looking at the things which are unseen —for making them the chief object of our attention. In so doing, we become conversant with the primal source of reality. We ascend to the original fountain of Being, from which the streams that flow forth receive their properties and their direction.

GEORGE RIPLEY (1802–1880)
Discourses on the Philosophy of Religion

Let them recognize that there are two kinds of people one can call reasonable; those who serve God with all their heart because they know Him, and those who seek Him with all their heart because they do not know Him.

BLAISE PASCAL (1623–1662)
Pensées

The nature of the living Being without me I can understand only through the living Being which is within me.

ALBERT SCHWEITZER (1875–1965)
Out of My Life and Thought

My spirit suddenly saw through all, and in and by all the creatures, even in herbs and grass, it knew God who he is, and how he is, and what his will is; and suddenly in that light my will was set on, by a mighty impulse, to describe the being of God.

JACOB BOEHME (1575–1624)
Aurora

Our conception of God must make meaningful the far-flung galaxies in space and time which science has revealed to us, if the soul is not to despair in loneliness under the stars. But our conception of God must also give inspiration and reality to our ideal creativeness in the social crisis in which we live.

JOHN ELOF BOODIN (1869–1950)
God: A Cosmic Philosophy of Religion

Be not ungrateful to Him Who hath made thee see, whereby thou mayest be able to believe what as yet thou canst not see. God hath given thee eyes in the body, reason in the heart; wake up the interior inhabitant of thine interior eyes, let it take to its window, examine the creature of God. SAINT AUGUSTINE (354–430)
Sermons

Thou, therefore, my invisible God, art seen of all and art seen in all seeing. Thou art seen by every person that seeth, in all that may be seen, and in every act of seeing, invisible as Thou art, and freed from all such conditions, and exalted above all for everymore.

NICHOLAS OF CUSA (1401–1464)
The Vision of God

Of this I am certain: if a soul understood the smallest thing that has isness, it would not turn away from it for an instant. The tiniest thing that one knows in God—if one even knew a flower, so far as it has its isness in God—that would be nobler than the whole world.

MEISTER ECKHART (1260–1327)
Works

Work to simplify the heart, that being immovable and at peace from any invading vain phantasms, thou mayest always stand fast in the Lord within thee, to that degree as if thy soul had already entered the always present now of eternity.

SAINT ALBERTUS MAGNUS (1206–1280)
De Adhaerendo Dei

And so I saw that God rejoices that he is our Father, and God rejoices that he is our Mother, and God rejoices that he is our true spouse, and that our soul is his beloved wife.

JULIAN OF NORWICH (1343–1416)
Showings

In a season of calm weather
Though inland far we be
Our souls have sight of that immortal sea
    which brought us hither.

WILLIAM WORDSWORTH (1770–1850)
Intimations of Immortality

There is one eternal Thinker, who though one, fulfilleth the desires of many. The wise who perceive Him within, to them belongeth eternal peace, to others not. *The Upanishads*

As for me, I will behold thy face in righteousness: I shall be satisfied, when I awake, with thy likeness.

The Old Testament
Psalms 17:15

If I feel God behind all existence, then there is a great identity established between all the utterances of Him throughout the length and breadth of human life. Let me know God, the source of all that man does anywhere, and then, O poet, sing your song! O sculptor, carve your statue! O builder, build your house! O engineer, roll out your railroad on the plain! O sailor, sail your ship across the sea! They are all mine. I am glad; I am proud of them all. PHILLIPS BROOKS (1835–1893)
Sermons

He who sees the Infinite in all things, sees God.

RICHARD HOOKER (1554–1600)
The Law of Ecclesiastical Polity

Equally perceiving the supreme mind in all beings, and all things in the supreme mind, the true worshipper sacrifices his own spirit by fixing it on the Spirit of God, and approaches the nature of the One, who shines by his own effulgence.

The Code of Manu

When, for a moment, after a long day's survey of the field, we lift our eyes and gaze towards the spiritual horizon, we perceive a region beyond the scope of science, where measurements fail, where explanations cease, and we catch a glimpse of an unfathomable glory.

SIR OLIVER LODGE (1851–1940)
Modern Scientific Ideas

The fact that man is unable or unwilling to acknowledge God, means only that he cannot accept ideas and beliefs about God framed by men, the false gods which obscure the living and ineffable God.

SARVEPALLI RADHAKRISHNAN (1888–1975)
Works

Real existence, real knowledge, and real love are eternally connected with one another, the three in one: where one of them is, the others must also be; they are the three aspects of the One without a second —the Existence-Knowledge-Bliss. When that existence becomes relative, we see it as the world; that knowledge becomes in its turn modified into the knowledge of the things of the world; and that bliss forms the foundation of all true love known to the heart of man.

SWAMI VIVEKANANDA (1863–1902)
Karma-Yoga

Can God be known? Yes, God can be known, since it is actually true and real that He is knowable through Himself. When that happens, man becomes free, he becomes empowered, he becomes capable —a mystery to himself—of knowing God.

KARL BARTH (1886–1968)
Dogmatics in Outline

I am not interested in any of the ways of building Babel-towers in the hope of reaching up to God, whether the towers are of brick and mortar, or whether they are of logic or of layers of Scripture texts, or of blocks from ancient creeds, or of sequences of causal proofs. All these man-built towers presuppose a remote and hidden god. The seeker, the tower-builder, on that supposition, must painfully rear his structure from below up by sheer human effort, with no sign of help, no evidence of cooperation from above. That kind of God could never be found, and such a quest would always end in confusion both of heart and of tongues.

RUFUS JONES (1863–1948)
Pathways to the Reality of God

The purpose and the way of knowledge are expressed in Augustine's famous words: "I wish to know God and the soul. Nothing else? Nothing at all."

PAUL TILLICH (1886–1965)
A History of Christian Thought

When I set myself to acquire wisdom and see all the activity taking place on the earth, I saw that though a man sleep neither by day nor by night he cannot discover the meaning of God's work which is done under the sun, for the sake of which a man may search hard, but he will not find it, and though a wise man may think he is about to learn it, he will be unable to find it.

The Old Testament
Ecclesiastes: 8:17

The wise man views that mysterious Being
In whom the universe perpetually exists,
Resting upon that sole support;
In him is the world absorbed;
From him it issues;
In creatures is he turned, and wove in various forms.
Let the wise man, versed in Holy Writ,
Promptly celebrate that immortal being,

Who is the mysteriously existing various
   abode.   *The Yajur Veda*

There is, apart from mere intellect, in
the make-up of every superior human
identity, a wondrous something that realizes without argument an intuition of the
absolute balance, in time and space, of the
whole of this multifariousness, this revel of
fools, and incredible make-believe and
general unsettledness, we call the world; a
soul-sight of that divine clue and unseen
thread which holds the whole congeries of
things, all history and time, and all events,
however trivial, however momentous,
like a leashed dog in the hand of the
hunter.
        WALT WHITMAN (1819–1892)
               Specimen Days

The superiority of man consists in his
being cognizant of divine attributes and
actions. Therein lies his perfection; thus
he may be worthy of admission to God's
presence.
  ABU-HAMID MUHAMMAD AL-GHAZZALI
              (1058–1111)
The Renovation of the Science of Religion

We doubt of the existence of God and
consequently of all else, so long as we have
no clear and distinct idea of God, but only
a confused one. For as he who knows not
rightly the nature of a triangle, knows not
that its three angles are equal to two right
angles, so he who conceives the Divine nature confusedly, does not see that it pertains to the nature of God to exist.
    BENEDICT SPINOZA (1632–1677)
      Theologico-Political Treatise

Revelation is natural religion enlarged
by a new set of disclosures communicated
by God immediately which reason vouches
the truth of.   JOHN LOCKE (1632–1704)
An Essay Concerning Human Understanding

When the sky is clear, and the wind
hums in the fir-trees, 'tis the heart of God
Who thus reveals himself.
        Oracle at Shinto Shrine

God himself culminates in the present
moment, and will never be more divine in
the lapse of all the ages.
  HENRY DAVID THOREAU (1817–1862)
               Walden

To make covenant with God is impossible, but by mediation of such as God
speaketh to, either by revelation supernatural or by His lieutenants that govern
under Him and in His name; for otherwise
we know not whether our covenants be accepted or not.
    THOMAS HOBBES (1588–1679)
              Leviathan

The fact that God can be revealed in a
personal life carries momentous implications. It may well be that God is all along
endeavoring to break through and reveal
His presence and character, the only difficulty being that He finds such poor, self-
filled instruments for any true revelation
to break through.
      RUFUS JONES (1863–1948)
A Preface to Christian Faith in a New Age

Know thou that every created thing is a
sign of the revelation of God. Each, according to its capacity, is, and will ever remain, a token of the Almighty.
      BAHA'U'LLAH (1817–1892)
          The Promised One

And I saw a new heaven and a new
earth: for the first heaven and the first
earth were passed away; and there was no
more sea.   *The New Testament*
            Revelation 21:1

Suppose a man in hiding stirs, showing his whereabouts there. God does the same. No one could ever have found God; He gave himself away.

MEISTER ECKHART (1260–1327)
Works

Inspiration, like God's omnipresence, is not limited to the few writers claimed by the Jews, Christians, or Mahometans, but is coextensive with the race. As God fills all space, so all spirit; as he influences and constrains unconscious and necessitated matter, so he inspires and helps free and conscious man.

THEODORE PARKER (1810–1860)
A Discourse of Matters Pertaining to Religion

To one in all, to all in one—
    Since Love the work began—
Life's ever widening circles run,
    Revealing God and man.

JOHN BANNISTER TABB (1845–1909)
Communion

There is nothing covered, that shall not be revealed, nor hid, which shall not be known; all will be examined in the searching, penetrating light of God's omniscience and glory, and by him whose eyes are as a flame of fire; and truth and right shall be made plainly to appear, being stripped of every veil.

JONATHAN EDWARDS (1703–1758)
Farewell Sermon

All that God ever reveals in revelation is —revelation. Or, to express it differently, he reveals nothing but himself to man. Whatever does not follow directly from this covenant between God and man, whatever cannot prove its direct bearing on the covenant, cannot be a part of it.

FRANZ ROSENZWEIG (1886–1929)
The Star of Redemption

If you say you have a revelation from God, I must have a revelation from God too, before I can believe you.

BENJAMIN WHICHCOTE (1609–1683)
Sermons

God hides nothing. His very work from the beginning is *revelation*—a casting aside of veil after veil, a showing unto men of truth after truth.

GEORGE MACDONALD (1824–1905)
Sermons

Providence is God's sermon. The things which we see about us are God's thoughts and God's words to us; and if we were but wise there is not a step that we take which we should not find to be full of mighty instruction.

CHARLES HADDON SPURGEON (1834–1892)
Sermons

Natural truths are truths of God's creation; supernatural truths are truths of God's revelation. Nothing is more knowable than natural truth; nothing is more credible than revealed truth.

BENJAMIN WHICHCOTE (1609–1683)
Aphorisms

Wondrous truths, and manifold as wondrous,
God hath written in those stars above;
But not less in the bright flowerets under us
Stands the revelation of his love.

HENRY WADSWORTH LONGFELLOW
(1807–1882)
Flowers

Man is the book in which all the mysteries are recorded; but this book is interpreted by God.

PARACELSUS (1493–1541)
Works

Revelation is God Himself in His self-manifestation within history; revelation is something that happens.

EMIL BRUNNER (1889–1966)
Revelation and Reason

A revelation is not made for the purpose of showing to indolent men that which, by faculties already given to them, they may show themselves; no, but for the purpose of showing that which the moral darkness of man will not, without supernatural light, allow him to perceive.

THOMAS DE QUINCEY (1785–1859)
*The True Relations of the Bible
to Merely Human Science*

The mysterious God, whom the world neither knows nor shows, whom I do not know and whom the inner man does not reveal, must reveal his mystery to the world—must tell his own name—by piercing into the world. He must assert himself over against the world as a being who is not-world, not-ego; who reveals his true name, the secret of his unknown will which is opposed to the world, contrary to our experience and, above all, to the thoughts and intents of our own heart.

EMIL BRUNNER (1889–1966)
The Theology of Crisis

The Eternal Gospel is the endless revelation to men of a spiritual Reality who is over all and in all, and at the same time vastly more than all things in space and time, a Reality both immanent and transcendent, as Spirit in its essential nature is bound to be.　RUFUS JONES (1863–1948)
The Eternal Gospel

The Purpose of the one true God, exalted be his glory, in revealing Himself unto men is to lay bare those gems that lie hidden within the mine of their true and inmost selves.　BAHA'U'LLAH (1817–1892)
Works

No age thinks of God quite as its predecessor did, or talks to him in quite the same language. Yet the same God reveals himself to each, speaking to each in the language it is fitted to understand. Piety is unity, but unity is not uniformity.

WILLIAM ADAMS BROWN (1865–1943)
The Life of Prayer in a World of Science

My life is completely and unmistakably determined by the mysterious experience of God revealing Himself within me as ethical Will and desiring to take hold of my life.

ALBERT SCHWEITZER (1875–1965)
Civilization and Ethics

Life is a perpetual Revelation of the Infinite, Invisible One. The undying Life is ever throbbing in the soul of Man, and investing him with the immortality which is its essential being. Man lives and is from God. He is, as it were, the fast-flitting pulse of the Divinity.

BRONSON ALCOTT (1799–1888)
Journals

Blind unbelief is sure to err and scan his
　　work in vain,
God is his own interpreter and he will
　　make it plain.

WILLIAM COWPER (1731–1800)
God Moves in a Mysterious Way

The revelation of God to man is always a two-fold one, a personal-individual revelation, and a revelation in the context of social-historical experience. Without the public and historical revelation the private experience of God would remain poorly defined and subject to caprice. Without the private revelation of God, the public and historical revelation would not gain credence.

REINHOLD NIEBUHR (1892–1971)
The Nature and Destiny of Man

God will eventually reveal his glory to all mankind as unmistakably as though he had placed his throne in the center of the heavens, and then moved it from one extreme end to the other, so that everybody should see and know it.   *The Midrash*

He who seeks for the divine revelation will not find God through the theory of cognition. First of all let him endeavor to create values. Let him liberate those who are oppressed, feed those who are in want, give sight to the blind, find a way to enrich the poor. Then will he be able to see divine revelations every day.

TOYOHIKO KAGAWA (1888–1960)
Meditations

If the revelation of God is a revelation of perfection, as well as an exhortation to what it should be, then the consciousness of guilt is man's discovery of his lack of likeness to God.

NIKOLAI F. FEDOROV (1828–1903)
Works

In all times, either men have spoken of the true God, or the true God has spoken to men.   BLAISE PASCAL (1623–1662)
Pensées

The knowledge of man is as the waters, some descending from above, and some springing from beneath; the one informed by the light of nature, and the other inspired by divine revelation.

FRANCIS BACON (1561–1626)
The Advancement of Learning

We must impress on our memory the infallible rule, that what God has revealed is incomparably more certain than anything else; and that we ought to submit our belief to the Divine authority rather than to our own judgment, even though perhaps the light of reason should, with the greatest clearness and evidence, appear to suggest to us something contrary to what is revealed.

RENÉ DESCARTES (1596–1650)
Meditations

· I AND THOU ·

Thou which within me art, yet Me! Thou
   Eye,
And Temple of his Whole Infinitie!
O what a World art Thou! a World
   within!

THOMAS TRAHERNE (1637–1674)
My Spirit

Bring into this great cup, which is full of wine, the essence of ambrosia produced from the essence of all that is in this world with its differing kinds of taste. I offer as oblation into the Fire of the Supreme Self the excellent nectar of Thisness with which the cup of I-ness is filled.

The Mahanirvana Tantra

The I of the revealing God, the I of the God Who accords to the mystic the intercourse with Him, and the I of God, in Whom the human I merges itself, are identical.

MARTIN BUBER (1878–1965)
Hasidism

Look where I may, still nothing I discern
But Thee throughout this Universe,
   wherein
Thyself Thou dost reflect, and through
   those eyes
Of him whom Man thou madest,
   scrutinize.

Do Thou my separate and derived Self
Make one with thy Essential! Leave me
   room
On that Divan which leaves no room for
   Twain;
Lest, like the simple Arab in the tale,
I grow perplext, O God! 'twixt 'Me' and
   'Thee.'

JAMI (1414–1492)
Salaman and Absal

The symbols "life," "spirit," "power,"
"grace," etc., as applied to God in devotional life, are elements of the two main
symbols of a person-to-person relationship
with God, namely, God as Lord and God
as Father. While Lord is basically the
expression of man's relation to the God
who is holy power, Father is basically the
expression of man's relation to the God
who is holy love. The concept "Lord" expresses the distance; the concept "Father,"
the unity.

PAUL TILLICH (1886–1965)
Systematic Theology

But when all madness and delusion fall
to dust, when they stand over against Him
in the loneliest darkness and no longer say
"He, He" but rather sigh "Thou," shout
"Thou," all of them the one word, and
when they add "God," is it not the real God
whom they all implore, the One Living
God, the God of the children of man?

MARTIN BUBER (1878–1965)
Eclipse of God

Thou shalt lose thy *thyness* and dissolve
is His *hisness*; thy *thine* shall be His *mine*, so
utterly one *mine* that thou in Him shalt
know eternalwise his *isness*, free from becoming: His nameless nothingness.

MEISTER ECKHART (1260–1327)
Works

There are three different paths to reach
the Highest; the path of I, the path of
Thou, and the path of Thou and I.

SRI RAMAKRISHNA (1834–1886)
Gospel of Sri Ramakrishna

Repeating "Thou, Thou," I became
Thou; in me no "I" remained. Offering
myself into Thy name, wherever I look
Thou art! KABIR (1450–1518)
The Adi Granth

God is experienced as "Thou" or "I," according to the spot in which consciousness
centers; but the man who experiences Him
as "I" experiences Him more profoundly.

HERMANN KEYSERLING (1880–1946)
The Travel Diary of a Philosopher

Through God, man becomes I, his particular self, someone special within the
world. He is that because he is someone to
whom God calls "Thou," someone called
forward by God and addressed by Him.
God says to him, "Thou," and thus makes
him I. From the eternal I, through the
"Thou shalt," a particular uniqueness enters into his life and makes him conscious
of his I. Now he can also speak to God, can
say to Him, "Thou art my God."

LEO BAECK (1873–1956)
This People Israel

All religion is in the change from He to
Thou. It is a mere abstraction as long as it
is He. Only with the Thou we know God.

THOMAS ERSKINE (1788–1870)
Letters

Can one still speak to God after Oswieçim and Auschwitz? Can one still, as an
individual and as a people, enter at all into
a dialogue relationship with Him? Dare we
recommend to the survivors of Oswieçim,
the Jobs of the gas chambers, "Call to Him,
for He is kind, for His mercy endureth
forever?" MARTIN BUBER (1878–1965)
Dialogue Between Heaven and Earth

Our eternal life is rooted in the "thou" of God who addresses us, not in the "I" which we speak to ourselves.

EMIL BRUNNER (1889–1966)
Man in Revolt

Ask the lovers of God and men alike: do they not all tell us, so far as they can tell the inexpressible, that there is no loss but an immense enhancement of being: that if "I" becomes "Thou" it is not by losing the real self but by finding it.

GERALD VANN (1906–1963)
The Heart of Man

The essence of man is contained only in the community, in the unity of man with his fellow man—a unity which, however, rests only on the reality of the distinctness of I and Thou.

LUDWIG FEUERBACH (1804–1872)
The Philosophy of the Future

In the relation of trust between I and Thou, I am asked only whether I believe the *Thou.* I cannot through my own feeling validate for myself the trust I have given him. This is equally true in man's relation to God. A faith which concentrates on itself is no more faith than a love which concentrates on itself is love.

RUDOLF BULTMANN (1884–1976)
Faith and Understanding

· LETTING GO OF SELF ·

The more the Self, the I, the Me, the Mine, that is, self-seeking and selfishness, abate in a man, the more doth God's I, that is, God Himself, increase in him.

Theologia Germanica

The best way to see divine light is to put out your own candle. *English Proverb*

When you get rid of selfishness, together with things and what pertains to them, and have transferred all to God, and united with him, and abandoned all for him in complete trust and love, then whatever your lot, whatever touches you, for better or worse, sour or sweet, none of it is yours but it is all God's, to whom you have left it. MEISTER ECKHART (1260–1327)
Sermons

Keep God in remembrance until self is
 forgotten,
That you may be lost in the Called,
 without distraction of caller and call.
JALAL-UD-DIN RUMI (1207–1273)
The Diwan

He who works without attachment, dedicating his actions to God, is untouched by sin, as a lotus leaf is not wetted by water.
The Bhagavad Gita

From the moment a creature becomes aware of God as God and itself as self, the terrible alternative of choosing God or self for the centre is opened to it.

C. S. LEWIS (1898–1963)
The Problem of Pain

He whose heart is unattached to objects of the senses, findeth that within which is very bliss; he who resteth in identity with the One Supreme, enjoyeth bliss eternal.
The Bhagavad Gita

Those who seek name and fame are under a delusion. They forget that everything is ordained by the Great Dispenser of all things and that all is due to the Lord and the Lord alone. The wise man says

always, "It is Thou, O Lord, it is Thou," but the ignorant and deluded say, "It is I, it is I."   SRI RAMAKRISHNA (1836–1886)
Sayings

When you stop willing and thinking self then the eternal hearing, seeing and speaking will be revealed within you, and God will see and hear through you. Your egocentric hearing, willing and seeing hinders you from seeing and hearing God.
JACOB BOEHME (1575–1624)
The Way to Christ

Love took up the harp of life,
And smote on all the chords with might;
Smote the chord of "self," which,
    trembling,
Passed in music out of sight.
ALFRED LORD TENNYSON (1809–1892)
Collected Poems

We must be ready to choose discomfort when Love demands it. And, of course, Love demands it, first of all because the self-seeking which is so deeply rooted in us is an offence against love.
GERALD VANN (1906–1963)
The Divine Pity

There is nothing contrary to God in the whole world, nothing that fights against him, but self-will. This is the strong castle that we all keep garrisoned against Heaven in every one of our hearts, which God continually layeth siege unto; and it must be conquered and demolished, before we can conquer Heaven.
RALPH CUDWORTH (1617–1688)
Sermons

Pluck out self-love as with the hand you pluck the autumn water-lily, and you will set your heart on the perfect path of peace.   *Buddhist Proverb*

God in Heaven, let me really feel my nothingness, not in order to despair over it, but in order to feel the more powerfully the greatness of Thy goodness.
SÖREN KIERKEGAARD (1813–1855)
Journals

The love of one's neighbor is the only door out of the dungeon of self. The man thinks his consciousness is himself; whereas his life consists of the inbreathing of God, and the consciousness of the universe of truth. To have himself, to know himself, to enjoy himself, he calls life; whereas, if he would forget himself, tenfold would be his life in God and his neighbors. The region of man's life is a spiritual region. God, his friends, his neighbors, his brothers all, is the wide world in which alone his spirit can find room. Himself is his dungeon.
GEORGE MACDONALD (1824–1905)
Unspoken Sermons

He who prays fervently knows not whether he prays or not, for he is not thinking of the prayer which he makes, but of God, to whom he makes it.
SAINT FRANCIS OF SALES (1567–1622)
Treatise on the Love of God

What we see, then, is that two societies have issued from two kinds of love. Worldly society has flowered from a selfish love which dared to despise even God, whereas the communion of saints is rooted in a love of God that is ready to trample on self. In a word, this latter relies on the Lord, whereas the other boasts that it can get along by itself.
SAINT AUGUSTINE (354–430)
The City of God

Whoever seeks, loves, and pursues the Good for the sake of the Good and for nothing but the love of the Good, not as from the Me, or as the I, Me, Mine, or for the sake of the Me, he will find it, for he seeks it aright.   *Theologia Germanica*

Prayer is nought but a rising desire of the heart into God by withdrawing of the heart from all earthly thoughts.
WALTER HILTON (1340–1395)
The Scale of Perfection

"The Kingdom of God is within you," yes, but only if we are prepared to let that powerful germ of eternal life grow, until it splits away and consumes this husk, our ego. Unless we, this person with his tightly bound triple self-love—love of his physical appetites and comforts, of his possessions, of his place, rank, and recognition—unless that hard and hardening nut is buried and rots and is eaten away by the new life's germ, there is no hope.
GERALD HEARD (1889–1971)
The Creed of Christ

· THE WONDERS OF CREATION ·

Any one thing in the creation is sufficient to demonstrate a Providence to a humble and grateful mind.
EPICTETUS (1st century)
Discourses

My library shall consist of the threefold book of God; my philosophy shall be, with David, to consider the heavens and the works of God; and to wonder that He, the Lord of so great a kingdom, should condescend to look upon a poor worm like me.   JOHN AMOS COMENIUS (1592–1670)
The Confession

If the stars should appear one night in a thousand years, how would men believe, and adore, and preserve for many generations, the remembrance of the city of God which had been shown? But every night come out these envoys of beauty, and light the universe with their admonishing smile.
RALPH WALDO EMERSON (1803–1882)
Journals

A man with God is always in the majority.   JOHN KNOX (1505–1572)
Sermons

However, you're a man, you've seen the
world—
The beauty and the wonder and the
power,
The shape of things, their colours, lights
and shades,
Changes, surprises—and God made it all!
ROBERT BROWNING (1812–1889)
Fra Lippo Lippi

If the Father deigns to touch with divine power the cold and pulseless heart of the buried acorn and to make it burst forth from its prison walls, will He leave neglected in the earth the soul of man made in the image of his Creator?
WILLIAM JENNINGS BRYAN (1860–1925)
The Prince of Peace

God is in all that liberates and lifts;
In all that humbles, sweetens, and
consoles
A mystery of purpose gleaming through
the secular confusion of the world,
Whose will we darkly accomplish, doing
ours.
JAMES RUSSELL LOWELL (1819–1891)
The Soul's Horizon

It was because the lion and the lamb first lay down together in the heart of God that the prophet declared that they shall yet do it on earth.

HENRY WARD BEECHER (1813–1887)
Sermons

In the breadth and depth of its cosmic stuff, in the bewildering number of the elements and events that make it up, and in the wide sweep, too, of the overall currents that dominate it and carry it along as one single great river, the world, filled by God, appears to our enlightened eyes as simply a setting in which universal communion can be attained and a concrete expression of that communion.

PIERRE TEILHARD DE CHARDIN (1881–1955)
Let Me Explain

· THE MEASURE OF ALL THINGS ·

Have thy tools ready; God will find thee work.

CHARLES KINGSLEY (1819–1875)
Sermons

The wise man therefore embraces God and enjoys Him, the Being that always endures, and as to whom one does not look forward to His coming to be, but through that very fact, *that* He truly is, He is always present.

SAINT AUGUSTINE (354–430)
De Ordine

Henceforth, please God, forever I forgo
The yoke of men's opinions. I will be
Light-hearted as a bird, and live with
    God.
I find him in the bottom of my heart.
I hear continually his voice therein.

The little needle always knows the North,
The little bird remembereth his note,
And this wise Seer within me never errs.
I never taught it what it teaches me;
I only follow when I act aright.

RALPH WALDO EMERSON (1803–1882)
Self-Reliance

Let us weigh the gain and the loss in wagering that God is. Let us estimate these two chances. If you gain, you gain all; if you lose, you lose nothing. Wager, then, without hesitation that He is.

BLAISE PASCAL (1623–1662)
Pensées

My prayers, my God, flow from what I
    am not;
I think thy answers make me what I am.
Like weary waves thought follows upon
    thought,
But the still depth beneath is all thine
    own,
And there thou mov'st in paths to us
    unknown.
Out of strange strife thy peace is
    strangely wrought;
If the lion in us pray—thou answerest the
    lamb.

GEORGE MACDONALD (1824–1905)
Unspoken Sermons

Then what life is agreeable to God and becoming in his followers? One only, expressed once for all in the old saying: Like agrees with like, with measure measure. Now God ought to be to us the measure of all things, and not man, as men commonly say. And he who would be dear to God must, as far as is possible, be like Him and such as He is.   PLATO (427–347 B.C.)
Laws

The first instance that I remember of that sort of inward, sweet delight in God and divine things that I have lived much in since, was on reading those words in 1 Timothy 1:17. "Now unto the King eternal, immortal, invisible, the only wise God, be honor and glory for ever and ever, Amen." As I read the words, there came into my soul, and was as it were diffused in it, a sense of the glory of the Divine Being; a new sense, quite different from anything I had ever experienced before.

JONATHAN EDWARDS (1703–1758)
Works

· IF GOD BE MY FRIEND ·

If God be my friend I cannot be wretched. OVID (43 B.C.–A.D. 17)
Tristia

He who is pure in heart, not on account of the commandments, but on account of his higher insight, he is a friend of God.

CLEMENT OF ALEXANDRIA (150–215)
Miscellanies

Hast thou a friend, as heart may wish at will?
Then use him so, to have his friendship still
Wouldst have a friend, wouldst know what friend is best?
Have God thy friend, who passeth all the rest.

THOMAS TUSSER (1524–1580)
Posies for a Parlour

It is no use to ask what those who love God do with him. There is no difficulty in spending our time with a friend we love; our heart is always ready to open to him; we do not study what we shall say to him, but it comes forth without premeditation; we can keep nothing back—even if we have nothing special to say, we like to be with him.

FRANÇOIS FÉNELON (1651–1715)
Golden Thoughts

Strong one, make me strong!
May all beings look on me with the eye of friend,

May I look on all beings with the eye of friend,
May we look on one another with the eye of friend.

The Rig-Veda

To the friends of God a dark night
Shines like the brilliant day.

SAADI (1184–1291)
Gulistan

Prayer is friendship with God. Friendship is not merely a generalized mood: every event is its occasion.

GEORGE ARTHUR BUTTRICK (1892–1979)
Prayer

The best preacher is the heart; the best teacher is time; the best book is the world; the best friend is God. *The Talmud*

I have no friend like God, Who gave me soul and body, and infused into me understanding. He cherisheth, and watcheth over, all creatures.

GURU NANAK (1469–1539)
Hymns

This, this is the God we adore,
Our faithful, unchangeable Friend;
Whose love is as great as his power,
And neither knows measure nor end.

PHILIP DODDRIDGE (1702–1751)
Hymns

I awoke this morning with devout thanksgiving for my friends, the old and the new. Shall I not call God, the Beautiful, who daily showeth himself so to me in his gifts?

RALPH WALDO EMERSON (1803–1882)
Friendship

Fellowship with God is the goal to which God calls us; it is fellowship with Love—utter, self-forgetful, and self-giving Love. The selfish cannot reach it, except they be first changed into what they are not; and if they could, they would detest it.

WILLIAM TEMPLE (1881–1944)
Christus Veritas

Hearts are linked to hearts by God. The friend on whose fidelity you count, whose success in life flushes your cheek with honest satisfaction, whose triumphant career you have traced and read with a heart throbbing almost as if it were a thing alive, for whose honour you would answer as for your own; that friend, given you by circumstances over which you had no control, was God's own gift.

FREDERICK WILLIAM ROBERTSON
(1816–1853)
Sermons

A friend is the gift of God, and He only who made hearts can unite them.

JOHN TILLOTSON (1630–1694)
Sermons

If God is God, the best knowledge of God must come through a higher kind of friendship. So the "proof" is in a venture: we dare to live as in the presence of the Unseen Companion who ever and again takes us unawares.

GEORGE ARTHUR BUTTRICK (1892–1979)
So We Believe, So We Pray

Every one has the key to God in himself; let him but seek it in the right place.

JACOB BOEHME (1575–1624)
Second Apology

If the heart wanders or is distracted, bring it back to the point quite gently and replace it tenderly in its Master's presence.

SAINT FRANCIS OF SALES (1567–1622)
Spiritual Conferences

Do you not know that you are God's temple and that God's Spirit dwells in you? If anyone destroys God's temple, God will destroy him. For God's temple is holy, and that temple you are.

New Testament
1 Corinthians 3:16–17

In every renewed man, the individual temple of God, the outward parts are allowed common to God and the world; the inwardest and secretest, which is the heart, is reserved only for the God that made it.

JOSEPH HALL (1574–1656)
Contemplations

· THE INDWELLING CAUSE OF ALL THINGS ·

All things
Are of one pattern made; bird, beast, and plant,
Song, picture, form, space, thought, and character,

Deceive us, seeming to be many things,
And are but one.

RALPH WALDO EMERSON (1803–1822)
Xenophanes

Life is the sacred spark of God in us, and the best of our race have reverenced it most.

WALTER RAUSCHENBUSCH (1861–1918)
Christianizing the Social Order

Some may ask what it is like to be a partaker of the Divine Nature? Answer: he who is imbued with or illuminated by the Eternal or Divine Light and inflamed and consumed with Eternal or Divine Love, he is a deified man and a partaker of the Divine Nature.

Theologia Germanica

God is the indwelling, not the transient, cause of all things.

BENEDICT SPINOZA (1632–1677)
Ethics

Supreme Bliss comes to the yogi whose mind is completely tranquil and whose passions are quieted, who is free from stain and who has become one with Brahman.
The Upanishads

When I thus rest in the silence of contemplation, thou, Lord, makest reply within my heart, saying: Be thou mine and

I too will be thine; Thou, Lord canst not be mine if I be not mine own.

NICHOLAS OF CUSA (1401–1464)
The Vision of God

Let none turn over books or scan the stars in quest of God who sees Him not in man.

JOHANN KASPAR LAVATER (1741–1801)
Aphorisms on Man

You have heard of Saint Chrysostom's celebrated saying in reference to the Shekinah, or Ark of Testimony, visible Revelation of God, among the Hebrews: "The true Shekinah is Man!" Yes, it is even so: this is no vain phrase, it is veritably so. The essence of our being, the mystery in us that calls itself "I,"—ah, what words have we for such things?—is a breath of Heaven; the Highest Being reveals Himself in man. This body, these faculties, this life of ours, is it not a vesture for the Unnamed?

THOMAS CARLYLE (1795–1881)
On Heroes and Hero-Worship

But 'tis God
Diffused through all, that doth make all one whole.

SAMUEL TAYLOR COLERIDGE (1772–1834)
Religious Musings

· THE LORD SHALL GUIDE THEE CONTINUALLY.... ·

Whosoever believes in God, and does righteousness, He will admit him to gardens underneath which rivers flow; therein they shall dwell for ever and ever. God has made for him a goodly provision.
The Koran

A man's heart deviseth the way, but the Lord directeth his steps.
The Old Testament
Proverbs 41:9

God shall be my hope,
My stay, my guide and lantern to my feet.
WILLIAM SHAKESPEARE (1564–1616)
Henry VI, Pt. 2

Let man beware against going forth upon his journeyings alone. That is to say, let him obey the Divine Will so that he shall not go forth without the accompanying Presence of God—which will sustain him and deliver him in every hour of need. *The Zohar (13th century)*

And the Lord shall guide thee continually, and satisfy thy soul in drought, and make fat thy bones: and thou shalt be like a watered garden, and like a spring of water, whose waters fail not.

The Old Testament
Isaiah 58:10

We look to Thee; Thy truth is still the
  Light
Which guides the nations, groping on
  their way,
Stumbling and falling in disastrous night,
Yet hoping ever for the perfect day.

THEODORE PARKER (1810–1860)
The Way, the Truth, and the Life

God bestows many benefits upon us, even against our wills; many also, and these greater, without our knowledge.

SAINT JOHN CHRYSOSTOM (345–407)
Homilies

God guides every individual destiny through the inspiration of the soul. This soul-inspiration is given to each one, and not only the elect, so that everyone may, in the exercise of his free will, reach to the higher reason which is the supreme level of the holy spirit.

SHOLEM ASCH (1880–1957)
What I Believe

My light Thou art; without Thy glorious
  sight,
Mine eyes are darken'd with perpetual
  night.

My God, Thou art my way, my life, my
  light.

FRANCES QUARLES (1592–1644)
Emblems: Divine and Moral

The pious man does not believe that the right course of action can be determined, except insofar as, at the same time, there is knowledge of the relations of man to God; and again right action, he holds, is necessary for right knowledge.

FRIEDRICH SCHLEIERMACHER (1768–1834)
On Religion

He whom God takes by the forelock is easily dragged up to heaven.

Finnish Proverb

On the whole, as this wondrous planet, Earth, is journeying with its fellows through infinite Space, so are the wondrous destinies embarked on it journeying through infinite Time, under a higher guidance than ours. Go where it will, the deep Heaven will be around it. Therein let us have hope and sure faith.

THOMAS CARLYLE (1795–1881)
Signs of the Times

Act up to your light, though in the midst of difficulties, and you will be carried on, you do not know how far. Abraham obeyed the call and journeyed, not knowing whither he went; so we, if we follow the voice of God, shall be brought on step by step into a new world, of which before we had no idea.

JOHN CARDINAL NEWMAN (1801–1890)
Sermons

· THE MYSTERY OF RESPONSE ·

He who ceases to make a response, ceases to hear the Word.

MARTIN BUBER (1878–1965)
Between Man and Man

God is not dumb, that He should speak
  no more;
If thou hast wanderings in the wilderness

And find'st not Sinai, 'tis thy soul is
poor.

JAMES RUSSELL LOWELL (1819–1891)
Bibliolatres

In all our prayers, th' Almighty does
regard
The judgment of the balance, not the
yard:
He loves not words, but matter; 'tis his
pleasure
To buy his wares by weight, and not by
measure.

FRANCIS QUARLES (1592–1644)
Divine Poems

Blessed is the soul that heareth the Lord
speaking within her, and receiveth from
his mouth the word of consolation.

Blessed are the ears that gladly receive
the pulses of the divine whisper, and heed
not the loud clamors of the world.

Blessed, indeed are those ears which listen not after the voices sounding without,
but to the truth teaching inwardly.

THOMAS À KEMPIS (1380–1471)
The Imitation of Christ

There is indeed something in the most
obstinate and willful soul that God can
hear. There is no man so far from God, so
utterly indifferent, that God does not hear
the appeal of his indifference itself calling
out to Him for pity and awakening.

PHILLIPS BROOKS (1835–1893)
The More Abundant Life

If the soul knows God in his creatures,
that is only evening light; if it knows His
creatures in God, that is morning light: but
if it know God as He who alone is Being,
that is the clear light of midday.

MEISTER ECKHART (1260–1327)
Works

In darkness the One appears as uni-
form; in the light the One appears as manifold.

RABINDRANATH TAGORE (1861–1941)
Stray Birds

Whoever thinks that the understanding
of things Divine rests upon strict proofs
has in his thought narrowed down the
wideness of God's mercy.

ABU-HAMID MUHAMMAD AL-GHAZZALI
(1058–1111)
From That Which Delivers from Error

The name of this infinite and inexhaustible depth and ground of all being is God.
That depth is what the word God means.
And if that word has not much meaning
for you, translate it, and speak of the
depths of your life, of the source of your
being, of your ultimate concern, of what
you take seriously without any reservation.
Perhaps, in order to do so, you must forget
everything traditional that you have
learned about God, perhaps even the word
itself. For if you know that God means
depth, you know much about him. You
cannot then call yourself an atheist or unbeliever. For you cannot think or say: Life
has no depth! Life is shallow. Being itself
is surface only. If you could say this in
complete seriousness, you would be an
atheist; but otherwise you are not. He who
knows about depth knows about God.

PAUL TILLICH (1886–1965)
The Shaking of the Foundations

Shall any one teach God knowledge,
Seeing that it is He that judges those on
high?

The Old Testament
Book of Job 21:22

God not only sees the actions of man as
future, but as present and already per-
formed: in the same way as one person,
seeing another do an act, would not say,

because he was looking on, it was obliged to be done, so God, because he sees the action as present, does not oblige him who performs it, to do it, but leaves him to his liberty and the operating contingency.

MENASSEH BEN ISRAEL (1604–1657)
The Conciliator

He fathoms the abyss and the heart of man; he is versed in their intricate secrets; for the Lord possesses all knowledge and observes the signs of all time.

The Old Testament Apocrypha
Ecclesiasticus 42:18

And so I saw most surely that it is quicker for us and easier to come to the knowledge of God than it is to know our own soul. For our soul is so deeply grounded in God and so endlessly treasured that we cannot come to knowledge of it until we first have knowledge of God, who is the creator to whom it is united.

JULIAN OF NORWICH (1343–1416)
Showings

Man should not have a God merely intellectually conceived. Rather, man must have an essential God, who is high above the thoughts of men.

MEISTER ECKHART (1260–1327)
Works

You must ask yourself what God is. You must see how at the very bottom of His existence, as you conceive of it, lie these two thoughts—purpose and righteousness; how absolutely impossible it is to give God any personality except as the fulfillment of these two qualities—the intelligence that plans in love, and the righteousness that lives in duty.

PHILLIPS BROOKS (1835–1893)
Sermons

God knows whether the hearts which seek him offer him all of which they are capable.   *The Talmud*

God knows all that is, and all that God knows is, and these two are not different, but one and the same, because God's knowledge and his almighty will are one and the same.

FRIEDRICH SCHLEIERMACHER (1768–1834)
Der Christliche Glaube

The outer actions and appearances of a man develop from the inner depths. If one tries to dig down from one layer to another one may still not reach the ultimate foundations of a man's behavior. The depths may be a bottomless abyss. But God sees. He sees right throught the tangled webs of human motives. He distinguishes between the real and the unreal, between the expression and the intention, the mask and the original. The roots, the foundations, the origins, all lie open to His sight.

ROMANO GUARDINI (1885–1968)
The Living God

God, whose knowledge is infinite, can alone read clearly into its recesses, and fathom its most secret foldings. He sees our thoughts, even before we have formed them; he discovers our most hidden paths, he views all our stratagems and evasions.

SAINT FRANCIS OF SALES (1567–1622)
Treatise on the Love of God

Just as we perceive Him in the light which He emanates upon us—as it is said: "In thy light we see light" (Psalm 36:9)—so God looks down upon us by the same light. Because of it God is perpetually with us, looking down upon us from above.

MAIMONIDES (1135–1204)
Guide for the Perplexed

The exhaustive knowledge possessed by God is a loving knowledge. To know that we are known to God is not merely to experience justice, it is also to experience mercy.   JACQUES MARITAIN (1882–1973)
Existence and the Existent

God never wrought miracle to convince atheism, because his ordinary works convince it.   FRANCIS BACON (1561–1626)
Of Atheism

The commonest event, say the fall of a leaf, is as supernatural in its causation as any miracle would be; for in both alike God would be equally implicated.
BORDEN P. BOWNE (1847–1910)
The Immanence of God

For every house is built by some man; but he that built all things is God.
The New Testament
Hebrews 3:4

Man flows at once to God when the channel of purity is opened.
HENRY DAVID THOREAU (1817–1862)
Walden

The ripened soul does not condemn but seeks to understand and master, does not cry out but accepts or toils to improve and perfect, does not revolt inwardly but labours to obey and fulfil and transfigure. Therefore we shall receive all things with an equal soul from the hands of the Master.   SRI AUROBINDO (1872–1950)
Pathamandir Annual

If God sees that heart corroded with the rust of cares, riddled into caverns and films by the worms of ambition and greed, then your heart is as God sees it, for God sees things as they are. And one day you will be compelled to see, nay, to feel your heart as God sees it.
GEORGE MACDONALD (1824–1905)
Unspoken Sermons

God's ways seem dark, but, soon or late,
 They touch the shining hills of day;
The evil cannot brook delay,
 The good can well afford to wait.
JOHN GREENLEAF WHITTIER (1807–1892)
Complete Verse

The God whom I adore is not a God of darkness; he hath not given me an understanding to forbid me the use of it. To bid me give up my reason, is to insult the author of it. The minister of truth doth not tyrannize over my understanding—he enlightens it.
JEAN JACQUES ROUSSEAU (1712–1778)
Emile

All finite things involve an untruth; they have a notion and an existence, but their existence does not meet the requirements of the notion. God alone is the thorough harmony of notion and reality.
GEORG WILHELM FRIEDRICH HEGEL
(1770–1831)
Philosophy of Religion

He who clearly and distinctly understands himself and his emotions loves God, and so much the more in proportion as he more understands himself and his emotions.   BENEDICT SPINOZA (1632–1677)
Of Human Freedom

God is not an abstract reality, an absolute Alone, at the far end of Bethel-ladders and Babel-towers. He is central in the stream of Life and Love and Truth and Beauty. The reason we can hope to find God is that He is here, engaged all the time in finding us.
RUFUS JONES (1863–1948)
Pathways to the Reality of God

There is a twofold knowledge of God: the general and the particular. All men have the general knowledge, namely, that God is, that He has created heaven and earth, that He is just, that He punishes the wicked, etc. But what God thinks of us, what he wants to give and to do to deliver us from sin and death and to save us—which is the particular and the true knowledge of God—this men do not know. Thus it can happen someone's face may be familiar to me, but I really do not know him, because I do not know what he has in mind. What good does it do you to know that God exists if you do not know what His Will is toward you?

MARTIN LUTHER (1483–1546)
Commentary to Galatians

· THERE SHALL BE A COVENANT BETWEEN US. . . . ·

I will betroth thee unto Me forever;
Yeah, I will betroth thee unto Me in
  righteousness, and in justice
And in loving kindness, and in
  compassion.
And I will betroth thee unto Me in
  faithfulness;
And thou shalt know the Lord.

The Old Testament
Hosea 2:21–22

Abide with me from morn till eve,
For without Thee I cannot live;
Abide with me when night is nigh,
For without Thee I dare not die.

JOHN KEBLE (1792–1866)
The Christian Year

For Mercy, Pity, Peace and Love
Is God, our Father dear,
And Mercy, Pity, Peace and Love
Is man, His child and care.

WILLIAM BLAKE (1757–1827)
The Divine Image

God, it is said, owes nothing to his creatures. For my part, I believe he owes them every thing he promised them when he gave them being. Now what is less than to promise them a blessing, if he gives them an idea of it, and has so constituted them as to feel the want of it? The more I look into myself, the more plainly I read these words written in my soul: *be just and thou wilt be happy.*

JEAN JACQUES ROUSSEAU (1712–1778)
Emile

There is a covenant between man and God, a covenant between freedom and eternity, a unity which lives in the opposition between the two.

LEO BAECK (1873–1956)
The Essence of Judaism

The spirit of this age is the Covenant and Testament of God. It is like the pulsating artery in the body of the world.

ABDU'L BAHA (1844–1921)
The Mysterious Forces of Civilization

The Lord made this covenant not with our fathers, but with us, even us who are all of us here alive this day.

The Old Testament
Deuteronomy 5:3

Not only around our infancy
Doth heaven with all its splendors lie;
Daily, with souls that cringe and plot,
We Sinais climb and know it not.

JAMES RUSSELL LOWELL (1819–1891)
Vision of Sir Launfal

By purity God is made captive in me; purity makes me God-conscious and conscious of naught beside God; purity begets detachment. The pure soul has a light-birth, as it were; purity is satisfied with God alone.

MEISTER ECKHART (1260–1327)
Works

· THE DEEP OCEAN OF GOD'S PATIENCE ·

The Infinite Goodness has such wide arms that it takes whatever turns to it.

DANTE (1265–1321)
The Divine Comedy

Sometimes the truth about God and His relation to our human life seems to shape itself exactly into this, that He stands waiting, in infinite patience, till His children out of their restlessness and wanderings come back to find the satisfaction of their souls in Him.

PHILLIPS BROOKS (1835–1893)
Sermons

Thus saith the Lord God, the Holy One: "In returning and rest shall ye be saved. In quietness and confidence shall be your strength."   *The Old Testament*
Isaiah 40:29–31

O ye who believe! Seek help with patience and with prayer; for God is with the patient.   *The Koran*

What glory is it if, when ye be buffeted for your faults, ye shall take it patiently? But if, when ye do well and suffer for it, ye take it patiently—this is acceptable with God.   *The New Testament*
1 Peter 2:20

The God of patience and consolation grant you to be like-minded one toward another!   *The New Testament*
Romans 15:5

Patience which is in remembrance of God is not bitter;
For bitterness from a friend's hand is sugar.

SAADI (1184–1291)
Bustan

Look at ourselves; our minds and hearts making funny little whirlpools in the deep Ocean of God's Patience, and consider whether this disposition goes well with being a reasonable, pure and living sacrifice.   EVELYN UNDERHILL (1875–1941)
The Mount of Purification

My soul, sit thou a patient looker-on;
Judge not the play before the play is done:
Her plot hath many changes; every day
Speaks a new scene; the last act crowns the play.

FRANCIS QUARLES (1592–1644)
Respice Finem

God is long-suffering, but He collects His due.   *The Talmud*

He who hears himself cursed and remains silent becomes a partner of God—for does not the Lord hear nations blame Him, yet remain silent?   *The Midrash*

· THE CONSCIOUSNESS OF GOD'S PRESENCE ·

That we should know ourselves and God so far as we are able, that is God's will. It behooves us therefore to be vastly careful not to hamper in any way the work which the exalted workman designs to carry out in us to his glory, but so to maintain ourselves that the material is always ready for the workman to do his work in us.

MEISTER ECKHART (1260–1327)
Works

What a full and pregnant thing life is when God is known; and what a weary emptiness it is without Him! The river of God is full of water, and he will moisten and fill these parched hearts of ours, out of the river of His own life.

THOMAS ERSKINE (1788–1870)
Letters

The consciousness of God's presence is the first principle of religion.

Hebrew Proverb

The knowledge of God is the blessedness of man. To know God, and to be known by him—to love God, and to be loved by Him—is the most precious treasure which this life has to give.

FREDERICK WILLIAM ROBERTSON
(1816–1853)
Sermons

What a noble privilege is it of human reason to attain the knowledge of the supreme being; and, from the visible works of nature, be enabled to infer so sublime a principle as its supreme Creator?

DAVID HUME (1711–1776)
The Natural History of Religion

God has given to man a cloak whereby he can conceal his ignorance, and in this cloak he can enwrap himself at any moment, for it always lies near at hand. This cloak is silence.

BHARTRIHARI (7th century)
The Nitti Sataka

A quiet Silent Person may possess
All that is Great or High in Blessedness.
The Inward Work is the Supreme.

THOMAS TRAHERNE (1637–1674)
Silence

He, who from zone to zone,
Guides through the boundless sky thy
    certain flight,
In the long way that I must tread alone,
    Will lead my steps aright.

WILLIAM CULLEN BRYANT (1794–1878)
To a Waterfowl

O God, I am thinking Thy thoughts after Thee.

JOHANNES KEPLER (1571–1630)
When Studying Astronomy

I know not where His islands lift
    Their fronded palms in air;
I only know I cannot drift
    Beyond His love and care.

JOHN GREENLEAF WHITTIER (1807–1892)
The Eternal Goodness

What causes you to perform a given action, which I call virtuous, rather than another? I reply, that I cannot know which method, out of the infinite methods at His disposal, God employs to determine you to the said action. It may be, that God has impressed you with a clear idea of Himself, so that you forget the world for love of Him, and love your fellow-men as yourself; it is plain that such a disposition is at variance with those dispositions which are called bad, and, therefore, could not co-exist with them in the same man.

BENEDICT SPINOZA (1632–1677)
Letters

If we know there is some real being, and that nonentity cannot produce any real being, it is an evident demonstration that from eternity there has been something; since what was not from eternity had a beginning; and what had a beginning must be produced by something else.

JOHN LOCKE (1632–1704)
An Essay Concerning Human Understanding

If the doors of perception were cleansed, everything would appear to man as it is, infinite.

WILLIAM BLAKE (1757–1827)
Marriage of Heaven and Hell

I I · The Gifts of God

Alas for us if God helped us only when we knew we needed Him and went to Him with full self-conscious wants! Alas for us if every need which we know not, had not a voice for Him and did not call Him to us!

—PHILLIPS BROOKS

Now we explore with the God Seekers the dimensions of the many gifts God has always vouchsafed to humankind, immeasurable gifts such as his grace, his forgiveness, and above all, his peace. Why we eschew these gifts for the momentary gifts of the materialistic world has always been a source of deep concern and sorrow to the God Seekers.

God is not impressed with our worldly baubles. As Ralph Waldo Emerson said in "Friendship," "The only money of God is God. He never pays with anything less or anything else." If you were so affluent that you could pile ten-thousand-dollar bills one atop the other until they reached the summit of Mount Everest, God would still not be impressed. When we equate God's love with his giving us an ever-increasing list of worldly goods, we demean God into some kind of benevolent bookie who must always pay off with a smile. The Sufi master Jalal-uddin Rumi asks where could we find anyone who is more liberal than God, "who buys the worthless rubbish which is your wealth, and pays you with the Light that illuminates your heart."

The real gifts God gives to us are infinitely various, we are told by Phillips Brooks: "His great arms can hold the infant like a mother, and build a strong wall about the mature man who is fighting the noonday fight of life, and lay the bridge of sunset over which the old man's feet may walk serenely into the eternal day."

One of the greatest of God's gifts is his willingness to share his ethical plan for the world through his messengers, the prophets. There is an ancient Arabian proverb that says God has given to *every* people a prophet in its own tongue. Although they are endowed with rare spiritual courage in the dedication of their lives to promulgating God's message, these prophets are almost invariably treated with apathy or scorn by the multitude. As Jesus of Nazareth knew so well, "A prophet is not without honor, save in his own country."

Thomas à Kempis, in defining prophets, said, "To the world they were aliens, but to God they were familiar friends. To themselves they seemed as naught and despised by the world, but in the eyes of God they seemed precious and chosen." To which Horace Bushnell, a nineteenth-century American clergyman, would add, "The tallest saints of God will often be those who walk in the deepest obscurity, and are even despised or quite overlooked by man."

Nikolai Berdyaev also noted the difficult path ahead when a person sets out in the elusive search for truth. Nevertheless, because the imperative of their life is to come face to face with the Divine Mystery, the prophets cannot do otherwise. Berdyaev understood that the prophet "not only cries in the wilderness, but also leaves himself open to attack by the pontiffs of both religion and science."

Perhaps it is the nature of all prophets at one time or another to feel uncertain and to ask themselves why God had chosen them to convey his eternal message to a seemingly uncaring people. Moses' bitter disappointment when he returned from Mount Sinai and found his people worshiping a golden calf surely must have made him doubt his mission. But like all great prophets he accepted this temporary defeat and continued with the mission God had enjoined him to accomplish. There is a commentary in the Midrash in which God says to Moses and Aaron: "My children are often obstinate, often tiresome. With this knowledge accept for yourself My mission, but be prepared for curses and stones."

Is it so bad to be misunderstood, Emerson asked in "Self-Reliance"? He points out that Pythagoras was misunderstood, and so were Socrates, Jesus, Luther, Copernicus, Galileo, Newton, indeed "every pure and wise spirit that ever took flesh." And in another essay, Emerson adds, "Beware when the great God lets loose a thinker on this planet."

Even when the collective mob kills a prophet, as history records on many occasions, the prophet's faith in God's mission negates any fear of death. Baha' u'llah, the founder of the Bahai religion, although persecuted and imprisoned, never turned his back on his mission. As he stated in *The Promised Day Is Come*, "Not one Prophet of God was made manifest who did not fall victim to the relentless hate, to the denunciation, denial and execration of the clerics of his day!"

Sri Aurobindo, a modern Indian religious philosopher, perceived the prophets as "the master men, the great spirits, the God-knowers, God-doers, God-lovers who can live in God and for God and do their work joyfully for him in the world, a divine work uplifted above the restless darkness of the human mind and the false limitations of the ego."

William Wordsworth also understood the spiritual kinship that in some ineffable way links every true prophet who has ever lived.

> Prophets, each with each
> Connected in a mighty scheme of truth,
> Have each for his peculiar dower, a sense

By which he is enabled to perceive
Something unseen before.

Paul Tillich, with the clarity that permeates so much of his writing, noted that although prophets are called individually, their messages are given to entire nations. He concludes that "God's purpose in history is to save individuals, not as individuals, but as participants in his kingdom, in the unity of all beings under God."

In his *Specimen Days,* Walt Whitman defined a prophet as "one whose mind bubbles up and pours forth as a fountain, from inner, divine spontaneities revealing God." To Whitman the word "prophecy" is misused when it refers to prediction alone, for the "great matter is to reveal and outpour the Godlike suggestions pressing for birth in the soul."

Thomas R. Kelly, in *A Testament of Devotion,* reiterated Whitman's thesis that only now and then a man or a woman emerges who, like John Woolman or Saint Francis of Assisi, is able to be completely obedient and to follow God's faintest whisper. But, *mirabile dictu,* when such a dedication does come to a human life "God breaks through, miracles are wrought, world-renewing divine forces are released, history changes."

Another dominant theme in this section is God's gift of grace to every one of his creations. The nineteenth-century Russian philosopher, Vissarion Belinski, was certain that God's grace "is not given to us from *above,* but lies like a seed *within ourselves.*" Martin Luther described it even more specifically in *Table-Talk.* To him God's grace is "something strong, mighty and busy; it is not something that lies inert in our souls, nay, it carries, it leads, it drives, it travels, it does everything in a man."

One of the most moving passages depicting God's grace is found in the Old Testament book of Ezekiel, in which God tells the errant Israelites, "And I will sprinkle clean water upon you and you shall be clean; from all your uncleannesses, and from all your idols, will I cleanse you. A new heart also will I give you, and a new spirit will I put within you; and I will take away the stony heart out of your flesh."

John Donne's conception of God's grace was encapsulated in one of his sermons: "We ask *panem quotidianum,* our daily bread, and God never says you should have come yesterday; He never says you must come again tomorrow, but 'today if you will hear his voice,' today He will hear you."

As Pascal viewed it, God puts religion into our minds by reason, but into our hearts by grace. If God were to use force or threats to put religion into our minds or hearts, he maintained, it would not be grace but rather terror.

To know the peace that comes from God is the greatest blessing any man or woman is ever given. In Albert Schweitzer's words, "Those who have experienced the peace of God can face all eventualities."

James Martineau, a nineteenth-century English religious philosopher, seems to have understood the essence of God's gifts to all of his created beings. In his book *Hours of Thought on Sacred Things,* Martineau wrote: "The great Creative Spirit is ever ready to touch the merest grain of manna in the heart, and make it numerous to shine on all the ground. He to whom space is the seed-plot of stars has in the human soul a tillage more lustrous in the sowing and more enduring in the fruits."

· EVERY GOOD GIFT ·

It is good and comely for one to eat and to drink and to enjoy the good of all his labor that he taketh under the sun all the days of his life which God giveth him; for, it is his portion. To rejoice in labor—this is the gift of God.   *The Old Testament*
Ecclesiastes 5:18–19

God the Father endowed man, from birth, with the seeds of every possibility and every life.

GIOVANNI PICO DELLA MIRANDOLA
(1463–1494)
On the Dignity of Man

What reward therefore shall I give the Lord for all the benefits that He has done to me? By His first work He gave me to myself; and by the next he gave Himself to me. And when He gave Himself, He gave me back myself that I had lost.

SAINT BERNARD OF CLAIRVAUX (1091–1153)
On the Love of God

Genius on earth is God giving Himself. Whenever a masterpiece appears, a distribution of God is taking place. The masterpiece is a variety of the miracle.

VICTOR HUGO (1802–1885)
William Shakespeare

That gift of his, from God descended.
Ah! friend, what gift of man's does not?
ROBERT BROWNING (1812–1889)
Christmas Eve

God's gifts put man's best gifts to shame.
ELIZABETH BARRETT BROWNING
(1806–1861)
Sonnets from the Portuguese

Put on the whole armor of God.
The New Testament
Ephesians 6:11

No man indeed shall fail to use the reason
That God has given him—in its proper
    place.
GOTTHOLD EPHRAIM LESSING (1729–1781)
Nathan the Wise

The more naked and empty the heart is when it falls on God and is supported by Him, the deeper man is placed in God and the more he becomes receptive of all the most valuable gifts of God.

MEISTER ECKHART (1260–1327)
The Talks of Instruction

God metes out many things, this to one man, that to another, to each his own. But the highest good is meted out to all of us equally—and that is the enjoyment of life on this earth.

PARACELSUS (1493–1541)
De Gradibus et Compositionibus Receptorum

Love all men, love everything. Seek that rapture and ecstasy; water the earth with the tears of your joy and love those tears. Don't be ashamed of that ecstasy; prize it, for it is a gift of God and a great one; it is not given to many but only to the elect.

FYODOR DOSTOEVSKY (1821–1881)
The Brothers Karamazov

What God sends is better than what men ask for. *Croatian Proverb*

If God be for us, who can be against us?
The New Testament
Romans 8:31

What man is there of you, whom if his son ask bread, will he give him a stone? Or if he ask a fish, will he give him a serpent? If ye then, evil as ye are, know how to give good gifts to your children, how much more shall your Father which is in heaven give good things to them that shall ask him. *The New Testament*
Matthew 7:9–11

When you eat and take pleasure in the taste and sweetness of the food, bear in mind that it is the Lord who has placed into the food its taste and sweetness. You will, then, truly serve Him by your eating.

BAAL SHEM TOV (1700–1760)
Sayings

God giveth to no man here all good things at once; but some we receive in hand and some in hope.

ZACHARY BOYD (1585–1655)
The Last Battle of the Soul in Death

No doubt in His graciousness, God gives us His gifts, even in intermittent commu-

nion, and touches us into flame, far beyond our achievements and deserts.

THOMAS R. KELLY (1893–1941)
A Testament of Devotion

Man finds it hard to get what he wants, because he does not want the best; God finds it hard to give, because He would give the best, and man will not take it.

GEORGE MACDONALD (1824–1905)
Sermons

The greatest pleasure in life is love; the greatest possession is health; the greatest ease is sleep; and the greatest medicine is a true friend.

SIR WILLIAM TEMPLE (1628–1699)
Miscellanea

All that I have is the Lord's; not mine to
give or withhold it;
His, not mine, are the gifts, and only so
far can I make them
Mine, as in giving I add my heart to
whatever is given.

HENRY WADSWORTH LONGFELLOW
(1807–1882)
Collected Poems

Never dare alienate God's gifts you hold
Simply in trust for him!

ROBERT BROWNING (1812–1889)
Parleyings with Certain People

Therefore I say that we must learn to look through every gift and every event to God and never be content with the thing itself. There is no stopping place in this life—no, nor was there ever one for any man, no matter how far along his way he'd gone. This above all, then, be ready at all times for the gifts of God and always for new ones.

MEISTER ECKHART (1260–1327)
Sermons

The man in whom is the faith that works through love, begins to delight in the law

of God after the inward man; and that delight is a gift not of the letter but of the spirit.   SAINT AUGUSTINE (354–430)
The Spirit and the Letter

The kingdom of God is neither an unconditional divine gift sent down from heaven all at once, nor a simple human task to be completed in a few generations. It is both a gift and a task: an infinitely difficult, infinitely glorious divine-human undertaking requiring all God's power and all man's devotion, and even so stretching on from age to age as though it were endless.

WALTER MARSHALL HORTON (1895–1966)
Our Christian Faith

From some unknown depth of the judgments of God, which we cannot scrutinize, all our ability proceeds. I see that I am able; but how I am able I see not:—this far only I see, that it is of God.

JOHN CALVIN (1509–1564)
Institutes of the Christian Religion

If I should be asked to make a list of all that is still treasured within me, and for me, I would not know how to end it: for, truly, God has created the world for me as much as for any one else.

OSCAR WILDE (1854–1900)
De Profundis

How silently, how silently, the wondrous
   gift is given!
So God imparts to human hearts the
   blessings of his heaven.
PHILLIPS BROOKS (1835–1893)
O Little Town of Bethlehem

I thank thee, Father, Lord of heaven and earth, for hiding these things from the learned and wise, and revealing them to the simple. Yes, Father, for such was thy choice.   *The New Testament*
Matthew 11:25–26

Behind us, behind each one of us, lie six thousand years of human effort, with its yet uncreated and unconquered Continents and Eldorados, which we, even we, have to conquer, to create; and from the bosom of Eternity there shine for us celestial guiding stars.

THOMAS CARLYLE (1795–1881)
Characteristics

Every man hath his proper gift of God, one after this manner, and another after that.   *The New Testament*
1 Corinthians 5:7

Think, therefore, with every morsel of bread which relieves thee from the pain of hunger, with every draught of wine which cheers thy cheer, of God, who confers these beneficent gifts upon thee,—think of Man!

LUDWIG FEUERBACH (1804–1872)
The Way of Christianity

Talent is a gift which God has given us secretly, and which we reveal without perceiving it.

CHARLES DE SECONDAT MONTESQUIEU
(1689–1755)
Pensées

Every good gift and every perfect gift is from above, and cometh down from the Father of Lights, with whom there is no variableness, neither shadow of turning.
The New Testament
James 1:17

God has no riches of his own; it's what he takes from the one that he gives to the other.   *Yiddish Proverb*

   'Tis God gives skill,
But not without men's hands: He could
   not make

Antonio Stradivari's violins
Without Antonio.

GEORGE ELIOT (1819–1880)
Stradivarius

The holy prophet Zoroaster said,
The Lord who made thy teeth shall give
    thee bread.

Persian Proverb

God puts something good and something lovable in every man His hands create.   MARK TWAIN (1835–1910)
The American Vandal

Whene'er I take my walks abroad,
    How many poor I see!
What shall I render to my God
    For all his gifts to me?

ISAAC WATTS (1674–1748)
Divine Songs

Whatever hour God has blessed you
with, take it with grateful hand, nor post-
pone your joys from year to year, so that,
in whatever place you have been, you may
say that you have lived happily.

HORACE (65–8 B.C.)
Epistles

Indeed, every man to whom God has
given wealth and possessions and granted
the power to enjoy them, taking his share
and rejoicing in his labour, that is the gift
of God, for it is God who provides him
with the joy in his heart.

The Old Testament
Ecclesiastes 5:19–20

Patience is a gift that God gives only to
those He loves.   *Moroccan Proverb*

God has given some gifts to the whole
human race, from which no one is excluded.

LUCIUS ANNAEUS SENECA (4 B.C.–A.D. 65)
De Beneficiis

Thou visitest the earth, and waterest it:
Thou greatly enrichest it with the river of
God, which is full of water.

The Old Testament
Psalms 65:9

For each new morning with its light,
    Father, we thank Thee,
For rest and shelter of the night,
    Father, we thank Thee.
For health and food, for love and friends,
For everything Thy goodness sends,
    Father, in heaven, we thank Thee.

RALPH WALDO EMERSON (1803–1882)
Thanksgiving

· GOD'S INFINITE WISDOM ·

God's wisdom is infinite; it transcends all
our powers of expression. So of his mercy
and his benevolence. Infinite existence is
everlasting existence. When we speak of
God as the Infinite Existence, we mean
that all his attributes are infinite.

JOSEPH ALDEN (1807–1885)
Conceptions of the Infinite

The pursuit of perfection, then, is the
pursuit of sweetness and light. He who
works for sweetness and light united,
works to make reason and the will of God
prevail.

MATTHEW ARNOLD (1822–1888)
Culture and Anarchy

We behold, then, by the sight of the
mind, in that eternal truth from which all
things temporal are made, the form according to which we are, and according to
which we do anything by true and right

reason, either in ourselves, or in things corporeal.   SAINT AUGUSTINE (354–430)
On the Trinity

All wisdom comes from the Lord and is with him forever. The sand of the sea, the drops of rain, and the days of eternity—who can count them? The height of heaven, the breadth of the earth, the abyss, and wisdom—who can search them out? Wisdom was created before all things, and prudent understanding from eternity.
The Old Testament Apocrypha
Ecclesiasticus 1:1–4

God has chosen the foolish things of the world to confound the wise; and God hath chosen the weak things of the world to confound the things that are mighty.
The New Testament
1 Corinthians 1:27

For wisdom is more mobile than any motion; because of her pureness she pervades and penetrates all things. For she is a breath of the power of God, and a pure emanation of the glory of the Almighty; therefore nothing defiled gains entrance into her. For she is a reflection of eternal light, a spotless mirror of the working of God, and an image of his goodness.
The Old Testament Apocrypha
The Wisdom of Solomon 7:24–27

God's wisdom and God's Goodness!—Ah, but fools
Misdefine thee, till God knows them no more.
Wisdom and Goodness they are God!—What schools
Have yet so much as heard this simple lore.
This no Saint preaches, and this no Church rules:
'Tis in the desert, now, and heretofore.
MATTHEW ARNOLD (1822–1888)
The Divinity

The wisdom of God, not content with embracing all the possibles, penetrates them, compares them, weighs them one against the other, to estimate their degrees of perfection or imperfection, the strong and the weak, the good and the evil. It goes even beyond the finite combinations; it makes of them an infinity of infinities, that is to say, an infinity of possible sequences of the universe, each of which contains an infinity of creatures.
GOTTFRIED WILHELM VON LEIBNIZ
(1646–1716)
Theodicy

With ten characteristics was the earth created: wisdom and understanding; knowledge and strength; rebuke and might; righteousness and justice; mercy and compassion.   *The Talmud*

Our life is founded not only in bread, but also in arts and words of wisdom that come from the mouth of God. We should fill ourselves with these, and look upon a full belly as mortal, but upon those other things as eternal. For all those who live on those things will shine like the sun in the kingdom of God.   PARACELSUS (1493–1541)
De Natura Rerum

The Wisdom of God created understanding, fit and proportionable to Truth the object, and end of it, as the eye to the thing visible. If our *understanding* have a film of *ignorance* over it, or be bleary with gazing on other false glisterings, what is that to Truth?
JOHN MILTON (1608–1674)
Of Reformation

God's wisdom is one, but it reveals itself in various forms; as, for instance, the sun is one but its rays show in various color when they go through a prism.
BAHYA IBN PAKUDA (11th century)
The Duties of the Heart

That your faith should not stand in the wisdom of men, but in the power of God. Howbeit we speak wisdom among them that are perfect: yet not the wisdom of this world, nor of the princes of this world, that comes to naught. But we speak the wisdom of God in a mystery, even the hidden wisdom, which God ordained before the world unto our glory.

The New Testament
1 Corinthians 2:5–7

If you delight in wisdom, then keep the commandments, and the Lord will give you it.   *The Old Testament Apocrypha*
The Wisdom of Jesus ben Sirach 1:26

Deepest wisdom in nearest. Not in the midst of the ages alone, but in the midst of every soul. Wouldst be wise, O man? Look then into thy soul, and thou shalt find wisdom.

BRONSON ALCOTT (1799–1888)
Journals

The wisdom that is from above is first pure, then peaceable, gentle, and easy to be entreated, full of mercy and good fruits, without partiality and without hypocrisy.   *The New Testament*
James 3:17

But Wisdom, whence does she come, And where is the place of Understanding? For she is hidden from the eyes of all living things, concealed even from the birds of the air. Destruction and Death say, "We have heard only her echo." But God understands her way and He knows her place, For He looks to the ends of the earth and sees everything under heaven.

The Old Testament
Job 28:20–24

The bounds of wisdom are large, and within them much is contained. . . . Whatsoever either men on earth or the angels of heaven do know, it is as a drop of that unemptiable fountain of wisdom; which wisdom hath diversely imparted her treasures unto the world.

RICHARD HOOKER (1554–1600)
The Laws of Ecclesiastical Polity

If any of you lack wisdom, let him ask of God, that giveth to all men liberally, and upbraideth not; and it shall be given him.

The New Testament
James 1:5

And this is the great delight of this awakening: to know creatures through God and not God through creatures, to know the effects through their cause and not the cause through the effects; for the latter knowledge is secondary and this other is essential.

SAINT JOHN OF THE CROSS (1542–1591)
Living Flame of Love

The world is the book where eternal Wisdom wrote its own ideas, and the living temple where, depicting its own acts and likeness, it decorated the height and the depth with living statues; so that every spirit, to guard against profanity, should read and contemplate here art and government, and each should say: "I fill the universe, seeing God in all things."

But we, souls bound to books and dead temples, copied with many mistakes from the living, place these things before such instruction. O ills, quarrels, ignorance, labours, pains, make us aware of our falling away: O let us, in God's name, return to the original.

TOMMASO CAMPANELLA (1568–1639)
Modo di Filosofare

· TO EVERY PEOPLE A PROPHET ·

I believe in the Hindu theory of Guru and his importance in spiritual realization. An imperfect teacher may be tolerable in mundane matters, but not in spiritual matters. Only a perfect gnani [seer] deserves to be enthroned as Guru. One gets the Guru that one deserves. Infinite striving after perfection is one's right. It is his own reward. The rest is in the hands of God.

MOHANDAS K. GANDHI (1869–1948)
Autobiography

A prophet is not without honour, save in his own country, and in his own house.

The New Testament
Luke 4:24

In course of time, there arose among men false prophets who asserted that God had commanded and expressly told them: "Worship that particular star, or worship all the stars. Offer up such and such sacrifices. Pour out such and such libations. Erect a temple. Make a figure, to which all the people—the women, children, and the rest of the folk—shall bow down."

MAIMONIDES (1135–1204)
Hilkhot Avoda Zarah

Beware of false prophets, which come to you in sheep's clothing, but inwardly they are ravening wolves. *The New Testament*
Matthew 8:15

Jesus astonishes and overpowers sensual people. They cannot unite Him to history or reconcile Him with themselves.

RALPH WALDO EMERSON (1803–1882)
History

Moses with his law is most terrible; there never was any equal to him in perplex-

ing, affrighting, tyrannizing, threatening, preaching, and thundering.

MARTIN LUTHER (1483–1546)
Table-Talk

Was Christ a man like us?—Ah! let us try
If we then, too, can be such men as he!

MATTHEW ARNOLD (1822–1888)
The Better Part

O servant of God's holiest charge,
The minister of praise at large.

CHRISTOPHER SMART (1722–1771)
A Song to David

Thus saith the Lord of hosts: Let your hands be strong, ye that hear in these days these words by the mouths of the prophets, which were in the day that the foundation of the house of the Lord of hosts was laid, that the temple might be built.

The Old Testament
Zechariah 8:9

When in the heart of a people there is spiritual perception, the face and voice of the prophet are as an evidentiary miracle.
When the prophet utters a cry from without, the soul of the people falls to worship within,
Because never in the world will the soul's ear have heard a cry of the same kind as his.
That wondrous voice is heard by the soul in exile—the voice of God calling, "Lo, I am nigh."

JALAL-UD-DIN RUMI (1207–1273)
The Masnawi

The characters that are great must, of necessity, be characters that shall be willing, patient and strong to endure for others. To hold our nature in the willing service of another is the divine idea of manhood, of the human character.

HENRY WARD BEECHER (1813–1887)
Sermons

I know nothing more moral, more sublime, more worthy of your preservation than David's description of the good men in the Fifteenth Psalm.

THOMAS JEFFERSON (1743–1826)
Letter to Isaac Englebrecht

Each religious genius spells out the mystery of God according to his own endowment, personal, racial, and historical.

SARVEPALLI RADHAKRISHNAN (1888–1975)
The Hindu Way of Life

God's Saints are shining lights: who stays
  Here long must passe
O'er dark hills, swift streams, and steep
  ways
  As smooth as glasse;
They are (indeed), our Pillar-fires
  Seen as we go,
They are that Cities shining spires
  We travell too.

HENRY VAUGHAN (1622–1695)
Joy of My Life

Is not every true reformer, by the nature of him, a priest first of all? He appeals to Heaven's invisible justice against earth's visible force; knows that it, the invisible, is strong and alone strong. He is a believer in the divine truth of things; a seer, seeing through the shows of things; a worshipper, in one way or the other, of the divine truth of things; a priest, that is.

THOMAS CARLYLE (1795–1881)
On Heroes and Hero-Worship

Then the word of the Lord came unto me, saying: Before I formed thee in the belly I knew thee; and before thou camest forth out of the womb I sanctified thee,

and I ordained thee a prophet unto the nations.   *The Old Testament*
Jeremiah 1:4–5

Most men are on the ebb; but now and then a man comes riding down sublimely in high hope from God on the flood tide of the soul, as she sets into the coasts of time, submerging old landmarks, and laying waste the labors of centuries.

BRONSON ALCOTT (1799–1888)
Orphic Sayings

The true prophet lives by the true word he hears, and must endure having it treated as though it only held true for some "ideological" sphere, "morals" or "religion," but not for the real life of the people.   MARTIN BUBER (1878–1965)
Israel and the World

God speaks through many men, in the Bible through the successive prophets of whom Jesus is the last. But no man can be God; God speaks exclusively through no man, and what is more, His speech through every man has many meanings.

KARL JASPERS (1883–1969)
The Perennial Scope of Philosophy

The sage is not egocentric in the sense of caring for his own soul, or altruistic in the sense of caring for others, or theocentric in the sense of wishing to enjoy God in the solitude of his soul. He is at the heart of the universe in which he himself and others live, move and have their being. He is conscious of the wider destiny of the universe.

SARVEPALLI RADHAKRISHNAN (1888–1975)
Eastern Religions and Western Thought

Great Men are the inspired Texts of that divine Book of Revelation, whereof a Chapter is completed from epoch to epoch, and by some named History; to which inspired Texts your numerous talented men, and your innumerable untalented men, are the better or worse exegetic Commentaries.

THOMAS CARLYLE (1795–1881)
Sartor Resartus

Greatness is not a teachable nor gainable thing, but the expression of the mind of a God-made man; teach or preach, or labor as you will, everlasting difference is set between one man's capacity and another's, and this God-given supremacy is the priceless thing, always just as rare in the world one time as another.

JOHN RUSKIN (1819–1900)
Fors Clavigera

God has introduced man to be a spectator of God and of His works; and not only a spectator of them, but an interpreter.

EPICTETUS (1st century)
Discourses

Tell me of Moses, Isaiah, Confucius, Zoroaster, Buddha, Pythagoras, Jesus, Paul, Mohamet, Aquinas, Luther, and Calvin—a whole calendar of saints. I give God thanks for them, and bare my brow, and do them reverence, and sit down at their feet to learn what they have to offer. They are but leaves and fruit on the tree of humanity which still goes on leafing, flowering, fruiting with other Isaiahs and Christs, whereof there is no end.

THEODORE PARKER (1810–1860)
*Lessons in the World of Matter
and the World of Men*

I say then, invoking the aid of God in the effort to reveal and clarify all this, that God has a special light which He creates and makes manifest to His prophets in order that they may infer therefrom that it is a prophetic communication, emanating from God they hear. When one of them sees his light, he says: "I have seen the glory of the Lord."

SAADIA BEN JOSEPH (892–942)
The Book of Beliefs and Opinions

An institution is the lengthened shadow of one man; as the Reformation, of Luther; Quakerism, of Fox; Methodism, of Wesley; Abolition, of Clarkson.

RALPH WALDO EMERSON (1803–1882)
Self-Reliance

Take, my brethren, the prophets, who have spoken in the name of the Lord, for an example of suffering, affliction, and patience. *The New Testament
James 5:10*

Beloved, believe not every spirit, but try the spirits whether they are of God: because many false prophets are gone out into the world. *The New Testament
1 John 4:1*

So rare, so intermittent, indeed, is the presence of divinity in human affairs that when it appears in any heavy concentration, it becomes the center of a new way of viewing the world and acting in it, in the person of an Ikhnaton, a Moses, a Zarathustra, a Buddha, a Confucius, a Jesus; and when such a person appears, a whole society takes on a new shape and reveals new possibilities in thought and action and the general conduct of life.

LEWIS MUMFORD (1895–)
The Conduct of Life

Having plunged into the ocean of life, the one God rises up at one point and is known as Krishna, and when after another plunge, He rises up at another point, He is known as Christ. The Incarnations are to Brahman, the Absolute, as waves are to the ocean.

SRI RAMAKRISHNA (1834–1886)
The Harmony of Religions

Could we but climb where Moses stood,
 And view the landscape o'er,
Not Jordan's stream nor death's cold
  flood
 Should fright us from the shore.
EMILY DICKINSON (1830–1886)
There Is a Land of Pure Delight

It is precisely among the heretics of every age that we find men who are filled with the highest kind of religious feeling and who were in many cases regarded by their contemporaries as atheists, sometimes also as saints. Looked at in this light, men like Democritus, Francis of Assisi, and Spinoza are closely akin to one another.   ALBERT EINSTEIN (1879–1955)
The World As I See It

The wakes of Moses, of Buddha, of Confucius, of Lao Tse, of Christ, probably exert a greater influence over humanity today than when these men were pondering over its fate and happiness. No man ever disappears completely if he strives to do good and expects no reward outside of the joy of having contributed to the progress of mankind.
PIERRE LECOMTE DU NOUY (1883–1947)
Human Destiny

Would God that all the Lord's people were prophets, that the Lord would put His spirit upon them.   <i>The Old Testament</i>
Numbers 11:29

All great mystics declare that they have the impression of a current passing from their soul to God, and flowing back again from God to mankind.
HENRI BERGSON (1859–1941)
The Two Sources of Morality and Religion

A rebellious man who has clamorously asked an explanation of life's ills as the price of faith in God, may well in shame consider God's real saints. When things were at their worst, when wrong was conqueror, these spiritual soldiers went out to fight. The winds of ill that blow out our flickering faith made their religion blaze— a pillar of fire in the night. The more evil they faced, the more religion they produced to answer it.
HARRY EMERSON FOSDICK (1878–1969)
The Meaning of Prayer

We do not go far wrong if we define a prophet as a man who, in the name of God, boldly contradicts the spirit of his time. A man who knows very well what people are saying, and how they reached their conclusions, but who himself has a hold of the great fact of God, which, for him, makes all things different—that is, often, how we become aware that there is a prophet in our midst.
JOHN A. HUTTON (1868–1947)
The Soul's Leap to God

Oh, these are they
Who on men's hearts with mightiest
  power can play—
The master-poets of humanity,
From heaven sent down to lift men to the
  sky.
RICHARD WATSON GILDER (1844–1909)
The Master Poets

This is that which the sad prophet Jeremiah laments: "Woe is me, my mother, that thou hast borne me, a man of strife and contention!" And although Divine inspiration must certainly have been sweet to those ancient prophets, yet the irksomeness of that truth which they brought was so unpleasant unto them that everywhere they call it a burden.
JOHN MILTON (1608–1674)
The Burden of the Lord

One of the greatest Gifts that God bestows upon us is to provide us always with

holy men who lead us and teach us and guide us in things eternal, in the blessed life. PARACELSUS (1493–1541)
The Divine Works and Secrets of Nature

Whenever a man stands on integrity and truth in the midst of men who are dishonest and knavish, he is the natural judge of those men, and God's appointed superior to them.
HENRY WARD BEECHER (1813–1887)
Sermons

Where I heard noise and you saw flame,
Some one man knew God called his
  name.
ROBERT BROWNING (1812–1889)
Christmas Eve

The weapons which your hands have
  found
Are those which heaven hath wrought,
Light, truth, and love; your battleground,
The free, broad field of thought.
JOHN GREENLEAF WHITTIER (1807–1892)
The Reformers

This is the vocation of the great *zaddikim*, the world's mighty men of righteousness —to raise religious faith from its lowly state, to purge it out of its dross, and to bring it to its authentic character. At all times they raise specific elements of the light of faith to their highest level, they redeem them from their captivity and liberate them from their exile.
ABRAHAM ISAAC KOOK (1865–1935)
The Moral Principles

All history bears witness that when God means to make a great man, He puts the circumstances of the world and the lives of lesser men under tribute. He does not fling His hero like an aerolite out of the sky. He bids him grow like an oak out of the earth. All earnest, pure, unselfish, faithful men who have lived their obscure

lives well, have helped make him. God has let none of them be wasted.
PHILLIPS BROOKS (1835–1893)
Sermons

A divine person is the prophecy of the mind; a friend is the hope of the heart. Our beatitude waits for the fulfilment of these two in one.
RALPH WALDO EMERSON (1803–1882)
Character

Take, my brethren, the prophets, who have spoken in the name of the Lord, for an example of suffering affliction, and of patience. *The New Testament*
James 5:10

The Prophets Isaiah and Ezekiel dined with me, and I asked them how they dared so roundly to assert that God spoke to them; and whether they did not think at the time that they would be misunderstood, and so be the cause of imposition.

Isaiah answer'd: "I saw no God, nor heard any, in a finite organical perception; but my senses discover'd the infinite in everything, and as I was then persuaded, and remain confirm'd, that the voice of honest indignation is the voice of God, I cared not for consequences, but wrote."
WILLIAM BLAKE (1757–1827)
A Memorable Fancy

As we look back upon the work of the early prophets, we stand in awe of their achievement. They transformed the world into a temple of the divine spirit, and man into a child of God. Without the moral reserve of an other-world, they balanced the accounts of virtue and reward, evil and retribution in this world. Only a passionate love of God and faith in divine justice could hold the precarious scales in balance. ABRAHAM A. NEUMAN (1890–1970)
In Search of God and Immortality

The prophets and saints of all the religions have been vividly conscious that in concrete experiences, definitely dateable, God has spoken to them in recognizable ways. Without this belief and this experience, no one of the great classics of religion would have had its birth. We should have no Vedas, no Koran, no Bible. St. Augustine would not have written his *Confessions* or Thomas à Kempis his *Imitation of Christ,* or Dante his *Divine Comedy,* or Milton his *Paradise Lost,* or Bunyan his *Pilgrim's Progress.*

WILLIAM ADAMS BROWN (1865–1943)
God at Work

If the influence of all whose work was motivated primarily by the ideal of obedience to the will of God were to be stricken from the world's history, the story would lose its richest elements. Moses, Isaiah, Socrates, Jesus, Paul, Augustine, Aquinas, Luther, Lincoln, Gandhi, and hundreds of lesser figures, have learned of God and moulded destiny.

GEORGIA HARKNESS (1891–1974)
Conflicts in Religious Thought

The prophet who first sinks to his knees with a sense of unworthiness, rises from his knees with new hope and resolution, willing to be a channel of the Power that has called him—"Here am I, send me."

WALTER MARSHALL HORTON (1895–1966)
The God We Trust

Alas! how full of fear
Is the fate of the Prophet and Seer!
For evermore, for evermore,
It shall be as it hath been heretofore;
The age in which they live will not forgive
The splendor of the everlasting light,
That makes their foreheads bright,

Nor the sublime
Fore-running of their time!

HENRY WADSWORTH LONGFELLOW
(1807–1882)
The Divine Tragedy

Upon the wastes, a lifeless clod,
I lay, I heard the voice of God;
"Arise, oh prophet, watch and hearken,
And with my Will thy soul engird
Through lands that din and seas that darken,
Burn thou men's hearts with this, my Word."

ALEXANDER PUSHKIN (1799–1837)
The Prophet

An Avatara is a human messenger of God. He is like the viceroy of a mighty monarch. As when there is any disturbance in some far-off province, the king sends the viceroy to quell it, so whenever there is any waning of religion in any part of the world, God sends His Avatara there to guard virtue and foster its growth.

SRI RAMAKRISHNA (1834–1886)
Sayings

When Elijah was waiting with impatience for the Divine Presence in the wilderness, he found that God was not clothed in the whirlwind or in the earthquake, but that He was in the still small voice of duty.

CHARLES EDWARD GARMAN (1850–1907)
Lectures

The foundations of the ocean, the vast realms of water which girdle the earth, are as tranquil and as silent in the storm as in a calm. So it is with the souls of holy men. They have a well of peace springing up within them unfathomable; and though the accidents of the hour may make them seem agitated, yet in their hearts they are not so.

JOHN CARDINAL NEWMAN (1801–1890)
Sermons

He who kindles the fire of genius on the altar of the young heart unites his own prayers for humanity with every ascending flame that is emitted from it through succeeding time. He prays with the Universal Heart, and his prayers bring down blessings on all the race below.

BRONSON ALCOTT (1799–1888)
Journals

When the earth is made poor for us, sometimes the heavens become rich. God closed the eyes of Milton to the beauty in the land and sea and sky, that he might see the companies of angels marching and countermarching on the hills of God. He closed the ears of Beethoven, that he might hear the music of St. Cecilia falling over heaven's battlements. He gave Isaiah a slave's hut, that he might ponder the house not made with hands, eternal in the heavens. How is it that this prophet and poet has become companion of the great ones of the earth?

NEWELL DWIGHT HILLIS (1858–1929)
Sermons

There come occasionally into our race those who create epochs in history, who set loose new forces that change the course of things, who become light-centers that fling their radiance far out into the surrounding darkness, whose life and teaching mold the thoughts and beliefs of generations. He who sends them takes care that they are supplied with the gifts and filled with the talents, the greatness and the difficulties that their mission demand.

WILLIAM G. MOORHEAD (1836–1914)
Sermons

And he said, "Hear now my words: if there be a prophet among you, I the Lord will make myself known unto him in a vision, and will speak unto him in a dream."

The Old Testament
Numbers 12:6

It is a grand thing when in the stillness of the soul, thought bursts into flame, and the intuitive vision comes like an inspiration; when breathing thoughts clothe themselves in burning words, winged as it were with lightning; or when a great law of the universe reveals itself to the mind of Genius, and where all was darkness, his single word lets Light be, and all is order where chaos and confusion were before.

FREDERICK WILLIAM ROBERTSON
(1816–1853)
Sermons

Three of the greatest teachers of the world, Buddha, Jesus, Muhammad, have left unimpeachable testimony that they found illumination through prayer and could not possibly live without it.

MOHANDAS K. GANDHI (1869–1948)
Young India

When the great comes by, as always there are angels walking in the earth.

RALPH WALDO EMERSON (1803–1882)
Aristocracy

They hear your words, but they will not do them: for with mouth they show much love, but their heart goes after their covetousness. You are like one who sings a lovely song with a beautiful voice and plays well on an instrument, for they hear what you say, but they will not do it.

The Old Testament
Ezekiel 33:22

Each age has its prophets and its God-inspired men, but they speak the language

of the age, and their word must not remain behind the width of the reflexion
that the perception of Godhead reaches in
them.   JOSEPH GORRES (1776–1848)
Mythic History of the Ancient World

The prophet hears God's voice and feels
His heart. He tries to impart the pathos of
the message together with its logos. An an
imparter his soul overflows, speaking as he
does out of the fullness of his sympathy.
     ABRAHAM JOSHUA HESCHEL (1907–1972)
                              The Prophets

What were Luther's mission and Wesley's but appeals to powers which even the
meanest of men might carry with them—
faith and self-despair—but which were
personal, requiring no priestly interme-
diation, and which brought their owner
face to face with God?
          WILLIAM JAMES (1842–1910)
                      The Will to Believe

O I am sure they really came from Thee,
The urge, the ardor, the unconquerable
     will,
The potent, felt, interior command,
     stronger than words,
A message from the Heavens whispering
     to me even in sleep,
These sped me on.
            WALT WHITMAN (1819–1892)
                      Prayer of Columbus

Jesus Christ belonged to the true race of
prophets. He saw with open eyes the mystery of the soul. Drawn by its severe harmony, ravished with its beauty, he lived in
it, and had his being there.
     RALPH WALDO EMERSON (1803–1882)
                   Divinity School Address

Above the generations the lonely
     prophets rise,
While truth flings dawn and day-star
     within their glowing eyes;

And other eyes beholding, are kindled
     from that light;
And dawn becomes the morning, the
     darkness put to flight.
   WILLIAM CHANNING GANNETT (1840–1923)
                  The Morning Hangs a Signal

Seers of the Infinite have ever been
quiet souls. They abide alone with themselves and the Infinite, or if they do look
around them, grudge to no one who understands the mighty word his own peculiar way. By means of this wide vision, this
feeling of the Infinite, they are able to look
beyond their own sphere.
   FRIEDRICH SCHLEIERMACHER (1768–1834)
                              On Religion

Discovering the true meaning of God's
love, the prophet becomes the great poet
of the love of mankind.
          HERMANN COHEN (1842–1918)
                          Jewish Writings

The prophet, even when he seems to be
speaking, is in truth quiescent: it is Another who uses his vocal organs, his mouth
and tongue, to show forth whatsoever he
desires. This Other plays on these instruments by an invisible art of consummate
music, and so achieves an utterance fair-
sounding, harmonious, full of all possible
symphony.
      PHILO JUDAEUS (30 B.C.–A.D. 40)
            Quis Rerum Divinarum Haeres

Come ye near unto me, hear ye this; I
have not spoken in secret from the beginning; from the time that it was, there am
I; and now the Lord God, and his Spirit,
hath sent me.   *The Old Testament*
                               Isaiah 48:16

Faith is a kind of winged intellect. The
great workmen of history have been men
who believed like giants.
       CHARLES H. PARKHURST (1842–1933)
                                  Sermons

The prophet is primarily the man, not to whom God has communicated certain divine thoughts, but whose mind is illuminated by the divine spirit to interpret aright the divine acts; and the act is primary. WILLIAM TEMPLE (1881–1944)
Daily Readings

He that negotiates between God and man,
As God's ambassador, the grand concerns
Of judgment and of mercy, should
  beware
Of lightness in his speech.
WILLIAM COWPER (1731–1800)
The Task

The divine voice was always in their ears. Often they misunderstood it. Often they thought they heard it when it was only the echo of their own thoughts and wishes that they heard; but the desire to hear it, the sense that life consisted in hearing it,—that never left them.
PHILLIPS BROOKS (1835–1893)
Sermons

"Resist not evil," "Love your enemies," these are saintly maxims of which men of this world find it hard to speak without impatience. Are the men of this world right, or are the saints in possession of the deeper range of truth?
WILLIAM JAMES (1842–1910)
The Varieties of Religious Experience

Still, still, though dead, they speak,
  And trumpet-tongued, proclaim,
To many a wakening land,
  The one availing name.
MARTIN LUTHER (1483–1546)
Hymns

Saints cannot arise where there have been no warriors, nor philosophers where a prying beast does not remain hidden in the depths.
GEORGE SANTAYANA (1863–1952)
The Life of Reason

What bard,
At the height of his vision, can deem
Of God, of the world, of the soul,
With a plainness as near,
As flashing as Moses felt
When he lay in the night by his flock
On the starlit Arabian waste?
MATTHEW ARNOLD (1822–1888)
Future

Hear the voice of the Bard!
Who Present, Past, and Future sees;
Whose ears have heard
The Holy Word
That walk'd among the ancient trees.
WILLIAM BLAKE (1757–1827)
Introduction to Songs of Experience

The prophet's mantle, ere his flight
  began,
Dropt on the world—a sacred gift to
  man.
THOMAS CAMPBELL (1777–1844)
The Pleasures of Hope

To the unraveling of human tangles we would gladly believe that God sends especial men—chosen vessels which come to the world's deliverance.
W. E. B. DU BOIS (1868–1963)
John Brown

Jesus of Nazareth was the most scientific man that ever trod the globe. He plunged beneath the material surface of things, and found the spiritual cause.
MARY BAKER EDDY (1821–1910)
Science and Health

Great men are they who see that spiritual is stronger than any material force; that thoughts rule the world.
RALPH WALDO EMERSON (1803–1882)
Progress of Culture

Justice Bennet of Denby, was the first that called us Quakers, because I bid them tremble at the word of the Lord. This was in the year 1650.

GEORGE FOX (1624–1691)
Journal

Servant of God, well done! Well has thou
  fought
The better fight, who single hast
  maintained
Against revolted multitudes the cause
Of truth, in word mightier than they in
  arms.

JOHN MILTON (1608–1674)
Paradise Lost

God has brought prophetism near to men in giving them all a state analogous to it. In the prophetic the sight is illumined by a light which uncovers hidden things and objects which the intellect fails to reach. It is like an immediate perception, as if one touched the objects with one's hand.

ABU-HAMID MUHAMMAD AL-GHAZZALI
(1058–1111)
The Revival of the Religious Sciences

Things here are but signs that show to the wise how the Supreme God is known; the enlightened priest reading the sign may enter the holy place and make the vision real.   PLOTINUS (205–270)
Enneads

God is equally gracious, merciful, and the rest, to all men; and as the function of the prophet was to teach men not so much the laws of their country, as true virtue, and to exhort them thereto, it is not doubted that all nations possessed prophets, and that the prophetic gift was not peculiar to the Jews. Indeed, history, both profane and sacred, bears witness to the fact.   BENEDICT SPINOZA (1632–1677)
Theologico-Political Treatise

The saints of God are sealed inwardly with faith, but outwardly with good works.

JOHN BOYS (1571–1625)
Sermons

Men's minds perceive second causes,
But only prophets perceive the action of
  the First Cause.

JALAL-UD-DIN RUMI (1207–1273)
The Masnawi

Those that reach the sphere of the higher saints become the messengers of the Master of the Universe, even as the Angels are.   *The Zohar*

O sages standing on God's holy fire
As in the gold mosaic of a wall,
Come from the holy fire, perne in a gyre,
And be the singing-masters of my soul.

WILLIAM BUTLER YEATS (1865–1939)
Sailing to Byzantium

· UNLESS THE LORD HAD BEEN MY HELP ·

When God shows a child a yam, he certainly will afford him a stick to dig it out from the ground.   *Ibo Proverb*

Be still awhile from thy own thoughts, searching, seeking, desires, imaginations, and be stayed on the principle of God in thee, that it may raise thy mind up to God, and stay it upon God; and thou wilt find

strength from Him, and find Him to be a God at hand, a present help in time of trouble and need.

GEORGE FOX (1624–1691)
Journal

I meet with difficulties, disappointments, humiliations, troubles and temptations of every kind; if I pray to God to come to my help and give me strength to bear them, I am asking as I ought and am therefore entitled to hope that he will grant my prayer.

JEAN NICHOLAS GROU (1730–1803)
The School of Jesus Christ

What matters who in earth or hell is against us, if He is for us? Omnipotence to defend us, Omnipresence to companion us, and Infinite Love to enfold and uplift and enrapture us.

THOMAS DE WITT TALMAGE (1832–1902)
Sermons

Deliver me, O Lord, from that evil man, *myself.*   SAINT AUGUSTINE (354–430)
Confessions

If I forget,
Yet God remembers! If these hands of mine
Cease from their clinging, yet the hands divine
Hold me so firmly that I cannot fall;
And if sometimes I am too tired to call
For him to help me, then he reads the prayer
Unspoken in my heart, and lifts my care.

ROBERT BROWNING (1812–1889)
Paracelsus

When lightning flashes like an arrow; when the wind rends the mountains, as though they were earthen pitchers; when at the sound of the abundance of rain, all ears grow deaf; then the beasts of the forests all together take refuge, and all the young doves flee into the clefts of rocks. But in a moment, with the radiance of its light, the sun shines forth, and breaks through, and dispels all clouds and darkness. Thus likewise God, who rules the world with might, causes relief from trou-

ble to spring forth within a moment unto the contrite.

MOSES LUZZATTO (1707–1747)
The Way of the Upright

O how comely it is, and how reviving
To the spirits of just men long opprest
When God into the hands of their deliverer
Puts invincible might.

JOHN MILTON (1608–1674)
Samson Agonistes

God prepares the cure before the hurt.
The Talmud

The God whom we seek will, I doubt not, give us the help we need, that our labor be not fruitless. Then shall we understand what is written in the Psalm: "Let the heart of them rejoice that seek the Lord: seek the Lord and be strengthened; seek his face always."

SAINT AUGUSTINE (354–430)
On the Trinity

God never makes us feel our weakness but that we may be led to seek strength from Him. What is involuntary should not trouble us; but the great thing is never to act against the light within us, and to desire to follow where God would lead us.

FRANÇOIS FÉNELON (1651–1715)
Letters and Reflections

The one thing which really befits God's nature is to come to the aid of those in need.

SAINT GREGORY OF NYSSA (331–396)
Address on Religious Instruction

Thou drewest near in the day that I called upon thee: thou saidst, Fear not. O Lord, thou hast pleaded the causes of my soul; thou hast redeemed my life.

The Old Testament
Lamentations 3:57–58

Blow, winds of God, awake and blow the
   mists of earth away;
Shine out, O Light divine, and show how
   wide and far we stray.
      JOHN GREENLEAF WHITTIER (1807–1892)
              The Worship of Nature

God takes a thousand times more pains
with us than the artist with his picture, by
many touches of sorrow, and by many colors of circumstance, to bring man into the
form which is the highest and noblest in
His sight, if only we receive His gifts and
myrrh in the right spirit.
          JOHANNES TAULER (1300–1361)
            Sermons on the Inner Way

No wounds like those a wounded spirit
   feels,
No cure for such, till God who makes
   them heals.
        WILLIAM COWPER (1731–1800)
                   Retirement

We may boldly say: "The Lord is my
helper! I will not fear what man shall do
unto me!"   *The New Testament*
                  Hebrews 13:6

God will heal the bosoms of a people
who believe, and will take away the wrath
of their hearts.   *The Koran*

Abide with me! Fast falls the eventide;
The darkness deepens: Lord, with me
   abide!
When other helpers fail, and comforts
   flee,
Help of the helpless, O abide with me!
      HENRY FRANCIS LYTE (1793–1847)
                     Hymn

God is our refuge and strength, a very
present help in trouble. Therefore will we
not fear, though the earth do change, and
though the mountains be moved into the
heart of the seas; though the waters
thereof roar and foam, though the mountains shake at the swelling thereof.
                The Old Testament
                  Psalms 46:2–4

The eternal God is a dwelling-place, and
underneath are the everlasting arms.
                The Old Testament
              Deuteronomy 33:27

Only for God wait thou in stillness, my
soul; for from Him cometh my hope. He
only is my rock and salvation, my high
tower; I shall not be moved.
                The Old Testament
                Psalms 62:6–7

Lay up for yourselves the wealth of
God's name, which fire will not burn,
which winds will not dry up, and which
thieves will not approach.
             KABIR (1440–1518)
             The Adi Granth

Unless the Lord had been my help, my
soul had almost dwelt in silence. When I
said, My foot slippeth, thy mercy, O Lord,
held me up.   *The Old Testament*
                Psalms 94:17–18

O thou, who dost weave the bonds of
Nature's self, look down upon this pitiable
earth! Mankind is no base part of this
great work, and we are tossed on Fortune's
wave. Restrain, our Guardian, the engulf-
ing surge, and as Thou dost the un-
bounded heaven rule, with a like bond
make true and firm these lands.
             BOETHIUS (480–524)
         Consolation of Philosophy

With God's protection even a cobweb is
a castle.   *Hungarian Proverb*

Courage, my mind. God is our helper. He made us, and not we ourselves. Press on where truth begins to dawn.

SAINT AUGUSTINE (354–430)
Confessions

Try first thyself, and after call in God;
For to the worker God himself lends aid.

EURIPIDES (480–406 B.C.)
Hippolytus

· O GIVE ME GRACE ·

I implore thy grace, adorable Lord. Bear with me, I pray, as a father with his son, friend with friend, lover with beloved.
The Bhagavad Gita

O Power Supreme!
Without Whose call this world would
cease to breathe,
Who from the fountain of Thy grace does
fill
The veins that branch through every
frame of life.

WILLIAM WORDSWORTH (1770–1850)
The Prelude

It argues more grace to grieve for the sins of others than for our own. We may grieve for our own sins out of fear of hell, but to grieve for sins of others is from a principle of love to God.

THOMAS WATSON (died 1686)
Sermons

These are thy wonders, Lord of love,
To make us see we are but flowers that
glide:
Which when we once can finde and
prove,
Thou hast a garden for us, where to bide.

GEORGE HERBERT (1593–1633)
The Flower

O give me Grace to see thy face, and be
A constant Mirror of Eternitie.

THOMAS TRAHERNE (1637–1674)
Desire

What counts is the presence of Grace. What counts is the evidence that there is "something else" than this flesh and this blood, and that He who made men of flesh and blood in His image has, from all eternity, consented to all the profanations that this resemblance implies.

FRANÇOIS MAURIAC (1885–1970)
Journal

People try to find out whether it is "grace" or "nature" that saves us and they never reach a solution. How foolish of them! Let God rule within you, leave the work to Him. Do not trouble thyself whether he does it naturally or supernaturally.

MEISTER ECKHART (1260–1327)
Sermons

You are told you should love your neighbor as yourself; but if you love yourself meanly, childishly, timidly, even so shall you love your neighbor. Learn therefore to love yourself with a love that is wise and healthy, that is large and complete.

MAURICE MAETERLINCK (1862–1949)
Wisdom and Destiny

God is freedom, and not necessity, not authority over man and the world. What the theologians call grace, placing it alongside human freedom, is this action in man of divine freedom. We might say that the existence of God is man's charter of liberty, his inner justification for his struggle for freedom against nature and society.

NIKOLAI BERDYAEV (1874–1948)
The Realm of Spirit and the Realm of Caesar

When our wills are united with the will of God, we never take all the goodness and beauty and people and things in life for granted, but we accept them again and again as a gift from him—given that we may serve him with still greater joy and thank him for it.

ALBERT SCHWEITZER (1875–1965)
Reverence for Life

The world has only rest upon the narrow
    space where God in peace dwells with
    his creature
In inward unity, and no one knows the
    beginning of his grace, and end of
    nature.

PAUL CLAUDEL (1868–1955)
Feuilles de Saints

Divine knowledge is not sought in mere words; to speak concerning it were hard as iron. By God's grace man obtains it; skill and order are useless therefore.

The Upanishads

There is no minor sin when His justice confronts you; and there is no major sin when His grace confronts you.

IBN 'ATA'ILLAH (died 1309)
The Book of Wisdom

If grace takes hold of us and remakes us in the depths of our being, it is so that all our action should feel its effects and be illuminated by it.

JACQUES MARITAIN (1882–1973)
True Humanism

With the Lord in thy heart take refuge with all thy being; by His grace thou shalt attain to the supreme peace and the eternal status. *The Bhagavad Gita*

Voltaire cynically said of the forgiveness of God: "C'est son metier—it is His job." But this is not so. Things are quite different from the popular assumption. The grace of God can also be silent.

HELMUT THIELICKE (1908–)
The Silence of God

A new heart also will I give you, and a new spirit will I put within you; and I will take away the stony heart out of your flesh, and I will give you a heart of flesh.

The Old Testament
Ezekiel 36:26

Truly that man knows something of religion who can only wonder, in all humility, how God is able to make such a weak and morally fragile vessel a creature worthy of His grace.

RICHARD ROTHE (1799–1867)
Still Hours

God works in us from within outwards; but all creatures work from without inwards. And thus it is that grace, and all the gifts of God, and the Voice of God, come from within, in the unity of our spirit; and not from without, into the imagination, by means of sensible images.

JAN VAN RUYSBROECK (1293–1381)
The Spiritual Espousals

God be gracious unto you and give you all a heart to serve him and to do his will with a good courage and a willing mind; and open your hearts in his law and commandments, and send you peace and hear your prayers, and be at one with you and never forsake you in time of trouble.

The Old Testament Apocrypha
2 Maccabees 1:2–5

In meeting and welcoming the divine grace, man's spirit is not passive but responsive; and the divine influence comes as a gift and not by compulsion.

WILLIAM RITCHIE SORLEY (1855–1935)
Moral Values and the Idea of God

That little word "grace" is like a small window that opens out on to a great landscape, for it gathers up into one encyclopedical expression the whole infinite variety of beneficences and bestowments which come showering down upon us.

ALEXANDER MACLAREN (1826–1910)
Sermons

· THE GIFT OF PEACE ·

If our peace be but the peace of the sensualist satisfying pleasure, if it be but the peace of mental torpor and inaction, the peace of apathy, or the peace of the soul dead in trespasses and sins, we may whisper to ourselves, "Peace, peace," but there will be no peace; *there* is not the peace of unity, nor the peace of God, for the peace of God is the living peace of love.

FREDERICK WILLIAM ROBERTSON
(1816–1853)
Sermons

The only authentic altruism is one that flows spontaneously from the heart that is already at peace with itself, and then only in the profounder sense in which being at peace with oneself is to be at peace with God.   JOHN BAILLIE (1886–1960)
The Sense of the Presence of God

If you are hopelessly upset by every transient ill fortune; if you are thrown off your balance by every threat of trouble in the future, however remote; if you are endlessly worried about the state of your own soul and the perils which may beset it, instead of trying to love God and living in the trust which is begotten of love; then, of course, you are not at peace.

GERALD VANN (1906–1963)
The Divine Pity

What will the spirit of man be like, when it has no vice at all, and gives way to no one, nor yields to any, nor fights even a praiseworthy battle against anything—when it is perfected in the most peaceful virtue? How sure then will its knowledge be of the grandeur and beauty of all things—a knowledge without error or labor, in which the wisdom of God will be drunk from its very source, accompanied by the highest happiness and stripped of all trouble?

SAINT AUGUSTINE (354–430)
The City of God

If thou take heed what thou art within thou shalt not reck what men say of thee: man looketh on the visage and God on the heart; man considereth the deeds and God praiseth the thoughts.

THOMAS À KEMPIS (1380–1471)
The Imitation of Christ

Calm soul of all things! make it mine
To feel, amid the city's jar,
That there abides a peace of thine,
Man did not make, and cannot mar.

MATTHEW ARNOLD (1822–1888)
Kensington Guard

Flowers every night
Blossom in the sky;

Peace in the Infinite;
At peace am I.
JALAL-UD-DIN RUMI (1207–1273)
The Masnawi

May the Lord of peace Himself give you peace at all times and in every way!
The New Testament
2 Thessalonians 3:16

To win true peace, a man needs to feel himself directed, pardoned, and sustained by a supreme power, to feel himself in the right road, at the point where God would have him be,—in order with God and the universe.
HENRI FRÉDÉRIC AMIEL (1821–1881)
Journal Intime

For I have known all along what I have intended for you, says God, a destiny of peace and not of evil, to give you a future and a hope.   *The Old Testament*
Jeremiah 29:11

Our age-old and noble dream of a world of peace may yet become a reality, but it will come neither by man working alone nor by God destroying the wicked schemes of men, but when men so open their lives

to God that he may fill them with love, mutual respect, understanding, and goodwill. Social salvation will come only through man's willing acceptance of God's mighty gift.
MARTIN LUTHER KING, JR. (1929–1968)
Strength to Love

How can the peace of God—the health, joy, and life of the soul—find room in a heart filled with bitter waters? Let us first seek out the spark of God's truth within us, which, lighting up our darkness, will bring us to the holy waters of Siloam to which the prophet summons us: "Wash you, make you clean, put away the evil of your doings."
GREGORY SAVVICH SKOVORODA
(1722–1794)
A Conversation Concerning Life's
True Happiness

How beautiful upon the mountains are the feet of him that bringeth good tidings, that publisheth peace; that bringeth good tidings of good, that publisheth salvation; that saith unto Zion, Thy God reigneth!
The Old Testament
Isaiah 52:7

· THE GIFT OF FORGIVENESS ·

Who is a God like unto Thee, pardoning iniquity and passing over transgression? He does not retain his anger for ever because he delights in mercy.
The Old Testament
Micah 7:18

God will forgive me; it is his trade.
HEINRICH HEINE (1797–1856)
On his deathbed

O Thou, who Man of baser Earth did make,

And ev'n with Paradise devise the Snake:
For all the Sin wherewith the face of Man
Is blacken'd—Man's forgiveness give—
and take!
OMAR KHAYYÁM (died c. 1123)
The Rubáiyát

And forgive us our trespasses as we forgive those who trespass against us; and what we do not forgive entirely, make thou, O Lord, that we should forgive, so that for thy sake we should sincerely love our enemies, and intercede devoutly for them with thee, and never render evil for evil, strive with thy help to be of assistance to all men.

SAINT FRANCIS OF ASSISI (1182–1226)
Exposition of the Lord's Prayer

For 'tis sweet to stammer one letter
Of the Eternal's language—on earth it is
called Forgiveness!

HENRY WADSWORTH LONGFELLOW
(1807–1882)
The Children of the Lord's Supper

"Forgive us," we say, "as we forgive those who have wronged us." What do we mean by that, if not that we offer to him our souls freed from revenge and rancor? Yet we invoke God and his assistance in plotting our iniquities and invite him to our wrongdoing.

MICHEL EYQUEM DE MONTAIGNE
(1533–1592)
Of Prayers

Then hear thou from heaven thy dwelling place, and forgive, and render unto every man according unto all his ways, whose heart thou knowest; for thou only knowest the hearts of the children of men.

*The Old Testament
2 Chronicles 6:30*

Be praised, my Lord, for those who for
Thy love forgive,
Contented unavenged in quiet to live.
Bless those who in the way of peace are
found—
By Thee, O Lord Most High, they shall
be crowned!

SAINT FRANCIS OF ASSISI (1182–1226)
The Canticle of the Sun

God destroyed Sodom, but in the world to come, when he heals Israel, he will heal her also, as it says, "I will give her her vineyards" (Hosea 2:15)—her vineyards are her prophets—"and her troubled valley for a gate of hope," the valley which I troubled in my wrath shall be their gate of hope. And then will Sodom "sing there as in the days of her youth," singing songs of thanksgiving to God. *The Mishnah*

God wishes man to ask forgiveness, and not to see him in his guilt. *The Midrash*

God in His inscrutable wisdom has appointed a term for the existence of perversity, and when the time of Inquisition comes, He will destroy it for ever. Then truth will emerge triumphant for the world, albeit now and until the time of the final judgment it will go sullying itself in the ways of wickedness owing to the domination of perversity.

The Dead Sea Scrolls

The acceptance by God, his forgiving or justifying act, is the only and ultimate source of a courage to be which is able to take the anxiety of guilt and condemnation into itself.

PAUL TILLICH (1886–1965)
The Courage to Be

When the sinner despairs of the forgiveness of sin, it is almost as if he were directly picking a quarrel with God.

SÖREN KIERKEGAARD (1813–1855)
Sickness unto Death

The righteousness of God is his forgiveness, the radical alteration of the relationship between God and man which explains why, though human unrighteousness and ungodliness have brought the world to its present condition and are intolerable to Him, He nevertheless continues to name us His people in order that we may *be* his people. Unlike any other verdict, His verdict is creative: He pronounces us, His enemies, to be His friends.

KARL BARTH (1886–1968)
The Epistle to the Romans

Only God can forgive, yet our response is needed. The pardon is without full effect until man accepts it and lives in its power, as music is null and void until a man opens his ears. The aural nerve is frail, yet without it symphonies are lost.

GEORGE ARTHUR BUTTRICK (1892–1979)
So We Believe, So We Pray

We must be willing to forgive without limit even as God forgives; otherwise we cannot be forgiven. Of course, we must be willing to live out our forgiveness in restoring and repairing where we have done wrong. Being forgiven means joining all others in the common responsibility of putting things right before God and with one another.

NELS F. S. FERRE (1908–1971)
The Living God of Nowhere and Nothing

What will it matter though you have fallen by the way, if you reach your journey's end safely at last? God will forgive the falls: they are often caused by undue haste, which prevents us from taking fitting precautions, or with timid souls from a perpetual looking round for imaginary dangers which cause them to stumble. Perhaps the holiest men are not always those who commit the fewest faults, but those who have the most courage, most love, and the most free spirit; those who make the heartiest efforts for conquering self and who are not afraid of a stumble, even of a fall, so long as their progress is certain.

JEAN NICHOLAS GROU (1731–1803)
The Hidden Life of the Soul

If we forgive God for his crime against us, which is to have us finite creatures, He will forgive our crime against him, which is that we are finite creatures.

SIMONE WEIL (1909–1943)
Notebooks

And Thou, O Lord! by whom are seen
    Thy creatures as they be,
Forgive me if too close I lean
    My human heart on Thee!

JOHN GREENLEAF WHITTIER (1807–1892)
The Eternal Goodness

When God forgives, he does not simply pronounce or simply record a sentence; when God forgives, the well-spring of life turns from bitter to sweet, the acid of sin ceases to corrode, and living waters irrigate the soul. We stop shriveling, we begin to grow.

AUSTIN FARRER (1904–)
A Faith of Our Own

What is the meaning of the Kingdom of Heaven? It is this: that we should forgive one another—then God will forgive us too; that we should love one another—then God will love us too. And if it is in this that we find our happiness on earth, then the Kingdom of Heaven is with us.

PARACELSUS (1493–1541)
Liber Principiorum

Oh, God! I say not hear my prayers! I say:
Blot with forgiving pen my sins away!

SAADI (1184–1291)
Gulistan

God has promised forgiveness to your repentance, but He has not promised tomorrow to your procrastination.

SAINT AUGUSTINE (354–430)
Sermons

God gives man a "new heart" and a "new life," but He does not render undone what has been done.

ROMANO GUARDINI (1885–1968)
Faith and the Modern Man

Forgiveness is the greatest and most incomprehensible miracle of the love of God because in it God communicates Himself to a human being who in the seeming ba-nality of everyday life has had the effrontery to say No to God.

KARL RAHNER (1904–)
Meditations on the Sacraments

· BLESSED IS THE MAN ·

Bless me in this life with but peace of my conscience, command of my affections, the love of Thyself and my dearest friends, and I shall be happy enough to pity Caesar.   SIR THOMAS BROWNE (1605–1682)
Religio Medici

God sendeth down water from Heaven, and causeth the earth to revive after it hath been dead, Verily, herein is a sign of the resurrection unto people who hearken.   *The Koran*

Blessed is the man who loveth Thee, and his friend in Thee, and his enemy for Thee. For he only loses none dear to him, to whom all are dear, in Him who cannot be lost. And who is that but our God, the God that made heaven and earth, and filleth them, even by creating them. None loseth but he who leaveth Thee.

SAINT AUGUSTINE (354–430)
Sermons

"God is thy portion," says David. David does not speak so narrowly, so penuriously, as to say, "God hath given thee thy portion, and thou must look for no more." But, "God is thy portion," and as long as He is God He hath more to give, and as long as thou art His, thou hast more to receive.

JOHN DONNE (1572–1631)
Sermons

God sheds his light upon the soul, gives it a radiance and a bliss that knows no end-ing; yet it is all done in such a hidden way, that it echoes the sacred text's description of Moses bidden alone to the summit of Mount Sinai, where he spoke to the Lord, and the Lord's voice was heard in answer.

SAINT FRANCIS OF SALES (1567–1622)
The Love of God

May He bless you with every good, and keep you from every evil. May He shine into your heart with life-giving wisdom and graciously grant you eternal knowledge. May He lift up his merciful face toward you for your eternal peace.

The Dead Sea Scrolls

He who blesses himself in the earth shall bless himself in the God of truth; and he that swears in the earth shall swear by the God of truth; because the former troubles are forgotten, and because they are hid from mine eyes.   *The Old Testament
Isaiah 65:16*

May it be thy will, O our God, to give every one his needs and to every being sufficient for his lack.   *The Talmud*

Perfect blessedness, which consists in a vision of God.

SAINT THOMAS AQUINAS (1225–1274)
Summa Theologica

In respect of blessedness—God was equally gracious to all.

BENEDICT SPINOZA (1632–1677)
Theologico-Political Treatise

May God reveal to you the true nature of His revelation, and grant you the greatness of His favour and graciousness. May he contain you by embracing you yourself in the fullness of His beneficences which, when they reach you, are the grace of His raising and exalting you.

ABU-L-QASIM AL-JUNAYD (died 910)
Letters

Blessed is the man who can love all men equally. Blessed is the man who is attached to nothing subject to corruption and time. Blessed is the mind which, passing by all creatures, constantly rejoices in God's beauty.

SAINT MAXIMUS THE CONFESSOR (580–662)
Mystagogia

· GOD PAYS BACK IN HIS OWN COIN ·

Whatever a man sows, that shall he reap. The law of Karma is inexorable and impossible of evasion. There is hardly any need for God to interfere. He laid down the rules and, as it were, retired.

MOHANDAS K. GANDHI (1869–1948)
Hindu Dharma

Good and evil do not befall men without reason. Heaven sends them happiness or misery according to their conduct.

CONFUCIUS (551–479 B.C.)
The Book of History

The soul takes nothing with her to the other world but her education and culture; and these, it is said, are of the greatest service or of the greatest injury to the dead man at the very beginning of his journey thither.

SOCRATES (470–399 B.C.)
Dialogues of Plato

God gives sense, but hope takes it away.
Finnish Proverb

The one eternal amid the transient, the one amid many, who grants their desires, to the wise who perceive Him as abiding in the soul, to them is eternal peace and to no others. *The Upanishads*

O God, who art Peace everlasting, whose chosen reward is the gift of peace, and who has taught us that the peacemakers are Thy children, pour Thy sweet peace into our souls, that everything discordant may utterly vanish, and all that makes for peace be sweet to us forever.

SAINT GELASIUS I (5th century)
Gelasian Sacramentary

What is fulness of joy but *peace?* Joy is tumultuous only when it is not full; but peace is the privilege of those who are "filled with the knowledge of the glory of the Lord, as the waters cover the sea."

JOHN CARDINAL NEWMAN (1801–1890)
Sermons

The prophet which prophesieth of peace, when the word of the prophet shall come to pass, then shall the prophet be known, that the Lord truly sent him.

The Old Testament
Jeremiah 28:9

Let us inquire of the just Job, who entered into a life-covenant with God before he himself was brought forth into life, what the most high God requires above all in those tens of hundreds of thousands who attend him. He will answer that it is

peace, in accord with what we read in him:
"He maketh peace in his high places."

GIOVANNI PICO DELLA MIRANDOLA
(1463–1494)
On the Dignity of Man

Send down thy peace, O Lord;
Earth's bitter voices drown in one deep
ocean of accord;
Thy peace, O God, send down.

EDWARD ROWLAND SILL (1841–1887)
Send Down Thy Truth

God hath this world for many made, 'tis
true:
But He hath made the world to come for
few.

ROBERT HERRICK (1591–1674)
Noble Numbers

Sometimes He gives while depriving
you, and sometimes He deprives you in
giving. When He opens up your understanding of deprivation, the deprivation
becomes the same as the gift.

IBN 'ATA'ILLAH (died 1309)
Kitab Al-Hakim

But men must know, that in this theater
of man's life it is reserved only for God
and angels to be lookers-on.

SIR FRANCIS BACON (1561–1626)
The Advancement of Learning

If only man were worthy of help as God
is able to provide it.   *Yiddish Proverb*

Think not that after thou hast gone
forth from the prison of thy body thou wilt
turn to correction from thy perpetual
backsliding; for it will not be possible for
thee then to turn away from backsliding
or to repent of wickedness, guilt, and
transgression. For that world has been established to render accounts—the book of
the hidden and concealed deeds which
every man commits is sealed—and it has
been prepared to grant a good reward to

them that fear the Lord and think upon
His name, and to execute the vengeance
of the covenant upon them that forget
God, who say unto God: "Depart from us,
for we desire not the knowledge of Thy
ways. What is the Almighty, that we should
serve Him? and what profit should we
have, if we pray to him?"

BAHYA IBN PAKUDA (11th century)
The Duties of the Heart

Beethoven composed his Mass in D
major while Napoleon was advancing on
Vienna; when he came to the last chorus
—"Dona nobis pacem"—he wrote above
his score, "Prayer for inward and outward
peace." It is seldom that the nature of
man's utmost need is presented to him in
a manner so vivid; but at all times it is true
that the need of man is for inward and
outward peace.

WILLIAM TEMPLE (1881–1944)
Christus Veritas

We might say of peace that it is the end
of all our good, especially since the sacred
psalmist says of the city of God, about
which our laborious work is written:
"Praise the Lord, Jerusalem, praise thy
God, O Zion; for he has strengthened the
bars of thy gates; he has blessed thy children within thee; he has made thy borders
peace."   SAINT AUGUSTINE (354–430)
The City of God

Get but that "peace of God, which passeth all understanding," and the questions
of the understanding will cease from puz-
zling, and pedantic scruples be at rest.

WILLIAM JAMES (1842–1910)
The Will to Believe

The peace of God is peace within ourselves. The unrest of human life comes
largely from our being torn asunder by
contending impulses. Conscience pulls this
way, passion that. Desire says, "Do this";

reason, judgment, prudence say "It is your peril if you do!" One desire fights against another. And so the man is rent asunder. There must be the harmonizing of all the being if there is to be real rest of spirit.

ALEXANDER MACLAREN (1826–1910)
Sermons

One ought to pray for peace even to the last clod of earth thrown over his grave.

The Talmud

The world will never be the dwelling-place of peace, till peace has found a home in the heart of each and every man, till every man preserves in himself the order ordained by God to be preserved.

POPE JOHN XXIII (1882–1963)
Pacem in Terris

I am a bird of God's garden, I do not belong to this dusty world. For a day or two they have locked me up in the cage of my body. I did not come here of myself, how should I return of myself? He who brought me must take me back again to my own country.

JALAL-UD-DIN RUMI (1207–1273)
The Masnawi

God waits a long time, but he pays with interest in the end. *Yiddish Proverb*

For whatsoever a man soweth, that shall he also reap. *The Old Testament*
Hosea 8:7

God will have no man pressed with an-other's inconveniences in matters spiritual and intellectual—no man's salvation to de-pend on another; and every tooth that eats sour grapes shall be set on edge for itself, and for none else.

JEREMY TAYLOR (1613–1667)
The Liberty of Prophesying

I cannot believe that the life eternal is one of endless idleness. If it were endless duration only, it would be endless bore-dom and scarcely willed by God. What we may be given to do in the next life we can-not say, and with so many forms of work in this life related to physical existence, it is useless to speculate. But if there is a fel-lowship of persons, God will give us tasks for their enrichment.

GEORGIA HARKNESS (1891–1974)
Understanding the Kingdom of God

· I DELIGHT TO DO THY WILL ·

How shall I now abandon wisdom, since God's spirit made a covenant between us? Or how shall she forsake me, since she is like a mother to me and I am the child of her old age?

SOLOMON IBN GABIROL (1021–1058)
The Fountain of Life

I delight to do Thy will, O my God: yea, Thy law is within my heart.

The Old Testament
Psalms 40:8

Few, but full of understanding, are the books of the library of God.

MARTIN FARQUHAR TUPPER (1810–1889)
Of Recreation

In the imperishable, infinite city of Brahman two things there are—Wisdom and unwisdom, hidden, established there. Perishable is unwisdom, but wisdom is immortal: Who over wisdom and un-wisdom rules He is Another.

The Upanishads

From all which I conclude, there is a Mind which affects me every moment with all the sensible impressions I perceive. And, from the variety, order, and manner of these, I conclude the Author of them to be wise, powerful, and good beyond comprehension. Mark it well; I do not say, I see things by perceiving that which represents them in the intelligible Substance of God. This I do not understand; but I say, the things by me perceived are known by the understanding, and produced by the will of an infinite Spirit.

GEORGE BERKELEY (1685–1753)
Three Dialogues

The wisdom of God says, "I alone can make you understand who you are." God has willed to make Himself quite recognizable to those who seek Him with all their heart, and to be hidden from those who flee from Him with all their heart. There is enough light for those who only desire to see, and enough obscurity for those who have a contrary disposition.

BLAISE PASCAL (1623–1662)
Pensées

Till your spirit filleth the whole world, and the stars are your jewels; till you are as familiar with the ways of God in all Ages as with your walk and table; till you are intimately acquainted with that shady nothing out of which the world was made: till you love men so as to desire their happiness, with a thirst equal to the zeal of your own: till you delight in God for being good to all: you never enjoy the world.

THOMAS TRAHERNE (1637–1674)
Centuries of Meditations

Indeed with foreign speech and a strange tongue
Will it be spoken to this people;
To whom God had said:

"This is the secret of rest—give rest to the weary;
And this means refreshment—"
But they would not hear.

The Old Testament
Isaiah 28:9–12

Man strives for reconciliation with God —could he aspire to anything higher? Since identity with God is a paradoxical notion, reconciliation with Him remains man's only goal because it represents no less than his redemption from the conflicting forces within his own nature.

HERMANN COHEN (1842–1918)
Jewish Writings

This then is the explication of the meaning of reconciliation, that God is reconciled with the world, or rather that God has shown Himself to be by his very nature reconciled with the world, that what is human is not something alien to His nature, but that this otherness, this self-differentiation, finitude, as it is sometimes expressed, is a moment in God Himself, though, to be sure, it is a vanishing moment.

GEORG WILHELM FRIEDRICH HEGEL
(1770–1831)
Lectures on the Philosophy of Religion

But the Lord said to Samuel, "Do not look on his appearance or the height of his stature, for the Lord sees not as man sees; man looks on the outward appearance, but the Lord looks on the heart."

The Old Testament
1 Samuel 16:7

Between the soul and God, between humanity and God, between the world and God, there stands a third element, or rather a third Person, who, although He unites man with God, yet equally maintains the absolute distinction between them; through Him alone that reconciliation takes place through which God reveals Himself: the Mediator.

EMIL BRUNNER (1889–1966)
The Mediator

Man is conscious of a universal soul within or behind his individual life, wherein, as in a firmament, the natures of Justice, Truth, Love, Freedom arise and shine. This universal soul he calls Reason: it is not mine, or thine, or his, but we are its; we are its property and men.

RALPH WALDO EMERSON (1803–1882)
Nature

There is no other reward but nearness to God, and there is no other punishment but estrangement from God. God does not reward us with wealth; God does not punish us with sickness. The good have suffered sickness and the evil have enjoyed wealth. The reward of the good life is goodness, and the reward of an evil life is evil. Kinship with God, or estrangement from God—that is Providence.

ABBA HILLEL SILVER (1893–1963)
Sermons

For a good deed by a man of good
   judgment—
For one, God writes ten.

SAADI (1184–1291)
Bustan

A pagan lady asked Rabbi Jose, "Can your God draw near to Him whom He wills?" He brought to her a basket of figs. She chose a good one and ate it. He said to her, "You know how to choose. Should not God know how to choose? Him whom He sees to be a doer of good deeds He chooses and brings near to Him."

The Talmud

God gives all men all earth to love,
   But since man's heart is small,

Ordains for each one spot shall prove
   Beloved over all.

RUDYARD KIPLING (1865–1936)
Sussex

The noblest of the gifts which God bestowed on His human creatures is Wisdom. This constitutes the life of their spirit, the lamp of their intellect. It secures them the favors of God, and saves them from His wrath both here and hereafter.

BAHYA IBN PAKUDA (11th century)
The Duties of the Heart

God who hath given the world to men in common, hath also given them reason to make use of it to the best advantage of life and convenience.

THOMAS HOBBES (1588–1679)
Human Nature

Every good gift and every perfect gift is from above, and cometh down from the Father of Lights, with whom is no variableness, neither shadow of turning.

The New Testament
James 1:17

The abounding goodness of God to us is manifested in the capacities of thought and perception with which he has uniquely endowed us and distinguished us from other living creatures.

BAHYA IBN PAKUDA (11th century)
The Duties of the Heart

Rabbi Johanan said: The Holy One, blessed be He, gives wisdom only to him who has wisdom.   *The Gemarah*

They in whose heart God is contained possess wisdom, honor, and wealth. What need is there of praising them? What further decoration can they obtain?

GURU NANAK (1469–1539)
The Adi Granth

God has stamp'd certain characters upon men's minds, which like their shapes, may perhaps be a little mended, but can hardly be totally alter'd and transformed into the contrary.

JOHN LOCKE (1632–1704)
Some Thoughts Concerning Education

God illuminates each man who enters this world in such a way that anybody thinks in God and through Him whatever he thinks, though dark minds may not comprehend Him, because they do not recognize that they see all things through Him.   MARSILIO FICINO (1433–1499)
Theologia Platonica

God has given man the eye of investigation by which he may see and recognise truth. He has endowed man with ears that he may hear the message of reality, and conferred upon him the gift of reason by which he may discover things for himself. Man is not intended to see through the eyes of another, hear through another's ears nor comprehend with another's brain. Each human creature has individual endowment, power and responsibility in the creative plan of God.

ABDUL BAHA (1844–1921)
The Mysterious Forces of Civilization

The seeds of all ages and all sciences are hidden in us from our birth, and that great workman, God, produceth out of the hidden all our faculties.

LUCIUS ANNAEUS SENECA (4 B.C.–A.D. 65)
God in Nature

The intellect which emanates from God to us is the link that joins us to God. You have it in your power either to strengthen or weaken that bond. It will become strong only when you make use of it in a spirit of love for God; it will be weakened when you direct your thoughts to other things.

MAIMONIDES (1135–1204)
Guide for the Perplexed

Where God gives hard bread he also gives sharp teeth.   *German Proverb*

God's works of providence are not disunited and jumbled, without connection or dependence, but are all united, just as the several parts of one building: there are many stones, many pieces of timber, but all are so joined, and fitly framed together, that they make but one building: they have all but one foundation, and are united at last in one top-stone.

JONATHAN EDWARDS (1703–1758)
A History of the Work of Redemption

Let not your spirit be troubled on account of the times; For the Holy and Great One has appointed days for all things.
*The Old Testament Apocrypha
The Book of Enoch*

God is equal to His purpose, but most men know it not.   *The Koran*

God has assigned to each man a director, his own good genius, and committed him to his care, a director who never sleeps and cannot be deceived. To what better, more careful guardian could He have committed us?

EPICTETUS (1st century)
Discourses

Let us not content ourselves with loving God for the mere sensible favors, however elevated, which He has done or may do us. Such favors, though never so great, cannot bring us so near to Him as faith does in one simple act.

BROTHER LAWRENCE (1605–1691)
The Practice of the Presence of God

Every wish
Is like a prayer, with God.
ELIZABETH BARRETT BROWNING
(1806–1861)
Aurora Leigh

No one is cast into the abyss unless he has first rejected, freed his heart from the terrible, yet gentle, hand of God. No one is abandoned unless he has first committed the fundamental sacrilege and denied God not in his justice but in his love.

GEORGES BERNANOS (1888–1948)
L'Imposture

Let us ask ourselves seriously and honestly, "What do I believe after all? What manner of man am I after all? What sort of show should I make after all, if the people round me knew my heart and all my secret thoughts? What sort of show, then, do I already make in the sight of Almighty God, who sees every man exactly as he is?"

CHARLES KINGSLEY (1819–1875)
Sermons

When goodness grows weak,
When evil increases,
I make myself as body.
In every age I come back
To deliver the holy,
To destroy the sin of the sinner,
To establish righteousness.

The Bhagavad Gita

In tragic life, God wot,
No villain need be! Passions spin the plot:
We are betrayed by what is false within.

GEORGE MEREDITH (1828–1909)
Modern Love

The Eternal One, your God, is no jealous God of revenge, but a God who reckons with your imperfections, to whom your inadequacy is known, who realizes that you must falter and that your road is long.

ARNOLD SCHOENBERG (1874–1951)
Jacob's Ladder

Unclasp thy conscience before God, and show thy wounds unto Him, and of Him ask a medicine. Show them to Him that will not reproach but heal thee, for although thou hold thy peace He knoweth all.   SAINT JOHN CHRYSOSTOM (345–407)
Sermons

Would aught avail us against a secret disease, if Thy healing hand, O Lord, watched not over us?

SAINT AUGUSTINE (354–430)
Confessions

The most High hath created medicines out of the earth, and a wise man will not abhor them.

The Old Testament Apocrypha
Ecclesiasticus 38:4

God gives food to every bird, but he does not throw it into the nest.

Hindu Proverb

Do not lie in a ditch and say, God help me; use the lawful tools He hath lent thee.

GEORGE CHAPMAN (1559–1634)
May-Day

God reaches us good things by our own hands.   THOMAS FULLER (1654–1734)
Gnomologia

The harder your undertaking, the easier God's help.   *Yiddish Proverb*

Verily, God will not change the conditions of men, until they change what is in themselves.   *The Koran*

Appeal to no one but Him to relieve you of a pressing need that He Himself has brought upon you. For how can someone else remove what He has imposed? And how can he who is unable to free himself of a pressing need free someone else of one?   IBN 'ATA'ILLAH (died 1309)
The Book of Wisdom

We can hardly suppose that God judges value by size. It is to surrender to an unreasonable worship of bigness to suppose that God cares less for human beings because they occupy little space in a vast material universe.

GEORGIA HARKNESS (1891–1974)
Conflicts in Religious Thought

I swear by the splendour of the light,
And by the silence of the night,
That the Lord shall never forsake thee.
The Koran

As God did not at first choose you because you were so high, so He will not forsake you because you are low.

JOHN FLAVEL (1630–1691)
Sermons

III · God's Love

The religion of love is apart from all
    religions.
The lovers of God have no religion but
    God alone.

—JALAL-UD-DIN RUMI

JALAL-UD-DIN RUMI wrote that "the astrolabe" of the mysteries of God is love. An astrolabe was the instrument used in ancient and medieval times to find the altitude of celestial bodies. Is it not significant that Jalal used the astrolabe as a symbolic way to search the infinite spaces above the earth's skies for God? Perhaps he is telling us that although no man-made instrument can penetrate the mysteries of God, love comes closest to showing us what they mean.

Jalal's striking metaphor could well serve as the central theme of this section of the anthology, in which the God Seekers, regardless of their nationality or religious persuasion, declare that love and God are in essence synonymous. Whether in the majestic strains of the Bhagavad Gita, the Gathas of Zoroaster, the hymns of Guru Nanak, the sermons of Martin Luther, or the wise sayings of the Baal Shem Tov, Kierkegaard, or Gandhi, the message is the same: discover, if you can, the full dimensionality of love and you will have taken the first steps to approaching the Living God.

This love, which must find its source in the most secret part of one's spirit, is not gained by mere lip service. As Pascal observed, "How far it is from the knowledge of God to a love of Him!" One of the greatest of contemporary theologians, Karl Rahner, in his *Meditations on the Sacraments,* says it this way:

In the last analysis we remain persons who must flee from ourselves and from the dark mystery of our threatening guilt in order to find our true selves in God. Whoever has understood the importance of this flight, this critical distancing of ourselves from ourselves, whoever has understood this knows that it comes about only by allowing oneself to be loved by an infinite and all-forgiving love, which is called God, and by believing, hoping and loving in this love.

To understand God's love is to accept that the very act of creation on his part was an act of divine love. If we cannot distinguish between a "giving" love, epitomized in the Greek word *agape,* and our earthbound physical *eros,* we are doomed from the start to misunderstand God's love. Only if these distinctions are clearly understood can we know that God does not need a reason for loving us, and certainly He does not *owe* us his love—such things are germane only within the confines of erotic love—but that his is a freely given love.

The philosopher Alfred North Whitehead believed that what is done in this world is translated into a reality in "heaven," and conversely that the reality of "heaven" passes back into the world. In *Process and Reality,* Whitehead saw that in this reciprocal relationship between God and people "the love in the world passes into the love in heaven, and floods back again into the world. In this sense, God is the great companion—the fellow-sufferer who understands."

In essence, Whitehead was restating what George Fox, founding father of the Quakers, had experienced on many occasions. Fox wrote in his *Journal* that he perceived there was an ocean of darkness and death, but like his contemporary, the poet Henry Vaughan, he also saw "an infinite ocean of light and love which flowed over the ocean of darkness." In this great ocean of eternity, George Fox believed, all could find the infinite love of God.

Few God Seekers have been as adept at using verbal symbolism to evoke religious emotions as John Donne. Like Saint Augustine in his youthful years, Donne's early life was spent in the worldly pursuit of pleasure that characterized his frenetic Elizabethan world. After his beloved wife, Anne, died, Donne poured his genius into spiritual endeavors, and eventually he became dean of St. Paul's Cathedral. Thereafter the eloquence of his sermons made him a court favorite of King James (himself no mean theologian), and later Donne preached the inaugural sermon opening the hapless reign of Charles I.

In one of his most notable sermons, Donne's metaphor for God's love is a circle—since a circle is endless, whomever God loves He loves endlessly. In a brilliant metaphysical conceit, which typified his poetry, Donne spins a variation on his theme, declaring "Whom God loves He loves to the end; and not only to their own end, to their death, but to His end, and His end is that He might love them still."

Saint Paul, in one of the most cherished and moving passages in the New Testament, says that even if we had the power to speak with the tongues of angels, but lacked the spirituality to deeply affirm our love of God, or to intuit his love for us, our words would be nothing more than cacophonous brass and clashing cymbals. Paul ends his incomparable definition of love in I Corinthians 13 with "There remain then, faith, hope, and love, these three; but the greatest of these is love."

Emil Brunner, a twentieth-century theologian, commented on the lasting implications of Saint Paul's luminous line. In *The Great Invitation,* Brunner points out that faith per se is not God, for, clearly, it is not incumbent on God to believe. By the same token, hope is not God, for He does not have to hope. But, Brunner says, "God is love because God Himself *loves and is love* in its changeless living reality. And because God is greater than all things, therefore love is greater than any other virtue, greater even than faith and hope."

Sören Kierkegaard wrote in his *Journal* that the only thing he knew for certain is that God is love: "Even if I have been mistaken on this or that point: God is nevertheless love." Kierkegaard believed that God resolves to communicate his love to us. Although we might think it would be a small matter for God, from whom all possibilities flow, to make his love understandable to us, Kierkegaard doubted that it can be easy, for "God is God, and we are men, sinful men."

The God Seekers are fully aware that our Creator has never *forced* us to love him. Instead, through the prophets and sages He has sent for thousands of years, God has been saying that He is willing, more than willing, to share through his love the greatest gift He can bestow on us, the gift of peace with ourselves and our fellow human beings.

As Henry Ward Beecher viewed it, when we plead with God for our daily bread, how shortsighted we are unless we realize that "love is God's loaf; and this is that feeding for which we ought to pray."

There is an old Serbian proverb that says if you love God you cannot fear him, and if you fear him you cannot love him. Like many proverbs, this bit of folk wisdom has deeper implications than appear on the surface. Though our lives would be barren without the need to love others—sweethearts, husbands and wives, friends, children, pets—we are always fearful that we might lose them, because of our own inability to love enough to allay their fears and they ours, or because of the mortal nature of all earthly relationships. We are loth to give ourselves completely to *eros* without some residual fears.

What our God Seekers tell us, however, is that we need not fear in reaching for the love of a Creator who established us and every living being in the universe out of the very core of his love. Indeed, if we seek the love of God with any reservations or anxieties we are merely extending our selfish, earthly concept of love and diminishing our chance of entering into the mystery of his love for us.

Why do we turn our backs on this gift of gifts? Why are we unable to assimilate that God loves every creature He has put in this universe? If we could take the sum of all human feelings of love and multiply it a billion times, the intensity of that love would still be infinitely small compared to God's inner core of love.

When will this Armageddon-prone earth begin to fulfill Saint Augustine's vision of a City of God, where people will love one another because their love of God and their acceptance of his love for them constitutes the supreme law? In *The City of God,* Augustine wrote: "Because a city is held together by some law, their very law is love. And that very love is God. For openly it is written 'God is love' (1 John 4:8). He, therefore, who is full of love is full of God."

Miguel de Unamuno implied in *The Tragic Sense of Life* that we cannot find God through the path of reason, since we can never free ourselves from the doubts and fears that vitiate this approach:

Not by the way of reason, but only by the way of love and of suffering, do we come to the living God, the human God. We cannot first know Him in order that afterwards we may love Him; we must begin by loving Him, longing for Him, hungering after Him before knowing Him. The knowledge of God proceeds from the love of God, and this knowledge has little or nothing of the rational in it.

If the day ever comes when this kind of love prevails in us all, when human-kind will accept Jalal-ud-din Rumi's bold declaration that the religion of love is apart from all religions and that the lovers of God need no religion but God alone, then the City of God that Saint Augustine envisioned in his prayers may become a reality. On the day when the various peoples of this earth are able collectively to *believe,* with no trace of doubt or fear, that God has a loving plan for every single one of us, on that miraculous day, as William Penn put it, "we shall all be Lovely, and in Love with God and one with another."

· THOU HIDDEN LOVE OF GOD ·

The Bible can say "God is love," but it could not say "God is wrath." For his wrath is but the shadow cast by his love rejected, and his judgment but the misery men make for themselves when his mercy is refused.   JOHN BAILLIE (1886–1960)
The Sense of the Presence of God

Creation is simply an act of divine love and cannot be accounted for on any other supposition than that of immense and eternal love.
FREDERICK WILLIAM FABER (1814–1863)
Creator and Creature

God, the Ground of Being, the Spirit Creator of all being, creates because he is love. Therefore he creates finite persons who are spirits, but have being, that they might learn love. To learn love man needs genuine self-being, genuine freedom; therefore man is put in an indirect relation to God within a pedagogical process where he can go his own partial, rebellious and faithless way until he discovers, through fear and frustration, indeed through all the opposite experiences from Love, that God's way, the way of love, is alone in accordance with man's deepest nature and alone can satisfy his deepest needs.
NELS F. S. FERRE (1908–1971)
The Living God of Nowhere and Nothing

Love is and was my lord and king,
    And in his presence I attend
    To hear the tidings of my friend,
Which every hour his couriers bring.
ALFRED LORD TENNYSON (1809–1892)
In Memoriam

For Thou lovest all the things that are, and abhorest nothing which Thou hast made: for never wouldst Thou have made anything, if Thou hadst hated it. But Thou sparest all: for they are Thine, O Lord, Thou lover of souls.

The Old Testament Apocrypha
The Wisdom of Solomon 11:24–26

To the soul which dares believe the vast and precious truth of God's personal love, all life becomes significant, and no past is so dreary that out of it there will not come up some ark of God to lead us to the richer things beyond.

PHILLIPS BROOKS (1835–1893)
The Light of the World

For the love of God is broader
Than the measure of man's mind;
And the heart of the Eternal
Is most infinitely kind.

FREDERICK WILLIAM FABER (1814–1863)
Hymns

Beloved, let us love one another: for love is of God; and every one that loveth is born of God, and knoweth God.

The New Testament
1 John 4:7

The Spirit of Love, wherever it is, is its own blessing and happiness, because it is the truth and reality of God in the soul; and therefore is in the same joy of life, and is the same good to itself everywhere and on every occasion.

WILLIAM LAW (1686–1761)
The Way to Divine Knowledge

Whoso is wise, and will observe these things, even they shall understand the loving-kindness of the Lord.

The Old Testament
Psalms 107:43

God is Love; and to love men till private attachments have expanded into a philan-thropy which embraces all—at last even the evil and enemies with compassion—that is to love God.

FREDERICK WILLIAM ROBERTSON
(1816–1853)
Sermons

God creates, governs, judges, punishes, pities, redeems, and saves; but love is the root of all. It was love that created this wondrous universe, to which science can set no bounds.

ROSWELL D. HITCHCOCK (1817–1887)
Sermons

The Lord hath appeared of old unto me, saying, Yea, I have loved thee with an everlasting love: therefore with loving-kindness have I drawn thee.

The Old Testament
Jeremiah 31:3

It is a divine thing, this kingdom of God. In it God's supreme purpose finds expression, His purpose to promote the reign of the spirit of love among men. It is for this that God is, and that is what God's love for the world means.

ARTHUR C. MCGIFFERT (1861–1933)
Sermons

Love "bears all things" and "endures all things" (1 Corinthians 13:7). These words say all there is to be said; nothing can be added to them. For we are in the deepest sense the victims and the instruments of cosmogonic "love."

CARL JUNG (1875–1961)
Memories, Dreams, Reflections

The One Word which God speaks is Himself. Speaking, He manifests Himself as infinite Love. His speaking and His hearing are One. So silent is His speech that, to our way of speaking, His speech is no-speech, His hearing is no-hearing. Yet, in his silence, in the abyss of His one Love, all words are spoken and all words are heard. Only in this silence of infinite Love do they have coherence and meaning.

THOMAS MERTON (1915–1968)
Thoughts in Solitude

All the joys of life which Thou holdest, O Mazda, the joys that were, the joys that are, and the joys that shall be, Thou dost apportion all in Thy love for us.

ZOROASTER (6th century B.C.)
The Gathas

As thy Love is discovered almighty, almighty be proved
Thy power, that exists with and for it, of being Beloved!

ROBERT BROWNING (1812–1889)
Saul

My God is Love;
My God is Love,
Tender and deep;
I feel His close, sweet presence
Looking down to see
The beggar-baby
Lying in my arms asleep.

TOYOHIKO KAGAWA (1888–1960)
Love

Thou hidden love of God, whose height, whose depth unfathomed no man knows.

GERHARD TERSTEEGEN (1697–1769)
Hymns

This is Hillel's teaching: it declares that the Love of God makes the loving heart realize that it can never live up to the lawful demands of that Love.

GERALD HEARD (1889–1971)
The Gospel According to Gamaliel

Agape is a unique type of Love, a Love that pours itself out regardless of merit, or desert—it floods out like the sun to reach the just and the unjust.

RUFUS JONES (1863–1948)
Pathways to the Reality of God

When our souls are utterly swept through and overturned by God's invading love, we suddenly find ourselves in the midst of a wholly new relationship with some of our fellow-men.

THOMAS R. KELLY (1893–1941)
A Testament of Devotion

Love is an image of God, and not a lifeless image, but the living essence of the divine nature which beams full of all goodness.

MARTIN LUTHER (1484–1546)
Sermons

We must know that love, which is God, and takes its existence in Him, affectionately loves nothing earthly, nothing material, nothing corruptible. For it is against its nature to love anything corruptible affectionately, since it is itself the source of incorruption.

ORIGEN (185–254)
Commentary on the Song of Songs

Only love can transform calculating justice into creative justice. Love makes justice just. Justice without love is always injustice.   PAUL TILLICH (1886–1965)
Systematic Theology

God is love, and the object of love: herein lies the whole contribution of mysticism. About this twofold love the mystic will never have done talking. His description is interminable, because what he wants to describe is ineffable. But what he does state clearly is that divine love is not a thing of God: it is God Himself.

HENRI BERGSON (1859–1941)
The Two Sources of Morality and Religion

God's nature is love, God's form is love, God's substance is love, God's color is love.   DADU (1554–1603)
The Bani

The world in its own way shows that the purposes of God are those of a Love that is perfect, and although they are not always seen to triumph in the lives of men, they are never seen defeated.

SIR HENRY JONES (1852–1922)
A Faith That Enquires

Moved by love, God is eternally resolved to reveal himself. But as love is the motive so love must also be the end; for it would be a contradiction for God to have a motive and an end which did not correspond.

SÖREN KIERKEGAARD (1813–1855)
Philosophical Fragments

That measureless love which is God Himself, dwells in the pure deeps of our spirit, like a burning brazier of coals. And it throws forth brilliant and fiery sparks which stir and enkindle heart and senses, will and desire, and all the powers of the soul, with a fire of love.

JAN VAN RUYSBROECK (1293–1381)
The Book of Supreme Truth

Only love, Charity, in its deep peacefulness and abiding joy, can embrace all human inconsistency and imperfection and see within it the stirring of the Perfect. But so God loves the world.

EVELYN UNDERHILL (1875–1941)
The Fruits of the Spirit

Love is the Spirit of Life, and Music the Life of the Spirit!

SAMUEL TAYLOR COLERIDGE (1772–1834)
Ad Vilmum Axiologum

O indestructible Love, O divine Minstrel,
Thou art both stay and refuge: a name
   equal to thee I have not found.
We are pieces of steel, and thy love is the
   magnet.

JALAL-UD-DIN RUMI (1207–1273)
The Diwan

Active love means hard work and tenacity, and for some people it is, perhaps, a

whole science. But I predict that at the very moment when you will realize with horror that, far from getting nearer to your goal, you are, in spite of all your efforts, actually further away from it than ever, I predict that at that very moment you will suddenly attain your goal and will behold clearly the miraculous power of the Lord who has all the time been loving and mysteriously guiding you.

FYODOR DOSTOEVSKY (1821–1881)
The Brothers Karamazov

The fullest life is the fullest love; and the love comes from the celestial light which streams forth from the Absolute One, the Absolute Good, that Supreme Principle which made life, and made spirit, the Source and Beginning, which gave spirit to all spiritual things and life to all living things.

PLOTINUS (205–270)
Enneads

In each soul, God loves and partly saves the whole world which that soul sums up in an incommunicable and particular way.

PIERRE TEILHARD DE CHARDIN (1881–1955)
The Divine Milieu

Even when He was silent, God suffered with us. In His silence He experienced the fellowship of death and the depths with us. Even when we thought He did not care, or was dead, He knew all about us and behind the dark wings He did His work of love.

HELMUT THIELICKE (1908–)
The Silence of God

What Joy in rosy waves outpoured,
Flows from the heart of Love, the Lord.

RALPH WALDO EMERSON (1803–1882)
May-Day

To ascribe love to God without making it a quality of his unalterable purpose, which must sweep on through costs in suffering however great, is to misread the gospel.

HARRY EMERSON FOSDICK (1878–1969)
The Meaning of Faith

On the whole, God's love for us is a much safer subject to think about than our love for Him. Nobody can always have devout feelings: and even if we could, feelings are not what God principally cares about. If we are trying to do His will we are obeying the commandment. "Thou shalt love the Lord thy God." He will give us feelings of love if He pleases. We cannot create them for ourselves, and we must not demand them as a right. But the great thing to remember is that, though our feelings come and go, his love for us does not. C. S. LEWIS (1898–1963)
Mere Christianity

Direct love toward God, and peace comes over the soul: turn it from God, and the heart becomes a broken fountain where tears fall "from the sighful branches of mind." FULTON J. SHEEN (1895–1979)
Peace of Soul

Maybe it's all men, and all women we love; maybe that's the Holy Spirit—the human spirit—the whole shebang. Maybe all men got one big soul ev'bodies a part of. JOHN STEINBECK (1902–1968)
The Grapes of Wrath

We and all men move
Under a canopy of love,
As broad as the blue sky above.

RICHARD CHENEVIX TRENCH (1807–1886)
The Kingdom of God

God's love for us is not the reason for which we should love him. God's love for us is the reason for us to love ourselves. How could we love ourselves without this

motive? It is impossible for man to love himself except in this roundabout way.

SIMONE WEIL (1909–1943)
Gravity and Grace

Of thy divine poem the first word is Reason, and the last is Man. And whoso shall trace the words from last to first shall find them the unbroken series of thy favours, the varied names of thy love.

JAMI (1414–1492)
Haft Aurang

The greatest idea that we can frame of God is when we conceive Him to be a Being of infinite love and goodness; using an infinite wisdom and power for the common good and happiness of all His creatures. WILLIAM LAW (1686–1761)
The Way to Divine Knowledge

The fact that God loves man proves that it is in the divine order of spiritual blessings that eternal love shall be given to the eternally unworthy.

OSCAR WILDE (1854–1900)
De Profundis

Love is the great subduing, transforming, and harmonizing emotion in human nature. And it is love alone by which responsive love is awakened, or on account of which love is felt in return. Ultimately, therefore, it is the love of God for man, and that alone, which redeems the man; because that love alone calls forth in return that love of man for God, by which man's whole nature is transformed.

S. H. HODGSON (1832–1912)
The Metaphysic of Experience

It is clear to us that human love is but an offshoot of the divine love, for without that divine love no love could be aroused within our heart.

NAHUM OF CZERNOBEL (1730–1798)
Meor Enayim

Whoever loves me beyond measure, him will I love beyond measure in return. Unable to bear separation from him, I cause him to possess me. This is my true promise: you will come to me.

The Bhagavad Gita

O Love, who formed me to wear
The image of thy Godhead here;
Who soughtest me with tender care
Through all my wanderings wild and
   drear;
O Love, I give myself to thee,
Thine ever, only thine to be.

ANGELUS SILESIUS (1624–1677)
Hymns

The beloved of the Lord shall dwell in safety by him, and the Lord shall cover him all the day long, and he shall dwell between his shoulders.

The Old Testament
Deuteronomy 33:12

True religion is to love, as God has loved them, all things, whether great or small.

The Hitopadesa

Love can forbear, and Love can forgive, though it can never be reconciled to an unlovely object. And hence it is that though you have so little considered the Works of God, and prized His love, yet you are permitted to live: and live at ease, and enjoy your pleasure.

THOMAS TRAHERNE (1637–1674)
Centuries of Meditations

To see the world as being ruled by a divine love which sets infinite value upon each individual and includes all men in its scope, and yet to live as though the world were a realm of chance in which each must fight for his own interests against the rest, argues a very dim and wavering vision of God's rule.   JOHN HICK (1922–)
Faith and Knowledge

God, from a beautiful necessity, is Love in all he doeth.

MARTIN FARQUHAR TUPPER (1810–1889)
Of Immortality

In youth I looked to these very skies,
And probing their immensities,
I found God there, his visible power;
   Yet felt in my heart, amid all its sense
   Of the power, an equal evidence
That his love, there too, was the nobler
   dower.

ROBERT BROWNING (1812–1889)
Christmas Eve

When I knew not his form, even then he fixed his love on me, planted himself within my thought and flesh and made me his.

With greater love than that of the mother who thoughtfully feeds with milk, melting the flesh of the sinner like me, flooding my soul with inner light, God bestows unweary, honeyed bliss.

MANIKKAVACAKAR (9th century)
Tiruvacakam

For God hath not given us the spirit of fear, but of power, and of love, and of a sound mind.   *The New Testament*
2 Timothy 1:7

From highest Brahman to the yonder
   worm,
And to the very minutest atom,
Everywhere is the same God, the All-
   Love;
Friend, offer mind, soul, body, at their
   feet.

SWAMI VIVEKANANDA (1863–1902)
In Search of God

Love is the emblem of eternity: it confounds all notion of time, effaces all memory of a beginning, all fear of an end.

MADAME DE STAËL (1766–1817)
Letters

Love, which is the essence of God, is not for levity, but for the total worth of man.

RALPH WALDO EMERSON (1803–1882)
Friendship

O Light divine! we need no fuller test
  That all is ordered well;
We know enough to trust that all is best
  Where Love and Wisdom dwell.

CHRISTOPHER PEARSE CRANCH
(1813–1892)
Oh, Love Supreme

The Love which moves the sun and the other stars. DANTE (1265–1321)
The Divine Comedy

With great love hast Thou loved us, O Lord our God; with great and overflowing pity hast Thou pitied us. O our Father, our King, for our fathers' sake, who trusted in Thee, and whom Thou didst teach the statutes of life, be gracious unto us too, and teach us.

The Ahabah, a traditional Hebrew prayer

God wisheth none should wreck on a
  strange shelf:
To him man's dearer than to himself.

BEN JONSON (1573–1637)
The Forest

There surely is a reason,
O Lord, for this rotation
And endless whirling: Love fills the entire
Space of heavens.

MOHAMMED TAQUI MIR (1723–1810)
The First Diwan

God gives us love. Something to love
  He lends us; but when love is grown
To ripeness, that on which it throve
  Falls off, and love is left alone.

ALFRED LORD TENNYSON (1809–1892)
To J.S.

How precious is thy steadfast love, O God! The children of men take refuge in the shadow of thy wings. They feast on the abundance of thy house, and thou givest them a drink from the river of thy delights. For with thee is the fountain of life; in thy light do we see light.

The Old Testament
Psalms 36:8–10

Love is indestructible,
Its holy flame for ever burneth,
From Heaven it came, to Heaven
  returneth.

ROBERT SOUTHEY (1774–1843)
The Curse of Kehama

O happy race of mortals, if your hearts are ruled as is the universe, by Love!

BOETHIUS (480–524)
The Consolation of Philosophy

Who has not found the heaven below
  Will fail of it above.
God's residence is next to mine,
  His furniture is love.

EMILY DICKINSON (1830–1886)
Who Has Not Found the Heaven Below

'Tis a motion of the Spirit that revealeth
  God to man.
In the shape of Love exceeding, which
  regards not taint or fall,
Since in perfect love, saith Scripture, can
  be no excess at all.

RUDYARD KIPLING (1865–1936)
Rahere

I sought the love which springs from the central profundities of being. I will have none of those passions of straw which dazzle, burn up, and wither; I invoke, I await, and I hope for the love which is great, pure, and earnest, which lives and works in all the fibres and through all the powers of the soul. And even if I go lonely to the end, I would rather my hope and my dream died with me, than that my soul should content itself with any meaner union.

HENRI FRÉDÉRIC AMIEL (1821–1881)
Journal Intime

With wide-embracing love
Thy Spirit animates eternal years,
  Pervades and broods above,
Changes, sustains, dissolves, creates, and
  rears.

EMILY BRONTË (1818–1848)
Last Lines

Love's secret life is in the heart, unfathomable, and it also has an unfathomable connection with the whole of existence. As the peaceful lake is grounded deep in the hidden spring which no eye can see, so a man's love is grounded even deeper in the love of God. If there were at the bottom no wellspring, if God were not love, then there would be no quiet lake or human love.   SÖREN KIERKEGAARD (1813–1855)
Works of Love

And He loves you; and, hourly, miracles
For you and such as you, is working
  now—
From all eternity, has worked them for
  you.

GOTTHOLD EPHRAIM LESSING (1729–1781)
Nathan the Wise

If I were to paint a picture of God, I would so draw him that there would be nothing else in the depth of his divine nature than that fire and passion which is called love for people. Correspondingly, love is such a thing that it is neither human, nor angelic, but rather divine, yes, even God itself.

MARTIN LUTHER (1483–1546)
Sermons

Love personalizes all that it loves. Only by personalizing it can we fall in love with an idea. And when love is so great and so vital, so strong and so overflowing, that it loves everything, then it personalizes everything and discovers that the total All, that the Universe, is also a Person possessing a Consciousness, a Consciousness which in its turn suffers, pities, and loves, and therefore is consciousness. And this Consciousness of the Universe, which love, personalizing all that it loves, discovers, is what we call God.

MIGUEL DE UNAMUNO (1864–1936)
The Tragic Sense of Life

The flame of the holy fire of the love of God is always burning in the human heart. It is this that warms the human spirit and illumines life; the delights it yields are endless, there is no measure by which to assess it.

ABRAHAM ISAAC KOOK (1865–1935)
The Moral Principles

Love is the crown of human nature; its regal chaplet of flowers; the bond by which the sentient universe is made one; the trait in which we most nearly resemble God— for God is love.

FREDERICK BROTHERTON MEYER
(1847–1929)
Our Daily Homily

Love took up the glass of Time, and
  turn'd it in his glowing hands;
Every moment, lightly shaken, ran itself
  in golden sands.

ALFRED LORD TENNYSON (1809–1892)
Locksley Hall

Be ye certain all seems love,
Viewed from Allah's throne above;
Be ye stout of heart, and come
Bravely onward to your home!
La Allah illa Allah! yea!
Thou love divine! Thou love alway!

SIR EDWIN ARNOLD (1832–1904)
After Death in Arabia

I will never thank God that he loves me, for he cannot do otherwise, whether he wishes it or not; his nature forces him to do it. I will rather thank him that in his goodness he cannot cease loving me.

MEISTER ECKHART (1260–1327)
Sermons

God from a beautiful necessity is Love.

MARTIN FARQUHAR TUPPER (1810–1889)
Proverbial Philosophy

There is only one standard that has any business being read into the heart of God and that is the ultimate standard of love.

REINHOLD NIEBUHR (1892–1971)
Education Adequate for Modern Times

If you want to see what real tenderness is, look at the love of God: you will not find in Him any sentimentality, you will find no weak humanitarian mildness in the infinite consuming Fire, no shielding us from the pain that can show us what life means; but you will find the tenderness that tempers the winds for the shorn lamb, that will do anything, short of violence to its own gift of free-will, to lead us back in spite of ourselves to wholeness.

GERALD VANN (1906–1963)
The Heart of Man

The work of creation finds its consummation, and the eternal will of the infinite mercy finds its fulfillment only in the restoration of the free creature to God and of an evil world to goodness, through love.

HENRI FRÉDÉRIC AMIEL (1821–1881)
Journal Intime

Love was the beginner of all the works of God, and from eternity to eternity nothing can come from God but a variety of wonders and works of love over all nature and creature.

WILLIAM LAW (1686–1761)
A Serious Call to a Devout and Holy Life

If there had not been love there would have not been any existence. Had it not been for pure love's sake, how should there be any reason for the creation of heavens?

JALAL-UD-DIN RUMI (1207–1273)
The Masnawi

That night I awoke lying upon my back and hearing a voice speaking above me and saying, "No human soul is like any other human soul, and therefore the love of God for any human soul is infinite, for no other soul can satisfy the same need in God."

WILLIAM BUTLER YEATS (1865–1939)
Celtic Twilight

God communicates himself in love: and this happens in the fullest sense only when his love is known in responding love. In the responding love of the human creature the will of God is first realized: in the "yes" to the self-giving love of God, fellowship first takes its rise.

EMIL BRUNNER (1889–1966)
Truth as Encounter

A lively faith in the love of God would warm and chafe our benumbed minds, and thaw our hearts frozen with self-love.

JOHN SMITH (1616–1652)
Discourses

God does not love, as it were, upon an agreement; He does not love simply upon the preception of a cause or of an occasion. There is a fulness of His love which is spontaneous. There is such richness, and depth, and treasure, and abundance of Divine feeling, that it tends to flow over immeasurably, unless there is something which absolutely stops it. This is the pulse that beats out from the heart of God through creation.

HENRY WARD BEECHER (1813–1887)
Sermons

God, thou art love! I build my faith on
   that.
I know thee who hast kept my path, and
   made
Light for me in the darkness, tempering
   sorrow
So that it reached me like a solemn joy
It were too strange that I should doubt
   thy love.
                    ROBERT BROWNING (1812–1889)
                                    Paracelsus

Love is the greatest thing that God can
give us; for Himself is love: and it is the
greatest thing we can give to God; for it
will also give ourselves, and carry with it
all that is ours. The apostle calls it the band
of perfection; it is the old, and it is the
new, and it is the great commandment,
and it is all the commandments; for it is
the fulfilling of the law.
                    JEREMY TAYLOR (1613–1667)
                            The Rule of Holy Living

This Life from the Lord is the life of
Love towards the Universal Human Race.
            EMANUEL SWEDENBORG (1688–1772)
                                Arcana Coelestia

The image under which the nature of
God can best be conceived is that of a
tender care that nothing can be lost.
        ALFRED NORTH WHITEHEAD (1861–1947)
                                Nature and Life

Love it is—not conscience—that is God's
regent in the human soul, because it can
govern the soul as nothing else can.
            HENRY WARD BEECHER (1813–1887)
                                        Sermons

One glorious chain of love, of giving and
receiving, unites all creatures; none is by
or for itself, but all things exist in continual reciprocal activity—the one for the all;
the all for the one.
                    SAMSON HIRSCH (1808–1888)
                                Nineteen Letters

Dearly beloved!
Let us go toward Union.
And if we find the road
That leads to separation,
We will destroy separation.
Let us go hand in hand.
Let us enter the presence of Truth.
Let it be our judge
And imprint its seal upon our union
For ever.
                        IBN ARABI (1165–1240)
                        The Book of Theophanies

If God is Love, He is, by definition,
something more than mere kindness. And
it appears, from all records, that though
He has often rebuked us and condemned
us, He has never regarded us with contempt. He has paid us the intolerable com-
pliment of loving us, in the deepest, most
tragic, most inexorable sense.
                        C. S. LEWIS (1898–1963)
                            The Joyful Christian

We attain the fullness of God's love as
His children when it is no longer happiness or misery, prosperity or adversity that
draws us to Him or keeps us back from
Him.   JOHANNES TAULER (1300–1361)
                                        Sermons

This identity out of the One into the
One and with the One is the source and
fountainhead and breaking forth of glowing Love.
                    MEISTER ECKHART (1260–1327)
                                        Sermons

(We need love's tender lesson taught
   As only weakness can;)
God hath His small interpreters;
   The child must teach the man.
        JOHN GREENLEAF WHITTIER (1807–1892)
                                        A Mystery

To see the universal and all-pervading
Spirit of Truth face to face one must be

able to love the meanest of creation as one-self. MOHANDAS K. GANDHI (1869–1948)
Autobiography

When I consider Thy heavens, the work of Thy fingers, the moon and the stars, which Thou hast ordained—what is man that Thou art mindful of him? and the son of man, that Thou visitest him?
The Old Testament
Psalms 8:3–4

God must be glad one loves His world so much! ROBERT BROWNING (1812–1889)
Pippa Passes

Keep me as the apple of Thine eye, and hide me under the shadow of Thy wings.
The Old Testament
Psalms 17:8

That measureless Love which is God Himself, dwells in the pure deeps of our spirit, like a burning brazier of coal. And it throws forth brilliant and fiery sparks which stir and enkindle heart and senses, will and desire, and all the powers of the soul, with a fire of love.
JAN VAN RUYSBROECK (1293–1381)
The Mirror of External Salvation

Fate, Time, Occasion, Chance, and
    Change? To these
All things are subject but eternal love.
PERCY BYSSHE SHELLEY (1792–1822)
Prometheus Unbound

He Who is wrapped in purple robes,
With planets in his care,
Had pity on the least of things
Asleep on a chair.
WILLIAM BUTLER YEATS (1865–1939)
Ballad of Father Gilligan

Every creature, since it is good, can be loved both well and badly: well, that is, when order is preserved; badly when

order is disturbed. If the Creator be truly loved, that is, if He Himself, not ought else instead of Him which is not He, be loved, He cannot be loved badly.
SAINT AUGUSTINE (354–430)
The City of God

Love harmonises the three powers of our soul, and binds them together. The will, with ineffable love, follows what the eye of the understanding has beheld; and, with its strong hand, it stores up in the memory the treasure that it draws from this love.
SAINT CATHERINE OF SIENA (1347–1380)
Letters

In His eternity, outside of time, outside of every other limit, as pleased Him, the eternal Love unfolded Himself in new loves. DANTE (1265–1321)
Paradiso

Love magnifies existence; love the
    world,—
Thy soul shall grow world-great in its
    sensation;
And 'neath the blaze of infinite life
    unfurl'd,
Pant with the passion of a whole creation,
O love then! love!
EBENEZER JONES (1820–1860)
A Plea for Love of the Universe

I loved you, so I drew these tides of men into my hands and wrote my will across the sky in stars.
T. E. LAWRENCE (1888–1935)
The Seven Pillars of Wisdom

Thou! whose best name on earth
Is Love—whose fairest birth
The freedom of the fair world thou hast
    made.
ALGERNON CHARLES SWINBURNE
(1837–1909)
Ode to Mazzini

If you love yourself, you love everybody else as you do yourself. As long as you love another person less than you love yourself, you will not succeed in loving yourself; but if you love all alike, including yourself, you will love them as one person and that person is both God and man.

MEISTER ECKHART (1260–1327)
Sermons

The Being that is in the clouds and air,
That is in the green leaves among the
    groves,
Maintains a deep and reverential care
For the unoffending creatures whom he
    loves.

WILLIAM WORDSWORTH (1770–1850)
Oxford

For if I ought to love myself in Thee who art my likeness, I am most especially constrained thereto when I see that Thou lovest me as Thy creature and Thine image.   NICHOLAS OF CUSA (1401–1464)
The Vision of God

He who acts out of the pure love of God, not only does he not perform his actions to be seen by men, but does not do them even that God may know them. Such a one, if he thought it possible that his good works might escape the eye of God, would still perform them with the same joy, and in the same pureness of love.

SAINT JOHN OF THE CROSS (1542–1591)
Sermons

The love of God and his creation—delight, joy, triumph, exultation in my own existence—though but an atom, a molecule *organique* in the universe—are my religion.   JOHN ADAMS (1735–1826)
Letter to Thomas Jefferson

How humble and yet how sublime are these two points—strength and love—which the Seraphim, in the first flush of his desire, fixed in their place like two rings which would unite the immeasurable spaces of the lower worlds to the vastness of the higher.

HONORÉ DE BALZAC (1799–1850)
Seraphita

The way to the love of God is folly to the world, but wisdom to the children of God. When the world perceiveth this fire of love in the children of God, it saith they are turned fools, but to the children of God it is the greatest treasure, so great that no life can express it, nor tongue so much as name what the fire of the inflaming love of God is.   JACOB BOEHME (1575–1624)
The Way to Christ

The law which we must obey, if we would know God as love, is itself a law of love. To those who obey the law come what St. Paul termed the three fruits of the spirit: peace, love, joy.

ALDOUS HUXLEY (1894–1963)
The Perennial Philosophy

It is manifest that the love of God and the love of man are enjoined by the law; and as the genuine love of the one comprehends that of the other, the apostle assures us that "love is the fulfilling of the law."   JOHN JAY (1745–1829)
Letter to John Murray

A good deed done without love is nothing, but if anything is done from love, however small and inconsiderable it may be, every bit of it is counted. God considers what lies behind the deed, and not what is actually done.

THOMAS À KEMPIS (1380–1471)
The Imitation of Christ

The keys of the gate of love are gilded with cares and desires, sighs and tears; the cord which binds them is woven of conscience, devotion, contrition and atonement; the door is kept open by justice and mercy.

RAYMOND LULLY (1235–1315)
The Book of the Lover and the Beloved

God's first word to the soul that unlocks itself to him is "Love me!" and everything which he may yet reveal to the soul in the form of law, therefore, without more ado turns into words which he commands *today*.   FRANZ ROSENZWEIG (1886–1929)
The Star of Redemption

Love is a great reality. It is the only one of all the movements, feelings, and affections of the soul in which the creature is able to respond to its Creator, though not upon equal terms, and to repay like with like.

SAINT BERNARD OF CLAIRVAUX (1091–1153)
Sermons

"The love," cried Caecilius, "which He inspires lasts, for it is the love of the Unchangeable. It satisfies, for He is inexhaustible. The nearer we draw to Him, the more triumphantly does He enter into us; the longer He dwells in us, the more intimately have we possession of Him. It is an espousal for eternity."

JOHN CARDINAL NEWMAN (1801–1890)
Callista

To love God with all our hearts and all our souls and all our minds means that every cleavage in human existence is overcome.   REINHOLD NIEBUHR (1892–1971)
Interpretation of Christian Ethics

We talk about men's reaching through Nature up to Nature's God. It is nothing to the way in which they may reach through manhood up to manhood's God, and learn the divine love by the human.

PHILLIPS BROOKS (1835–1893)
The Light of the World

Love the pride of God beyond all things, and the pride of your neighbor as your own.   ISAK DINESEN (1885–1962)
Out of Africa

Fulfill His commands out of love, for one who acts out of love is not like one who acts out of fear. He who serves his master out of fear, if he troubles him overmuch, leaves him and goes away.

RASHI (1040–1105)
Commentaries

We must love God with a hopeless love, despairing of our ever being able to love Him as we ought. We must love Him with a brave love, which indeed calculates grace but does not calculate difficulties. We must love Him with a swift, pushing love which, like a tree, is fastening itself deeper in the ground with its roots, while it is also climbing higher into the blue sky.

FREDERICK WILLIAM FABER (1814–1863)
Spiritual Conferences

We cease to pray to God as soon as we cease to love Him, as soon as we cease to thirst for His perfections. The coldness of our love is the silence of our hearts toward God. Without this we may pronounce prayers, but we do not pray; for what shall lead us to meditate upon the laws of God if it be not the love of Him who has made these laws? Let our hearts be full of love, then, and they will pray.

FRANÇOIS FÉNELON (1651–1715)
Sermons

And we know that all things work together for good to them that love God, to them who are the called according to his purpose.   *The New Testament*
Romans 8:28

And this is love, that we walk after his commandments. This is the commandment, That as ye have heard from the beginning, ye should walk in it.

The New Testament
2 John 1:6

If we long with love for the Creator himself alone, we shall speedily flame up with His consuming fire into a Seraphic likeness. Whoso is a Seraph, that is, a lover, is in God and God in him, nay, rather God and himself are one.

GIOVANNI PICO DELLA MIRANDOLA
(1463–1494)
On the Dignity of Man

Brothers, love is a teacher; but one must know how to acquire it, for it is hard to acquire, it is dearly bought, it is won slowly by long labor. For we must love not only occasionally, for a moment, but forever. Everyone can love occasionally, even the wicked can.

FYODOR DOSTOEVSKY (1821–1881)
The Brothers Karamazov

When man loves God with a love that is fitting he automatically carries out all the precepts in love. What is the love that is fitting? It is that man should love God with an extraordinary powerful love to the extent that his soul becomes tied to the love of God and he longs for it all the time.

MAIMONIDES (1135–1204)
Yesodei-ha-Torah

The Law of God exact he shall fulfill
Both by obedience and by love, though
    love
Alone fulfill the Law.

JOHN MILTON (1608–1674)
Paradise Lost

He that loves God and man, and lives in accordance with that love, need not fear what man can do to him. His religion comes to him in his hour of sadness, it lays its hand on him when he has fallen among thieves, and raises him up, heals and comforts him.

THEODORE PARKER (1810–1860)
Transient and Permanent Discourses
on the Philosophy of Religion

They who would love mould themselves in likeness to their beloved. In the same way the soul loves God, being stirred by Him to love from the beginning.

PLOTINUS (205–270)
Enneads

We know Thee, each in part—
    A portion small;
But love Thee, as Thou art—
    The All in all:
For Reason and the rays thereof
Are starlight to the noon of Love.

JOHN BANNISTER TABB (1845–1909)
All in All

The lover ascends to the highest beauty, to the love and knowledge of the Divinity, by steps on this ladder of created souls.

RALPH WALDO EMERSON (1803–1882)
Love

Love is the instructor who teaches us more certainly what belongs to the mysteries of the soul, than the utmost metaphysical subtlety.

MADAME DE STAËL (1766–1817)
Germany

God is love; for who does not love him, does not know him; for how can we know love without loving?

FRANÇOIS FÉNELON (1651–1715)
On the Knowledge and Love of God

The highest proof of the Spirit is love. Love is the eternal thing which men can already on earth possess as it really is.

ALBERT SCHWEITZER (1875–1965)
Out of My Life and Thought

Men may know their God and fear him; instead of seeking him, they may wish to flee and hide from him. But they cannot worship a "loveless God." They recognize that "a loving worm within its clod" were diviner than such a deity. For love is one of those facts which has ultimate and absolute and unborrowed value.

SIR HENRY JONES (1852–1922)
A Faith That Enquires

In this life it is impossible to know God in his fullness; piously and ardently to love Him is possible. This love is a blessing at all times whatsoever; this knowledge sometimes makes us miserable—as does that knowledge the demons have, who tremble below in hell before Him they have learned to know.

PETRARCH (1304–1374)
On His Own Ignorance

That Love which is and was
My father, and my brother, and my God.

ALFRED LORD TENNYSON (1809–1892)
Doubt and Prayer

We must love God more than our neighbor, more than man, and from this love of God we must draw strength for love of man.

NIKOLAI BERDYAEV (1874–1948)
The Destiny of Man

If thou be among people, make for thyself love, the beginning and end of the heart. The man who is great of heart is one of God's men. He hearkeneth unto the command of his heart, his enemy becometh his possession.

PTAHHOTEP (*c.* 2400 B.C.)
The Proverbs of Ptahhotep

Love interprets between human and divine. Through Love all the intercourse and converse of God with man, whether asleep or awake, is carried on.

PLATO (427–347 B.C.)
The Symposium

The holy man is the true lover by whom the Truly Beloved is found. Man is then happy night and day, and naturally absorbed in God. The holy man may laugh; the holy man may weep. Whatever he does, is in God's service.

GURU NANAK (1469–1539)
Hymns

Consider whether more depends upon God's love to you, or your love to Him. From His love all the things in Heaven and Earth flow unto you; but if you love neither Him nor them, you bereave yourself of all, and make them infinitely evil and hurtful to you, and yourself abominable.

THOMAS TRAHERNE (1637–1674)
Centuries of Meditations

Whosoever offers to Me with devotion a leaf, a flower, a fruit or water, that offering of love of the pure in heart I accept.

The Bhagavad Gita

Love is our highest word, and the synonym of God.

RALPH WALDO EMERSON (1803–1882)
Love

He that loves God will soar aloft and take him wings; and, leaving the earth, fly up to heaven, wander with the sun and moon, stars, and that heavenly troop, God himself being his guide.

PHILO JUDAEUS (30 B.C.–A.D. 40)
On Nobility

The sum of all is, thou shalt love,
If any body, God above:
At any rate shall never labour
More than thyself to love thy neighbor.

ARTHUR HUGH CLOUGH (1819–1861)
The Latest Decalogue

Great works do not always lie in our way, but every moment we may do little ones excellently, that is, with great love.

SAINT FRANCIS OF SALES (1567–1622)
On the Love of God

Thrice blest whose lives are faithful
   prayers,
Whose loves in higher love endures.
   ALFRED LORD TENNYSON (1809–1892)
   In Memoriam

Whoever does not draw near to God as
a result of the caresses of love is shackled
to Him with the chains of misfortune.
   IBN 'ATA'ILLAH (died 1309)
   The Book of Wisdom

He who loves brings God and the world
together.   MARTIN BUBER (1878–1965)
   At the Turning

The more that the knowledge of God is
simultaneously felt to be love of God, the
more passionate becomes the battle for
faith, the struggle for the knowledge of
God and for love of God.
   HERMANN COHEN (1842–1918)
   Religion and Morality

If a man lives a hundred years, and en-
gages the whole of his time and attention
in religious offerings to the gods, sacrific-
ing elephants and horses and other things,
all this is not equal to one act of pure love
in saving life.   *The Dhammapada*

Through the higher love the whole life
of man is to be elevated from temporal
selfishness to the spring of all love, to God:
man will again be master over nature by
abiding in God and lifting her up to God.
   MEISTER ECKHART (1260–1327)
   Sermons

If you keep your heart immersed always
in the ocean of divine love, your heart is
sure to remain ever full to overflowing
with the waters of the divine love.
   SRI RAMAKRISHNA (1834–1886)
   Sayings

Love is the fairest and most profitable
guest that a reasonable creature can entertain. To God it is the most acceptable and
pleasing of all things.
   RICHARD ROLLE OF HAMPOLE (1290–1349)
   Incendium Amoris

Upon love depends all of God's com-
mandments and both the Old and New
Testaments—that thou shalt love God,
and shalt love thy neighbor as thyself.
   JOHANNES TAULER (1300–1361)
   Union with God

Man's hostility to God proves indisputa-
bly that he belongs to him. Where there is
the possibility of hate, there and there
alone is the possibility of love.
   PAUL TILLICH (1886–1965)
   The Meaning of Existence

When all the people in the world love
one another, then the strong will not over-
power the weak, the many will not oppress
the few, the wealthy will not mock the
poor, and the honoured will not disdain
the humble, and the cunning will not deceive the simple. And it is all due to natural love that calamities, strifes, complaints,
and hatred are prevented from arising.
   MO-TZU (470–391 B.C.)
   The Mo Tzu

O man! entertain such love for God as
the lotus has for the water. Such love does
it bear it, that it blooms even when dashed
down by the waves. O man! How shall you
be delivered without love?
   GURU NANAK (1469–1539)
   Hymns

God does not bombard me with instruc-
tions for carrying out his commandments
in every possible case, so that I could follow them blindly and mindlessly, because
he prefers to require only one thing of me
—that I love him.
   HELMUT THIELICKE (1908–)
   How to Believe Again

The object and aim of all divine commands is to love God truly, and to cleave to him.　　RABBI BEN EZRA (1098–1164)
Commentaries

I understand, finally, why the love of God created men responsible for one another and gave them hope as a virtue. Since it made each of them the ambassador of the same God, in the hands of each rested the salvation of all.

ANTOINE DE SAINT-EXUPÉRY (1900–1945)
Flight to Arras

Religion is nothing else but love of God and man.　　WILLIAM PENN (1644–1718)
Some Fruits of Solitude

There must be for me a deep sense of relatedness to God. This relatedness is the way by which there shall open for me more and more springs of energy and power, which will enable me to thread life's mysteries with life's clue. I shall not waste any effort in trying to reduce God to my particular logic. Here in the quietness, I shall give myself in love to God.

HOWARD THURMAN (1899–1981)
Meditations of the Heart

The more a man loves, the deeper he penetrates the divine purposes. Love is the astrolabe of heavenly mysteries, the eye-salve which clears the spiritual eye and makes it clairvoyant.

JALAL-UD-DIN RUMI (1207–1273)
The Masnawi

Love unites the mind more quickly, more closely, and more stably with God than does knowledge, because the force of knowledge consists more in distinction, that of love in union.

MARSILIO FICINO (1433–1499)
Theologia Platonica

Those who construct a raft in the name of Rama can cross over the ocean of love in this world.　　KABIR (1450–1518)
Bijak

Life without love in one's heart is like a withered tree flowering in the barren sand.　　TIRUVALLUVAR (2nd century)
Kural

In a human context, love means sharing an experience, showing compassion, and helping one another. But our love of God is akin to reverent love. God is infinite life. Thus the most elementary ethical principle, when understood by the heart, means that out of reverence for the unfathomable, infinite, and living Reality we call God, we must never consider ourselves strangers toward any human being.

ALBERT SCHWEITZER (1875–1965)
Reverence for Life

Eye hath not seen, nor ear heard, neither have entered into the heart of man, the things which God hath prepared for them that love him.　　*The New Testament*
1 Corinthians 2:9

There is always a danger of intense love destroying what I might call the polyphony of life. What I mean is that God requires that we should love him eternally with all our hearts, yet not so as to compromise or diminish our earthly affections, but as a kind of cantus firmus to which the other melodies of life provide the counterpoint.

DIETRICH BONHOEFFER (1906–1945)
Letters and Papers from Prison

Yes, love indeed is light from heaven;
　A spark of that immortal fire
With angels shared, by Allah given,
　To lift from earth our low desire.

GEORGE GORDON, LORD BYRON
(1788–1824)
Giaour

Love is a circle that doth restless move
In the same sweet eternity of Love.
        ROBERT HERRICK (1591–1674)
                Hesperides

There are some people who do not like
the word, "love." It embarrasses them, because it has become hackneyed, and because we hear it as well from lips that have
gone to rot, or from hearts that worship
themselves. God is not so squeamish. The
Apostle John tells us that God is self-sub-
isting Love.
        JACQUES MARITAIN (1882–1973)
                Ransoming the Time

Love fits the soul with wings, and bids her
        win
Her flight aloft nor e'er to earth decline;
'Tis the first step that leads her to the
        shrine
Of Him who slakes the thirst that burns
        within.
        MICHELANGELO BUONARROTI (1475–1564)
                Sonnet 53

Love rules the court, the camp, the grove,
And men below, and saints above;
For love is heaven and heaven is love.
        SIR WALTER SCOTT (1771–1832)
                The Lay of the Last Minstrel

Who knows if love and its beatitude,
clear manifestation as it is of the universal
harmony of things, is not the best demonstration of a fatherly and understanding
God, just as it is the shortest road by which
to reach Him? Love is a faith, and one
faith leads to another.
        HENRI FRÉDÉRIC AMIEL (1821–1881)
                Journal Intime

If thou dost love to see thy God, if in this
exile thou sighest with that love; behold
the Lord thy God maketh trial of thee, saying, "Do what thou wilt, fulfill thy desires,
prolong wickedness, augment luxurious-
ness, think whatever pleaseth lawful. I will
not punish thee for this, I will not send
thee to hell; I will only deny thee My face."
If thou hast been horrorstruck, thou hast
loved! If at this that was said to thee, "Thy
God will deny thee His face," if at these
words thy whole heart hath trembled, if in
the not seeing thy God thou hast imagined
a great punishment—thou hast loved
truly.   SAINT AUGUSTINE (354–430)
                Sermons

The ways to realize God are not many,
but only one—love.   *Sikh Proverb*

Blessedness consists in love towards
God, a love which springs from the highest
kind of knowledge.
        BENEDICT SPINOZA (1632–1677)
                Ethics

Of all earthly music, that which reaches
farthest into heaven is the beating of a
truly loving heart.
        HENRY WARD BEECHER (1813–1887)
                Sermons

If a man who was rich enough in this
world's goods saw that one of his brothers
was in need, but closed his heart to him,
how could the love of God be living in
him? My children, our love is not to be just
words or mere talk, but something real
and active.   *The New Testament*
                1 John 3:17–18

A great cry in the ears of God is that
burning affection of soul that saith "My
God, my love, thou art all mine and I
thine."   THOMAS À KEMPIS (1380–1471)
                The Imitation of Christ

The ways are two: love and want of love.
That is all.   MENCIUS (371–288 B.C.)
                The Book of Mencius

Loving-kindness is greater than law; and the charities of life are more than all the ceremonies. *The Talmud*

King David said: I, what am I in this world? I have been fearful in the midst of my joy, and have rejoiced in the midst of my fear, and my love has surpassed them both. *The Talmud*

An eternal growth is an unchangeable peace, an ever profounder depth of apprehension, a possession constantly more intense and more spiritual of the joy of heaven—this is happiness. Happiness has no limits, because God has neither bottom nor bounds, and because happiness is nothing but the conquest of God through love.

HENRI FRÉDÉRIC AMIEL (1821–1881)
Journal Intime

Do I find love so full in my nature, God's
ultimate gift,
That I doubt His own love can compete
with it?

ROBERT BROWNING (1812–1889)
Saul

Just as one cannot love God too much, so one cannot trust Him too much. However much you love Him, be sure that He loves you incomparably more and is incomparably more faithful.

MEISTER ECKHART (1260–1327)
Sermons

Science is the power of man, and love his strength; man *becomes* man only by the intelligence, but he *is* man only by the heart.

HENRI FRÉDÉRIC AMIEL (1821–1881)
Journal Intime

Man can creatively reinstate God's image in the living object of his love only by reinstating that image in himself as well; but he has no power of his own to do it, for if he had, he would not need any

reinstatement; and not having the power, he must receive it from God.

VLADIMIR SOLOVIËV (1853–1900)
Beauty and Love

The goal of personal life is known to you beyond all question, and consists in the realization in you of the highest perfection of love, which is essential for the realization of the Kingdom of God. And this goal is always known to you and is always attainable.

LEO TOLSTOY (1828–1910)
The Law of Violence and the Law of Love

The art of arts is the art of loving. Nature itself and God, nature's author, are its teachers. For love itself is given by the creator of nature, and unless its natural purity has been soiled by some adulterous affection, love teaches itself, I say, to its own disciples, to the disciples of God.

WILLIAM OF SAINT THIERRY (1070–1148)
On the Contemplation of God

If we believe that mankind has steadily progressed towards ahimsa (i.e., love), it follows that it has to progress towards it still further. Nothing in this world is static, everything is kinetic. If there is no progression, then there is inevitable retrogression. No one can remain without the eternal cycle, unless it be God Himself.

MOHANDAS K. GANDHI (1869–1948)
Selected Addresses

God is love, and the fount of love: for this the great John declares that "love is of God," and "God is love": the Fashioner of our nature has made this to be our feature too: for "hereby," He says, "shall all men know that ye are my disciples, if ye love one another": thus, if this be absent, the whole stamp of the likeness is transformed.

SAINT GREGORY OF NYSSA (331–396)
On the Making of Man

The rose and the lily, the moon and the
　　dove,
Once loved I them all with a perfect love.
I love them no longer, I love alone
The Lovely, the Graceful, the Pure, the
　　One
Who twines in one wreath all their beauty
　　and love,
And rose and lily, and moon and dove.

　　　　　　HEINRICH HEINE (1797–1856)
　　　　　　The Rose, the Lily, the Dove

It is love alone by which responsive love
is awakened, or on account of which love
is felt in return. Ultimately, therefore, it is
the love of God for man, and that alone,
which redeems the man; because that love
alone calls forth in return that love of man
for God, by which the man's whole nature
is transformed. But to be efficacious in
man, it must be appropriated by man, that
is, believed in and reciprocated by conscious acts of will.

　　　　　　S. H. HODGSON (1832–1912)
　　　　　　The Metaphysic of Experience

I believe that it is difficult to love God
truly when one, having the power to
change his disposition, is not disposed to
wish for that which God desires. In fact,
those who are not satisfied with what God
does seem to me like dissatisfied subjects
whose attitude is not very different from
that of rebels. I hold therefore, that to act
conformably to the love of God it is not
sufficient to force oneself to be patient; we
must be really satisfied with all that comes
to us according to his will.

　　　GOTTFRIED WILHELM VON LEIBNIZ
　　　　　　　　(1646–1716)
　　　　　　Metaphysical Discourses

Our salvation, or blessedness, or liberty
consists in a constant and eternal love towards God, or in the love of God towards

men. This love or blessedness is called
Glory in the sacred writings, and not without reason.

　　　　　BENEDICT SPINOZA (1632–1677)
　　　　　　　　　　　Ethics

Love then the Lord thy God with the
entire and full affection of the heart; love
him with all the vigilance and all the fore-
sight of the reason; love him with the full
strength and vigor of the soul, so that for
his love you would not fear even to die; as
it is written: Love is strong as death, jeal-
ousy as hard as hell.

　　SAINT BERNARD OF CLAIRVAUX (1091–1153)
　　　　　　On the Love of God

Eternal life begins here upon earth, and
the soul of man lives and breathes where
it loves; and love, in living faith, has
strength enough to make the soul of man
experience unity with God—two natures
in a single spirit and love.

　　　　　JACQUES MARITAIN (1882–1973)
　　　　　　The Range of Reason

If the love of truth be pursued in artifi-
cial abstraction from the other claims
which life makes on us, it is likely to degen-
erate into the love of error. God in His
own indivisible nature is the only reality
that must be sought and loved for its own
sake alone.　　JOHN BAILLIE (1886–1960)
　　　　　　Invitation to Pilgrimage

True love asks no reward but deserves
one.
　　SAINT BERNARD OF CLAIRVAUX (1091–1153)
　　　　　　On the Love of God

Love, says the New Testament, keeps
everything going in perfect harmony.
Paul's hymn to love in his I Corinthians 13
is indirectly the height of man's description of God. Faith and hope will remain
because the great of all realities, Love, re-

mains forever without disappearing or failing.   NELS F. S. FERRE (1908–1971)
Know Your Faith

It is the consciousness of love by which man reconciles himself with God, or rather with his own nature as represented in the moral law.
LUDWIG FEUERBACH (1804–1872)
The Essence of Christianity

From the beginning until the ending of time, there is love between Thee and me; and how shall such love be extinguished
Kabir says: "As the river enters into the ocean, so my heart touches Thee."
KABIR (1440–1518)
Song

The truths of love are like the sea
For clearness and for mystery.
COVENTRY PATMORE (1823–1896)
The Wedding Sermon

All true science begins in the love, not the dissection, of your fellow-creatures; and it ends in the love, not the analysis, of God.   JOHN RUSKIN (1819–1900)
Deucalion

A single atom of the love of God in a heart is worth more than a hundred thousand paradises.
BAYAZID AL-BISTAMI (9th century)
Tadhkirat

I know of no redeeming qualities in me but a sincere love for some things, and when I am reproved I have to fall back on to this ground. This is my argument in reserve for all cases. My love is invulnerable. Meet me on that ground, and you will find me strong. When I am condemned, and condemn myself utterly, I think straightway, "But I rely on my love for some things." Therein I am whole and entire. Therein I am God-propped.
HENRY DAVID THOREAU (1817–1862)
Journals

I always think that the best way to know God is to love many things. Love a friend, a wife, something—whatever you like— you will be on the way to knowing more about Him; that is what I say to myself. But one must love with a lofty and serious intimate sympathy, with strength, with intelligence; and one must always try to know deeper, better and more. That leads to God, that leads to unwavering faith.
VINCENT VAN GOGH (1853–1890)
Letters

So far as we can, let us always rejoice to strengthen each other's hands in God. Above all, let us each take heed to himself (since each must give an account of himself to God) that he fall not short of the religion of love; that he be not condemned in that he himself approveth.
JOHN WESLEY (1703–1791)
A Letter to a Roman Catholic

Maintain the root of love at all times in yourself through faith and then nothing can proceed from you except good and you will begin to fulfill the commandments of God, which are all contained in love.
JOHANN ARNDT (1555–1621)
True Christianity

All other feelings write their memories upon glass with crayons. Love writes upon crystal with a diamond. For of all the heart's powers, this alone is sovereign, and, being sovereign, God has crowned it with immortality.
HENRY WARD BEECHER (1813–1887)
Sermons

It is love that asks, that seeks, that knocks, that finds, and that is faithful to what it finds.

SAINT AUGUSTINE (354–430)
Sermons

Love is not a possession but a growth. The heart is a lamp with just oil enough to burn for an hour, and if there be no oil to put in again its light will go out. God's grace is the oil that fills the lamp of love.

HENRY WARD BEECHER (1813–1887)
Sermons

A love that has no silence has no depth. "Methinks the lady doth protest too much." There are people whose love we instinctively distrust because they are always telling us about it. And perhaps it is simple because God is love, in all the glorious fulness of that word, that we have to be still if we would know him.

GEORGE HERBERT MORRISON (1866–1928)
Sermons

Not with doubting, but with assured consciousness, do I love Thee, Lord. Thou hast stricken my heart with Thy word, and I loved Thee.

SAINT AUGUSTINE (354–430)
Confessions

What more can one ask for than to be swallowed up on the great tidal wave of Love, to go down defeated as a man and be born again as a lover—a lover of man, a lover of woman, a lover of all God's creatures large or small! Is it too much to hope for? I cannot think it thus. It is what will be, must be, else this precious spark of life which is you or me has no reason to exist.

HENRY MILLER (1891–1980)
Love

Love is the fountain and the end of all, without which there can be no beauty nor goodness in any of the virtues. Love to one self, Love to God, Love to man, Love to felicity, a clear and intelligent Love is the life and soul of every virtue.

THOMAS TRAHERNE (1637–1674)
Christian Ethics

You ask me what the voice of the heart is. How can I put it into words and how could you understand me? It is love which is the voice of the heart. Love God and you will be always speaking to him.

JEAN NICHOLAS GROU (1730–1803)
The School of Jesus Christ

Love is the high nobility of Heaven, the peaceful home of man. To lack love, when nothing hinders us, is to lack wisdom.

MENCIUS (371–288 B.C.)
The Book of Mencius

Love for God is a fruit of faith. Out of love for God is born love for our neighbor also, when we desire to serve God in all his creatures.

PHILIPP MELANCHTHON (1497–1560)
Loci Communes

Here on earth we must first love, and love will open our eyes as well as our hearts, and we shall then see and perceive and understand.

JEREMY TAYLOR (1613–1667)
Via Intelligentiae

Love cannot be hid any more than light; and least of all when it shines forth in action, when ye exercise yourselves in the labor of love, in beneficence of every kind.

JOHN WESLEY (1703–1791)
Sermons

One who knows himself and his passions clearly and distinctly, loves God, and that all the more, the greater this understanding is. BENEDICT SPINOZA (1632–1677)
Ethics

Between whom there is hearty truth, there is love; and in proportion to our truthfulness and confidence in one another, our lives are divine and miraculous, and answer to our ideal.

HENRY DAVID THOREAU (1817–1862)
A Week on the Concord and Merrimack Rivers

Love God and you will be humble; love God and you will throw off the love of self; love God and you will love all that He gives you to love for love of him.

FRANÇOIS FÉNELON (1651–1715)
Sermons

Show me what thou truly lovest, show me what thou seekest with thy whole heart, and thou hast thereby shown me thy life. This love is the root and central part of thy being.

JOHANN GOTTLIEB FICHTE (1762–1814)
The Way Towards the Blessed Life

To love God, and to be beloved by Him; to love our fellow-men, and to be beloved by them: there is the whole of religion and morality; in both, love is everything—end, principle, means.

JOSEPH JOUBERT (1754–1824)
Pensées

Love is God, and to die means that I, a particle of love, shall return to the general and eternal source.

LEO TOLSTOY (1828–1910)
War and Peace

The nearest way to God
Leads through love's open door;
  The path of knowledge is
  To slow for evermore.

ANGELUS SILESIUS (1624–1677)
The Pilgrim of Truth

What is it, Lord, that prevents our hearts from running to Thee? What bonds could be so strong that they hold us captive and prevent us from reaching Thee? If it is a love for the things of this world, how can such fragile and passing things hold back the impetus of our love for Thee? Will a little blade of grass be sufficient to resist a stone that comes hurtling down a mountain side?

FRAY LUIS DE GRANADA (1504–1588)
Book of Prayer

If a man loveth, he knoweth what his voice crieth. For the ardent affection of the soul is a great clamour in the ears of God, and it saith: My God, my Beloved! Thou art mine, and I am thine.

THOMAS À KEMPIS (1380–1471)
The Imitation of Christ

God is a lover of hearts and communes directly and not through anything external. God desires an inner living love. There is more truth in such a one than in a man who sings so lustily that his song reaches heaven.

JOHANNES TAULER (1300–1361)
Sermon on the Feast of St. Matthew

Unless you lead me, Lord, I cannot
  dance.
Would you have me leap and spring,
You yourself, dear Lord, must sing.
So shall I spring with your love,
From your love to understanding,
From understanding to delight.

MECHTILD OF MAGDEBURG (1217–1287)
*The Book of the Flowing Light
of the Godhead*

And we are put on earth a little space,
That we may learn to bear the beams of
  love.

WILLIAM BLAKE (1757–1827)
The Little Black Boy

Was not man made in high Jehovah's
  image?
Did God not love what he had made?
  And what

Do we but imitate and emulate
His love unto created love?

GEORGE GORDON, LORD BYRON
(1788–1824)
Heaven and Earth

One unquestioned text we read,
All doubt beyond, all fear above;
Nor crackling pile nor cursing creed
Can burn or blot it: *God is love.*

OLIVER WENDELL HOLMES
(1809–1894)
What We All Think

I touch God in my song
   as the hill touches the far-away sea with
      its waterfall.
Love remains a secret even when spoken,
   for only a lover truly knows that he is
      loved.
In love I pay my endless debt to thee
   for what thou art.

RABINDRANATH TAGORE (1861–1941)
Fireflies

Yet, though I have not seen, and still
Must rest in faith alone;
I love Thee, dearest Lord, and will,
Unseen but not unknown.

EMILY BRONTË (1818–1848)
Legends of Angria

Love (not in the least for my slight
worth, but in his nobleness) set me in a life
so delightful and sweet that I heard people
say behind me many times: "God, by what
grace is that man's heart so lightsome?"

DANTE (1265–1321)
O You Who Pass Along the Way of Love

The soul lives by that which it loves
rather than in the body which it animates.
For it has not life in the body, but rather
gives it to the body and lives in that which
it loves.

SAINT JOHN OF THE CROSS (1542–1591)
Sermons

He that lives in love lives in God, says
the beloved disciple. And, to be sure, a
man can live nowhere better.

WILLIAM PENN (1644–1718)
Some Fruits of Solitude

For to faith and hope shall succeed at
once the very substance itself, no longer to
be believed in and hoped for, but to be
seen and grasped. Love, however, which is
the greatest among the three, is not to be
superseded but increased and fulfilled—
contemplating in full vision what it used to
see by faith, and acquiring in actual fruition what it once only embraced in hope.

SAINT AUGUSTINE (354–430)
On the Perfection of Man's Righteousness

When he, too, who abhors the name,
and believes himself to be godless, gives
his whole being to addressing the Thou of
his life, as a Thou that cannot be limited
by another, he addresses God.

MARTIN BUBER (1878–1965)
I and Thou

Love is the fountain of life, love is the
   flashing sword of death.
The hardest rocks are shivered by love's
   glance:
Love of God at last becomes wholly God.

MAHOMED IQBAL (1873–1938)
Secrets of the Self

This symphony is concerned with another kind of love than that which you
imagine. It is supposed to symbolize the
peak, the highest level from which we can
view the world. I could almost call the
movement "What God tells me!"—in the
sense that God can only be comprehended
as Love.   GUSTAV MAHLER (1860–1911)
Letter to Anna von Mildenburg

True love's the gift which God has given
To man alone beneath the heaven:
It is the secret sympathy,

The silver link, the silken tie,
Which heart to heart and mind to mind
In body and in soul can bind.

SIR WALTER SCOTT (1771–1832)
The Lay of the Last Minstrel

My brothers, the love of God is a hard love. It demands total self-surrender.

ALBERT CAMUS (1913–1960)
The Plague

This need to be the creator of what we love is a need to imitate God. But the divinity toward which it tends is false unless we have recourse to the model seen from the other, the heavenly side.

SIMONE WEIL (1909–1943)
Gravity and Grace

When we find love songs in the Bible, we must understand that the love of God for this world is revealed through the depths of love human beings can feel for one another.

MARTIN BUBER (1878–1965)
Die Schrift und ihre Verdeutschung

The Bridegroom is God; the bride is the soul. The Bridegroom is at home, when He fills the mind through internal joy; He goeth away, when He withdraws the sweetness of contemplation.

HUGH OF SAINT VICTOR (1096–1141)
De Amore Sponsi ad Sponsam

And the Lord God said, It is not good that the man should be alone; I will make a helpmeet for him.

The Old Testament
Genesis 2:18

IV · Union with God

If the soul opens itself to the will and gift of God, whom it loves more than its own existence, then it is granted what it has loved. It enters forever into the joy of the uncreated Being; it sees God face to face and knows Him as it is known by Him, intuitively.

—JACQUES MARITAIN

THE GOD SEEKERS, as we see throughout this anthology, constitute a rare company of men and women endowed with such a depth of spiritual sensibility that they transcend the barriers of time, culture, and creed. They share an unswerving desire to confront the most fundamental questions inherent in humankind's tenuous search for God.

One common goal of the God Seekers has been not only to search for the way God manifests himself to us but to joyously accept God's imperative—that when we have fulfilled his plan for us in this particular place of his universe we shall all again be united with him.

The God Seekers seldom waver in their faith in God's inscrutable plan, nor do they question why He created them as human beings rather than as praying mantises or wildflowers blossoming in a meadow. They never fail to marvel at the mystery of why He put them here on this little fleck of a planet amidst the countless billions upon billions of other dwelling places in His universe. Their spiritual strength, as we see in the many beautiful passages in this section of our anthology, comes from their ability to reach into the depths of their souls and affirm that *all* of God's creations will return to their universal Father in joyous unity.

The concept that humankind possesses a soul has been found in all ages and among all peoples. Whether it was called *psyche* by the ancient Greeks, *atman* by the Hindus, *anima* by the Romans, or *neshama* by the Hebrews, people have always sought to define this most undefinable aspect of themselves. However, as Henry David Thoreau wrote in his *Journal,* "With all your science, can you tell me how and whence it is that light comes into the soul?"

William Law, an eighteenth-century English mystic, believed that the ever-present God exists for each individual only in the deepest and most central part of the soul. In his view, this "depth" is the unity, the eternity: "I had almost said the infinity of thy soul; for it is so infinite that nothing can satisfy it or give it rest but the infinity of God."

Law was reiterating, of course, what Jewish scholars had perceived hundreds of years before in the Talmud. They believed that as God fills the whole world, the soul fills the whole body. Carrying the analogy further, they said that just as

God sees but cannot be seen, the soul sees, even though we cannot see it. These Talmudists concluded, "As God nourishes the whole world, so also the soul nourishes the whole body."

To the modern Russian philosopher Nikolai Chaikovski, our individual soul merges with the soul of the whole universe and enables us to conceive that the entire cosmos is a single whole. When this happens, Chaikovski says, "We hear God—first in ourselves, then in others, in nature, and in the heavens."

In another major theme in this section, the collective thoughts of such varied God Seekers as George Fox, Epictetus, Chuang-tze, and Rabindranath Tagore tell us that death is a natural part of God's plan for all of his creations. This view of death as the perfect corollary to an earthly life inevitably bounded by time and space is expressed to perfection by Rainer Maria Rilke, in his poem "Requiem."

> Life is only a part . . . of what?
> Life is only a note . . . in what?
> Life is only the dream of a dream
> But the state of awakeness is elsewhere.

Samuel Taylor Coleridge had expressed this thought in a similar vein in his "Anima Poetae." Pondering the thought that he could pass "through Paradise in a dream, and have a flower presented to him as a pledge that his soul had really been there," Coleridge asked himself what if the same flower were in his hand when he awoke? Might he not then wonder whether the dream and the reality were the same?

Miguel de Unamuno reminds us in his *Life of Don Quixote and Sancho* that life and death are relative terms imposed on us "in this prison of time and space." We can take solace that both terms have a common root, which grows in the eternity of the infinite, in the Consciousness of the Universe, God.

This is not to say that our awareness that all whom we love must die does not cause us agony. It is an agony that, as Karl Jaspers perceived, we must acknowledge and accept without delusion. We can find the strength to accept the presence of death if we believe that it is part of God's plan for us, and that in some way we shall be united with the one eternal God who created us in the first place.

Carl Jung echoed this thought in *Memories, Dreams, Reflections,* pointing out that when the seeming cruelty and wantonness of death is experienced we become so bitter that we conclude that the God of mercy, justice, and kindness is no more. Look at it from another point of view, he says, and death will appear as a joyful event. In the light of eternity, "it is a wedding, a *mysterium coniunctionis,*" in which the soul finds its missing half and achieves wholeness. Only then can we see, in the words of Rabindranath Tagore, that "death is not extinguishing the light; it is putting out the lamp because the dawn has come."

A central theme in this section is the search for unity, the knowledge, as Jan van Ruysbroeck saw it, that "we are all one, united in our eternal image which is the image of God." Ruysbroeck's contemporary, Johannes Tauler, declared: "All creatures seek after unity; all multiplicity struggles toward it—the universal aim of all life is always toward this unity. All that flows outward is to flow backward into its source—God."

Whether in the words of the ancient Hindu Upanishads; or those of the Latin poet Vergil; Maimonides in medieval Spain; Guru Nanak in fifteenth-century India; or William Blake in the eighteenth century; this inmost thought is expressed, for as the greatest of Sufi poets, Jalal-ud-din Rumi, wrote, "God is the cupbearer, the cup and the wine."

That gentlest of misunderstood men, the philosopher Benedict Spinoza, reviled and excommunicated by his orthodox brethren and even accused of being an atheist, wrote, "I say that all things are in God and move in God, thus agreeing with Paul, and perhaps, with all the ancient philosophers, though the phraseology may be different; I will even venture to affirm I agree with all the ancient Hebrews."

Humankind's union and reunion with God are dominant themes in Hindu and Muslim scriptures, to be found in the Bhagavad Gita and the Koran as well as in the Bible of the Jews and Christians. They are major components in the writings of Philo Judaeus, Plotinus, and such Christian mystics as Meister Eckhart and Madame Guyon.

In one of his sermons Eckhart said, "The eye with which I see God is the same as that with which He sees me." In her *Autobiography*, the French mystic Jeanne Marie de la Motte-Guyon commented on the psalmist David's line, "He brought me forth into a large place." What is this large place, she asks, other than God himself, "that infinite Being in whom all other beings and all other streams of life terminate." In what must be more than a veiled illusion to the suffering she endured for her *quietism*, Madame Guyon adds, "God is a large place indeed, and it was through humiliation, through abasement, through nothingness, David was brought into it."

Another significant theme in this section is seeking the Kingdom of God, surely one of the most beautiful metaphors for achieving union with him. To Nikolai Berdyaev, the Kingdom of God can be realized in every moment of our lives, for it existed before He created a single being, it existed before there were earthly measures of time and space, and it will exist throughout eternity. When Meister

Eckhart reflected on the pervasiveness of God's kingdom he often became mute with the awesome wonder of its greatness, for how could it be anything less than the totality of God?

Leo Tolstoy, best known for such epic novels as *War and Peace*, should also be remembered for the depth of his spiritual quest, particularly his plea to human-kind to break down the corrosive walls of hate and fear that still remain God-denying barriers. Tolstoy often reiterated that the reason for life "is for each of us simply to grow in love," because he believed "that this growth in love will contribute more than any other force to establish the Kingdom of God on earth."

Dr. Albert Schweitzer, in *The Conception of the Kingdom of God*, echoed Tolstoy's thoughts, insisting that there could be no Kingdom of God in this world without the Kingdom of God in our hearts. As long as the "spirit of the world" with its focus of material treasures prevails in our hearts, Dr. Schweitzer says, we will be deprived of the spiritual victory that will establish the foundations of God's king-dom here on earth. As Jesus of Nazareth observed, the Kingdom of God is within every man and woman, but few are willing to give up the glitter of their few fragmented years on earth to even try to establish its precepts.

In seeking union with God, another term that has been used to denote his abode, and therefore the "place" where we can "live" with him, is heaven. Para-celsus wondered how can we begin to explore the mathematics of heaven? Can we find anything that could be measured if "heaven has no beginning and no end, and no one knows the middle"?

Jacob Boehme, a sixteenth-century German mystic, wrote in his *Confessions* that "the true heaven is everywhere, even in that very place where thou standest and goest." If our spirit is able to go beyond the physical bounds that so often seem to chain us to earth, and if, as Boehme adds, we "apprehend the innermost moving of God," then clearly we are in heaven.

The story is told that during the last moments of his life, the composer Rich-ard Strauss declared, "Fifty years ago I wrote *Death and Transfiguration.* I was not mistaken; it is indeed that." Again, since the earliest days, men and women have longed for, dreamed of, and believed that there would be a resurrection with God after their physical death. But no one has ever been able to describe the nature of that union with God, except in the broadest sense.

As the master realist, Montaigne, put it in his *Apology for Raimond Sebond,* if the joys we are to receive in another "life" are like those we have known here below, they surely will have nothing in common with infinity. If we are to be resurrected, he says, even with our five physical senses "overflowing with glad-ness" it would still be nothing. In short, Montaigne logically concludes, "If it be at all human, there is nothing divine. If it is other than what appertains to our present condition, it cannot be computed."

Miguel de Unamuno suggested in *The Tragic Sense of Life* that we are all "ideas" in a Universal and Supreme Consciousness. Since it is impossible for any idea of God, the Supreme Consciousness, to be completely blotted out, even after we have died He will go on remembering us. Thus, concludes Unamuno, "to be remembered by God, to have my consciousness sustained by the Supreme Consciousness, is not that, perhaps, to be?"

Angelus Silesius, whose short book of mystic poetry, *The Cherubic Wanderer,* is unique in religious literature, conceived of resurrection by using a metaphor that goes back to the time of the Upanishads:

> Here still I flow to God, a brook in time's abyss;
> There I will be the sea of everlasting bliss.

Rabbi Pincus Goodblatt tells of a prayer that one of the six million Jews who died in Nazi death camps during those five dark years from 1940 to 1945 inscribed on the wall of his prison: "I believe in the sun even when it is not shining; I believe in love even when feeling it not; I believe in God, even when He is silent." This testament by the unknown Jew demonstrates what the God Seekers have been saying for thousands of years: when we truly *trust* God we are in his presence. According to Thomas Carlyle, we must believe that we are all in God's hand, "otherwise this world, which is but wholly a valley of the shadow of death, were too frightful."

There is an English proverb that says the best way to see divine light is to put out your own candle. In this section we learn that there is no quality more vigorously sought by the God Seekers than that of humility. Ralph Waldo Emerson in his essay "Spiritual Laws" does not equivocate on this matter when he urges us to "take our bloated nothingness out of the path of the divine circuits." As the sages who wrote the Midrash pointed out, our late appearance on earth should be a lesson in humility, so "Be not proud, O man, for the gnat was created before you."

Walk in humility. Put all your trust in God's plan for the world and your role in it. Do not fear death, even as you should not fear life. Find the Kingdom of God within your soul. In these ways, the God Seekers tell us, we shall achieve a joyful reunion with God.

· THE LAMP OF GOD IS THE SOUL OF MAN ·

Life is the one universal soul, which by virtue of the enlivening Breath, and the informing Word, all organized bodies have in common, each after its kind.

SAMUEL TAYLOR COLERIDGE (1772–1834)
Aids to Reflection

I think the soul will never stop, or attain to any growth beyond which it shall not go. When I walked at night by the seashore and looked up at the countless stars, I asked of my soul whether it would be filled and satisfied when it should become God enfolding all these and the answer was plain to me: No, when I reach there, I shall want to go further still.

WALT WHITMAN (1819–1892)
Notebooks

None but God can satisfy the longings of an immortal soul; that as the heart was made for Him, so He only can fill it.

RICHARD CHENEVIX TRENCH (1807–1886)
Notes on the Parables

The soul within me is greater than this earth and the sky and the heaven and all these united. That which performs and wills all, to which belong all sweet juices and fragrant odors, which envelops the world and is silent and is no respecter of persons, that is the soul within me. It is Brahma.   *The Upanishads*

We cannot kindle when we will
The fire which in the heart resides;
The spirit bloweth and is still,
In mystery our soul abides.

MATTHEW ARNOLD (1822–1888)
Morality

Great souls are always loyally submissive, reverent to what is over them; only small, mean souls are otherwise.

THOMAS CARLYLE (1795–1881)
Heroes and Hero Worship

O my soul, be not as the horse, or as the mule, which have no understanding; nor shouldst thou be as a drunkard that is fast asleep, or as a man that is stupified; for out of the fountain of understanding thou wast formed; and from the spring of wisdom was thou taken; from a holy place wast thou brought forth, and from the city of the mighty, from heaven, wast thou taken out by God.

BAHYA IBN PAKUDA (11th century)
The Duties of the Heart

The lamp of God is the soul of man, searching all the inward parts.

The Old Testament
Proverbs 20:27

Let no one presume either to kill, teach, judge, or give life to the human spirit or soul. Rather, let external instruments and teachers stick to the external man and not try to reach into God's region to rule, teach, and master the conscience and heart or instruct and enlighten the soul. Rather, let this inner work be left completely to God's management, so that everything may remain in its own order.

SEBASTIAN FRANCK (1449–1542)
Chronicles

Our birth is but a sleep and a forgetting:
The soul that rises with us, our life's star,

Hath had elsewhere its setting,
And cometh from afar
WILLIAM WORDSWORTH (1770–1850)
Intimations of Immortality

Each bud flowers but once and each flower has but its minute of perfect beauty; so, in the garden of the soul each feeling has, as it were, its flowering instant, its one and only moment of expansive grace and radiant kingship.
HENRI FRÉDÉRIC AMIEL (1821–1881)
Journal Intime

My soul, drink deep of understanding and eat your fill of wisdom! Without your consent you came here, and unwillingly you go away; only a brief span of life is given to you. O Lord above, if I may be allowed to approach you in prayer, plant a seed in our hearts and minds, and make it grow until it bears fruit, so that fallen man may obtain life. For you alone are God, and we are all shaped by you in one mould, as your word declares.
The Old Testament Apocrypha
2 Esdras 8:4–6

Let the humblest of men never cease to cherish and lift up his soul, even as though he were fully convinced that this soul of his should one day be called to console or gladden a God. When we think of preparing our soul, the preparation should never be other than befits a mission divine.
MAURICE MAETERLINCK (1862–1949)
Wisdom and Destiny

Since the soul is indeed other than God and yet from God, she loves and longs for Him of necessity; and when she tarries there she possesses Heavenly Love, whereas straying here below she becomes, as it were, a common courtesan.
PLOTINUS (205–270)
Enneads

That which oppresses me, is it my soul trying to come out in the open, or the soul of the world knocking at my heart for its entrance?
RABINDRANATH TAGORE (1861–1941)
Stray Birds

Hands of invisible spirits touch the strings
Of that mysterious instrument, the soul,
And play the prelude of our fate.
HENRY WADSWORTH LONGFELLOW
(1807–1882)
The Spanish Student

Again into the same cup in which he had blended and mixed the soul of the Universe the Creator poured what was left of the elements, mingling them in much the same manner, yet no longer so pure as before, but one or two degrees less pure. And when he had the whole compound, he divided it into souls equal in number to the stars, and assigned each soul to a star, and placing them in the stars as in a chariot, he showed them the nature of the Universe, and told them the laws of Fate—how that their first birth would be ordained the same for all, lest any should suffer wrong at his hands; and how, after being sown into the instruments of time, each into that appropriate to it, they must be born the most God-fearing of animals.
PLATO (427–347 B.C.)
Timaeus

Star to star vibrates light; may soul to soul
Strike thro' a finer element of her own?
ALFRED LORD TENNYSON (1809–1892)
Aylmer's Field

I swear I think now that everything
    without exception has an eternal
    soul—
The trees have, rooted in the ground;

the weeds of the sea have; the animals.

WALT WHITMAN (1819–1892)
To Think of Time

These two things are common to God's soul and to man's, that is, to the soul of every reasonable creature: not to be subject to another's hindrance, to find his good in righteous act and disposition, and to terminate his desire in what is right.

MARCUS AURELIUS (121–180)
Meditations

To the religious man religion is inwardly justified. God has no need of natural or logical witnesses, but speaks himself within the heart, being indeed that ineffable attraction which dwells in whatever is good and beautiful, and that persuasive visitation of the soul by the eternal and incorruptible by which she feels herself purified, rescued from mortality, and given an inheritance in the truth.

GEORGE SANTAYANA (1863–1952)
The Life of Reason

There is a deeper fact in the soul than compensation, to wit, its own nature. The soul is not a compensation but a life. The soul is. Under all this running sea of circumstance, whose waters ebb and flow with perfect balance, lies the aboriginal abyss of real Being. Existence, or God, is not a relation or a part, but the whole. Being is the vast affirmative, excluding negation, self-balanced, and swallowing up all relations, parts, and times within itself.

RALPH WALDO EMERSON (1803–1882)
Compensation

My soul knows that I am part of the human race, my soul is an organic part of the great human soul, as my spirit is part of my nation. There is nothing of me that is alone and absolute except my mind, and we shall find that the mind has no existence by itself; it is only the glitter of the sun on the surface of the waters.

D. H. LAWRENCE (1885–1930)
Apocalypse

For what is a man profited, if he shall gain the whole world and lose his own soul? Or what shall a man give in exchange for his soul? *The New Testament*
Matthew 16:26

In the choral dance of life the Soul sees the fountain of life and the fountain of Spirit, the Source of Being, the cause of Good, the root of Soul. For we are not cut off from our source nor separated from it, but we are more truly alive when we turn towards it, and in this lies our well-being.

PLOTINUS (205–270)
Enneads

A crystal is the soul, divinity its gleam:
The body where you dwell is cupboard
  for them both.

ANGELUS SILESIUS (1624–1677)
The Cherubic Wanderer

To regard it merely as the stern award of a Judge, the anger of an irritated Ruler or even the mechanical recoil of result of evil upon cause of evil is to take the most superficial view possible of God's dealings with the soul and the law of its evolution.

SRI AUROBINDO (1872–1950)
The Human Cycle

The soul of man has been brought hither in order to cause it to see—to see the writing of God.

RABBI BEN EZRA (1098–1164)
Commentaries

The moral law has its seat in the soul of man. Truth is within ourselves. There is an inmost center in us all where Truth abides in fullness.

MOHANDAS K. GANDHI (1869–1948)
Ethical Religion

He who wakes in the night and travels on the road alone, and turns his heart to vanity, is guilty of the death of his own soul.   *The Mishnah*

Immortal, lasting, alone, completely real is the soul. The world is only a majestic fireworks. The soul is an entire universe and her sun is love.

HENRI FRÉDÉRIC AMIEL (1821–1881)
Journal Intime

Unlovely, nay, frightful, is the solitude of the soul which is without God in the world.

RALPH WALDO EMERSON (1803–1882)
Journal

No weapons hurt the soul; no fire burns it; no waters moisten it; no wind dries it up. It is imperishable, perpetual, immovable, eternal. Therefore, knowing it thus, you should not grieve.

The Bhagavad Gita

Nothing is more difficult than to realize that every man has a distinct soul, that every one of all the millions who live or have lived, is as whole and independent a being in himself, as if there were no one else in the whole world but he.

JOHN CARDINAL NEWMAN (1801–1890)
Parochial and Plain Sermons

We should consider that God gave the sovereign part of the human soul to be the divinity of each one, being that part which, inasmuch as we are a plant not of an earthly but of a heavenly growth, raises us from earth to our kindred who are in heaven.   PLATO (427–347 B.C.)
The Meno

Since then the soul is so precious and divine a thing, be persuaded that by it thou canst attain to God; with it raise thyself to Him. Be sure that thou wilt not have to go far afield; there is not much between.

PLOTINUS (205–270)
Enneads

"The human soul is a lamp of God," says a wise Hebrew proverb. Man is a weak, miserable animal until in his soul there burns the fire of God.

LEO TOLSTOY (1828–1910)
My Religion

More minute than the minute,
    Greater than the great,
Is the Soul that is set in the heart of a
    creature here.

The Upanishads

It seems as if the Deity dressed each soul which he sends into nature in certain virtues and powers not communicable to other men, and sending it to perform one more turn through the cycle of beings, wrote *"not transferable"* and *"good for this trip only,"* on these garments of the soul.

RALPH WALDO EMERSON (1803–1882)
Representative Men

The entire striving of our soul is that it become God. Such striving is no less natural to men than the effort to flight is to birds. For who but God, Himself, whom we seek, would have inserted this into our souls? who, since He alone is the author of the species, inserts a proper appetite into the species.

MARSILIO FICINO (1433–1499)
Theologia Platonica

May that soul of mine, which mounts aloft in my waking and sleeping hours, an ethereal spark from the light of lights, be united by devout meditation with the Spirit supremely blest and supremely intelligent!   *The Rig-Veda*

As a man in the arms of the woman beloved feels only peace all around, even so the Soul in the embrace of Atman, the Spirit of vision, feels only peace all around. All desires are attained, since the Spirit that is all has been attained, no desires are there, and there is no sorrow.

The Upanishads

In the first minute that my soul is infused, the Image of God is imprinted in my soul; so forward is God in my behalf, and so early does he visit me.

JOHN DONNE (1572–1631)
Sermons

The soul has nothing in common with anything else. It is unconscious of the yesterday or the day before, and of tomorrow and the day after, for in eternity there is no yesterday nor any tomorrow, but only Now, as it was a thousand years ago and as it will be a thousand years hence, and is at this moment, and as it will be after death.

MEISTER ECKHART (1260–1327)
Sermons

Our soul's house forms part of the vast City of God. Though it may not be an important mansion with a frontage on the main street, nevertheless it shares all the obligations and advantages belonging to the city as a whole.

EVELYN UNDERHILL (1875–1941)
Concerning the Inner Life

If I err in my belief that the souls of men are immortal, I err gladly, and I do not wish to lose so delightful an error.

MARCUS TULLIUS CICERO (106–43 B.C.)
De Senectute

Love is the essence of the soul, and must be strengthened and cleansed of ill-feeling, irritation, irony, against every individual.
LEO TOLSTOY (1828–1910)
Emblems

Even as a mirror stained by dirt shines bright when it has been cleansed, so also the embodied soul on seeing the true nature of the Self, becomes one, its goal attained, free from sorrow.

The Upanishads

You furnish your parts toward eternity
Great or small, you furnish your parts
   toward the soul.

WALT WHITMAN (1819–1892)
Crossing Brooklyn Ferry

Man is a soul informed by divine ideas, and bodying forth their image.

BRONSON ALCOTT (1799–1888)
Tablets

The soul is its own witness; yea, the soul itself is its own refuge; grieve thou not, O man, thy soul, the great internal Witness.

The Code of Manu

There are no souls without bodies. God alone is wholly without body.

GOTTFRIED WILHELM VON LEIBNIZ
(1646–1716)
Monadologie

Only for the soul that is reconciled to God is nature as a whole renewed; difficult moral questions, which are insoluble for the mind, resolve themselves without the least struggle; life once more becomes beautiful and lofty.

NICHOLAS STANKEVICH (1813–1840)
Letters

As the web issues from the spider, as little sparks proceed from fire, so from the One Soul proceed all breathing animals, all the gods, and all beings.

The Upanishads

I trust in my own soul, that can perceive
The outward and the inward, Nature's
   good
And God's.

ROBERT BROWNING (1812–1889)
A Soul's Tragedy

The soul is not only equal with God, but it is the same as He is.

MEISTER ECKHART (1260–1327)
Sermons

Every man has an open gate to God in his soul.   WILLIAM LAW (1686–1761)
The Way to Divine Knowledge

The original human soul is the oldest thing, more correctly an oldest thing, for it has always been, before time and before form, just as God has always been.

THOMAS MANN (1875–1955)
Joseph and His Brothers

That which is the finest essence—this the whole world has that is its soul. That is Reality. That is Atman. That art Thou.

The Rig-Veda

God is throughout. God mingles in all
  things.
The beginning, the end, and the center of
  life.
All things enclose His soul, and are made
  vigorous
By it, in the way our souls infuse our
  bodies.

PIERRE DE RONSARD (1524–1585)
The Cats

God is man's soul; man's soul a spark of
  God:
By God in man the dull terrestrial clod
Becomes a thing of beauty; thinking man
Through God made manifest, outrival
  can
His handiwork of nature.

JOHN ADDINGTON SYMONDS (1840–1893)
New and Old

Souls are like unto mirrors, and the bounty of God is like unto the sun. When the mirrors pass beyond all coloring and attain purity and polish, and are con-

fronted with the sun, they will reflect in full perfection its light and glory.

ABDU'L BAHA (1844–1921)
The Loom of Reality

I already possess all that is granted to me in eternity. For God in the fullness of his Godhead dwells eternally in his image —the soul.

MEISTER ECKHART (1260–1327)
Sermons

And the Lord God formed man of the dust of the ground, and breathed into his nostrils the breath of life, and man became a living soul.   *The Old Testament*
Genesis 2:7

God loves from Whole to Parts: but
  human soul
Must rise from Individual to the Whole.
Self-love but serves the virtuous mind to
  wake,
As the small pebble stirs the peaceful
  lake.

ALEXANDER POPE (1688–1744)
Essay on Man

By its trust, the faith of the soul attests the love of God and endows it with enduring being. The lover who sacrifices himself in love is recreated anew in the trust of the beloved, and this time forever. When the soul is first overcome by the tremors of love, it hears an "unto eternity" within itself which is no self-delusion. The soul is at peace in the love of God, like a child in the arms of its mother, and now it can reach beyond "the uttermost parts of the sea" and to the portals of the grave—and yet is ever with Him.

FRANZ ROSENZWEIG (1886–1929)
The Star of Redemption

The eyes of my soul were opened, and I discerned the fullness of God, in which I understood the whole world, here and beyond the sea, the abyss, the ocean, everything. My soul was brimming over with wonder and cried out in a loud voice "The whole world is full of God."

ANGELA OF FOLIGNO (1258–1309)
Book of Visions

But (ah!) my soul with too much stay
Is drunk, and staggers in the way.
Some men a forward motion love,
But I by backward steps would move,
And when this dust falls to the urn
In that state I came return.

HENRY VAUGHAN (1622–1695)
The Retreat

Belief consists in accepting the affirmations of the soul; unbelief in denying them.

RALPH WALDO EMERSON (1803–1882)
Representative Men

Do not say any more that your soul is united to your body more intimately than to anything else; since its immediate union is with God alone, since the divine decrees are the indissoluble bonds of union between the various parts of the universe and of the marvellous network of all the subordinate clauses.

NICOLAS MALEBRANCHE (1638–1715)
Dialogues on Metaphysics and Religion

Out of the depths have I called upon Thee, O Lord. . . . My soul waiteth for the Lord, more than watchmen for the morning, yea, more than watchmen for the morning.   *The Old Testament*
Psalms 130:1, 6

Like as the hart desireth the waterbrooks, so longeth my soul after Thee, O God.   *The Old Testament*
Psalms 42:1

And thus the poet knows that the silent rows of stars carry God's own invitation to the individual soul.

RABINDRANATH TAGORE (1861–1941)
Gitanjali

As the one fire has entered the world
And becomes corresponding in form to
  every form,
So the Inner Soul of all things is
  corresponding in form to every form,
  and yet is outside.
As the sun, the eye of the world, is not
  sullied by the external faults of the
  eyes,
So the one Inner Soul of all things is
  not sullied by the evil in this world,
  being external to it.

The Upanishads

The soul's dark cottage, batter'd and
  decay'd
Lets in new light through chinks that time
  has made;
Stronger by weakness, wiser men become,
As they draw near their eternal home.

EDMUND WALLER (1606–1687)
Divine Poems

O we can wait no longer,
We too take ship, O soul,
Joyous we too launch out on trackless
  seas,
Fearless for unknown shores on waves of
  ecstasy to sail,
Amid the wafting winds (thou pressing
  me to thee, I thee to me, O soul),
Caroling free, singing our song of God,
Chanting our chant of pleasant
  exploration.

WALT WHITMAN (1819–1892)
Passage to India

The soul,
Remembering how she felt, but what she
felt

Remembering not, retains an obscure
  sense
Of possible sublimity.
> WILLIAM WORDSWORTH (1770–1850)
> *The Prelude*

As for my soul, I simply don't and never did understand how I could "save" it. One can save one's pennies. But how can one save one's soul? One can only live one's soul. The business is to live, really live. And this needs wonder.
> D. H. LAWRENCE (1885–1930)
> *Phoenix*

Herein lies the soul's purity, that it is purified from a life that is divided and that it enters into a life that is unified. All that is divided in lower things, will be unified so soon as the perceptive soul climbs up into a life where there is no contrast.
> MEISTER ECKHART (1260–1327)
> *German and Latin Works*

There is no great and no small
To the Soul that maketh all.
> RALPH WALDO EMERSON (1803–1882)
> *Epigraph to History*

Nothing is so like a soul as a bee. It goes from flower to flower as a soul from star to star, and it gathers honey as a soul gathers light.
> VICTOR HUGO (1802–1885)
> *Ninety-Three*

Great Truths are portions of the soul of
  man;
Great souls are portions of Eternity.
> JAMES RUSSELL LOWELL (1819–1891)
> *Sonnet VI*

God visits the soul in a manner which prevents its doubting, on returning to itself, that it dwelt in him and that he was within it.
> SAINT TERESA (1515–1582)
> *The Interior Castle*

Though inland far we be,
Our souls have sight of that immortal sea
Which brought us hither.
> WILLIAM WORDSWORTH (1770–1850)
> *Intimations of Immortality*

Make, Love, the universe our solitude,
And, over all the rest, oblivion roll—
Sense quenching Soul!
> ROBERT BROWNING (1812–1889)
> *Ferishtah's Fancies*

As the drop poured into the ocean is the ocean, not the ocean the drop, so the soul drawn into God is God, not God the soul. There the soul is in God as God is in himself.
> MEISTER ECKHART (1260–1327)
> *German Works*

To any vision must be brought an eye adapted to what is to be seen, and having some likeness to it. Never did eye see the sun unless it had first become sunlike, and never can the soul have vision of the First Beauty unless itself be beautiful.
> PLOTINUS (205–270)
> *Enneads*

The property of the universal soul is love. When it contemplated intellect and saw its beauty and splendor, it loved it as the passionate lover loves the object of his passion, and desired to unite with it, and reached out toward it.
> AL-SHAHRASTANI (died 1153)
> *Kitab al-Milal*

There is a spiritual sun that enlightens the soul more fully than the material sun does the body. This sun of truth leaves no shadow, and it shines upon both hemispheres. It is as brilliant in the night as in the daytime; it is not without that it sheds its rays; it dwells within each of us.
> FRANÇOIS FÉNELON (1651–1715)
> *On the Existence of God*

When all the stars have revolved they only produce Now again. The continuity of Now is for ever. So that it appears to me purely natural, and not supernatural, that the soul whose temporary frame was interred in this mound should be existing as I sit on the sward. How infinitely deeper is thought than the million miles of the firmament! The wonder is here, not there; now, not to be, now always.

RICHARD JEFFERIES (1848–1887)
The Story of My Heart

Darest thou now, O Soul,
Walk out with me toward the Unknown Region,
Where neither ground is for the feet nor any path to follow?

WALT WHITMAN (1819–1892)
Leaves of Grass

The vitalizing soul of man is one aspect of the vitalizing source of all living and created being, namely of the Holy One himself, as it were. When a man meditates on the thought that he is rooted in the divine, and he prays to God, then he performs an act of true unification.

BAAL SHEM TOV (1700–1760)
Sayings

The soul, when it shall have driven away from itself all that is contrary to the Divine Will, becomes transformed in God in love —the soul then becomes immediately enlightened by and transformed in God, because He communicates His own supernatural being in such a way that the soul seems to be God Himself and to possess the things of God, the soul seems to be God rather than itself and indeed is God by participation.

SAINT JOHN OF THE CROSS (1542–1591)
The Ascent of Mount Carmel

Deep within us all there is an amazing inner sanctuary of the soul, a holy place, a Divine Center, a speaking Voice, to which we may continuously return. Eternity is at our hearts, pressing upon our time-torn lives, warming us with intimations of an astounding destiny, calling us home to Itself.

THOMAS R. KELLY (1893–1941)
A Testament of Devotion

The uniqueness of the inner soul, in its own authenticity—this is the highest expression of the seed of divine light, the light planted for the righteous, from which will bud and blossom the fruit of the tree of life.

ABRAHAM ISAAC KOOK (1865–1935)
Lights of Holiness

Everywhere the human soul stands between a hemisphere of light and another of darkness; on the confines of two everlasting hostile empires, necessity and free will.

THOMAS CARLYLE (1795–1881)
Goethe

The Masters say that the soul has two faces. The higher one always sees God, the lower one looks downward and informs the senses. The higher one is the summit of the soul, it gazes into eternity. It knows nothing about time and body.

MEISTER ECKHART (1260–1327)
Sermons

When the true beauty and amiableness of the holiness or true moral good that is in divine things is discovered to the soul, it opens a new world to its views.

JONATHAN EDWARDS (1703–1758)
Concerning Religious Affections

We see the world piece by piece, as the sun, the moon, the animal, the tree; but the whole, of which these are the shining parts, is the soul. From within or from behind a light shines through us upon

things, and makes us aware that we are
nothing, but the light is all.

RALPH WALDO EMERSON (1803–1882)
Collected Essays

The soul is the mirror of an indestructible universe.

GOTTFRIED WILHELM VON LEIBNIZ
(1646–1716)
Monadologie

The sphere that is deepest, most unex-
plored, and most unfathomable, the wonder and glory of God's thought and hand,
is our own soul!

HENRY WARD BEECHER (1813–1887)
Sermons

The soul of man is still oracular. The
God Who is Spirit is still, as always, a revealing God, and man, who is essentially
spirit, is a recipient of tidings from beyond.   RUFUS JONES (1863–1948)
A Call to What Is Vital

Every man recognizes within himself a
free and rational spirit, independent of his
body. This spirit is what we call God.

LEO TOLSTOY (1828–1910)
The Gospel in Brief

And you, O my soul, where you stand,
Surrounded, detached, in measureless
      oceans of space,
Ceaselessly musing, venturing, throwing,
      seeking the spheres to connect them,
Till the bridge you will need be form'd,
      till the ductile anchor hold,
Till the gossamer thread you fling catch
      somewhere, O my soul.

WALT WHITMAN (1819–1892)
A Noiseless, Patient Spider

Up then, noble soul! Put on thy jumping
boots which are Intellect and Love, and
overleap thy mental powers, overleap
thine understanding, and spring into the
heart of God, into the hiddenness where
thou art hidden from all creatures.

MEISTER ECKHART (1260–1327)
Sermons

A soul, free from the tumults of passion,
is an impregnable fortress, in which man
may take refuge and defy all the powers of
earth to enslave him. He that does not see
this must be very ignorant: and he who
sees it, and does not avail himself of this
privilege, must be very unhappy.

MARCUS AURELIUS (121–180)
Meditations

There is always a radiance in the soul of
man, untroubled like the light in a lantern
in a wild turmoil of wind and tempest.

PLOTINUS (205–270)
Enneads

In the most noble part of the soul, the
domain of our spiritual powers, we are
constituted in the form of a living and
eternal mirror of God; we bear in it the
imprint of his eternal image and no other
image can enter here.

JAN VAN RUYSBROECK (1293–1381)
The Mirror of Eternal Salvation

The human soul is a silent harp in God's
quire, whose strings need only to be swept
by the divine breath to chime in with the
harmonies of creation.

HENRY DAVID THOREAU (1817–1862)
Journals

In the Soul of Man there are innumerable infinities. One soul in the immensity of
its intelligence, is greater and more excellent than the whole world. The Ocean is
but the drop of a bucket to it, the Heavens
but a centre, the Sun obscurity, and all
Ages but one day. It being by its understanding a Temple of Eternity, and God's

omnipresence between which and the whole world there is no proportion.

THOMAS TRAHERNE (1637–1674)
Centuries of Meditations

The soul, tempted, tried, humbled, wearied, badgered, cast to and fro, longs to feel the very touch of God, and to know that it is played upon by nothing less than the soul-power of God Himself.

HENRY WARD BEECHER (1813–1887)
Sermons

The one thing in the world of value, is the active soul,—the soul, free, sovereign, active. This every man is entitled to; this every man contains within him, although in almost all men, obstructed, and as yet unborn. The soul active sees absolute truth; and utters truth, or creates.

RALPH WALDO EMERSON (1803–1882)
The American Scholar

The finite is but the return of the soul on the path of the infinite—the wheeling orb attracted toward, and yet preserved in the cycle of, the central sphere.

BRONSON ALCOTT (1799–1888)
Journals

Man is conscious of a universal soul within or behind his individual life, wherein, as in a firmament, the natures of Justice, Truth, Love, Freedom, arise and shine. This universal soul he calls Reason: it is not mine, or thine, or his, but we are its; we are its property and men.

RALPH WALDO EMERSON (1803–1882)
Nature

I know that my soul is the better part of me, because it animates the whole of my body. It gives it life, and this is something that no body can give to another body. But God is even more. He is the Life of the life of my soul.   SAINT AUGUSTINE (354–430)
Confessions

The soul in the body is the life of the flesh; but God, who gives life to all, is the life of souls. And if life that is communicated is of such greatness that it cannot be comprehended, who will be able to comprehend by his intellect of how great majesty is the Life that gives life?

GREGORY THE GREAT 540–604)
Homily on Ezekiel

When the soul enters into her Ground, into the innermost recesses of her being, divine power suddenly pours into her.

MEISTER ECKHART (1260–1327)
Sermons

Of the progress of the souls of men and women along the grand roads of the universe, all other progress is the needed emblem and sustenance.

WALT WHITMAN (1819–1892)
Song of the Open Road

He who has seen It, knows whereof I speak: that the soul has another life as it nears God, and is now come to Him, and has a share in Him so that, restored, it knows that the Dispenser of true life is here present, it needs naught else; and on the other hand we must put aside everything else and abide in This alone, and become This alone—detached from all temporal things.   PLOTINUS (205–270)
Enneads

I have come to the conclusion that, seeing the general pattern of the world bearing upon man's conduct, small and insignificant as man's body may be—his soul is greater than the skies and earth, for his power of cognition encompasses everything that fills them.

SAADIA BEN JOSEPH (892–942)
Sefer Yezira

The Soul of man, a traveller, wanders in the cycle of Brahman, huge, a totality of lives, a totality of states, thinking itself different from the Impeller of the journey. Accepted by Him, it attains its goal of Immortality.   *The Upanishads*

Spirit that knows no insulated spot,
No chasm, no solitude; from link to link
It circulates, the Soul of all the worlds.
WILLIAM WORDSWORTH (1770–1850)
The Excursion

It must not be supposed that they who assert the natural immortality of the soul are of the opinion that it is absolutely incapable of annihilation, even by the infinite power of the Creator who first gave it being.   GEORGE BERKELEY (1685–1753)
Principles of Human Knowledge

Unlovely, nay, frightful, is the solitude of the soul which is without God in the world.
RALPH WALDO EMERSON (1803–1882)
The Preacher

Doubt is the trouble left to itself, which wants to see what God hides from it, and out of self-love seeks impossible securities.
FRANÇOIS FÉNELON (1651–1715)
Spiritual Letters

Our soul sits in God in true rest, and our soul stands in God in sure strength, and our soul is naturally rooted in God in endless love.
JULIAN OF NORWICH (1343–1416)
Showings

A man has many skins in himself, covering the depths of his heart. Why, thirty or forty skins or hides, just like an ox's or a bear's, so thick and hard, cover the soul. Go into your own ground and learn to know yourself there.
MEISTER ECKHART (1260–1327)
Sermons

In how many churches, by how many prophets, tell me, is man made sensible that he is an infinite Soul; that the earth and heavens are passing into his mind; that he is drinking from the soul of God?
RALPH WALDO EMERSON (1803–1882)
Divinity School Address

If the soul is immortal, it demands our care not only for that part of time which we call life, but for all time; and indeed it would seem now that it will be extremely dangerous to neglect it. If death were a release from everything it could be a boon for the wicked, because by dying they would be released not only from the body but also from their own wickedness together with the soul; but as it is, since the soul is clearly immortal it can have no escape or security from evil except by becoming as good and wise as it possibly can.
PLATO (427–347 B.C.)
Phaedo

Why dost thou wonder, O man, at the
    height of the stars or the depth of the
    sea?
Enter into thine own soul, and wonder
    there.
FRANCIS QUARLES (1592–1644)
Emblems

Eternal and most glorious God, suffer me not so to undervalue myself as to give away my soul, thy soul, thy dear and precious soul, for nothing; and all the world is nothing, if the soul must be given for it.
JOHN DONNE (1572–1631)
Sermons

The human soul has had a primordial experience in the infinite Spirit. The finite is but the return of the soul on the path of the infinite—the wheeling orb attracted toward, and yet, preserved in the cycle of, the central sphere.
BRONSON ALCOTT (1799–1888)
Journals

Let not that expression—filling the soul with God—pass away without a distinct meaning. God is love and goodness. Fill the soul with goodness, and fill the soul with love, *that* is the filling it with God.

FREDERICK WILLIAM ROBERTSON
(1816–1853)
Sermons

Just as the soul fills the body, so God fills the world; as the soul bears the body, so God endures the world; as the soul sees but is not seen, so God sees but is not seen.

The Talmud

Gently did my soul
Put off her veil, and self-transmuted
  stood
Naked, as in the presence of her God.

WILLIAM WORDSWORTH (1770–1850)
The Prelude

All souls are equal before God, so far as mere worldly eminence is concerned.

Their inequality rests solely upon the degree that they have realized the eternal will by their own choice.

WILLIAM TORREY HARRIS (1835–1909)
The Last Judgment

We were created once in majesty, to find enjoyment in God, and if our hearts are empty now, there is nothing in it but to fill up the hollowness of the soul with God.

FREDERICK WILLIAM ROBERTSON
(1816–1853)
Sermons

Verily, this soul is *Brahma*, made of knowledge, of mind, of breath, of seeing, of hearing, of earth, of water, of wind, of space, of energy and of non-energy, of desire and of non-desire, of anger and of non-anger, of virtuousness and of non-virtuousness. It is made of everything.

The Upanishads

· O DEATH, WHERE IS THY STING? ·

So when this corruptible shall have put on incorruption, and this mortal shall have put on immortality, then shall be brought to pass the saying that is written, Death is swallowed up in victory. O Death, where is thy sting? O grave where is thy victory?

The New Testament
I Corinthians 15:54–55

I saw there was an ocean of darkness and death, but an infinite ocean of light and love which flowed over the ocean of darkness.   GEORGE FOX (1624–1691)
Epistles

One cannot die hidden from God.

Italian Proverb

Should the trumpet sound tomorrow for the Judgment Day, men and women would stand before Him with countenance pale. But I would approach with love in my hands, saying, "Consider all my deeds, O Lord, naught do I fear."

JALAL-UD-DIN RUMI (1207–1273)
The Masnawi

If you really understand Him that governs the universe, and if you carry Him about within you, do you still long for paltry stones and pretty rock? What will you do, then, when you are going to leave the very sun and moon? Shall you sit crying like little children?

EPICTETUS (1st century)
Discourses

Wherefore is light given to him that is in misery, and life unto the bitter in soul—

who long for death, but it cometh not; and dig for it more than for hid treasures; who rejoice unto exultation, and are glad, when they can find the grave?

> *The Old Testament*
> *Job 3:20–23*

That is the road we all have to take—over the Bridge of Sighs into eternity.

> SÖREN KIERKEGAARD (1813–1855)
> *Journals*

And a voice said in mastery, while I
    strove,—
"Guess now who holds thee?"—"Death," I
    said, but, then,
The silver answer rang, "Not Death, but
    Love."

> ELIZABETH BARRETT BROWNING
> (1806–1861)
> *Sonnets from the Portuguese*

O thou soul of my soul! I shall clasp thee
    again,
And with God be the rest!

> ROBERT BROWNING (1812–1889)
> *Prospice*

Life and death are a part of Destiny. Their sequence, like day and night, is beyond the interference of man. These all lie in the inevitable nature of things. The Great gives me this form, this toil in manhood, this repose in old age, this rest in death. And surely that which is such a kind arbiter of my life is the best arbiter of my death.

> CHUANG-TZE (died 300 B.C.)
> *The Chuang-tze*

One short sleep past, we wake eternally,
And death shall be no more; death thou
    shalt die.

> JOHN DONNE (1572–1631)
> *Holy Sonnets*

Blessed are the dead which die in the Lord from henceforth: Yea, saith the Spirit, that they may rest from their labours; and their works do follow them.

> *The New Testament*
> *Revelation 14:13*

In this playhouse of infinite forms I have had my play and here have I caught sight of Him that is formless. My whole body and my limbs have thrilled with His touch, who is beyond touch; and if the end comes here, let it come—let this be my parting word.

> RABINDRANATH TAGORE (1861–1941)
> *Gitanjali*

Love is God, and to die means that I, a particle of love, shall return to the general and eternal source.

> LEO TOLSTOY (1828–1910)
> *War and Peace*

I love thee with a love I seemed to lose
With my lost saints,—I love thee with the
    breath,
Smiles, tears, of all my life!—and if God
    choose,
I shall but love thee better after death.

> ELIZABETH BARRETT BROWNING
> (1806–1861)
> *Sonnets from the Portuguese*

God employs several translators; some pieces are translated by age, some by sickness, some by war, some by justice; but God's hand is in every translation; and his hand shall bind up all our scattered leaves again for that library where every book shall lie open to one another.

> JOHN DONNE (1572–1631)
> *Meditations*

There was a Door to which I found no
    Key:
There was a veil past which I could not
    see:
    Some little Talk awhile of Me and Thee

There seemed—and then no more of
Thee and Me.

OMAR KHAYYÁM (died c. 1123)
The Rubáiyát

The Lord who gave us Earth and Heaven
Takes that as thanks for all He's given
The book he lent is given back
All blotted red and smutted black.

JOHN MASEFIELD (1878–1967)
Everlasting Mercy

When we have wandered all our ways,
Shut up the story of our days,
And from the earth, this grove, this dust,
My God shall raise me up, I trust.

SIR WALTER RALEIGH (1552–1618)
Written the night before his death;
discovered in his Bible in the gatehouse
at Westminster

Return, O my soul, unto thy rest; for the
Lord hath dealt bountifully with thee. For
Thou hast delivered my soul from death,
mine eyes from tears, and my feet from
stumbling. I shall walk before the Lord in
the lands of the living.

The Old Testament
Psalms 116:7–9

That nothing walks with aimless feet;
That not one life shall be destroy'd,
Or cast as rubbish to the void,
When God hath made the pile complete.

ALFRED LORD TENNYSON (1809–1892)
In Memoriam

There is not room for Death,
Nor atom that his might could render
void:
Thou—Thou art Being and Breath,
And what Thou art may never be
destroy'd.

EMILY BRONTË (1818–1848)
Last Lines

What is death? A mask. Turn it and be
convinced. See, it doth not bite. This little
body and spirit must be again, as once they
were, separated, either now or later. And
when Nature, which gave the body, takes
it away, will you not bear that? You say,—
"I love it." This very love has Nature given
you, but she also says,—"Now let it go, and
be troubled with it no longer." Another,
Whose care it is, provides you with food,
with clothes, with senses and ideas. Whenever, He doth not provide what is necessary for that body, He sounds a retreat. He
opens the door and says,—"Come."
Whither? To nothing dreadful; but to that
whence you were made,—to what is
friendly and congenial, to the elements.
What in you was fire, goes away to fire;
what was earth, to earth; what was air, to
air; what water, to water. There is no
Hades; but all is full of God and Divine
Beings.

EPICTETUS (1st century)
Discourses

Master, I've filled my contract, wrought in
many lands;
Not by my sins wilt Thou judge me, but
by the work of my hands.
Master, I've done Thy bidding, and the
light is low in the west,
And the long, long shift is over. . . .
Master, I've earned it—Rest.

ROBERT W. SERVICE (1874–1958)
Song of the Wage Slave

Do not invite death by the error of your
life, nor bring on destruction by the work
of your hands; because God did not make
death, and he does not delight in the death
of the living.

The Old Testament Apocrypha
The Wisdom of Solomon 1:12–13

Of all the thoughts of God that are
Borne inward into souls afar,
Along the Psalmist's music deep,
Now tell me if that any is,

For gift or grace, surpassing this:
"He giveth his beloved—sleep."
                 ELIZABETH BARRETT BROWNING
                              (1806–1861)
                                 The Sleep

Then shall the dust return to the earth
as it was; and the spirit shall return unto
God who gave it.   *The Old Testament*
                            Ecclesiastes 12:7

All flesh is grass, and all its beauty is like
the flower of the field: The grass withers,
the flower fades, when the breath of the
Lord blows upon it: surely the people is
grass. The grass withers, the flower fades;
but the word of our God will stand for
ever.   *The Old Testament*
                             Isaiah 40:6–8

The One remains, the many change and
   pass;
Heaven's light forever shines, Earth's
   shadows fly;
Life, like a dome of many-coloured glass,
Stains the white radiance of Eternity,
Until Death tramples it to fragments.
           PERCY BYSSHE SHELLEY (1792–1822)
                                   Adonais

The one soul in the midst of this world—
This surely is the fire which has entered
   into the ocean.
Only by knowing Him does one pass over
   death.
This whole world is illumined with his
   light.
                    The Svetsvatar Upanishad

The problem of personal survival per se
doesn't worry me much. Once the fruit of
my life is received up into one who is immortal, what can it matter whether I am
egotistically conscious of it or have joy of
it? To be happy it is enough to know that
the best of me passes on for ever into
one who is more beautiful and greater
than I.
        PIERRE TEILHARD DE CHARDIN (1881–1955)
                                   Letters

God's finger touched him, and he slept.
           ALFRED LORD TENNYSON (1809–1892)
                               In Memoriam

For I say, this is death, and the sole death,
When a man's loss comes to him from his
   gain,
Darkness from light, from knowledge
   ignorance,
And lack of love from love made
   manifest.
                 ROBERT BROWNING (1812–1889)
                         A Death in the Desert

And many of those who sleep in the dust
of the earth shall awake, some to everlasting life, and some to shame and everlasting contempt. And those who are wise
shall shine like the brightness of the firmament; and those who turn many to
righteousness, like the stars for ever and
ever.   *The Old Testament*
                              Daniel 12:2–3

   Our journey had advanced;
   Our feet were almost come
   To that odd fork in Being's road,
   Eternity by term.
               EMILY DICKINSON (1830–1886)
                    Our Journey Had Advanced

And the earth shall restore those that
are asleep in her, and so shall the dust
those that dwell therein in silence, and the
secret places shall deliver up those souls
that were committed unto them. And the
Most High shall be revealed upon the seat
of judgment, and compassion shall pass
away, and long-suffering shall be with-
drawn: but judgment only shall remain.
                The Old Testament Apocrypha
                            2 Esdras 7:32–34

When a man dies they who survive him ask what property he has left behind. The angel who bends over the dying man asks what good deeds he has sent before him.

The Koran

This dying has many degrees, and so has this life. A man might die a thousand deaths in one day and find at once a joyful life corresponding to each of them. This is at it must be: God cannot deny or refuse this to death. The stronger the death the more powerful and thorough is the corresponding life; the more intimate the death, the more inward the life.

JOHANNES TAULER (1300–1361)
Sermons

Like the hand which ends a dream,
Death, with the might of his sunbeam,
Touches the flesh, and the soul awakes.

ROBERT BROWNING (1812–1889)
The Flight of the Duchess

Death stands above me, whispering low
I know not what into my ear:
Of his strange language all I know
Is, there is not a word of fear.

WALTER SAVAGE LANDOR (1775–1864)
Last Fruit Off an Old Tree

Many a life has been injured by the constant expectation of death. It is life we have to do with, not death. The best preparation for night is to work diligently while the day lasts. The best preparation for death is life.

GEORGE MACDONALD (1824–1905)
Unspoken Sermons

Death? Translated into the heavenly tongue, that word means life!

HENRY WARD BEECHER (1813–1887)
Sermons

Who knows that 'tis not life which we call death,
And death our life on earth?

EURIPIDES (480–406 B.C.)
Phrixus

Hope is held out here for man for everything. If he is in abject poverty, he *may* become rich; if he is sickly, it is not beyond the range of possibility for him to become robust; if he is captive, he may regain his liberty. Death is the only thing which man cannot hope to escape. But let man take comfort in the thought that even so great a man as Moses, who spoke with God face to face, the head of all prophets, did not escape death.   *The Midrash*

Life and death are brothers that dwell together; they cling to each other and cannot be separated. They are joined by the two extremes of a frail bridge over which all created beings travel. Life is the entrance; death is the exit.

BAHYA IBN PAKUDA (11th century)
The Duties of the Heart

When good people die, they are not truly dead, for their example lives on.

The Talmud

Thou canst not soar where he is sitting
     now,
     Dust to the dust—but the pure spirit
     shall flow
Back to the burning fountain whence it
     came,
     A portion of the Eternal, which must
     glow
Through time and change, unquenchably
     the same.

PERCY BYSSHE SHELLEY (1792–1822)
Adonais

Spend your brief moment according to nature's law, and serenely greet the journey's end as an olive falls when it is ripe, blessing the branch that bare it, and giving thanks to the tree that gave it life.

MARCUS AURELIUS (121–180)
Meditations

God is life essential, eternal, and death cannot live in His sight; for death is corruption, and has no existence in itself, living only in the decay of the things of life.

GEORGE MACDONALD (1824–1905)
Unspoken Sermons

"Blessed be God, for he created Death!"
    The mourners said, "and Death is rest
        and peace";
Then added, in the certainty of faith,
    "And giveth Life that nevermore shall
        cease."

HENRY WADSWORTH LONGFELLOW
(1807–1882)
The Jewish Cemetery at Newport

Refrain thy voice from weeping, and thine eyes from tears: for thy work shall be rewarded, saith the Lord; and there is hope in thine end, saith the Lord, that thy children shall come again to their own border. *The Old Testament*
Jeremiah 31:16–17

Death is but Crossing the World, as Friends do the Seas; They live in one another still.   WILLIAM PENN (1644–1718)
Some Fruits of Solitude

There is not room for Death,
Nor atom that his might could never void
Since thou art Being and Breath,
And what thou art may never be
    destroyed.

EMILY BRONTË (1818–1848)
No Coward Soul of Mine

Now I will lie down in peace and sleep; for thou alone, O Lord, makest me live unafraid.   *The Old Testament*
Psalms 4:8

The wish that of the living whole
No life may fail beyond the grave,
Derives it not from what we have,
The likest-God within the soul?

ALFRED LORD TENNYSON (1809–1892)
In Memoriam

Is there any doctrine of immortality that can say anything more simple yet definitive about man's fate after death? He has come from God and returns to God. From the very beginning, man is bound up with God; and this bond continues to exist, unaffected by death which befalls the body only. God's creation of man's spirit, then, must be understood as a principle whose consequence is immortality.

HERMANN COHEN (1842–1918)
Jewish Writings

We can believe that what lies beyond this earthly life in terms of God's further teaching and unfolding of his endless riches is consistent with his wisdom and his love, but cannot finally be spelled out by us within this life.

NELS F. S. FERRE (1908–1971)
The Finality of Faith

We do not know what lies beyond death, but we know that God is last as well as first, the Eternal One who outlives the universe he has made, whose days have no end; and we are confident that any life once anchored in him is safe against whatever storm may beat upon it, in this world or the next.

WALTER MARSHALL HORTON (1895–1966)
Our Christian Faith

Peace, peace! he is not dead, he doth not
    sleep—
He hath awakened from the dream of
    life—

'Tis we who, lost in stormy visions, keep
  with phantoms an unprofitable strife.
PERCY BYSSHE SHELLEY (1792–1822)
Adonais

In this life, with all its miseries and sorrows, its joys and smiles and tears, one thing is certain: that all things are rushing towards their goal and it is only a question of time when you and I, plants and animals, and every particle of life that exists, must reach the infinite Ocean of Perfection, must attain to Freedom, to God.
SWAMI VIVEKANANDA (1863–1902)
Jnana-Yoga

Ye are not bound! The Soul of Things is
  sweet,
The Heart of Being is celestial rest;
Stronger than woe is will; that which was
  Good
Doth pass to Better—Best.
SIR EDWIN ARNOLD (1832–1904)
The Light of Asia

Then long Eternity shall greet our bliss
With an individual kiss;
And Joy shall overtake us as a flood,
When everything that is sincerely good
And perfectly divine,
With Truth, and Peace, and Love, shall
  ever shine
About the supreme Throne.
JOHN MILTON (1608–1674)
On Time

God's thought, made conscious through
  man's mortal life,
Resumes through death the eternal unity.
JOHN ADDINGTON SYMONDS (1840–1893)
The Prism of Life

We cannot part with our friends; we cannot let our angels go.
RALPH WALDO EMERSON (1803–1882)
Compensation

When the soul has returned to its rest, that is, to the fatherland in paradise, it will be taught more truly and will understand more truly what the meaning of its pilgrimage was. The prophet contemplated this in the form of a mystery and said, "Return, O my soul, to your rest; for the Lord has dealt bountifully with you."
ORIGEN (185–254)
Homily on Numbers

Far, far beneath, the noise of tempests
  dieth,
  And silver waves chime ever peacefully;
And no rude storm, how fierce soe'er it
  flieth,
  Disturbs the Sabbath of that deeper sea.
HARRIET BEECHER STOWE (1811–1896)
The Secret

The soul that flows out into God does not die; death is alien to what is submerged in life. The soul is alive, but not to itself. Stars are ever giving light, but they do not shine in the daytime; the sun shines in them, and they are hidden away in the sun's rays. So it is with the soul: still alive, but now its life is bound up with God; or rather, it is God who lives in it.
SAINT FRANCIS OF SALES (1567–1622)
The Love of God

Yea, though I walk in the valley . . .
a timeless prayer echoing at gravesides,
as if death were in fear of heights
and never scaled the uplands;
as if overawed by foaming seas
death never ventured far from still
  waters;
as if the Shepherd could not long
for the return of formlessness
to an earth again engulfed in silence
and a firmament bereft of stars.
MICHAEL BRAUDE (1911–)
Requiem

To whatever worlds He carries our souls when they shall pass out of these imprisoning bodies, in those worlds these souls of ours shall find themselves part of the same great Temple; for it belongs not to this earth alone. There can be no end of the universe where God is, to which that growing Temple does not reach.

PHILLIPS BROOKS (1835–1893)
Sermons

Our brains are seventy-year clocks. The Angel of Life winds them up once and for all, then closes the case, and gives the key into the hand of the Angel of the Resurrection.

OLIVER WENDELL HOLMES (1809–1894)
The Autocrat of the Breakfast-Table

Your dead shall live, your dead bodies shall rise. Awake and sing, you that sleep in the dust, for your dew is a dew of light, and on the land of the shades you will let it fall.

The Old Testament
Isaiah 26:19

Death, thy servant, is at my door. He has crossed the unknown sea and brought thy call to my home. The night is dark and my heart is fearful—yet I will take up the lamp, open my gates and bow to him my welcome. It is thy messenger who stands at my door.

RABINDRANATH TAGORE (1861–1941)
Gitanjali

When the day that he must go hence was come, many accompanied him to the riverside; into which as he went he said, Death, where is thy sting? And as he went down deeper he said, Grave, where is thy victory? So he passed over, and all the trumpets sounded for him on the other side.   JOHN BUNYAN (1628–1688)
The Pilgrim's Progress

And the spirits of you who have died in righteousness shall live and rejoice, and your spirits shall not perish, nor their memorial from before the face of the Great One, unto all the generations of the world.

The Old Testament Apocrypha
Enoch 103:4

One should part from life as Odysseus parted from Nausicaä—blessing it rather than in love with it.

FRIEDRICH NIETZSCHE (1844–1900)
Beyond Good and Evil

Dear, beauteous death! the Jewel of the
    Just,
  Shining nowhere but in the dark;
What mysteries do lie beyond thy dust;
  Could man outlook that mark!

HENRY VAUGHAN (1622–1695)
Silex Scintillans

Death is a great adventure, but none need go unconvinced that there is an issue to it. The man of faith may face it as Columbus faced his first voyage from the shores of Spain. What lies across the sea, he cannot tell; his special expectations all may be mistaken; but his insight into the clear meanings of present facts may persuade him beyond doubt that the sea has another shore.

HARRY EMERSON FOSDICK (1878–1969)
Assurances of Immortality

One Being there is who knows us now, who knows us perfectly, who has always known us. When we die we shall for the first time know ourselves, even as also we are known. We shall not have to await the Judge's sentence; we shall read it at a glance, whatever it be, in this new apprehension of what we are.

HENRY PARRY LIDDON (1829–1890)
Sermons

To pass through the valley of the shadow of death is the way home, but only thus, that as all changes have hitherto led us nearer to this home, the knowledge of God, so this greatest of all outward changes—for it is but an outward change—will surely usher us into a region where there will be fresh possibilities of drawing nigh in heart, soul and mind to the Father of us all.

GEORGE MACDONALD (1824–1905)
Unspoken Sermons

Blessed shalt thou be when thou comest in, and blessed shalt thou be when thou goest out (Deuteronomy 37:6). May thy departure from this world be like thy coming into this world. Even as thou didst enter into this world without sin, so mayest thou depart from this world without sin.

The Talmud

Servant of God, well done, well hast thou
    fought
The better fight, who singly hast
    maintained
Against revolted multitudes the cause
Of truth, in word mightier than they in
    arms.

JOHN MILTON (1608–1674)
Paradise Lost

I consider myself in the hands of my Creator, and that He will dispose of me after this life consistently with His justice and goodness. I leave all these matters to Him, as my Creator and friend, and I hold it to be presumption in man to make an article of faith as to what the Creator will do with us hereafter.

THOMAS PAINE (1737–1809)
An Examination of the Prophecies

This Soul of mine in the heart is Brahman, and when I go from here I shall merge into it.   *The Upanishads*

This is thy hour, O soul, thy free flight
    into the wordless,
Away from books, away from art, the day

erased, the lesson done,
Thee fully forth emerging, silent, gazing,
    pondering the themes thou lovest
    best,
Night, sleep, death and the stars.

WALT WHITMAN (1819–1892)
A Clear Midnight

The door of death is made of gold,
    That mortal eyes cannot behold;
But, when the mortal eyes are closed,
And cold and pale the limbs reposed,
The soul awakes; and, wondering, sees
In her mild hand the golden keys.

WILLIAM BLAKE (1757–1827)
Songs of Experience

He will swallow up death in victory; and the Lord God will wipe away tears from all faces; and the rebuke of his people shall he take away from off all the earth: for the Lord hath spoken it.   *The Old Testament*
Isaiah 25:8

Man with his burning soul
Has but an hour of breath
To build a ship of Truth
In which his soul may sail,
Sail on the sea of death;
For death takes toll
Of beauty, courage, youth,
Of all but Truth.

JOHN MASEFIELD (1878–1967)
Truth

And when, in the final hour of suffering, death at last approaches us, we smile at him, and hear our hearts say: Come, death of sleep, come, brother, and lead me away. Take the oar of my frail bark and guide me safely to port. Some may dread you, but you are making me glad. For you are the gateway to my Father's everlasting home.

ALBERT SCHWEITZER (1875–1965)
Reverence for Life

"Life is a passing shadow," says Scripture. The shadow of a tower or a tree? No: the shadow of a bird—for when a bird flies away, there is neither shadow nor bird.

The Midrash

There are brave and fortunate deaths. I have seen death cut the thread of the progress of a marvellous advancement, and that in the flower of its growth; and with an ending so magnificent that, in my opinion, the man's ambitious and courageous designs had nothing in them so high as their interruption. He reached, without moving, the place he was aiming at, more grandly and gloriously than he could either have hoped or desired. By his fall he carried his power and name beyond the point to which he aspired in his career.

MICHEL EYQUEM DE MONTAIGNE
(1533–1592)
Essays

Lights of infinite pity star the gray dusk
    of our days:
Surely here is soul: with it we have eternal
    breath:
In the fire of love we live, or pass by
    many ways,
    By unnumbered ways of dream to
    death.

GEORGE WILLIAM RUSSELL ("A.E.")
(1867–1935)
Immortality

Then star nor sun shall waken,
    Nor any change of light:
Nor sound of waters shaken,
    Nor any sound or sight:
Nor wintry leaves nor vernal,
    Nor days nor things diurnal:
Only the sleep eternal
    In an eternal night.

ALGERNON CHARLES SWINBURNE
(1837–1909)
The Garden of Proserpine

When Death summons a man to appear before his Creator, three friends are his: The first, whom he loves most, is money, but money cannot accompany him one step; his second friend is relatives, but they can only accompany him to the grave, and cannot defend him before the Judge. It is his third friend, whom he does not highly esteem, his good deeds, who can go with him, and can appear before the King, and can obtain his acquittal.   *The Talmud*

Fear no more the heat o' the sun,
    Nor the furious winter's rages;
Thou thy worldly task hast done,
Home art thou gone, and ta'en thy wages.
Golden lads and girls all must,
As chimney-sweepers, come to dust.

WILLIAM SHAKESPEARE (1564–1616)
Cymbeline

Death is for many of us the gate of hell; but we are inside on the way out, not outside on the way in.

GEORGE BERNARD SHAW (1856–1950)
Parents and Children

When a man dies, his voice goes into the fire, his breath into the wind, his eye to the sun, his thought to the moon, his ear to the heavens, his body to the earth, his ego to the ether, the hair of his head and body to the plants and the trees; his blood and his seed flow into the waters.

The Upanishads

Death reads the title clear—
What each soul for itself conquered from
    out things here.

ROBERT BROWNING (1812–1889)
Fifine at the Fair

He was exhal'd; his great Creator drew
His spirit, as the sun the morning dew.

JOHN DRYDEN (1631–1700)
On the Death of a Very Young Gentleman

And when, at eventide, the fray is done,
My soul to death's bed chamber do Thou
  light,
And give me, be the field or lost or won,
Rest from the fight.

PAUL LAURENCE DUNBAR (1872–1906)
The Warrior's Prayer

The night comes down, the lights turn
  blue;
And at my door the Pale Horse stands,
To bear me forth to unknown lands.

JOHN HAY (1838–1905)
The Stirrup Cup

For Death and Time bring on the prime
  Of God's own chosen weather,
And we lie in the peace of the Great
    Release
As once in the grass together.

WILLIAM ERNEST HENLEY (1849–1903)
In Memoriam R. L. S.

The Lightning reached a fiery rod,
And on Death's fearful forehead wrote
The autograph of God.

JOAQUIN MILLER (1841–1913)
With Love to You, and Yours

Yet some there be that by due steps aspire
To lay their just hands on that golden key
That opes the palace of Eternity.

JOHN MILTON (1608–1674)
Comus

For when he dieth he shall carry nothing
away: his glory shall not descend after
him.   *The Old Testament*
                Psalms 49:17

On the grass of the cliff, at the edge of
  the steep,
God planted a garden, a garden of sleep.

CLEMENT WILLIAM SCOTT (1841–1904)
The Garden of Sleep

Will you not allow that I have as much
of the spirit of prophecy in me as the
swans? For they, when they perceive that
they must die, having sung their life long,
do then sing more lustily than ever, rejoicing in the thought that they are going to
the god they serve.

SOCRATES (470–399 B.C.)
Dialogues of Plato

God bless them all who die at sea!
If they must sleep in restless waves,
God make them dream they are ashore,
With grass above their graves.

SARAH ORNE JEWETT (1849–1909)
The Gloucester Mother

There is, if one may say so, no rejoicing
before God at the destruction of the
wicked. But if there is no rejoicing before
Him at the death of the wicked, how much
less at the death of the righteous, of whom
even one is worth the whole world.

The Talmud

Every morning the day is reborn among
the newly blossomed flowers with the same
message retold and the same assurance renewed that death eternally dies, that the
waves of turmoil are on the surface, and
that the sea of tranquility is fathomless.

RABINDRANATH TAGORE (1861–1941)
Sadhana

So live, that when thy summons comes to
  join
The innumerable caravan which moves
To that mysterious realm where each
    shall take
His chamber in the silent halls of death,
Thou go not, like the quarry-slave at
    night,
Scourged to his dungeon, but sustained
    and soothed
By an unfaltering trust, approach thy
    grave
Like one who wraps the drapery of his
    couch

About him, and lies down to pleasant
dreams.

WILLIAM CULLEN BRYANT (1794–1878)
Thanatopsis

I saw a dead man's finer part
Shining within each faithful heart
Of those bereft. Then said I, "This must
be His immortality."

THOMAS HARDY (1840–1928)
His Immortality

We sometimes congratulate ourselves at
the moment of waking from a troubled
dream; it may be so the moment after
death.

NATHANIEL HAWTHORNE (1804–1864)
Journal

I strove with none, for none was worth
my strife;
Nature I loved; and next to Nature, Art.
I warm'd both hands against the fire of
life;
It sinks, and I am ready to depart.

WALTER SAVAGE LANDOR (1775–1864)
Dying Speech of an Old Philosopher

The grave itself is but a covered bridge,
Leading from light to light, through a
brief darkness!

HENRY WADSWORTH LONGFELLOW
(1807–1882)
The Golden Legend

Have you ever considered how dreadful
it would be if our lives had no appointed
end but went on forever? Can you imagine
that as far as the eye can see into the future we should remain enmeshed in the
desires and troubles of this life and that all
the ensuing envy, hatred and malice, our
own and other people's, should continue
to pile up undiminished? If you have ever
considered how intolerable the burden of
our life would be without the understood
certainty that it has an appointed end, you

know that death comes to all, even the
most fortunate, not as an enemy but as a
deliverance.

ALBERT SCHWEITZER (1875–1965)
Reverence for Life

Life makes the soul dependent on the
dust; Death gives her wings to mount
above the spheres.

EDWARD YOUNG (1683–1765)
Night Thoughts

And may we find, when ended is the
page,
Death but a tavern on our pilgrimage.

JOHN MASEFIELD (1878–1967)
The Word

God has counted and fixed for man all
his days and breathings: these cannot be
increased or diminished the length of a
sesame seed.   GURU ARJAN (1563–1606)
The Adi Granth

With thy rude ploughshare, Death, turn
up the sod,
And spread the furrow for the seed we
sow;
This is the field and Acre of our God,
This is the place where human harvests
grow!

HENRY WADSWORTH LONGFELLOW
(1807–1882)
God's-Acre

When the hour of man's departure
hence arrives, nothing will save him from
it. If he had the wings of an eagle and
could soar high up above the earth, he
would, of his own accord, come down to
meet his fate. Death is a new gate for the
righteous to enter in.   *The Midrash*

During Rabbi Meier's absence from
home two of his sons died. Their mother,
hiding her grief, awaited the father's return, and then said to him:

"My husband, some time since two jewels of inestimable value were placed with me for safe keeping. He who left them with me called for them today, and I delivered them into his hands."

"That is right," said the Rabbi approvingly. "We must always return cheerfully and faithfully all that is placed in our care."

Shortly after this the Rabbi asked for his sons, and the mother, taking him by the hand, led him gently to the chamber of death. Meier gazed upon his sons, and realizing the truth, wept bitterly.

"Weep not, beloved husband," said his noble wife; "didst thou not say to me we must return cheerfully, when 'tis called for, all that has been placed in our care? God gave us these jewels; he left them with us for a time, and we gloried in their possession; but now that he calls for his own, we should not repine." *The Talmud*

Do not, then, grudge your brother his rest; he has at last become free, safe, and immortal, and ranges joyous through the boundless heavens; he has left this low-lying region and has soared upwards to that place which receives in its happy bosom the souls set free from the chains of matter. Your brother has not lost the light of day, but has obtained a more enduring light. He has not left us, but has gone on before.

LUCIUS ANNAEUS SENECA (4 B.C.–A.D. 65)
Consolatio ad Polybium

All mankind is of one Author, and is one volume; when one Man dies, one Chapter is not torn out of the book, but translated into a better language; and every Chapter must be so translated.

JOHN DONNE (1572–1631)
Devotions

What better can the Lord do for a man, then take him home when he has done his work? CHARLES KINGSLEY (1819–1875)
Westward Ho!

The day of death is when two worlds meet with a kiss: this world going out, the future world coming in. *The Talmud*

The souls of the righteous are in the hand of God, and there shall no torment touch them. In the sight of the unwise they seemed to die: and their departure is taken for misery, and their going from us to be utter destruction: but they are in peace. *The Old Testament Apocrypha*
The Wisdom of Solomon 3:1–3

Those who love me will not perish; those who love me will be delivered from their evil. This was my promise from the beginning: he who loves me does not perish.
The Isvara Gita

As death comes on we are like trees growing in the sandy bank of a widening river. BHARTRIHARI (7th century)
The Vairagya Sataka

When death, the great Reconciler, has come, it is never our tenderness that we repent of, but our severity.
GEORGE ELIOT (1819–1880)
Adam Bede

The Lord gave, and the Lord hath taken away; blessed be the name of the Lord.
The Old Testament
Job 1:21

If a man die, can he live again? All the days of my service I would wait, till my hour of release should come. You would call and I would answer You; you would be longing for the work of Your hands.
The Old Testament
Job 14:14–15

The splendors of the firmament of time
May be eclipsed, but are extinguished
  not;
Like stars to their appointed height they
  climb,
And death is a low mist which cannot blot
The brightness it may veil.

PERCY BYSSHE SHELLEY (1792–1822)
Adonais

Father, when we suffer in our hearts, when our houses are hung with blackness, and the shadow of death falls on the empty seat of those dear and once near to us, we know that there is mercy in all that thou sendest, and through the darkness we behold thy light, and thank thee for the lilies of Solomon that spring out of the ground which Death has burned over with his blackness and sprinkled with the ashes of our sorrow.

THEODORE PARKER (1810–1860)
Sermons

There is no suffering for him who has finished his journey, and abandoned grief, who has freed himself on all sides, and thrown off all fetters. *The Dhammapada*

And now that your errand is ended,
  And now that your steps go afar,
What strong soul will catch up the splendid
High dream that your spirit attended—
  The purpose of God for our star?

EDWIN MARKHAM (1852–1940)
The Shoes of Happiness

· LIFE, A MOMENT BETWEEN ETERNITIES ·

Thou perceivest the Flowers put forth
  their precious Odours,
And none can tell how from so small a
  center comes such sweets,
Forgetting that within that center Eternity
  expands
Its ever during doors.

WILLIAM BLAKE (1757–1827)
Milton

Life is a fragment, a moment between two eternities, influenced by all that has preceded, and to influence all that follows. The only way to illumine it is by extent of view.

WILLIAM ELLERY CHANNING (1780–1842)
Journals

The time will come when every change
  shall cease,
This quick revolving wheel shall rest in
  peace:

No summer then shall glow, nor winter
  freeze;
Nothing shall be to come, and nothing
  past,
But an eternal now shall ever last.

PETRARCH (1304–1374)
The Triumph of Eternity

We perish but thou endurest. Ours is not thy eternity. But in thy eternity we would be remembered, not as blots on the face of this part of thy infinite reality, but as healthy leaves that flourished for a time on the branches of the eternal tree of life, and that have fallen, though not into forgetfulness. For to thee nothing is forgotten.

JOSIAH ROYCE (1855–1916)
The Religious Aspect of Philosophy

'Tis the divinity that stirs within us;
'Tis Heaven itself that points out an
  hereafter,

And intimates eternity to man.
Eternity! thou pleasing, dreadful
   thought!
                JOSEPH ADDISON (1672–1719)
                                    Cato

Eternity is the great atonement of finitude. The earthly is reconciled with the
endless. All atonement is fundamentally
this: reconciliation of the finite and the infinite.   LEO BAECK (1873–1956)
                        The Essence of Judaism

The Timeless and Eternal is the *I am*
towards which we reach out in spiritual regard. Thus truth, beauty, and goodness—
rational, aesthetic, and ethical values—are
raised to a higher status for those in whom
the spiritual attitude is supervenient, since
they have their ultimate being in God.
                CONWAY LLOYD MORGAN (1852–1936)
                                Life, Mind and Spirit

Behind us, behind each one of us, lie Six
Thousand Years of human effort, human
conquest: before us is the boundless Time,
with its yet uncreated and unconquered
Continents and Eldorados, which we, even
we, have to conquer, to create; and from
the bosom of Eternity there shine for us
celestial guiding stars.
                THOMAS CARLYLE (1795–1881)
                                Characteristics

· GOD MADE ALL THE CREATURES ·

We indeed created man; and We know
what his soul whispers within him, for we
are nearer to him than the jugular vein.
                                    The Koran

The Lord created me at the beginning
of his way, the first of his acts of old. Ages
ago I was set up, at the first, before the
beginning of the earth. When he established the heavens, I was there, when he
drew a circle on the face of the deep, when
he marked out the foundations of the
earth, then was I beside Him, like a master
workman.   *The Old Testament*
                        Proverbs 8:22–23

Creation happens to us, burns itself into
us, recasts us in burning—we tremble and
are faint, we submit. We take part in creation, meet the Creator, reach out to Him,
helpers and companions.
                MARTIN BUBER (1878–1965)
                                    I and Thou

He, the great father, kindled at one flame
The world of rationals; one spirit pour'd
From spirit's awful fountain; pour'd
   himself
Through all their souls.
                EDWARD YOUNG (1683–1765)
                                Night Thoughts

God made all the creatures, and gave
   them our love and our fear,
To give sign, we and they are his
   children, one family here.
                ROBERT BROWNING (1812–1889)
                                    Saul

In the creative vision of God the individual is present as a whole in his essential
being and inner teleos and at the same
time in the infinity of the special moments
of his life process. Of course this is said
symbolically, since we are unable to have a
perception of or even an imagination of
that which belongs to the divine life. The
mystery of being beyond essence and ex-

istence is hidden in the mystery of the creativity of the divine life.

PAUL TILLICH (1886–1965)
Systematic Theology

I believe that our Heavenly Father invented man because he was disappointed in the monkey.

MARK TWAIN (1835–1910)
Letters

All created things are but the crumbs which fall from the table of God.

SAINT JOHN OF THE CROSS (1542–1591)
The Ascent of Mount Carmel

We believe that God hath made all things out of nothing: because even although the world hath been made of some material, that very same material hath been made out of nothing.

SAINT AUGUSTINE (354–430)
Of the Faith and of the Creed

The whole Creation is a mystery and particularly that of man. At the blast of His mouth were the rest of the creatures made; and at His bare Word they started out of nothing: but in the frame of men (as the text describes it) he played the sensible operator, and seemed not so much to create as make him.

SIR THOMAS BROWNE (1605–1682)
Religio Medici

It is so impossible for the world to exist without God that if God should *forget* it, it would immediately cease to be.

SÖREN KIERKEGAARD (1813–1855)
Journals

At the beginning all things were in the mind of Wakonda. All creatures, including man, were spirits. They moved about in space between the earth and the stars. They were seeking a place where they could come into a bodily existence.

Omaha Indian Ritual

From all eternity God knew that he could make a great number of creatures past all counting, endowed with different perfections, different characteristics, to which he could give himself. Realizing that he could give himself in no better fashion than by uniting himself with a created nature—in such a way as to engraft the creature into the godhead, so as to form one person—his infinite goodness, naturally self-sharing, decided on that method.

SAINT FRANCIS OF SALES (1567–1622)
The Love of God

God the Creator becomes the molder of man's heart and spirit. "He that fashioneth the hearts of them all" (Psalms 33:15), and He "who stretched forth the heavens, and laid the foundation of the earth, and formed the spirit of man within him" (Zechariah 12:1). As the calling-into-being of heaven and earth is a special act of creation, so is the forming of man's spirit within him.

HERMANN COHEN (1842–1918)
Jewish Writings

I can know myself as a person only where I feel my existence grounded in responsibility, and that means where I know myself to be created by and in the Word of God.

EMIL BRUNNER (1889–1966)
The Word and the World

Creation—happens to us, burns into us, changes us, we tremble and swoon, we submit. Creation—we participate in it, we encounter the creator, offer ourselves to him, helpers and companions.

MARTIN BUBER (1878–1965)
I and Thou

Imagine yourself alone in the world, a musing, wondering, reflecting spirit, lost in thought, and imagine thereafter the creation of man!—man made in the image of God!

HENRY DAVID THOREAU (1817–1862)
Journals

If I were the author of my being, I should doubt of nothing, I should desire nothing, and, in fine, no perfection would be awanting me; for I should have bestowed upon myself every perfection of which I possess the idea, and I should thus be God.   RENÉ DESCARTES (1596–1650)
Principles of Philosophy

As God Himself planted this seed and pressed it in and begat it, it can quite well be covered and hidden and yet never destroyed nor extinguished in itself. It glows and sparkles and burns and turns without intermission to God.   ORIGEN (185–254)
Homiliae in Genesim

O rich and various man! thou palace of sight and sound, carrying in thy senses the morning and the night, and the unfathomable galaxy; in thy brain, the geometry of the city of God; in thy heart, the power of love and the realms of right and wrong. An individual man is a fruit which it cost all the foregoing ages to form and ripen.

RALPH WALDO EMERSON (1803–1882)
Collected Essays

The greatness of God is infinite; for while with one die man impresses many coins and all are exactly alike, the King of Kings, the Holy One—blessed be He!— with one die impresses the same image on all men, and yet not one of them is like his neighbor. So that every one ought to say, "For myself is the world created."

The Talmud

· THE UNITY OF GOD ·

Because God is One, all our lives have various and unique places in the harmony of the divine life. And because God attains and wins and finds this uniqueness, all our lives win in our union with him the individuality which is essential to their true meaning.   JOSIAH ROYCE (1855–1916)
The Conception of Immortality

That which is One, the wise call it in diverse manners. Wise poets, by words, make the beautiful-winged manifold, though he is One.   *The Rig-Veda*

He who would see the Divinity must see him in his Children.

WILLIAM BLAKE (1757–1827)
Jerusalem

In the light of the eternal we are manifest, and even this very passing instant pulsates with a life that all the worlds are needed to express. In vain would we wander in the darkness; we are eternally at home in God.   JOSIAH ROYCE (1855–1916)
The World and the Individual

The brain is just the weight of God,
    For, lift them pound for pound,
And they will differ, if they do,
    As syllable from sound.

EMILY DICKINSON (1830–1886)
The Brain Is Wider Than

Sublime and Living Will, named by no name, compassed by no thought! I may well raise my soul to Thee, for Thou and I are not divided. Thy voice sounds within me, mine resounds in Thee; and all my thoughts, if they be but good and true, live in Thee also.

JOHANN GOTTLIEB FICHTE (1762–1814)
The Vocation of Man

Listen not to me, but to reason, and confess the true wisdom that All things are One.

HERACLITUS (c. 535–c. 475 b.c.)
Fragments

One Life through all the immense
 creation runs,
One Spirit is the moon's, the sea's, the
 sun's;
All forms in the air that fly, on the earth
 that creep,
And the unknown nameless monsters of
 the deep—
Each breathing thing obeys one Mind
 control,
And in all substance is a single Soul.

VERGIL (70–19 b.c.)
The Aeneid

The Lord shall be King over all the earth; in that day shall the Lord be One and His Name, One.   *The Old Testament*
Zechariah 14:9

Finite and fragmentary we certainly are, "broken lights" of the one light, as Tennyson puts it, but in any case God and man are not sundered in the sense that mind and matter have been held to be separated by an impassable "divide." The divine and the human are not two diverse and incompatible realities, one exclusive of the other.

RUFUS JONES (1863–1948)
New Studies in Mystical Religion

As the one fire, having entered the world, assumes the forms of all that is in it, so the One inmost Self of all beings takes on their manifold forms outside.

The Upanishads

God as the absolute first foundation or first principle is a total-unity, apart from which nothing is conceivable. If the world is something "wholly other" with respect to God, then this otherness flows from God and is grounded in God.

SIMON L. FRANK (1877–1950)
The Unfathomable

Is not God the sole and highest unity? Is it not God alone before whom and in whom all particularity vanishes? And if you regard the world as a whole and a totality, can you do it otherwise than in God?

FRIEDRICH SCHLEIERMACHER (1768–1834)
Sermons

We live in succession, in division, in parts, in particles. Meantime within man is the soul of the whole; the wise silence; the universal beauty, to which every part and particle is equally related; the eternal One. And this deep power in which we exist and whose beatitude is all accessible to us, is not only self-sufficing and perfect in every hour, but the act of seeing and the thing seen, the seer and the spectacle, the subject and the object, are one.

RALPH WALDO EMERSON (1803–1882)
The Over-Soul

We are partakers of the life of God; and though we differ from Him in that we are individualized spirits, while He is the Infinite Spirit, including us, as well as all else beside, yet in essence the life of God and the life of man are identically the same, and so are one. They differ not in essence or quality; they differ in degree.

WILLIAM JAMES (1842–1910)
The Varieties of Religious Experience

The sum total of religion is to feel that, in its highest unity, all that moves us in feeling is one; to feel that aught single and particular is only possible by means of this unity; to feel, that is to say, that our being and living is a being and living in and through God.

FRIEDRICH SCHLEIERMACHER (1768–1834)
On Religion

Verily, this whole world is Brahma. Tranquil, let one worship It as that from which he came forth, as that into which he will be dissolved, as that in which he doth breathe. *The Upanishads*

Life is the one universal soul, which by virtue of the enlivening Breath, and the informing Word, all organized bodies have in common, each after its kind.
SAMUEL TAYLOR COLERIDGE (1772–1834)
Aids to Reflection

There is one Mind, one omnipresent Mind,
Omnific. His most holy name is Love.
SAMUEL TAYLOR COLERIDGE (1772–1834)
Religious Musings

In the endless self-repeating
    For evermore flows the Same.
Streams from all things love of living,
    Grandest star and humblest clod.
All the straining, all the striving
    Is eternal peace in God.
JOHANN WOLFGANG VON GOETHE
(1749–1832)
Collected Poems

That God, which ever lives and loves,
    One God, one law, one element,
    And one far-off divine event,
To which the whole creation moves.
ALFRED LORD TENNYSON (1809–1892)
In Memoriam

Know all this, whatever moves in this moving world, is enveloped by God. Therefore find your enjoyment in renunciation; do not covet what belongs to others. *The Upanishads*

I recognize the distinction of the outer and the inner self; the double consciousness that within this erring, passionate, mortal self sits a supreme, calm immortal mind, whose powers I do not know; but it is stronger than I; it is wiser than I; it

never approved me in any wrong; I seek counsel of it in my doubt; I repair to it in my dangers; I pray to it in my undertakings. It seems to me the face which the creator uncovers to his child.
RALPH WALDO EMERSON (1803–1882)
Sermons

The form ever changes, ever perishes, the informing spirit neither changes nor perishes. True love consists in transferring itself from the body to the dweller within and then necessarily realizing the oneness of all life inhabiting numberless bodies.
MOHANDAS K. GANDHI (1869–1948)
Letters

The strength of unity bring me from distraction to myself. I want to be one with myself. The binding forces of my life grow in the same measure as my links with the source of unity. Unity for me is the one Transcendence as well as myself.
KARL JASPERS (1883–1969)
Philosophical Truth and Revelation

God is the cupbearer, the cup and the wine. He knows what manner of love is mine. JALAL-UD-DIN RUMI (1207–1273)
The Masnawi

There is not one realm of spirit and another of nature; there is only the growing realm of God. God is not spirit, but what we call spirit and what we call nature hail equally from the God who is beyond and equally conditioned by both, and whose kingdom reaches its fulness in the complete unity of spirit and nature.
MARTIN BUBER (1878–1965)
Israel and the World

It must be that when God speaketh he should communicate, not one thing, but all things; should fill the world with his voice; should scatter forth light, nature, time, souls, from the center of the present thought; and new date and new create the whole.

RALPH WALDO EMERSON (1803–1882)
Self-Reliance

Is not God the highest, the only unity? Is it not God alone before whom and in whom all particular things disappear? And if you see the world as a Whole, a Universe, can you do it otherwise than in God? If not, how could you distinguish the highest existence, the original and eternal Being from a temporal and derived individual?

FRIEDRICH SCHLEIERMACHER (1768–1834)
On Religion

We need, what Genius is unconsciously seeking, and, by some daring generalization of the universe, shall assuredly discover, a spiritual calculus, a novum organon, whereby nature shall be divined in the soul, the soul in God, matter in spirit, polarity resolved into unity; and that power which pulsates in all life shall manifest itself as one universal deific energy.

BRONSON ALCOTT (1799–1888)
Orphic Sayings

Let us build altars to the Beautiful Necessity, which secures that all is made of one piece; that plaintiff and defendant, friend and enemy, animal and plant, food and eater are of one kind. In astronomy is vast space but no foreign system; in geology, vast time but the same laws as today.

RALPH WALDO EMERSON (1803–1882)
Fate

He, the Highest Person, who is awake in us while we are asleep, shaping one lovely sight after another, that indeed is the Bright, that is Brahman, that alone is called the Immortal. All worlds are contained in it, and no one goes beyond.

The Upanishads

Think not of God, my children, as a great tyrant sitting away up there in Heaven removed from you. Why, look down! There is a flower, and a blade of grass, and a stream, and a grain of sand— and that is God, too! He is there! He is everywhere!

BAAL SHEM TOV (1700–1760)
Discourses

We are not only the sons of God; so far as we are wise our lives are hid in God, we are in Him, of Him.

JOSIAH ROYCE (1855–1916)
The Spirit of Modern Philosophy

Why should there be so many different faiths? The Soul is one, but the bodies which she animates are many. We cannot reduce the number of bodies, yet we recognize the unity of the Soul. Even as a tree has a single trunk, but many branches and leaves, so is there one true and perfect Religion, but it becomes many as it passes through the human medium.

MOHANDAS K. GANDHI (1869–1948)
Yervada Mandir

All things are gathered together in one with the divine sweetness, and the man's being is so penetrated with the divine substance that he loses himself therein.

JOHANNES TAULER (1300–1361)
Sermons

He who is one, and who dispenses the inherent needs of all peoples and all times, who is in the beginning and end of all things, may He unite us with the bond of Truth, of common fellowship, and of righteousness.   *The Upanishads*

All is concenter'd in a life intense,
Where not a beam, nor air, nor leaf is
    lost,
But hath a part of being, and a sense

Of that which is of all Creator and
defence.

GEORGE GORDON, LORD BYRON
(1788–1824)
Childe Harold

So shalt thou see and hear
The lovely shapes and sounds intelligible
Of that eternal language, which thy God
Utters, who from eternity doth teach
Himself in all, and all things in himself.
Great universal Teacher! he shall mould
Thy spirit, and by giving make it ask.

SAMUEL TAYLOR COLERIDGE (1772–1834)
Frost at Midnight

When a man has learned to understand
the workings of the universe and has realized that there is nothing so great or all-
inclusive as this frame of things wherein
men and God are united, and that from it
come the seeds from which are sprung not
only my own father or grandfather, but all
things that grow upon the earth, why
should he not call himself a citizen of the
universe and son of God?

EPICTETUS (1st century)
Discourses

How present and sensible to my inner
sense is the unity of everything! It seems
to me that I am able to pierce to the sublime motive which, in all the infinite
spheres of existence, and through all the
modes of space and time, every created
form reproduces and sings within the
bond of an eternal harmony.

HENRI FRÉDÉRIC AMIEL (1821–1881)
Journal Intime

All that a man has here externally in
multiplicity is intrinsically One. Here all
blades of grass, wood and stone, all things
are one. This is the deepest depth and
thereby am I completely captivated.

MEISTER ECKHART (1260–1327)
Sermons

Why do you go to the forest to find God?
He lives in all and yet remains distinct. He
dwells in you as well, as fragrance resides
in a flower or the reflection in a mirror.
See him, therefore, in your own heart.

GURU TEGH BAHADUR (1621–1675)
The Adi Granth

There can be nothing truly alone and by
itself, which is not truly one; and such is
only God; all others do transcend a unity,
and so by consequence are many.

SIR THOMAS BROWNE (1605–1682)
Religio Medici

The contemplation of the pious is the
immediate consciousness of the universal
existence of all finite things in and
through the Infinite and of all temporal
things in and through the Eternal. Religion is a life in the infinite nature of the
Whole, in the One and in the All, in God,
having and possessing all things in God
and God in all.

FRIEDRICH SCHLEIERMACHER (1768–1834)
On Religion

This is the truth: as from a blazing fire
sparks, being like unto fire, fly forth a
thousandfold, thus are various beings
brought forth from the Imperishable, my
friend, and return thither also.

The Upanishads

It was the insight of great prophets proclaiming that across all human alienations
there was *one* God, and every son of man
his child. "Have we not all one father?"
cried the prophet. "Hath not one God created us? Why do we deal treacherously
every man against his brother?" Across all
lines that men have drawn, it goes, saying
first of all and deepest of all: "Have we not
one father?"

HARRY EMERSON FOSDICK (1878–1969)
Riverside Sermons

I believe with perfect faith that the Creator, praised be He, is a Unity, and that there is no unity like His in any manner, and that He alone is our God, who was, is, and will be.

MAIMONIDES (1135–1204)
Sanhedrin

The universal Spirit floweth through every form of humanity, never losing its own essential life, yet assuming, to the external sense, every variety of manifestation without marring or fracturing the divine unity.   BRONSON ALCOTT (1799–1888)
Journals

God is the substratum of all souls. Is not that the solution of the riddle?

RALPH WALDO EMERSON (1803–1882)
Journals

God is everywhere as absolutely and entirely as if He were nowhere else; and it seems to be essential to the existence of every creature, rational and irrational, good and evil, in heaven and hell, that in some sense or other He should be present with it and be its life.

JOHN CARDINAL NEWMAN (1801–1890)
Lectures on Justification

If thou speakest, bear in mind that thy power of speech comes from thy soul which is part of God, and when thou hearest bear in mind that thy power of hearing comes from thy soul. Thus thou wilt be able to unite thy soul with the Shekinah.

BAAL SHEM TOV (1700–1760)
Sayings

How, then, am I to love the Godhead? Thou shalt love Him as He is: not as a God, not as a Spirit, not as a Person, not as an image, but as a sheer pure One. And in this One we are to sink from nothing to nothing, so help us God.

MEISTER ECKHART (1260–1327)
Sermons

The world and my being, its life and mine, were one. The microcosm and macrocosm were at length atoned, at length in harmony. I lived in everything; everything entered and lived in me. To be aware of a thing, was to know its life at once and mine, to know whence we came, and where we were at home—was to know that we are all what we are, because Another is what He is.

GEORGE MACDONALD (1824–1905)
Lilith

We are not aliens in a strange universe governed by an outside God; we are parts of a developing whole, all enfolded in an embracing and interpenetrating love, of which we too, each to other, sometimes experience the joy too deep for words.

SIR OLIVER LODGE (1851–1940)
Man and the Universe

As an actor in a play appears in many
     guises
So God when His play is ended abandons
     the guise
And appears as the One only.

GURU ARJAN (1563–1606)
The Adi Granth

In order to know the world as a totality, and in order himself to become a totality in or over it by the help of God, man needs the idea of the oneness of God, and of the consummation of the world in an end which is for man both knowable and realizable.

ALBRECHT RITSCHL (1822–1889)
*The Christian Doctrine of Justification
and Reconciliation*

The system of the world is entirely one; small things and great are alike part of one mighty whole. As the flower is gnawed by frost, so every human heart is gnawed by faithlessness. And as surely—as irrevocably—as the fruit-bud falls before the east wind, so fails the power of the kindest human heart, if you meet it with poison.

JOHN RUSKIN (1819–1900)
Modern Painters

The sum total of Religion is to feel that, in its highest unity, everything that stirs our emotions is one in feeling; to feel that aught single and particular is only possible by means of this unity; to feel that our being and living is a being and living in and through God.

FRIEDRICH SCHLEIERMACHER (1768–1834)
On Religion

Deep strike thy roots, O heavenly vine
  Within our earthly sod,
Most human and yet most divine,
  The flower of man and God.

JOHN GREENLEAF WHITTIER (1807–1892)
Immortal Love, Forever Full

If it be true that Spirit is involved in Matter and apparent Nature is secret God, then the manifestation of the divine in himself and the realisation of God within and without are the highest and most legitimate aims possible to man upon earth.

SRI AUROBINDO (1872–1950)
The Life Divine

To look upon the world as undivine is a speculative aberration. God is not jealous of his own works. The world is an abyss of nothingness, if we take away its roots in the Divine.

SARVEPALLI RADHAKRISHNAN (1888–1975)
Fragments of a Confession

In the heart of all things, of whatever there is in the universe, dwells the Lord.

The Upanishads

There is but One God, whose name is True, the Creator, devoid of fear and enmity, immortal, unborn, self-existent, great and bountiful; The True One was in the beginning, the True One was in the primal age. The True One is, was, O Nanak, and the True One shall also be.

GURU NANAK (1469–1539)
The Japji

Nothing in this world is single;
  All things by a law divine
In one another's being mingle.

PERCY BYSSHE SHELLEY (1792–1822)
Love's Philosophy

Blessedness is to rest and remain in the One. Misery is to be dispersed into multiplicity and differentiation. Therefore the condition of becoming blessed is the withdrawal of our love from the Many back to the One.

JOHANN GOTTLIEB FICHTE (1762–1814)
The Guide to the Blessed Life

There is but one God, and they that serve Him should be one. There is nothing that would render the true religion more lovely, or make more proselytes to it, than to see the professors of it tied together with the heart-strings of love.

THOMAS WATSON (died 1686)
Sermons

Unity is, in truth, but Becoming-unity; it is—only as it becomes. And it becomes—only as unity of God. Only God is—nay, precisely only God becomes the unity which consummates everything.

FRANZ ROSENZWEIG (1886–1929)
Kleine Schriften

Say you: "We believe in God, and in that which has been sent down on us and sent down of Abraham, Ishmael, Isaac, and Jacob, and the Tribes, and that which was given to Moses and Jesus and the Prophets, of their Lords we make no division between any of them, and to Him we surrender."

The Koran

Our monistic God, the all-embracing essence of the world, the nature-god of Spinoza and Goethe, is identical with eternal, all-inspiring energy, and one, in eternal and infinite substance.

ERNST HAECKEL (1834–1919)
Der Kampf unden Entwicklungs Gedanken

God present is at once in every place,
Yet God in every place is ever one.

ROBERT SOUTHWELL (1561–1595)
Of the Blessed Sacrament of the Altar

In Mind, this is to be noted: there is no plurality here whatever; he who sees any plurality here is ensnared from death to death.   *The Upanishads*

After having exercised our powers to the full, and having given a charm and sacredness to our temporary life, we shall at last be for ever incorporated into the Supreme Being, of whose life all noble natures are necessarily partakers.

AUGUSTE COMTE (1798–1857)
System of Positive Polity

God's endeavor is to give himself to us entirely. Just as fire seeks to draw the wood into itself and itself into the wood, it first finds the wood unlike itself. It takes a little time. Fire begins by warming it, then heating it, and then it smokes and crackles because the two are so unlike each other. The hotter the wood becomes, the more still and quiet it grows. The more it is likened to the fire, the more peaceful it is, until it becomes entirely flame. That the wood be transformed into fire, all dissimilarity must be chased out of it.

MEISTER ECKHART (1260–1327)
Sermons

Every man has and has had from everlasting his true and perfect being in the Divine Consciousness.

ALFRED LORD TENNYSON (1809–1892)
Memoir

The unconsciousness of a man is the consciousness of God, the end of the world.

HENRY DAVID THOREAU (1817–1862)
Journals

The spirit of the worm beneath the sod
In love and worship, blends itself with God.

PERCY BYSSHE SHELLEY (1792–1822)
Epipsychidion

I have put duality away, I have seen that the two worlds are one;
One I seek, One I know; One I see, One I call.
He is the first, He is the last, He is the outward, He is the inward.

JALAL-UD-DIN RUMI (1207–1273)
The Diwan

Constantly think of the Universe as one living creature, embracing one being and one soul; how all is absorbed into the one consciousness of this living creature; how it compasses all things with a single purpose, and how all things work together to cause all that comes to pass, and their wonderful web and texture.

MARCUS AURELIUS (121–180)
Meditations

I believe in the absolute oneness of God and therefore also of humanity. What though we have many bodies? We have but one soul. The rays of the sun are many through refraction. But they have the same source.

MOHANDAS K. GANDHI (1869–1948)
Selected Addresses

That God, which ever lives and loves,
One God, one law, one element,
And one far-off divine event.
To which the whole creation moves.

ALFRED LORD TENNYSON (1809–1892)
In Memoriam

To us also, through every star,
through every blade of grass, is not a
God made visible, if we will open our
minds and eyes?

THOMAS CARLYLE (1795–1881)
On Heroes and Hero-Worship

Lord, I am like the mistletoe,
Which has no root and cannot grow
Or prosper, but by that same tree
It clings about: so I by Thee.

ROBERT HERRICK (1591–1674)
To God

Tumult and peace, the darkness and the
    light
Were all like workings of one mind, the
    features
Of the same face, blossoms upon one
    tree,
Characters of the great Apocalypse,
The types and symbols of Eternity,

Of first and last, and midst, and without
    end.

WILLIAM WORDSWORTH (1770–1850)
The Prelude

I saw no difference between God and
our substance, but as it were all God; and
yet mine understanding took it that our
substance is in God; that is to say, God is
God, and our substance is a creature of
God.   JULIAN OF NORWICH (1343–1416)
Revelations

We are united immediately and directly
to God. It is in the light of his wisdom that
he makes us see the magnificence of His
works, the model upon which He forms
them, the immutable art which regulates
their mechanism and movements, and it is
through the efficacy of His will that He
unites us to our body, and through our
body to all those in our environment.

NICOLAS MALEBRANCHE (1638–1715)
Investigation of Truth

· UNION WITH GOD ·

By his God thou knowest the man, and
by the man his God; the two are identical.
Whatever is God to a man, that is his heart
and soul; and conversely, God is the manifested inward nature, the expressed self
of a man—religion the solemn unveiling
of a man's hidden treasures, the revelation
of his intimate thoughts.

LUDWIG FEUERBACH (1804–1872)
The Essence of Christianity

The spiritually physical process of the
reinstatement of the image of God in material humanity cannot possibly happen of
itself, apart from us. Like all that is best in
this world it begins in the dark realm of
unconscious processes and relations; the

germ and the roots of the tree of life are
hidden there, but we must tend its growth
by our own conscious action.

VLADIMIR SOLOVIËV (1853–1900)
The Meaning of Love

There the soul unites with God, as food
with man, which turns in eye to eye, in ear
to ear; so does the soul in God turn into
God.   MEISTER ECKHART (1260–1327)
Works

We may not be God, but we are of God
even as a little drop of water is of the
ocean. Imagine it torn away from the
ocean and flung millions of miles away; it
becomes helpless, torn from its surround-
ings, and cannot feel the might and maj-

esty of the great ocean. But if someone could point out to it that it was of the ocean, its faith would revive, it would dance with joy and the whole might and majesty of the ocean would be reflected in it.

MOHANDAS K. GANDHI (1869–1948)
Harijan

You have subsisted as part of the Whole, and you shall vanish into that which begat you, or rather shall be taken again into its Seminal Reason by a process of change.

MARCUS AURELIUS (121–180)
Fragments

To unite the heart with Brahman and then to act: that is the secret of non-attached work. In the calm of self-surrender, the seers renounce the fruits of their actions, and so teach enlightenment.

The Bhagavad Gita

I call that mind free which escapes the bondage of matter, which, instead of stopping at the material universe and making it a prison wall, passes beyond to its Author, and finds in the radiant signatures which it everywhere bears of the Infinite Spirit, helps to its own spiritual enlargement.

WILLIAM ELLERY CHANNING (1780–1842)
Sermons

To be truly united in knowledge, love, and service with all beings, and thus to realise one's self in the all-pervading God is the essence of goodness, and this is the keynote of the teachings of the Upanishads: Life is immense!

RABINDRANATH TAGORE (1861–1941)
Creative Unity

Sometimes He opens the door of obedience for you, but not the door of acceptance; or sometimes He condemns you to

sin, and it turns out to be a cause for union with God. IBN 'ATA'ILLAH (died 1309)
The Book of Wisdom

He who is a seraph, that is a lover, is in God, and more, God is in him, and God and he are one.

GIOVANNI PICO DELLA MIRANDOLA (1463–1494)
On the Dignity of Man

We are not only the sons of God; so far as we are wise our lives are hid in God, we are in Him of Him.

JOSIAH ROYCE (1855–1916)
The Spirit of Modern Philosophy

The union of all seas, all tides, all beings, of man and God is ineffable. Yet the simplest person who lovingly and with integrity worships God, becomes God.

RALPH WALDO EMERSON (1803–1882)
Journal

Uncover the soul of its sensuality, selfishness, sin; there is nothing between it and God, who flows into man as light into air. THEODORE PARKER (1810–1860)
Discourses on Matters Pertaining to Religion

In our simple being, where we are one with God in His love, there begins a praeternatural contemplation and experience, the highest that man can express in words.

JAN VAN RUYSBROECK (1293–1381)
Sermons

The heart, once it becomes united to its God, if nothing divert it from this union, it sinks still deeper by an insensible progress of union, till it is wholly in God.

SAINT FRANCIS OF SALES (1567–1622)
Treatise

On this couch sits Brahman and he who knows himself one with Brahman, sitting on the couch, mounts it first with one foot only. Then Brahman says to him: "Who are thou?" and he shall answer: "I am like a season, and the child of the seasons, sprung from the womb of endless space, from the light, from the luminous Brahman. The light, the origin of the year, which is the past, which is the present, which is all living things, and all elements, is the Self. Thou art the Self. What thou art, that am I." Brahman says to him: "Who am I?" He shall answer: "That which is, the true."   *The Upanishads*

O my brothers, God exists. There is a soul at the center of nature, and over the will of every man, so that none of us can wrong the universe. It has so infused its strong enchantment into nature, that we prosper when we accept its advice; and when we struggle to wound its creatures, our hands are glued to our sides, or they beat our own breasts. The whole course of things goes to teach us faith.

RALPH WALDO EMERSON (1803–1882)
Spiritual Laws

God's Being is my life, but if it is so, then what is God's must be mine and what is mine God's. God's is-ness is my is-ness, and neither more nor less.

MEISTER ECKHART (1260–1327)
Sermons

Our union with a Being whose activity is world-wide and who dwells in the heart of humanity cannot be a passive one. In order to be united with Him we have to divest our work of selfishness and become *Visvakarma*, "the world-worker," we must work for all. In order to be one with this Mahatma, "the Great Soul," one must cultivate the greatness of soul which identifies itself with the soul of all peoples and not merely with that of one's own.

RABINDRANATH TAGORE (1861–1941)
The Religion of Man

All creatures seek after unity; all multiplicity struggles toward it—the universal aim of all life is always this unity. All that flows outward is to flow backward into its source—God.

JOHANNES TAULER (1300–1361)
Sermons

There is not a private meeting of three but God is a fourth in it, nor of five but he is a sixth, nor of a lower number than that, nor a higher, but he is with them wherever they may be.   *The Koran*

You can only apprehend the Infinite by a faculty superior to reason, by entering into a state in which you are your finite self no longer—in which the divine essence is communicated to you. This is ecstasy. It is the liberation of your mind from its finite consciousness. Like only can apprehend like; when you thus cease to be finite, you become one with the Infinite, In the reduction of your soul to its simplest self, its divine essence, you realise this union—this identity.

PLOTINUS (205–270)
Enneads

And let me know the living Father cares
For me, even me; for this one of his
    children.
Hast Thou no word for me? I am Thy
    thought.
God, let Thy mighty heart beat unto
    mine,
And let mine answer as a pulse of Thine.

GEORGE MACDONALD (1824–1905)
Within and Without

The mystery, and the unexpressed hope of God, lies in the union, in the genuine penetration of the spirit into the world of the soul, in a hallowing of the one through the other which should bring about a present humanity blessed with blessing from

heaven above and from the depths beneath.   THOMAS MANN (1875–1955)
Joseph and His Brothers

If then a man sees himself become one
with the One, he has in himself a likeness
of the One, and if he passes out of himself,
as an image to its archetype, he has
reached the end of his journey. And when
he comes down from his vision, he can
again awaken the virtue that is in him, and
seeing himself fitly adorned in every part
he can again mount upward through virtue to Spirit, and through wisdom to the
One itself.   PLOTINUS (205–270)
Enneads

To the masses, who could not conceive
of anything higher than a Personal God,
he said, "Pray to your Father in heaven."
To others, who could grasp a higher idea,
he said, "I am the vine and ye are the
branches." But to his disciples, to whom he
revealed himself more fully, he proclaimed the highest truth, "I and my Father are one."
SWAMI VIVEKANANDA (1863–1902)
Jnana-Yoga

All mysticism teaches that the depths of
man are more than human, that in them
lurks a mysterious contact with God and
with the world. The true escape from oneself, from one's self-imprisonment and
separation from the world, is hidden
within one's own self, rather than outside.
NIKOLAI BERDYAEV (1874–1948)
The Meaning of the Creative Act

As a hawk or an eagle having soared
high in the air, wings its way back to its
resting-place, being so far fatigued, so
does the soul, having experienced the phe-
nomenal, return into itself where it can
sleep beyond all desires, beyond all
dreams.   *The Upanishads*

If a drop of water, thrown into an ocean
of some priceless essence, were alive and
could speak and declare its condition,
would it not cry out with great joy: "O
mortals, I live indeed but I live not in myself, but this ocean lives in me and my life
is hidden in this abyss."
SAINT FRANCIS OF SALES (1567–1622)
The Love of God

He who flees from God, flees into himself. For there are two kinds of mind, the
mind of the universe, and that is God, and
the mind of the individual man. And the
one flees from his own mind to the mind
of the universe—for whoever leaves his
own mind, avows therewith that the works
of the mortal mind are as nothing, and
ascribes everything to God.
PHILO JUDAEUS (30 B.C.–A.D. 40)
Legum Sacrarum Allegoriarum Libri

To end that eternal conflict between our
self and the world, to restore the peace
that passeth all understanding, to unite
ourselves with nature so as to form one
endless whole—that is the goal of all our
striving.
FRIEDRICH HOLDERLIN (1770–1843)
Hyperion

Dead were God himself, if he moved his
world only from the outside, if he were a
"thing in himself" and not the One in all,
the Creator of all things visible and invisible, the beginning and the ending.
KARL BARTH (1886–1968)
The Word of God and the Word of Man

Whether we be young or old,
Our destiny, our being's heart and home,
Is with infinitude, and only there.
WILLIAM WORDSWORTH (1770–1850)
The Prelude

Men confess that He is infinite, yet they
start and object, as soon as His infinitude

comes in contact with their imagination and acts upon their reason. They cannot bear the fulness, the superabundance, the inexhaustible flowing forth, and "vehement rushing," and encompassing flood of the Divine attributes. They restrain and limit them by their own standard, they fashion them by their own model; and when they discern aught of the unfathomable depth, the immensity, of any single excellence or perfection of the Divine Nature, His love, or His justice, or His power, they are at once offended, and turn away, and refuse to believe.

JOHN CARDINAL NEWMAN (1801–1890)
Discourses to Mixed Congregations

God is Infinite; and to love the boundless, reaching on from grace to grace, adding charity to faith, and rising upwards ever to see the Ideal still above us—that is to love God.

FREDERICK WILLIAM ROBERTSON
(1816–1853)
Sermons

The decisive question for man is: Is he related to something infinite or not? That is the telling question of his life. Only if we know that the thing which truly matters is the infinite can we avoid fixing our interest upon futilities, and upon all kinds of goals which are not of real importance.

CARL JUNG (1875–1961)
Memories, Dreams, Reflections

If God is infinite today, and then should change and be infinite tomorrow, there would be two infinities. But that cannot be. Suppose he is infinite and then changes, he must become finite, and could not be God; either he is finite today and finite tomorrow, or infinite today and finite tomorrow, or finite today and infinite tomorrow—all of which suppositions are equally absurd. The fact of his being an infinite being at once quashes the thought of his being a changeable being. Infinity has written on its very brow the word "immutability."

CHARLES HADDON SPURGEON (1834–1892)
Sermons

That which is infinite is as much above what is great as it is above what is small. Thus God, being infinitely great, He is as much above kings as He is above beggars; He is as much above the highest angel as He is above the meanest worm.

JONATHAN EDWARDS (1703–1758)
Sermons

Every moment of life is fulfilled being, infinitely significant for its own sake, self-appointed and self-satisfied—an unlimited affirmation of itself; each moment drains the beaker of infinity, which like Oberon's magic cup is forever filled anew.

LUDWIG FEUERBACH (1804–1872)
Theogonie

The feeling of life endless, the great
  thought
By which we live, Infinity and God.

WILLIAM WORDSWORTH (1770–1850)
The Prelude

· THE ETERNAL BEING IS FOREVER ·

From the beginning of time, through
　　eternities
I was among his hidden treasures.
From Nothing he called me forth, but at
　　the end of time
I shall be reclaimed by the King.
　　　　　　　NAHMANIDES (1194–1270)
　　　　　　　Commentary on the Pentateuch

What is eternal? What escapes decay?
A certain faultless, matchless, deathless
　　line,
Curving consummate. Death, Eternity,
Add nought to it, from it take nought
　　away;
'Twas all God's gift and all man's mastery,
God become human and man grown
　　divine.
　　　　　　　ARTHUR O'SHAUGHNESSY (1844–1881)
　　　　　　　The Line of Beauty

The eternal Being is forever if he is at
all. 　　　　　BLAISE PASCAL (1623–1662)
　　　　　　　Pensées

He is eternal, He alone is eternal, He is
the eternal *per se*. In His mouth "I am" is
like "I shall be" and finds His explanation
only in it.
　　　　　　　FRANZ ROSENZWEIG (1886–1929)
　　　　　　　Kleinere Schriften

He who bends to himself a joy
Does the winged life destroy;
But he who kisses the joy as it flies
Lives in eternity's sunrise.
　　　　　　　WILLIAM BLAKE (1757–1827)
　　　　　　　Eternity

Nothing is there to come, and nothing
　　past,
But an eternal Now does always last.
　　　　　　　ABRAHAM COWLEY (1618–1667)
　　　　　　　Davideis

Thou, Lord, in the beginning hast laid
the foundation of the earth; and the heavens are the works of thine hands: They
shall perish; but Thou remainest; and they
all shall wax old as doth a garment; and
as a vesture shalt thou fold them up, and
they shall be changed: but thou art the
same and thy years shall not fail.
　　　　　　　The New Testament
　　　　　　　Hebrews 1:10–12

I dimly guess what Time in mists
　　confounds;
Yet ever and anon a trumpet sounds
From the hid battlements of Eternity.
　　　　　　　FRANCIS THOMPSON (1859–1907)
　　　　　　　The Hound of Heaven

Renewal befalls all creatures under
God; but for God there is no renewal, only
all eternity. What is eternity?—It is char-
acteristic of eternity that in it youth and
being are the same, for eternity would not
be eternal could it newly become and were
not always.
　　　　　　　MEISTER ECKHART (1260–1327)
　　　　　　　Sermons

Our noisy years seem moments in the
　　being
Of the eternal Silence.
　　　　　　　WILLIAM WORDSWORTH (1770–1850)
　　　　　　　Intimations of Immortality

Through the yawning fissures of human
rationality one glimpses the sky-blue of
Eternity.
　　　　　　　PAUL A. FLORENSKI (1882–1943)
　　　　　　　The Universally Human

He hath made everything beautiful in its time. Also He hath set eternity in their heart.
The Old Testament
Ecclesiastes 3:11

Eternity is Thine emanation. Thou Thyself art alone, but there are millions of powers of life in Thee to make thy creatures live. Buds burst into flower, the plants that grow on waste lands send up shoots at Thy rising.
IKHNATON (14th century B.C.)
Hymn of Praise

Until the life of men in time is, in every relation, shot through with Eternity, the Blessed Community is not complete.
THOMAS R. KELLY (1893–1941)
A Testament of Devotion

Like a drop of water from the sea and a grain of sand, so are a few years in the day of eternity. *The Old Testament Apocrypha*
Ecclesiasticus 18:10

It is contrary to true philosophy to affirm that the little flowers do not partake of eternity; although they wither away, they will nevertheless appear in the assembly of all the generations. And nothing has been created in the *mysterium magnum*, in God's great marvellous world, that will not also be represented in eternity.
PARACELSUS (1493–1541)
Intimatio Theophrasti

The world is a mirror of infinite Beauty, yet no man sees it. It is a Temple of Majesty, yet no man regards it. It is a region of Light and Peace, did not men disquiet it. It is the Paradise of God.
THOMAS TRAHERNE (1637–1674)
Centuries of Meditations

"God came down to see [the Tower of Babel]" (Genesis 11:5). But did He need to come down? Is not all patent and revealed to Him who "knoweth what is in the dark-

ness, and with whom light dwells" (Daniel 2:22)? The answer is that God did this to teach to mankind not to pass sentence, yea, not even to utter a single word, on hearsay, but to look with their own eyes.
The Midrash

We are actors in a great historical drama. It rests upon us to decide if a new era is to dawn in the transformation of the world into the kingdom of God, or if Western civilization is to descend to the graveyard of dead civilizations and God will have to try once more.
WALTER RAUSCHENBUSCH (1861–1918)
Christianity and the Social Crisis

The world is a great stage on which God displays His many wonders.
SAINT FRANCIS OF SALES (1567–1622)
Introduction to the Devout Life

The expression "God's world," may sound sentimental to some ears. For me it did not have this character at all. To "God's world" belonged everything superhuman—dazzling light, the darkness of the abyss, the cold impassivity of infinite space and time, and the uncanny grotesqueness of the irrational world of chance. CARL JUNG (1875–1961)
Memories, Dreams, Reflections

It is God's world still. It has been given to man not absolutely, but in trust, that man may work out in it the will of God; given—may we not say?—just as a father gives a child a corner of his great garden, and says, "There, that is yours; now cultivate it." PHILLIPS BROOKS (1835–1893)
Visions and Tasks

This visible World is wonderfully to be delighted in, and highly to be esteemed, because it is the theater of God's righteous Kingdom.
THOMAS TRAHERNE (1637–1674)
Centuries of Meditations

Slowly the Bible of the race is writ,
And not on paper leaves nor leaves of
stone;
Each age, each kindred, adds a verse to it,
Texts of despair or hope, of joy or moan.
JAMES RUSSELL LOWELL (1819–1891)
Bibliolatres

We have peace with God as soon as we
believe, but not always with ourselves. The
pardon may be past the prince's hand and
seal, and yet not put into the prisoner's
hand. WILLIAM GURNELL (1617–1679)
Sermons

There is nothing which God cannot ef-
fect.
MARCUS TULLIUS CICERO (106–43 B.C.)
De Natura Deorum

For the word of God is quick, and powerful, and sharper than any two-edged
sword, piercing even to the dividing asunder of soul and spirit.
The New Testament
Hebrews 4:12

God speaks all languages.
FRANZ ROSENZWEIG (1886–1929)
Letters

"Deep" in its spiritual use has two meanings: it means either the opposite of "shallow," or the opposite of "high." Truth is
deep and not shallow; suffering is depth
not height. The light of truth and the
darkness of suffering, both are deep.
There is a depth in God, and there is a
depth out of which the psalmist cries to
God. PAUL TILLICH (1886–1965)
The Shaking of the Foundations

To protect the righteous, to destroy the
wicked, and to establish the Kingdom of
God, I am re-born from age to age.
The Bhagavad Gita

And if we believe that God is everywhere, why should we not think Him present even in the coincidences that
sometimes seem so strange? For, if He be
in the things that coincide, He must be in
the coincidence of those things.
GEORGE MACDONALD (1824–1905)
Unspoken Sermons

The things which are impossible with
men are possible with God.
The New Testament
Luke 18:27

For thou hast been a strength to the
poor, a strength to the needy in his distress, a refuge from the storm, a shadow
from the heat, when the blast of the terrible ones is as a storm against the wall.
The Old Testament
Isaiah 25:4

"Thine is the kingdom, and the power,
and the glory, for ever and ever." This is a
wonderful gnomic saying summing up the
essential truth of the Omnipresence and
the Allness of God. It means that God is
indeed All in All, the doer, the doing, and
the deed, and one can also say the spectator. The Kingdom in this sense means all
creation, on every plane, for that is the
Presence of God—God as manifestation or
expression.
EMMET FOX (1886–1951)
Power Through Constructive Thinking

God's sovereignty is not in his right
hand; God's sovereignty is not in his intellect; God's sovereignty is in his love.
HENRY WARD BEECHER (1813–1887)
Sermons

There are four things God cannot do:
He cannot lie; He cannot die; He cannot
deny Himself; and He cannot look favor-
ably on sin. *Arab Proverb*

· SEEKING THE KINGDOM OF GOD ·

God sent us into the world to create something, and to enrich our own personality in the process. In our wrestling with intractable material, we have to draw on what is *above* ourselves. We have to rely on God's help to make anything worth making. And in the drawing upon this power above ourselves, we take this higher power *into* ourselves; we raise ourselves above ourselves. This is how creativeness and inner growth mutually condition each other.

WILLIAM RALPH INGE (1860–1954)
Personal Religion and the Life of Devotion

It would be an error to try to build the Kingdom of Heaven upon envy. For nothing that is founded on envy can thrive; it must have another root.

PARACELSUS (1493–1541)
Intimatio Theophrasti

Since God is in it, the Kingdom of God is always both present and future. Like God it is in all tenses, eternal in the midst of time.

WALTER RAUSCHENBUSCH (1861–1918)
A Theology for the Social Gospel

The kingdom of God for any soul is that condition, anywhere in the universe, where God is that soul's king, where it seeks and obeys the highest, where it loves truth and duty more than comfort and luxury.   PHILLIPS BROOKS (1835–1893)
Sermons

In the Kingdom of Heaven all is in all, all is one, and all is ours.

MEISTER ECKHART (1260–1327)
Sermons

In the Kingdom of God there are no claims, but only love, which, as something which cannot be coordinated into a given structure, knows no calculations. All claimfulness is overcome because it is realized that complete dependence and freedom, human dignity and divine grace, are not opposites as the autonomous self-centered man supposes.

EMIL BRUNNER (1889–1966)
Eternal Hope

The kingdom of God is our ultimate challenge and our ultimate hope. Thus, it is not surprising that Jesus found in it his central message. It remains for us to discover, to declare, and to live by all that is good and true in what the term implies.

GEORGIA HARKNESS (1891–1974)
Understanding the Kingdom of God

The kingdom of God is as a grain of mustard-seed:—we can sow of it; it is as a foam-globe of leaven:—we can mingle it; and its glory and its joy are that even the birds of the air can lodge in the branches thereof.   JOHN RUSKIN (1819–1900)
On the Old Road

The Kingdom of Heaven, which is within us as is the healing blood that pulses against the walls of our arteries, is also around us as the waves which beat against the shore. The influences of the transcendent God impinge upon us at every pore of the human spirit.

RALPH W. SOCKMAN (1889–1970)
The Highway of God

The kingdom of God must descend to earth: it is not the earth which must ascend to the kingdom of God, for this kingdom

must be a realm of the living and not of the dead. And this kingdom, whose coming we pray for every day, must be created, not only with prayer, but through struggle.   MIGUEL DE UNAMUNO (1864–1936)
The Life of Don Quixote and Sancho

In the Church of the Spirit the eternal Gospel will be read. When we draw near to the eternal Kingdom of the Spirit the torturing contradictions of life will be overcome and sufferings which towards the end will be increased, will pass into their antithesis, into joy.
NIKOLAI BERDYAEV (1874–1948)
Slavery and Freedom

Where God is not he never can be brought. The Kingdom of God is within you, says the truth. It does not come to him who looks for it outside himself.
JOHANNES DENCK (1495–1527)
Sermons

The kingdom of God is to come for all and the requirements of repentance, of a new way of thinking, of a new attitude to life, of doing God's will, of love, forgiveness, service, renunciation, are in principle the same for all.   HANS KÜNG (1928–)
On Being a Christian

The kingdom of God cometh not with observation; neither shall they say, Lo, here! or there, for, lo, the kingdom of God is within you.   *The New Testament*
Luke 17:20–21

The products of great creative minds prepare the way for the Kingdom of God, and enter into it. Greek tragedy, the pictures of Leonardo, Rembrandt, Botticelli; Michelangelo's sculpture and Shakespeare's dramas; the symphonies of Beethoven and the novels of Tolstoy;

the philosophical thought of Plato, Kant, and Hegel; the creative suffering of Pascal, Dostoevsky, and Nietzsche; the quest for freedom and for what is true and right in the life of society—all enter into the Kingdom of God.
NIKOLAI BERDYAEV (1874–1948)
The Beginning and the End

The kingdom of heaven is like unto a man that is a merchant seeking goodly pearls: and having found one pearl of great price, he went and sold all that he had, and bought it.   *The New Testament*
Matthew 13:45–46

We, having lived through, and still living in, a time of appalling and meaningless events, feel as if a terrible tidal wave had flung us back, far away from the harbor of the Kingdom of God, towards which we now have to start out afresh, rowing hard against storm and tide, without being certain of really making headway.
ALBERT SCHWEITZER (1875–1965)
Christianity and the Religions of the World

The overall purpose for which God created man was to set up a kingdom in which His righteous will would be freely done "on earth as it is in heaven"—a kingdom in which the earth would be beautified and dignified by its human managers instead of being scarred and uglified.
WALTER MARSHALL HORTON
(1895–1966)
The God We Trust

He alone enters the Kingdom of Heaven who is not a thief of his own thoughts. In other words, guilelessness and simple faith are the roads to that Kingdom.
SRI RAMAKRISHNA (1834–1886)
Sayings

"The kingdom of heaven is within you," says Jesus. So says Vedanta and every great teacher.

SWAMI VIVEKANANDA (1863–1902)
Jnana-Yoga

The kingdom of God means that He, the Father, the Brother, the Friend, is near, in the depths of the spirit, in the core of the heart; that love rules perceptibly in our goings and our comings, our dispensing and our receiving; that the whole of existence is transfigured by it, and that, while everything is transfigured into this one thing, the essential beauty and character of each blossoms forth.

ROMANO GUARDINI (1885–1968)
The Lord's Prayer

The Kingdom of God is the Sovereignty of Love, and the subordination of power to Love is the principle of that Kingdom.

WILLIAM TEMPLE (1881–1944)
The Hope of a New World

· HEAVEN HAS NO BEGINNING, NO END ·

God's in His Heaven—
All's right with the world!

ROBERT BROWNING (1812–1889)
Pippa Passes

There is a place beyond that flaming hill,
From whence the stars their thin
 appearance shed,
A place beyond all place, where never ill,
Nor impure thought was ever harbored.

GILES FLETCHER (1588–1623)
*Christ's Victory and Triumph
in Heaven and Earth*

Silently one by one, in the infinite
 meadows of heaven
Blossomed the lovely stars, the forget-me-
 nots of angels.

HENRY WADSWORTH LONGFELLOW
(1807–1882)
Evangeline

The kingdom of heaven is like treasure hidden in the field, which a man found and covered up; then in his joy he goes and sells all that he has and buys that field.

*The New Testament
Matthew 13:44*

Take all the pleasures of all spheres
And multiply each through endless
 years,—
One minute of heaven is worth them all.

THOMAS MOORE (1779–1852)
Lalla Rookh

I never spoke with God,
Nor visited in heaven;
Yet certain am I of the spot
As if the chart were given.

EMILY DICKINSON (1830–1886)
Lest This Be Heaven

I think
If through some chink in me could shine
But once—O, but one ray
From that all-hallowing and eternal day,
Asking no more of Heaven,
 I would go hence.

SIEGFRIED SASSOON (1886–1967)
Sequences

God never meant that man should scale
 the Heavens
By strides of human wisdom. In his
 works, though wondrous,

He commands us in his word to seek him
   rather where his mercy shines.
                    WILLIAM COWPER (1731–1800)
                                     The Task

Yes, Heaven is thine; but this
Is a world of sweets and sours;
Our flowers are merely—flowers,
And the shadow of thy perfect bliss
Is the sunshine of ours.
                    EDGAR ALLAN POE (1809–1849)
                                     Israfel

A mind enlightened is heaven; a mind
darkened is hell.   *Chinese Proverb*

Heaven is not a remote, transcendental
and unattainable sphere; it is a part of the
inmost depths of our spiritual life.
                    NIKOLAI BERDYAEV (1874–1948)
                                The Meaning of History

A man's heaven exists for him not outside of himself. If heaven is in him, then
will he be in heaven, wherever he may be.
Heaven is throughout the whole world
and outside of it; it is nothing but a manifestation of the Eternal One.
                    JACOB BOEHME (1575–1624)
                                 Supersensual Life

The Kingdom of Heaven cometh not by
observation. It comes by the appreciation
of the signs of the presence and power of
God in our inner experience.
                    EDGAR S. BRIGHTMAN (1884–1953)
                                     Is God a Person?

All places that the eye of heaven visits
Are to a wise man ports and happy
   havens.
                    WILLIAM SHAKESPEARE (1564–1616)
                                     Richard II

O never star
Was lost; here

We all aspire to heaven and there is
   heaven
Above us.
If I stoop
Into a dark tremendous sea of cloud,
It is but for a time; I press God's lamp
Close to my breast; its splendor soon or
   late
Will pierce the gloom. I shall emerge
   some day.
                    ROBERT BROWNING (1812–1889)
                                     Paracelsus

What does Heaven want and what does
it hate? Heaven wants men to love and be
profitable to each other, and does not want
men to hate and maltreat each other. How
do we know that Heaven wants men to
love and be profitable to each other? Because it embraces all in its love of them,
embraces all in its benefits to them.
                    MO-TZU (470–391 B.C.)
                                     The Mo-tzu

In heaven there is laid up a pattern of
it, methinks, which he who desires may behold, and beholding may set his own
house in order.   PLATO (427–347 B.C.)
                                     The Apology

Your enjoyment of the world is never
right, till every morning you awake in
Heaven; see yourself in your Father's Palace, and look upon the skies, the earth,
and the air as Celestial Joys.
                    THOMAS TRAHERNE (1637–1674)
                                Centuries of Meditations

As the flowing rivers in the ocean
Disappear, quitting name and form,
So the knower, being liberated from
   name and form,
Goes unto the heavenly Person, higher
   than the high.   *Mundaka Upanishad*

Above the battling rock-storm of this
   world

Lies heaven's great calm, through which
  as through a bell,
Tolleth the tongue of God eternally,
Calling to worship.
> PHILIP JAMES BAILEY (1816–1902)
> *Festus*

Revere the Maker; fetch thine eye
Up to his style, and manners of the sky.
Not of adamant and gold
Built he heaven stark and cold;
No, but a nest of bending reeds,
Flowering grass and scented weeds.
> RALPH WALDO EMERSON (1803–1882)
> *Threnody*

I can hardly think there was ever any scared into Heaven; they go the fairest way to Heaven that would serve God without a Hell; other Mercenaries, that crouch into Him in fear of Hell, though they term themselves the servants, are indeed but the slaves, of the Almighty.
> SIR THOMAS BROWNE (1605–1682)
> *Religio Medici*

A man may go to Heaven with half the pains which it costs him to purchase Hell.
> HENRY FIELDING (1707–1754)
> *Jonathan Wild*

For behold, I create news heavens and a new earth. Former things shall no more be remembered nor shall they be called to mind. Rejoice and be filled with delight, you boundless realms which I create.
> *The Old Testament*
> *Isaiah 65:17–18*

If God hath made this world so fair,
  Where sin and death abound,
How beautiful beyond compare
  Will paradise be found!
> JAMES MONTGOMERY (1771–1854)
> *The Earth Full of God's Goodness*

The world, well known, will give our
  hearts to Heaven,
Or make us demons, long before we die.
> EDWARD YOUNG (1683–1765)
> *Night Thoughts*

Let me enjoy the earth no less
Because the all-enacting Might
That fashioned forth its loveliness
Had other aims than my delight

And some day hence, towards Paradise
And all its blest—if such should be—
I will lift glad, afar-off eyes,
Though it contain no place for me.
> THOMAS HARDY (1840–1928)
> *Let Me Enjoy*

It is easier for a camel to pass through the eye of a needle, than for a rich man to enter into the kingdom of heaven.
> *The New Testament*
> *Matthew 19:24*

Heaven is my Father, Progenitor!
There is my origin.
> *The Rig-Veda*

In heaven is no war-fare, but all well-fare.
> JOHN BOYS (1571–1625)
> *Sermons*

There's heaven above, and night by night
I look right through its gorgeous roof.
> ROBERT BROWNING (1812–1889)
> *Johannes Agricola in Meditation*

Heaven does not choose its elect from among the great and wealthy.
> WILLIAM MAKEPEACE THACKERAY
> (1811–1863)
> *The Virginians*

· DEATH AND TRANSFIGURATION ·

At the round earth's imagin'd corners,
   blow
Your trumpets, angels, and arise, arise
From death, you numberless infinities
Of souls.

JOHN DONNE (1572–1631)
Holy Sonnets VII

For souls that of His own good life
   partake
He loves as His own self; dear as His eye
They are to Him. He'll never them
   forsake.
When they shall die, then God Himself
   shall die.
They live, they live in blest eternity.

BRONSON ALCOTT (1799–1888)
Orphic Sayings

In the life to be, there is neither envy
nor hatred, nor contention, but the righteous rejoice in the light of God's countenance.   *The Talmud*

O my heart, believe! nothing art thou
   losing.
What is yours remains, yes, remains
   forever,
All that was thy waiting, thy love, thy
   struggle.

GUSTAV MAHLER (1860–1911)
Chorale from the Resurrection Symphony

I stand under the golden canopy of
thine evening sky and I lift my eager eyes
to thy face. I have come to the brink of
eternity from which nothing can vanish—
no hope, no happiness, no vision of a face
seen through tears.

RABINDRANATH TAGORE (1861–1941)
Gitanjali

My rendezvous is appointed, it is certain,
The Lord will be there and wait till I
   come on perfect terms,
The great Camerado, the lover true for
   whom I pine will be there.

WALT WHITMAN (1819–1892)
Song of Myself

Thy dead men shall live, together with
my dead body shall they arise. Awake and
sing, ye that dwell in dust: for thy dew is
as the dew of herbs, and the earth shall
cast out the dead.   *The Old Testament*
                              Isaiah 26:19

All this earthy grossness quit,
Attired with stars we shall for ever sit,
Triumphing over Death, and Chance,
   and thee, O Time.

JOHN MILTON (1608–1674)
On Time

God knows in what part of the world
every grain of every man's dust lies. He
whispers, He hisses, He beckons for the
bodies of His saints, and in the twinkling
of an eye, that body that was scattered over
all the elements is sate down at the right
hand of God, in a glorious resurrection.

JOHN DONNE (1572–1631)
Sermons

When Earth's last picture is painted, and
   the tubes are twisted and dried,
When the oldest colours have faded, and
   the youngest critic has died,
We shall rest, and, faith, we shall need it
   —lie down for an aeon or two,
Till the Master of All Good Workmen
   shall put us to work anew.

RUDYARD KIPLING (1865–1936)
When Earth's Last Picture Is Painted

The dream that fires man's heart to
    make,
   To build, to do, to sing or say
A beauty Death can never take,
    An Adam from the crumbled clay.
                JOHN MASEFIELD (1878–1967)
                                Fragments

          So he gained
On earth a foretaste of Nirvana, not
The void of eastern dream, but the desire
And goal of all of us, whether through
    lives
Innumerable, by slow degrees, we near
The death divine, or from the breaking
    body
Of earthly death we flash at once to God.
                ALFRED NOYES (1880–1958)
                            Michael Oaktree

          Why shrinks the soul
Back on herself, and startles at
    destruction?
'Tis the divinity that stirs within us;
'Tis Heaven itself that points out an
    hereafter,
And intimates eternity to man.
Eternity! thou pleasing, dreadful
    thought!
                JOSEPH ADDISON (1672–1719)
                                     Cato

And many more, whose names on Earth
    are dark,
But whose transmitted effluence cannot
    die
So long as fire outlives the parent spark,
Rose, robed in dazzling immortality.
          PERCY BYSSHE SHELLEY (1792–1822)
                                  Adonais

I hope to see my Pilot face to face
When I have crossed the bar.
          ALFRED LORD TENNYSON (1809–1892)
                          Crossing the Bar

   The hand of Divine bounty proffereth
unto you the Water of Life. Hasten and
drink your fill. Whoso hath been reborn in
this Day, shall never die; whoso remaineth
dead, shall never live.
                BAHA'U'LLAH (1817–1892)
                            The Promised One

   Crossing this bridge, the blind cease to
be blind, the wounded to be wounded, the
afflicted to be afflicted, and on crossing
this bridge nights become days; forever re-
fulgent in the region of the Universal
Spirit.   *The Upanishads*

Our noisy years seem moments in the
    being
Of the eternal Silence: truths that wake,
To perish never.
          WILLIAM WORDSWORTH (1770–1850)
                  Intimations of Immortality

   The trumpet shall be heard on high
   The dead shall live, the living die
   And Music shall untune the sky!
                JOHN DRYDEN (1631–1700)
                  A Song for Saint Cecilia's Day

God keeps His holy mysteries
    Just on the outside of man's dream.
          ELIZABETH BARRETT BROWNING
                            (1806–1861)
                      Human Life's Mystery

   I awakened out of the body into myself
and came to be external to all other things
and contained within myself, when I saw a
marvelous beauty and was confident, then
if ever, that I belonged to the higher
order, when I actively enjoyed the noblest
form of life, when I had become one with
the Divine and stabilized myself in the Divine.   PLOTINUS (205–270)
                                 Enneads

   He commanded you in this world to reflect upon His creations; but in the Here-

after He will reveal to you the Perfection of his Essence.

IBN 'ATA'ILLAH (died 1309)
Kitab Al-Hakim

O knowing, glorious spirit! when
Thou shalt restore trees, beasts and men,

When thou shalt make all new again,
Destroying only death and pain,
Give him amongst thy works a place,
Who in them lov'd and sought thy face!

HENRY VAUGHAN (1622–1695)
The Book

· REVELATION OF THE DIVINE ·

In God there is a creative dynamic process which is accomplished in eternity. This must not be understood as meaning that God depends upon the world and the process that goes on in the world, but that the process which goes on in the world is inwardly linked with the process which goes on in God, in eternity not in time.

NIKOLAI BERDYAEV (1874–1948)
The Beginning and the End

Man uses many means to one end; God one means to many ends.

GUSTAV THEODOR FECHNER (1801–1887)
Life After Death

Every created thing is finite because all things are from Jehovah God through the sun of the spiritual world, which most nearly encompasses Him; and that sun is composed of the substance that has gone forth from Him, the essence of which is love.

EMANUEL SWEDENBORG (1688–1772)
The True Christian Religion

Those who have thus possessed the calm within can perceive always welling out from its silence the perennial supply of the energies which work in the universe.

SRI AUROBINDO (1872–1950)
The Life Divine

How can you expect God to speak in that gentle and inward voice which melts the soul, when you are making so much noise with your rapid reflections? Be silent and God will speak again.

FRANÇOIS FÉNELON (1651–1715)
Spiritual Letters

The first creature of God, in the works of the days, was the light of the sense: the last was the light of reason: and his sabbath work ever since is the illumination of his Spirit.

FRANCIS BACON (1561–1626)
Of Truth

The I of the revealing God, the I of the God Who accords to the mystic the intercourse with Him, and the I of God, in Whom the human I merges itself, are identical.

MARTIN BUBER (1878–1965)
Hasidism

Let him that glorieth glory in this: that he understands and knows Me, that I am the Eternal who exercises mercy, justice and righteousness on the earth.

The Old Testament
Jeremiah 9:32–33

Wisdom is the breath of the power of God, and a pure influence flowing from the glory of the Almighty; for she is the brightness of the everlasting light, the unspotted mirror of the power of God, and the image of his goodness. And in all ages entering into holy souls, she maketh them friends of God and prophets.

The Old Testament Apocrypha
The Wisdom of Solomon 7:25–27

The wisdom of this world is foolishness with God. *The New Testament*
1 Corinthians 3:19

The basis of all health, sinlessness, and immortality is the great fact that God is the only Mind; and this Mind must be not merely believed, but it must be understood. MARY BAKER EDDY (1821–1910)
Science and Health

There is surely a piece of divinity in us, something that was before the elements, and owes no homage unto the sun.

SIR THOMAS BROWNE (1605–1682)
Religio Medici

Only through the primal certainty of divine being can we come into contact with the mysterious meaning of divine becoming. MARTIN BUBER (1878–1965)
Talks on Judaism

Think you, 'mid all this mighty sum
Of things forever speaking,
That nothing of itself will come
But we must still be seeking?
WILLIAM WORDSWORTH (1770–1850)
Expostulation and Reply

Fear God, and where you go, men shall think they walk in hallowed cathedrals. And so I look on those sentiments which make the glory of the human being, love, humility, faith, as being also the intimacy of Divinity in the atoms.

RALPH WALDO EMERSON (1803–1882)
Worship

Follow you the star that lights a desert pathway, yours or mine. Forward, till you see the Highest Human Nature is divine.

ALFRED LORD TENNYSON (1809–1892)
Locksley Hall Sixty Years After

The divine in man is our sole ground for believing that there is anything divine in the universe outside of man. Man is the revealer of the divine.

FELIX ADLER (1851–1933)
Sermons

Let none turn over books or scan the stars in quest of God who sees Him not in man.

JOHANN KASPAR LAVATER (1741–1801)
Aphorisms on Man

If the eye were not by nature solar,
How should we be able to look at the light?
If God's own power did not live in us,
How would the divine be able to carry us off in ecstasy?
JOHANN WOLFGANG VON GOETHE
(1749–1832)
Farbenlehre

But 'tis God
Diffused through all, that doth make all one whole.
SAMUEL TAYLOR COLERIDGE (1772–1834)
Religious Musings

Some may ask what it is like to be a partaker of the Divine Nature? Answer: he who is imbued with or illuminated by the Eternal or Divine Light and inflamed and consumed with Eternal or Divine Love, he is a deified man and a partaker of the Divine Nature. *Theologia Germanica*

God is the indwelling not the transient cause of all things.

BENEDICT SPINOZA (1632–1677)
Ethics

Supreme Bliss comes to the yogi whose mind is completely tranquil and whose passions are quieted, who is free from stain and who has become one with Brahman. *The Upanishads*

Life is the sacred spark of God in us, and the best of our race have reverenced it most.

WALTER RAUSCHENBUSCH (1861–1918)
Christianizing the Social Order

All things
Are of one pattern made; bird, beast, and
plant,
Song, picture, form, space, thought, and
character,
Deceive us, seeming to be many things,
And are but one.

RALPH WALDO EMERSON (1803–1882)
Xenophanes

When I thus rest in the silence of contemplation, Thou, Lord, makest reply within my heart, saying: Be thou mine and I too will be thine; Thou, Lord, canst not be mine if I be not mine own.

NICHOLAS OF CUSA (1401–1464)
The Vision of God

There is an indefinable, mysterious power that pervades everything. I feel it though I do not see it. It is this Unseen Power which makes itself felt and yet defies all proof because it is so unlike all that I perceive through my senses.

MOHANDAS K. GANDHI (1869–1948)
Young India

God is not external to anyone, but is present with all things, though they are ignorant that He is so.

PLOTINUS (205–270)
Enneads

God as being-itself transcends nonbeing absolutely. On the other hand, God as creative life includes the finite and, with it, nonbeing, although nonbeing is eternally conquered and the finite is eternally reunited within the infinity of the divine life. The certainty of God's directing creativity is based on the certainty of God as the ground of being and meaning. The confidence of every creature, its courage to be, is rooted in faith in God as its creative ground.

PAUL TILLICH (1886–1965)
Systematic Theology

When Moses heard his doom, he urged every argument to secure a remission of his sentence. Amongst other things he said, "Sovereign of the universe, arise from the judgment seat, and sit on the throne of mercy, so that I die not. Let my sins be forgiven by reason of bodily sufferings which may come upon me. But put me not in the power of the angel of death. If thou wilt do this, then will I proclaim thy praise before all the inhabitants of the world, as David said I shall not die, but live, and declare the works of the Lord" (Psalms 118:17). Then God said to Moses, "Hear the rest of the verse, This is the gate of the Lord, through which the righteous shall enter." For all creatures death has been prepared from the beginning.

The Mishnah

Whenever spirituality decays and materialism is rampant, then, O Arjuna, I reincarnate myself. To protect the righteous, to destroy the wicked, and to establish the Kingdom of God, I am reborn from age to age. The ignorant think of Me, who am the Unmanifested Spirit, as if I were really in human form. They do not understand that my Supreme Nature is changeless and most excellent. *The Bhagavad Gita*

Fear not the future, but the present. God orders us to take care of the present. Whoever is darkened by dread of the future has already renounced the sacred power. Whoever is with God sees the light before him and in the present is the creator of a brilliant future.

NIKOLAI GOGOL (1809–1852)
To a Myopic Friend

If you see a man unterrified in the midst of dangers, untouched by desires, happy in adversity, peaceful amid the storm, will you not say: A divine power has descended upon that man?

LUCIUS ANNAEUS SENECA (4 B.C.–A.D. 65)
The End of Being

The contemplation of the pious is the immediate consciousness of the universal existence of all finite things, in and through the Infinite, and of all temporal things in and through the Eternal.

FRIEDRICH SCHLEIERMACHER (1768–1834)
On Religion

Everything that lives is holy.

WILLIAM BLAKE (1757–1827)
The Marriage of Heaven and Hell

Divine am I inside and out, and I make holy whatever I touch or am touch'd from.

WALT WHITMAN (1819–1892)
Song of Myself

A sense of the goodness of God is for us the true teacher of that piety from which religion takes its birth. What I call piety is a love united with reverence, produced in us by the recognition of His benefits.

JOHN CALVIN (1509–1564)
Institutes of the Christian Religion

Each moment holy is, for out from God
Each moment flashes forth a human soul.
Holy each moment is, for back to him
Some wandering soul each moment home
    returns.

RICHARD WATSON GILDER (1844–1909)
The Great Remembrance

Holiness is of a twofold nature; it begins as a quality of the service rendered to God, but it ends as a reward for such service. It is at first a type of spiritual effort, and then a kind of spiritual gift.

MOSES LUZZATTO (1707–1747)
The Way of the Upright

· YET WILL I TRUST ·

Put all your trust in the Lord and do not rely on your own understanding. Think of Him in all your ways, and he will smooth your path. Do not think how wise you are, but fear the Lord and turn from evil. Let that be the medicine to keep you in health, the liniment for your limbs.

The Old Testament
Proverbs 3:5–8

It is the assurance that God is fulfilling us individually as well as Himself, and fulfilling us for ourselves as well as for Himself, that makes human life in this bittersweet world endurable by the sensitively and delicately minded, the tender-hearted believer. It is because a being of the earth,

yet so God-like as man, could not be moulded into the image of God save from within himself, as a person or a free agent, that man can account the payment of the sometimes exorbitant price of learning love inevitable.

F. R. TENNANT (1866–1957)
Philosophical Theology

Take short views, hope for the best, and trust in God.

SYDNEY SMITH (1771–1845)
Lady Holland's Memoir

All I have seen teaches me to trust the Creator for all I have not seen. Whatever it be which the great Providence prepares for us, it must be something large and generous, and in the great style of his works. The future must be up to the style of our faculties,—of memory, of hope, of imagination, of reason.

RALPH WALDO EMERSON (1803–1882)
Letters and Social Aims

In God the word does not differ from the intention, for He is true; nor the word from the effect, for He is powerful; nor the means from the effect, for He is wise.

BLAISE PASCAL (1623–1662)
Pensées

I am sustained by a sense of the worthwhileness of what I am doing; a trust in the good faith of the process which created and sustains me. That process I call God.

UPTON SINCLAIR (1878–1968)
What God Means to Me

For him who puts his trust in Him, God will be all-sufficient. Truly God will attain His purpose.   *The Koran*

In God have I put my trust. I will not be afraid what man can do unto me.

The Old Testament
Psalms 56:11

Only that which is apart from my own being is capable of being doubted by me. How then can I doubt of God, who is my being? To doubt of God is to doubt myself.

LUDWIG FEUERBACH (1804–1872)
The Essence of Christianity

No one can show God greater disrespect than not to trust Him. By lack of reverence and faith, the soul holds Him to be incompetent, deceptive, and shallow, and, as far as she is concerned, she disclaims Him by such unbelief.

MARTIN LUTHER (1483–1546)
The Freedom of a Christian

If all the world were on our side, and God against us, what could the world avail us? Therefore let us set our whole faith and trust in God, and neither the world, the devil, nor all the power of them, shall prevail against us.

THOMAS CRANMER (1489–1556)
Miscellaneous Writings and Letters

Shall not the heart which has received so much, trust the Power by which it lives? May it not quit other leadings, and listen to the Soul that has guided it so gently, and taught it so much, secure that the future will be worthy of the past?

RALPH WALDO EMERSON (1803–1882)
Works

We sleep in peace in the arms of God, when we yield ourselves up to His providence, in a delightful consciousness of His tender mercies; no more restless uncertainties, no more anxious desires, no more impatience at the place we are in; for it is God who has put us there, and who holds us in His arms. Can we be unsafe where He has placed us?

FRANÇOIS FÉNELON (1651–1715)
Maximes des Saints

The Lord is thy keeper; the Lord is the shade upon thy right hand. The sun shall not smite thee by day, nor the moon by night. The Lord shall keep thee from all evil.   *The Old Testament*
Psalms 121:5–7

Belief in God is belief in the highest Truth and Right, exalted above the wrongness of the world. But this Truth demands the creative participation of man and the world. It is divine-human; in it the ideal humanity operates.

NIKOLAI BERDYAEV (1874–1948)
The Beginning and the End

God knows the truth, and lets it rest there.

MIGUEL DE CERVANTES (1547–1616)
Don Quixote

If God were to hold out enclosed in His right hand all Truth, and in His left hand just the active search for Truth, though with the condition that I should ever err therein, and should say to me: Choose! I should humbly take His left hand and say: Father! Give me this one; absolute Truth belongs to Thee alone.

GOTTHOLD EPHRAIM LESSING (1729–1781)
Wolfenbuttler Fragmente

Before Time itself there was truth.
When time began to run its course He
  was the truth.
Even now, He is the truth.
Evermore shall Truth prevail.

GURU NANAK (1469–1539)
The Adi Granth

Let reason be encouraged by the senses to seek for the truth, and draw its first principles from thence. Even the all-embracing universe and God who is its guide extends Himself forth into outward things, and yet altogether returns from all sides back to Himself. Let our minds do the same thing.

LUCIUS ANNAEUS SENECA (4 B.C.–A.D. 65)
Essays

I trust in nature for the stable laws
Of beauty and utility.—Spring shall plant,
And Autumn garner to the end of time:
I trust in God—the right shall be the
  right
And other than the wrong, while he
  endures:
I trust in my own soul, that can perceive

The outward and the inward—Nature's
  good
And God's.

ROBERT BROWNING (1812–1889)
A Soul's Tragedy

Wait on the Lord: be of good courage, and he shall strengthen thine heart: wait, I say, on the Lord.   *The Old Testament*
Psalms 27:14

Trust the soul that dwells in every soul,
Into one brave friendship let men enter;
All the stars and planets as they roll
Find in one great sun their common
  centre.

WATHEN MARK WILKS CALL (1817–1890)
Romantic Poems

The more miserable we know ourselves to be, the more occasion we have to confide in God, since we have nothing in ourselves in which to confide.

SAINT FRANCIS OF SALES (1567–1622)
Consoling Thoughts

If our heart condemn us, God is greater than our heart, and knoweth all things. Beloved, if our heart condemn us not, then have we confidence toward God.

The New Testament
1 John 3:20–21

"To have a God means that I trust him with my whole heart"—so says Luther. The definition of a "God" would therefore not be "a highest Spirit," "a supermundane Being," not any other ontological thing, but "the absolutely trustworthy Being."   RUDOLF OTTO (1869–1937)
India's Religion of Grace

There is nothing to test the perfection of love better than trust. Wholehearted love for another person carries confidence with it. Whatever one dares to trust God for, he really finds in God and a thousand times more.

MEISTER ECKHART (1260–1327)
Sermons

Blessed is the man who trusts in the Lord, whose hope is in the Lord. He is like a tree planted beside the waters that stretches out its roots to the stream; it fears not the heat when it comes, its leaves stay green; in the year of drought it shows no distress, but still bears fruit.

The Old Testament
Jeremiah 17:7–8

One who does not believe in God will not believe in God's people. He who believes in God's people will see His Holiness too, even though he had not believed in it till then.

FYODOR DOSTOEVSKY (1821–1881)
The Brothers Karamazov

Cast all your cares on God; that anchor holds.

ALFRED LORD TENNYSON (1809–1892)
Enoch Arden

We shall fall into the hands of the Lord, and not into the hands of men: for as his majesty is, so is his mercy.

The Old Testament Apocrypha
Ecclesiasticus 2:18

O Light divine! we need no further test
   That all is ordered well;
We know enough to trust that all is best
   Where love and wisdom dwell.

CHRISTOPHER PEARSE CRANCH (1813–1892)
Compensation

Trust in God is greater than the magical power of the alchemist who creates treasures of gold by his art; for he alone who confides in God is independent and satisfied with what he has, and enjoys rest and peace without envying anyone.

BAHYA IBN PAKUDA (11th century)
The Duties of the Heart

For the calamities of mortal life
Exists—one only—an assured belief
That the procession of our fate, however
Sad or disturbed, is ordered by a Being
Of infinite benevolence and power,
Whose everlasting purposes embrace
All accidents, converting them to good.

WILLIAM WORDSWORTH (1770–1850)
The Excursion

In a virtuous action, I properly *am;* in a virtuous act I add to the world; I plant into deserts conquered from Chaos and Nothing, and see the darkness receding on the limits of the horizon.

RALPH WALDO EMERSON (1803–1882)
Compensation

We properly know what is Good and what is Evil; and may be as certain in morals as in mathematics.

THOMAS FULLER (1654–1734)
Gnomologia

Many a man acquainted with the higher branches of mathematics is not able to do a plain sum in the Gospel arithmetic: "What shall it profit a man if he gain the whole world and lose his soul?"

THOMAS DE WITT TALMAGE (1832–1902)
Sermons

Are we not, all of us, God's ministers on earth and the arms by which His justice is done? And if we could convince ourselves of this truth, would that not be the true way to purify and ennoble our actions?

MIGUEL DE UNAMUNO (1864–1936)
The Life of Don Quixote and Sancho

Trust in God's mercies, and His kindness will encompass you. Fear God's punishments, and His strict judgment will surround you. Wherever your mind abides, you will find yourself cleaving unto it. Serve the Lord in love and in complete trust, and you will receive his mercies.

BAAL SHEM TOV (1700–1760)
Sayings

The person who has a firm trust in the Supreme Being is powerful in his power, wise by his wisdom, happy by his happiness. JOSEPH ADDISON (1672–1719)
The Spectator

I stretch lame hands of faith, and grope,
  And gather dust and chaff, and call
  To what I feel is Lord of all,
And faintly trust the larger hope.

ALFRED LORD TENNYSON (1809–1892)
In Memoriam

Here in the maddening maze of things,
When tossed by storm and flood,
To one fixed ground my spirit clings:
I know that God is good.

JOHN GREENLEAF WHITTIER (1807–1892)
Hymn

Even as David says, in Psalm XXXIV, "O taste and see that the Lord is sweet: blessed is the man who trusts in Him." He puts tasting before seeing, because this sweetness cannot be known unless one has experienced and felt it for oneself; and no one can attain to such experience unless he trusts in God with his whole heart, when he is in the depths and in sore straits.

MARTIN LUTHER (1483–1546)
The Magnificat

Though he slay me, yet will I trust in him: but I will maintain mine own ways before him. He also shall be my salvation: for a hypocrite shall not come before him.

The Old Testament
Job 13:15–16

Whatever a man fears may happen to him is only a matter of probability—either it will happen or it will not happen. And just as it is possible that something painful, worrisome and fearful may happen, it is also possible that, because of his reliance on God, the reverse of what he feared may happen. MAIMONIDES (1135–1204)
Preservation of Youth

I, who saw Power, see now Love perfect too:
Perfect I call Thy plan:
Thanks that I was a Man!
Maker, remake, complete,—I trust what Thou shalt do!

ROBERT BROWNING (1812–1889)
Rabbi Ben Ezra

Whoever says when clouds are in the sky,
"Be patient, heart, light breaketh by and by,"
Trusts the Most High.

EDWARD BULWER-LYTTON (1803–1873)
Faith

· GOD WALKS WITH THE HUMBLE ·

God walks with the humble; he reveals himself to the lowly; he gives understanding to the little ones; he discloses his meaning to pure minds, but hides his grace from the curious and proud.

THOMAS À KEMPIS (1380–1471)
The Imitation of Christ

I am overwhelmed by his kindness, I bless him and his gifts, but I do not pray to him. What should I ask of him—to change the order of nature, to work miracles on my behalf? Should I, who am bound to love above all things the order which he has established in his wisdom and maintained by his providence, should I desire the disturbance of that order on my own account?

> JEAN JACQUES ROUSSEAU (1712–1778)
> *Emile*

Humility stems from the inner recognition made in the true Light that being, life, knowledge, wisdom, and power are truly rooted in God, not in the created world.

> *Theologia Germanica*

The voice of humility is God's music and the silence of humility is God's rhetoric.

> FRANCIS QUARLES (1592–1644)
> *Emblems*

You should practise humility first toward man, and only then toward God. He who despises men has no respect for God.

> PARACELSUS (1493–1541)
> *Works*

It is my humility that gives God his divinity and the proof of it is this. God's peculiar property is giving. But God cannot give if he has nothing to receive his gifts. Since I make myself receptive to his gifts by my humility so I by my humility do make God giver and since giving is God's own peculiar property I do by my humility give God his property.

> MEISTER ECKHART (1260–1327)
> *Sermons*

Prayer needs no speech. It is itself independent of any sensuous effort. I have not the slightest doubt that prayer is an unfailing means of cleansing the heart of passions. But it must be combined with utmost humility.

> MOHANDAS K. GANDHI (1869–1948)
> *Young India*

I dwell in the high and holy place and also with him who is of a contrite and humble spirit, to revive the spirit of the humble and to revive the heart of the contrite.

> *The Old Testament*
> *Isaiah 57:15*

Rabbi Aba said in the name of Rabbi Alexandri: "He who hears himself cursed, and is able to stop the curser, yet remains silent, he makes himself a partner with God. Does not God hear how the nations blaspheme Him, yet remain silent?"

> *The Midrash*

Reverence for the Eternal trains men to be wise. And to be humble is the way to honor.

> *The Old Testament*
> *Proverbs 15:33*

The man who knows God is the most exalted of the exalted; yet his mind is the most humble of all.

> GURU ARJAN (1563–1606)
> *Hymns*

The last words of Luther after his great Christian life were not: "Look, Lord, how much I have progressed in love for you. For your sake I have known the greatest distress of conscience, the deepest loneliness and supreme achievement. Now you must open heaven to me." Luther did not speak in such terms. His last words were simply: "We are beggars, that is true."

> HELMUT THIELICKE (1908–)
> *The Silence of God*

Humility is the fittest glass of the Divine Greatness, and the fittest Womb for the conception of all felicity; for it hath a double heaven. It is the way to full and perfect sublimity.

> THOMAS TRAHERNE (1637–1674)
> *Christian Ethics*

As God is incapable of any envy, so he is incapable of wantonness. Having no "worlds to conquer," no possible "ambition" (if one may so speak), he can, as we have already seen, go only one way, the way of self-diminishment, which is the way of love. So he comes in meekness because he *is* meek, in humility because he *is* humble. Yet that meekness, that humility, is the greatest possible moral splendor and the greatest of all power.

GEDDES MACGREGOR (1909–)
He Who Lets Us Be

Humility is the most excellent natural cure for anger in the world, for he, that by daily considering his own infirmities and failings, makes the error of his servant or neighbor to be his own case, and remembers that he daily needs God's pardon and his brother's charity, will not be apt to rage at the levities, or misfortunes, or indiscretions of another.

JEREMY TAYLOR (1613–1667)
Sermons

God is not to be the valet for my private wishes; he is not to disrupt for human ends the order of Nature established by him from the foundation of the world.

WILLIAM ERNEST HOCKING (1873–1966)
Science and the Idea of God

It is God's nature to give; and He lives and moves that He may give unto us when we are humble. If we are not lowly, and yet desire to receive, we do Him violence, and kill Him, so to speak; and though we may not wish to do this, yet we do it as far as in us lies. That thou mayest truly give Him all things, see to it that thou castest thyself in deep humility at the feet of God, and beneath all created things.

JOHANNES TAULER (1300–1361)
The Inner Way

The humble soul is a temple of God, a seat of wisdom, a throne of the word, a house of the consoler, a room of the Bridegroom, the receiver of the covenant, a golden throne of grace, a tabernacle of holiness, a place of holy peace, a paradise of pleasure, a closed garden, a sealed fountain, a heavenly dwelling place.

JOHANN ARNDT (1555–1621)
True Christianity

He who knows himself to be insignificant, even among the uncultured and the ignorant, who lives in darkness, shall have the Divine Light dwell within him.

BAAL SHEM TOV (1700–1760)
Sayings

A man needs to have faith in himself and believe that he is beloved in the eyes of God. Feeling unimportant and distant from God is not humility, and a person should always ask God to be worthy of true humility.

RABBI NAHMAN OF BRATZLAV (1772–1811)
Likkute Mahoran

If you constantly accustom yourself to the way of modesty, that you feel humility before every man, and fear God and fear sin, then the Divine Presence will rest upon you with the light of its splendor, and you will live the life in the coming world.

NAHMANIDES (1195–1270)
Letter to His Son

Humility did not cast down the individual, it raised him up. As it obliged him to respect the presence of God in others, so it obliged him to respect the presence of God in himself, to make himself the messenger of God or the path taken by God.

ANTOINE DE SAINT-EXUPÉRY (1900–1945)
Flight to Arras

Many who pray for humility would be extremely sorry if God were to grant it to them. They forget that to love, desire, and ask for humility is loving, desiring, and asking for humiliations, for these are the companions, or rather the food of humility, and without them it is no more than a beautiful but meaningless idea.

JEAN NICHOLAS GROU (1730–1803)
The School of Jesus Christ

I see clearly that God reserved for Himself those who serve him in secret. For He said to Elias: I love the unknown adorers in the world.

BLAISE PASCAL (1623–1662)
Pensées

He that is in obscurity will lead a private life without discontent so as not to desert the station in which God has placed him. It will be no small alleviation of his cares, labors, troubles, and other burdens, when a man knows that in all these things he has God for his guide.

JOHN CALVIN (1509–1564)
Institutes of the Christian Religion

The man who considers all beings as existing even in the Supreme Spirit, and the Supreme Spirit as pervading all beings, henceforth views no creature with contempt.   *The Upanishads*

Being beautiful one should not be charmed by it: it is the light of the Lord, that shines in all bodies.   *The Adi Granth*

Dost thou wish to rise? Begin by descending. You plan a tower that shall pierce the clouds? Lay first the foundations on humility.

SAINT AUGUSTINE (354–430)
Sermons

The Lord will happiness divine
On contrite hearts bestow;
Then tell me, gracious God, is mine
A contrite heart, or no?

WILLIAM COWPER (1731–1800)
A Contrite Heart

And be clothed with humility: for God resisteth the proud, and giveth grace to the humble. Humble yourselves therefore under the mighty hand of God, that he may exalt you in due time.

The New Testament
1 Peter 5:5–6

Be modest and circumspect. Regard in silence what cannot be either disproved or comprehended, and humble thyself before the Supreme Being who alone knoweth the truth.

JEAN JACQUES ROUSSEAU (1712–1778)
Emile

I thought I could become wise, but it is much beyond me. Far away is all that has come into being and very, very deep; who can find it? With all my heart I turned to learn, explore and seek after wisdom and thought, and I saw that wickedness is foolishness, and folly is madness.

The Old Testament
Ecclesiastes 7:24–25

The sacrifices of God are a broken spirit: a broken and a contrite heart, O God, thou wilt not despise.

The Old Testament
Psalms 51:17

· TIME CANNOT BEND THE LINE ·

The invisible things of Him from the creation of the world are clearly seen, being understood of the things that are made.   *The New Testament*
Romans 1:20

Our conception of God must make meaningful the far-flung galaxies in space and time which science has revealed to us, if the soul is not to despair in loneliness under the stars. But our conception of

God must also give inspiration and reality to our ideal creativeness in the social crisis in which we live.

JOHN ELOF BOODIN (1869–1950)
God: A Cosmic Philosophy of Religion

God is the perfect poet,
Who in his person acts his own creations.

ROBERT BROWNING (1812–1889)
Paracelsus

And the Maker infinite,
Whose poem is Time,
He need not weave in it
A forced stale rhyme.

ABU-AL-ALA AL-MA'ARRI (973–1057)
Meditations

A day in the mind of God is like a millennium in the reckoning of man.

The Old Testament
Psalms 90:4

Nothing is void of God; He Himself fills His work.

LUCIUS ANNAEUS SENECA (4 B.C.–A.D. 65)
De Beneficiis

The Infinite Being is not complete if He remains absolutely infinite. He must realize Himself through the finite; that is, through creation. The impulse to realize comes from the fullness of joy; but the process must be through pain. You cannot ask why it should be—why the Infinite should attain truth by passing through the finitude; why the joy should be the cause of suffering, in order to come back to itself —for it is so. And when our minds are illumined, we feel glad that it is so.

RABINDRANATH TAGORE (1861–1941)
Letters to a Friend

Time cannot bend the line which God has writ.

HENRY DAVID THOREAU (1817–1862)
Inspiration

God created man in his own image and likeness, i.e., made him a creator too, calling him to free spontaneous activity and not to formal obedience to His power. Free creativeness is the creature's answer to the great call of its creator. Man's creative work is the fulfilment of the Creator's secret will.

NIKOLAI BERDYAEV (1874–1948)
The Destiny of Man

God never leaves off making, but even as it is the property of fire to burn and of snow to chill, so it is the property of God to make: nay, more so by far, since he is to all besides the source of action.

PHILO JUDAEUS (30 B.C.–A.D. 40)
Allegories of the Sacred Laws

In God there is a creative dynamic process which is accomplished in eternity. This must not be understood as meaning that God depends upon the world and the process that goes on in the world, but that the process which goes on in the world is inwardly linked with the process which goes on in God, in eternity not in time.

NIKOLAI BERDYAEV (1874–1948)
The Beginning and the End

Every created thing is finite because all things are from Jehovah God through the sun of the spiritual world, which most nearly encompasses Him; and that sun is composed of the substance that has gone forth from Him, the essence of which is love.

EMANUEL SWEDENBORG (1688–1772)
The True Christian Religion

Not as man's capacity is God's capacity. A man cannot say two words at one and the same moment, but God said all the Ten Commandments at one and the same moment. Man cannot hearken to two people who cry before him together, but God can hearken to all the inhabitants of the world if they cry before Him simultaneously, as it is said, "O thou that hearest prayer, unto thee does all flesh come" (Psalms 65:2). *The Talmud*

If in carnal wealth, how much more in spiritual does God love a cheerful giver.

SAINT AUGUSTINE (354–430)
Of the Catechizing of the Unlearned

God plays and laughs in good deeds, whereas all other deeds, which do not make for the glory of God, are like ashes before Him.

MEISTER ECKHART (1260–1327)
Sermons

What am I? I am myself a word spoken by God. Can God speak a word that does not have any meaning? Yet, am I sure that the meaning of my life is the meaning God intends for it? Does God impose a meaning on my life from the outside, through event, custom, routine, law, system, impact with others in society? Or am I called to create from within, with him, with his grace, a meaning which reflects his truth and makes me his "word" spoken freely in my personal situation? My true identity lies hidden in God's call to my freedom and my response to him.

THOMAS MERTON (1915–1968)
Contemplative Prayer

· ALL SENTIENT BEINGS ARE HOLY ·

To say we love God as unseen, and at the same time exercise cruelty toward the least creature moving by His life, or by life derived from Him, was a contradiction in itself. JOHN WOOLMAN (1720–1772)
Journal

I want to realise brotherhood or identity not merely with the beings called human, but with all life, even with such things as crawl upon earth. I want to realise identity with even the crawling things upon earth, because we claim descent from the same God, and that being so, all life in whatever form it appears must be essentially one.

MOHANDAS K. GANDHI (1869–1948)
Works

So did the Lord try Moses. While keeping the flock of his father-in-law in the wilderness a lamb left the flock and ran away. The merciful shepherd pursued it, and found it quenching its thirst at a spring by the roadside. "Poor lamb," said Moses, "I did not know that thou wast thirsty"; and

after the lamb had finished drinking, he took it up tenderly in his arms and carried it back to the flock. Then said God, "Moses, merciful Moses, if thy love and care are so great for an animal, how much greater will they be, exerted for thy fellow-being!" *The Gemarah*

Life is as dear to all beings as it is to oneself; feel compassion for every being, taking thy own Self as the measure.

The Upanishads

Every creature that exists, exists first of all in its own right. Its destiny may be to serve some other creature greater than itself, but that service does not comprehend its destiny. The ultimate purpose of all creatures is to sing to God. Therefore, whenever I try to say of anything "This is wholly mine and wholly for me," I do violence to the thing as well as to myself.

GERALD VANN (1906–1963)
The Heart of Man

Show love to all creatures and thou wilt be happy, for when thou lovest all things thou lovest the Lord, for he is in all.

TULSI DAS (1543–1623)
Ramcaritmanas

God is in every created being or thing: be cruel towards none, neither abuse any by intemperance.

JEREMY TAYLOR (1613–1667)
Holy Living

Whoso would carelessly tread one worm that crawls on earth, that heartless one is darkly alienated from God; but he that, living, embraceth all things with his love, to dwell with him God bursts all bounds above, below.　　*The Code of Manu*

> God knows no distinctions,
> All to him have equal worth;
> He holds as much in common
> With the fly as with you.

ANGELUS SILESIUS (1624–1677)
The Cherubic Wanderer

A man is ethical only when life, as such, is sacred to him, that of plants and animals as that of his fellowman, and when he devotes himself helpfully to all life that is in need of help.

ALBERT SCHWEITZER (1875–1965)
Out of My Life and Thoughts

Thus say all the perfect souls and blessed ones, whether past, present or to come—thus they speak, thus they declare, thus they proclaim: All things breathing, all things existing, all things living, all beings whatever, should not be slain or treated with violence, or insulted, or tortured or driven away.

Acuranga Sutra (Book of Good Conduct)

Reason discovers the bridge between love for God and love for men—love for all creatures, reverence for all being, compassion with all life, however dissimilar to our own.

ALBERT SCHWEITZER (1875–1965)
Reverence for Life

If thine heart were right, then every creature should be to thee a mirror of life and a book of holy doctrine. There is no creature so little nor so vile but it represents the goodness of God.

THOMAS À KEMPIS (1380–1471)
The Imitation of Christ

> Seest thou the little winged fly, smaller
>   than a grain of sand?
> It has a heart like thee, a brain open to
>   heaven and hell,
> Withinside wondrous and expansive: its
>   gates are not clos'd;
> I hope thine are not.

WILLIAM BLAKE (1757–1827)
Auguries of Innocence

> These are his manifold forms before
>   thee,
> Rejecting them, where seekest thou for
>   God?
> Who loves all beings, without distinction,
> He indeed is worshipping best his God.

SWAMI VIVEKANANDA (1863–1902)
In Search of God

The world globes itself in a drop of dew. The microscope cannot find the animalcule which is less perfect for being little. Eyes, ears, taste, smell, motion, resistance, appetite, and organs of reproduction that take hold on eternity—all find room to consist in the small creature. So do we put our life into every act. The true doctrine of omnipresence is that God reappears with all his parts in every moss and cobweb.

RALPH WALDO EMERSON (1803–1882)
Compensation

There are as many different species of animals and plants as there were different forms created by God in the beginning.

CAROLUS LINNAEUS (1707–1778)
The Study of Nature

These rivers flow, the eastern towards the West and the western towards the East; from ocean to ocean they flow. They actually become the ocean. And as they do not know which one they are, so all these creatures here, though they have come forth from Being, do not know they have come forth from Being. Whatever they are, whether tiger, lion, wolf, boar, worm, fly, gnat, or mosquito, they all become That. That which is the subtlest of the subtle, the whole world has as its self. That is reality. That is the Self, and that art thou.

The Upanishads

· BLESSED ARE THE PURE IN HEART ·

He that sees the beauty of holiness, or true moral good, sees the greatest and most important thing in the world, which is the fullness of all things, without which the world is empty, no better than nothing, yea, worse than nothing. He that sees not the beauty of holiness is ignorant of the greatest works of God, and in effect is ignorant of the whole spiritual world.

JONATHAN EDWARDS (1703–1758)
Concerning Religious Affections

Mankind is one, seeing that all are equally subject to the moral law. All men are equal in God's eyes.

MOHANDAS K. GANDHI (1869–1948)
Ethical Religion

Blessed are the pure in heart, for they shall see God.   *The New Testament*
Matthew 5:8

The origin of truth lies in the Fountain of Light, and that of perversity in the Wellspring of Darkness. All who practice righteousness are under the domination of the Prince of Lights, and walk in ways of light; whereas all who practice perversity are under the domination of the Angel of Darkness and walk in ways of darkness.

The Dead Sea Scrolls

It is in God that morality has its foundation and guarantee.

LEO BAECK (1873–1956)
Essence of Judaism

The end of morality is to give personal, human finality to the Universe; to discover the finality that belongs to it—if indeed it has any finality—and to discover it by acting.   MIGUEL DE UNAMUNO (1864–1936)
The Tragic Sense of Life

When the God idea is divorced from mythology, anthropomorphism and supernaturalism, Godhood will become identified with all human conduct that strives for the creative survival of the human species in a warless world.

MORDECAI M. KAPLAN (1881–1983)
The Religion of Ethical Nationhood

There are many religions, but there is only one morality.

JOHN RUSKIN (1819–1900)
Lectures on Art

A good character is, verily, the best mantle for men from God. With it He adorneth the temples of His loved ones. The light of a good character surpasseth the light of the sun and the radiance thereof.

BAHA'U'LLAH (1817–1892)
The Advent of Divine Justice

God does not merely provide us with the ground rules by which to control our passions. He is the archetype of morality, as revealed to historical man.

> HERMANN COHEN (1842–1918)
> *Jewish Writings*

What the compass is to navigation, that is moral principle to our affairs. We need not fear shipwreck when God is the pilot.

> HENRY WARD BEECHER (1813–1887)
> *Sermons*

There is no man suddenly either excellently good or extremely evil.

> SIR PHILIP SIDNEY (1554–1586)
> *Arcadia*

Reading, reflection and time have convinced me that the interests of society require the observation of those moral precepts only in which all religions agree (for all forbid us to murder, steal, plunder, or bear false witness) and that we should not intermeddle with the particular dogmas in which all religions differ, and which are totally unconnected with morality.

> THOMAS JEFFERSON (1743–1826)
> *Letter to J. Fishback*

All service ranks the same with God—
With God, whose puppets, best and worst,
Are we: there is no last nor first.

> ROBERT BROWNING (1812–1889)
> *Pippa Passes*

A hideously frightful idea is, that the One only good, the One only unselfish, thinks a great deal of Himself, and looks strictly after His rights in the way of homage. God is the one great Servant of all, and the only way to serve Him is to be a fellow-servant with Him.

> GEORGE MACDONALD (1824–1905)
> *Unspoken Sermons*

As whom did God bring you here? Was it not as a mortal? Was it not as one to live with a little portion of flesh upon earth, and to see His administration; to behold the spectacle with Him, and partake of the festival for a short time? After having beheld the spectacle and the solemnity then, as long as it is permitted you, will you not depart when He leads you out, adoring and thankful for what you have heard and seen?

> EPICTETUS (1st century)
> *Discourses*

There is no peace except where I am,
  saith the Lord—
Though you have health—that which is
  called health—yet without me it is only
  the fair covering of disease;
Though you have love, yet if I be not
  between and around the lovers, is their
  love only torment and unrest;
Though you have wealth and friends and
  home—all these shall come and go—
  there is nothing stable or secure, which
  shall not be taken away.
But I alone remain—I do not change.

> EDWARD CARPENTER (1844–1929)
> *Towards Democracy*

Without God, meaning is simply a human speciality, the vast universe is devoid of meaning. With God, the world has sense, perhaps a direction. And the wide frame of meaning returns upon our small lives to lend them significance; for meaning descends from the whole to the parts.

> WILLIAM ERNEST HOCKING (1873–1966)
> *Science and the Idea of God*

It seems as if life might all be so simple and so beautiful, so good to live, so good to look at, if we could only think of it as one long journey, where every day's march had its own separate sort of beauty to travel through; and so if we could go on clinging to no past, accepting every new present as it comes, finding everything beautiful in its time, and suiting ourselves to each new beauty with continual growth. And that can come to pass in the soul that really loves and lives in a living, loving God.

PHILLIPS BROOKS (1835–1893)
Visions and Tasks

I believe that at the beginning God made a world for each separate man, and in that world which is within us one should seek to live.　　OSCAR WILDE (1854–1900)
Letters

That I am a man, this I share with other men. That I see and hear and that I eat and drink is what all animals do likewise. But that I am I is only mine and belongs to me and to nobody else; to no other man nor to an angel nor to God—except inasmuch as I am one with Him.

MEISTER ECKHART (1260–1327)
Fragments

Are we not spirits, that are shaped into a body, into an Appearance; and that fade away again into air and Invisibility? Oh, Heaven, it is mysterious, it is awful to consider that we not only carry a future Ghost within us; but are, in very deed, Ghosts! These Limbs, whence had we them; this stormy Force; this life-blood with its burning Passion? They are dust and shadow; a Shadow-system gathered round our Me; wherein, through some moments or years, the Divine essence is to be revealed to the Flesh.　　THOMAS CARLYLE (1795–1881)
Sartor Resartus

The meaning and purpose of the world remain to a large extent inexplicable. But one thing is clear: the purpose of all events is spiritual. The purpose of existence is that we human beings, all nations and the whole of humanity, should constantly progress toward perfection. If we do this, our finite spirit will be in harmony with the infinite. If we have this yearning, we shall attain to the peace of God.

ALBERT SCHWEITZER (1875–1965)
Reverence for Life

What are we here for? As we view our evolution from life's primitive beginnings, we can see, though dimly, the outline of a great plan. If this is true, are we not of value to the Planner? I doubt whether there is any objective for life that is ultimately more satisfying than trying to live the life that one comes to feel God wants him to live.

ARTHUR HOLLY COMPTON (1892–1962)
*The Idea of God as Affected
by Modern Knowledge*

V · God and Ethics

If you do not wish for His kingdom, don't pray for it. But if you do, you must do more than pray for it; you must work for it.

—JOHN RUSKIN

THE DOMINANT MESSAGE of the God Seekers in this section of our anthology is that the most significant way to achieve rapport with him is through good works and the practice of charity throughout our lives. In his Sermon on the Mount, Jesus of Nazareth went right to the heart of this lesson: "Let your light so shine before men, that they may see your good works, and glorify your Father which is in heaven."

Henry Ward Beecher believed that one of the most difficult problems of human life is to "unfold what God has put into you, how to make it more and more, how to live more by the power of the spiritual world than by the power of the senses in this material world." The Baal Shem Tov recalled the Torah commandment that a fire shall be kept burning continually upon any altar glorifying God. With his characteristically direct manner of getting to the core of things, the Baal Shem Tov said, "Our heart is the altar. In every occupation let a spark of the holy fire remain within you, so that you may fan it into a flame."

Rainer Maria Rilke, in one of the poems in his *Book of Hours,* has God say that if we use the senses He has endowed us with we can get to the edge of our yearning to make our lives meaningful. To Rilke, God asks us to do this, to give him the garment of our effort.

The God Seekers constantly urge us to understand the uplifting spiritual challenge of doing useful deeds. Madame Guyon observed that if we can perform our apportioned work and serve God with "joyousness of Spirit" no yoke can prove too unbearable.

Prayers, to be sure, can be important in helping us to establish rapport with God, but as Martin Luther noted in one of his sermons, "Dear friends, the kingdom of God—and we are that kingdom—consists not in speech or in words, but in deeds, in works and exercises."

Few writers have praised the nobility of God-inspired work as wholeheartedly as Thomas Carlyle. In his best-known work, *Sartor Resartus,* Carlyle boldly exclaims: "The God-given mandate, *Work Thou in Welldoing,* lies mysteriously written, in Promethean Prophetic Characters, in our hearts; and leaves us no rest, night or day, till it be deciphered and obeyed; till it burn forth, in our conduct, a visible, acted Gospel of Freedom."

These same thoughts were echoed by Robert Louis Stevenson in his essay "Pulvis et Umbra," where his counsel was "do not grasp at the stars, do life's plain, common work as it comes, certain that daily duties and daily bread are the sweetest things of life."

How we may best serve God is another theme explored by the God Seekers in this section. They tell us in many eloquent passages that we should serve him with a joyousness of spirit and that we serve him most ably when, in Thomas Paine's words, we are "contributing to the happiness of the living creation that God has made."

In sum, we serve God, the great Servant of all, by being a fellow servant with him and by not detaching ourselves from his world or ever hating the precious gift of life He has given us. On the contrary, says Judah Halevi, whoever serves "loves the world and a long life because it affords him opportunities of deserving the world to come."

Perhaps the most palpable way of serving, the God Seekers reiterate throughout this portion of our anthology, is by being charitable to the needy. The word *charity* is derived from the Latin word *caritas*, meaning "love." As late as the King James version of the New Testament in the seventeenth century, the word for love in Saint Paul's timeless commentary in 1 Corinthians 13 was translated charity instead of love.

The practice of charity is so universal among the world's religions that one must conclude that it is one of the undeniable truths God has implanted in humankind. With so many references to charity in the Talmud there can be no doubt that it is a central precept of Jewish ethics. Sometimes the lesson is as short as a proverb, for example, "Charity knows no race, no creed"; at other times the Talmud turns to a lively anecdote to make its point. Rabbi Akiba was asked by a Roman general, "Why does your God who loves the needy not provide for their support Himself?" Akiba answered, "God, the father of both rich and poor, wants the one to help the other so as to make the world a household of love."

The God Seekers of all religions agree that the practice of charity benefits the giver as much, if not more, than the receiver. The Koran says, "Who is there that will lend to God a good loan? He will redouble it many a double; God closes His hand and holds it out, and unto Him shall ye return." The Midrash enjoins us to remember that when the poor stand before our door, "their Maker stands at their right hand, so consider it a high privilege to help them."

The noblest form of charity, the God Seekers repeatedly tell us, is when the donor seeks no self-aggrandizement for his or her generosity. A Talmudic proverb claims that "he who gives alms in secret is greater than Moses." Ralph Waldo Emerson expressed the same thought this way: "The magnanimous know very well that they who give time, or money, or shelter, to the stranger—so be it done for love, and not for ostentation—do, as it were, put God under obligation to them, so perfect are the compensations of the universe."

Charity is the most visible way we can express our love for God, because it tests whether we are merely offering lip service when we say that God's love reposes in the soul of every living being. Moreover, what better way is there for God to distinguish those who profess devoutness by chanting it at the top of their lungs from those who quietly practice it?

Antoine de Saint-Exupéry believes that the person who practices charity expedites God's work. As he says in *Flight to Arras*, "It was a thing owed to God, however insignificant the individual who was its recipient. Charity never humiliated him who profited from it, nor ever bound him by the chains of gratitude, since it was not to him but to God the gift was made."

We often look at our lives and wonder why God has given us our share, or even what may seem more than our share, of worldly goods. When we look at the less fortunate, whether they live in the run-down sections of our cities or in some impoverished country in Africa, where slow starvation afflicts hundreds of thousands of children, we are sometimes overwhelmed at what seems so unfair. At these moments we are being challenged—perhaps God's greatest challenge to us —to express our love for him.

There is a rabbinical legend that Job's house was open to the north and to the south, to the east and to the west. Job, according to this tale, had made four doors into his house so that the poor and needy would not be troubled to go to a back door, and that all would find a door facing them as they approached.

When the great suffering was inflicted on Job he cried out, "O Lord of the world, did I not feed the hungry and clothe the naked?" God told Job, yes, you did sit in your house and if a poor wayfarer came there you gave him bread and meat and wine. But look what my servant Abraham did: he went out and wandered about and when he found poor wayfarers he *brought* them to his house and fed and clothed them. And, even more, Abraham built large inns on the road and put meat and drink within them for the needy.

A modern Abraham appeared in our time to practice the truest form of charity. Dr. Albert Schweitzer left the comfort of his affluent home, his high position in the academic world, his worldwide reputation as a Bach scholar and organ virtuoso, to succor the helpless and the needy. Like Abraham, he, too, wandered forth to the most impoverished regions; he didn't wait until some half-dead native of Lambaréné knocked on the back door of his spacious house in Alsace.

The real test, then, when we affirm how much we seek God's love, is whether the true spirit of charity is in our hearts. An ancient Indian proverb enjoins us to cast our bread upon the waters, for God will know of it even if the fishes do not. It has often been said that charity is an expression of faith, but that is an understatement. It is the ultimate manifestation that we have achieved rapport with God's love; it is the ultimate expression of faith.

· DUTY AND FULFILLMENT ·

The heart has everywhere the same duties; on the steps of the throne of God, if He has a throne, and at the bottom of the great abyss, if there be an abyss.

VOLTAIRE (1694–1778)
Philosophical Dictionary

God requires of us the sacrifice of all we would conserve and grants us gifts we had not dreamed of—the forgiveness of our sins rather than our justification, repentance and sorrow for our transgressions rather than forgetfulness, faith in him rather than confidence in ourselves, instead of rest an ever-recurrent torment that will not let us be content.

REINHOLD NIEBUHR (1892–1971)
The Meaning of Revelation

We can only judge a man by his works. If a man abounds in the fruits of the Spirit, charity, joy, peace, long-suffering, kindness, goodness, faith, gentleness, chastity, against which, as Paul says (Galatians 5:22), there is no law. Such a one, whether he be taught by reason only, or by the Scripture only, has been in very truth taught by God, and is altogether blessed.

BENEDICT SPINOZA (1632–1677)
Theologico-Political Treatise

The needs of this great life—which alone manifests God's spiritual presence in our nature—require the utmost conceivable intensity of human freedom; require, in other words, that man should be spontaneously good of himself, good without any antagonism of evil, infinitely good even as God is good.

HENRY JAMES, SR. (1811–1882)
Substance and Shadow

So nigh is grandeur to our dust,
    So near is God to man,
When Duty whispers low, Thou must,
    The youth replies, I can.

RALPH WALDO EMERSON (1803–1882)
Voluntaries

I cannot afford to relax discipline because God is on my side, for He is on the side of discipline. There is more of God and divine help in a man's little finger than in idle prayer and trust.

HENRY DAVID THOREAU (1817–1862)
Journal

The Divine Presence does not dwell in the midst of idleness, sadness, jocularity, levity or idle chatter, but rather in the joy derived from a virtuous deed.

The Talmud

To pay homage to God by every outward and inward act, this is the first and
dearest work of humility, the most savory
among those of charity, and the most meet
among those of righteousness.

JAN VAN RUYSBROECK (1293–1381)
The Adornment of the Spiritual Marriage

Be ye steadfast, unmovable, always
abounding in the work of the Lord; foras-
much as ye know that your labor is not in
vain in the Lord.   *The New Testament*
1 Corinthians 15:58

Perform all thy duties with thy hands,
but let thy heart be with God.

KABIR (1440–1518)
Sayings

To do our duty in our own sphere, to
try to create something worth creating, as
our life's work, is the way to understand
what joy is in this life, and by God's grace
to earn the verdict: "Well done, good and
faithful servant; enter thou into the joy of
thy Lord."

WILLIAM RALPH INGE (1860–1954)
Personal Religion and the Life of Devotion

There is but one way in which man can
ever help God—that is, by letting God
help him; and there is no way in which His
name is more guiltily taken in vain, than
by calling the abandonment of our work
the performance of His.

JOHN RUSKIN (1819–1900)
The Ethics of the Dust

When a man does the work God gives
him, no sin can touch this man.

The Bhagavad Gita

God did not call you to be canary-birds
in a little cage, and to hop up and down
three times, within a space no larger than
the size of the cage. God calls you to be

eagles, and to fly from sun to sun, over
continents.

HENRY WARD BEECHER (1813–1887)
Sermons

Let the dead past bury its dead!
Act,—act in the living Present!
Heart within, and God o'erhead!

HENRY WADSWORTH LONGFELLOW
(1807–1882)
A Psalm of Life

It is clear that "to serve God" is equiva-
lent to serving "every living thing." It is for
this that the best among the Jewish people,
especially the prophets, including Jesus,
ceaselessly battled.

ALBERT EINSTEIN (1879–1955)
The World As I See It

God asks no man whether he will accept
life. That is not the choice. You *must* take
it. The only choice is *how*.

HENRY WARD BEECHER (1813–1887)
Life Thoughts

When you make a vow to God, do not
delay paying it, for He takes no pleasure
in fools—what you vow, be sure to pay!
Better not to vow at all than to vow and
fail to pay.   *The Old Testament*
Ecclesiastes 5:5–6

What asks our Father of His children,
    save
Justice and mercy and humility?

JOHN GREENLEAF WHITTIER (1807–1892)
Requirement

People may excite in themselves a glow
of compassion, not by toasting their feet at
the fire and saying, "Lord, teach me more
compassion," but by going out and seeking
an object that requires compassion.

HENRY WARD BEECHER (1813–1887)
Sermons

And only the Master shall praise us, and
  only the Master shall blame;
And no one shall work for money, and no
  one shall work for fame;
But each for the joy of the working, and
  each, in his separate star,
Shall draw the Thing as he sees It, for the
  God of Things as they are!

       RUDYARD KIPLING (1865–1936)
    When Earth's Last Picture Is Painted

To love our God with all our strength and
  will;
To covet nothing; to devise no ill
Against our neighbors; to procure or do
Nothing to others which we would not to
Our very selves; not to revenge our
  wrong;
To be content with little; not to long
For wealth and greatness; to despise or
  jeer
No man, and, if we be despised, to bear;
To feed the hungry; to hold fast our
  crown;
To take from others nought; to give our
  own,—
These are his precepts, and, alas, in these
What is so hard but faith can do with
  ease?

       HENRY VAUGHAN (1622–1695)
         Silex Scintillans

We are living in the midst of death.
What is the value of working for our own
schemes when they might be reduced to
naught? But we feel as strong as a rock, if
we could truthfully say we work for God
and His schemes. Then nothing perishes.

    MOHANDAS K. GANDHI (1869–1948)
        Selected Addresses

Ultimate concern is the abstract translation of the great commandment: "The
Lord, our God, the Lord is one; and you
shall love the Lord your God, with all your
heart, and with all your soul and with all
your mind, and with all your strength."
The religious concern is ultimate; it ex-
cludes all other concerns from ultimate
significance; it makes them preliminary.

       PAUL TILLICH (1886–1965)
        Systematic Theology

So, let him wait God's instant men call
  years;
Meantime hold hard by truth and his
  great soul,
Do out the duty! Through such souls
  alone
God stooping shows sufficient of his light
For us i' the dark to rise by.

      ROBERT BROWNING (1812–1889)
            Pomphilia

Allegiance to the Creator and Governor
of the Milky-Way, and the Nebulae, and
benevolence to all his creatures, is my Religion.   JOHN ADAMS (1735–1826)
      Letter to Thomas Jefferson

How can he will to die for God who will
not live according to God?

  SAINT FRANCIS OF SALES (1567–1622)
            Treatise

The supreme commandment that arises
out of love towards God, and the foundation of all morality, is this: Yield yourself
up entirely, give your spirit to the end that
you may save it, that you may eternalize it.

    MIGUEL DE UNAMUNO (1864–1936)
       The Tragic Sense of Life

Love's secret is to be always doing things
for God, and not to mind because they are
such little ones.

  FREDERICK WILLIAM FABER (1814–1863)
            Sermons

I shall study how so to love myself that,
in my attitude toward myself, I shall be
pleasing to God and face with confidence
what He requires of me. Here in the qui-

etness, I give myself over to the kind of self-regard that would make me whole and clean in my own sight and in the sight of God.

HOWARD THURMAN (1899–1981)
Meditations of the Heart

What if God awaits from man a feat of free creativeness and demands of man the manifestation of all the powers with which he is endowed? This is the will of God, and man must fulfill it.

NIKOLAI BERDYAEV (1874–1948)
Freedom and the Spirit

If you accept your thoughts as inspiration from the Supreme Intelligence, obey them when they prescribe difficult duties, because they come only so long as they are used.

RALPH WALDO EMERSON (1803–1882)
Courage

When a man's duty looks like an enemy, dragging him into the dark mountains, he has no less to go with it than when, like a friend with a loving face, it offers to lead him along green pastures by the river side.

GEORGE MACDONALD (1824–1905)
Unspoken Sermons

When God wanted sponges and oysters, He made them, and put one on a rock, and the other in the mud. When He made man, He did not make him to be a sponge or an oyster; He made him with feet, and hands, and head, and heart, and vital blood, and a place to use them, and said to him, "Go, work!"

HENRY WARD BEECHER (1813–1887)
Royal Truths

Never to tire, never to grow cold; to be patient, sympathetic, tender; to look for the budding flower and the opening heart; to hope always; like God, to love always,— this is duty.

HENRI FRÉDÉRIC AMIEL (1821–1881)
Journal Intime

Duty—that passion of the soul which
    from the sod
Alone lifts man to God.

RICHARD WATSON GILDER (1844–1909)
Pro Patria

Man's greatest duty is to love God: that is the first commandment. The second is to love his neighbor. And it is possible for two creatures to love one another only because God exists and is their common Father—it is the divine image and likeness that is lovable in our fellow-men.

NIKOLAI BERDYAEV (1874–1948)
Dostoevski

God laughs at a man who says to his soul, Take thy ease.

ABRAHAM COWLEY (1618–1667)
Of Myself

It is not from God's strictness that he requires so much of man, but rather from his kindness that he expects the soul to progress to the point where it may receive much, as he gives so much to it.

MEISTER ECKHART (1260–1327)
Sermons

If you mean to act nobly and seek to know the best things God has put within reach of men, you must learn to fix your mind on that end, and not on what will happen to you because of it.

GEORGE ELIOT (1819–1880)
Romola

· TO SERVE GOD'S AIMS ·

In His will is our peace.

DANTE (1265–1321)
The Divine Comedy

If the Maker of all things, who has done nothing without design, has furnished this earthly globe like a museum, with the most admirable proofs of His wisdom and power, it follows that man is made for the purpose of studying the Creator's works, that he may be the publisher and interpreter of the wisdom of God.

CAROLUS LINNAEUS (1707–1778)
The Study of Nature

Like a swift moving fire which ceases not nor rests, until it has accomplished its purpose, so must man's energy be in the service of God.

MOSES LUZZATTO (1707–1747)
The Way of the Upright

Every believer in this world of ours must be a spark of light, a center of love, a vivifying leaven amidst his fellowmen, and he will be all this more perfectly the more closely he lives in communion with God and in the intimacy of his own soul.

POPE JOHN XXIII (1881–1963)
Pacem in Terris

Be like a lighted candle which itself gives light, burning with earthly fire, and lights other candles, without losing its own flame, so that they can give light elsewhere. If this is so of earthly fire, what can we say of the fire of grace of the All-Holy Spirit of God?

SAINT SERAPHIM OF SAROV (1759–1833)
Sermons

Perfect devotedness requires, not only that we do the will of God, but that we do it with love. God would have us serve Him with delight; it is our hearts that He asks of us.

FRANÇOIS FÉNELON (1651–1715)
Maximes des Saints

Only the One God can be served with *all* that we are and have. It was just because men, in their innermost beings, found themselves pledged to the eternally binding and inviolable law, because they realized the commandment of God to be the true and only law-giving authority, and because they discovered in it the meaning of their lives, that they recognized Him as the One Lord, the Holy One.

LEO BAECK (1873–1956)
The Essence of Judaism

We cannot all be friars, and many are the ways by which God bears his chosen to heaven.

MIGUEL DE CERVANTES (1547–1616)
Don Quixote

Our life is but a little holding, lent
To do a mighty labour: we are one
With heaven and the stars when it is spent
To serve God's aim: else die we with the
  sun.

GEORGE MEREDITH (1828–1909)
Vittoria

Sick or well, blind or seeing, bond or free, we are here for a purpose and however we are situated, we please God better with useful deeds than with many prayers or pious resignation. The temple or church is empty unless the good of life fill it. The altar is holy if only it represents the altar of our heart upon which we offer the only sacrifices ever commanded—the love that is stronger than hate and the faith that overcometh doubt.

HELEN KELLER (1880–1968)
My Religion

For what is happier, what either more worthy of man and more similar to God than to help and serve as many as possible? Whoever is able to do this and does not, seems to me to have rejected the highest duty of humanity and for that reason to have abandoned the name and nature of man.

PETRARCH (1304–1374)
De Vita Solitaria

Man's ultimate aim is the realization of God, and all his activities, social, political, religious, have to be guided by the ultimate aim of the vision of God. The immediate service of all human beings becomes a necessary part of the endeavor, simply because the only way to find God is to see Him in His creation and be one with it.

MOHANDAS K. GANDHI (1869–1948)
Selected Addresses

Burn, then, little lamp; glimmer straight
  and clear—
Hush! a rustling wing stirs, methinks the
  air:
He for whom I wait, thus ever comes to
  me;
Strange Power! I trust thy might; trust
  thou my constancy.

EMILY BRONTË (1818–1848)
The Visionary

Th' Almighty, from his throne, on earth
  surveys
Nought greater than an honest, humble
  heart.

EDWARD YOUNG (1683–1765)
Night Thoughts

He who in his own activity serves the God Who reveals Himself—even though he may by nature be sprung from a mean earthly realm—is transplanted by the streams of water of the Direction.

MARTIN BUBER (1878–1965)
Good and Evil

For so is the will of God, that with well doing ye may put to silence the ignorance of foolish men. Live as free men, yet not using your liberty for a cloak of maliciousness, but as the servants of God.

The New Testament
1 Peter 2:15

Who falls for love of God, shall rise a star.

BEN JONSON (1573–1637)
Epistle to a Friend

From faith flow forth love and joy in the Lord, and from love a joyful, willing and free mind that serves one's neighbor willingly and takes no account of gratitude or ingratitude, of praise or blame, of gain or loss.

MARTIN LUTHER (1483–1546)
Concerning Christian Liberty

We give to God the flower that is out of reach.

Indian Proverb

Be as strong as a leopard, as swift as an eagle, as fleet as a stag, and as mighty as a lion in doing the will of thy Father in heaven.

Ethics of the Fathers

If a man truly loves God and has no will but to do God's will the whole force of the Rhine River may run at him and will not disturb him nor break his peace.

JOHANNES TAULER (1300–1361)
Sermons

· HE THAT GIVETH TO THE POOR ·

When a needy person stands at your door God himself stands at his side.

Hebrew Proverb

God is treasurer to the charitable man.

Italian Proverb

Give alms of thy substance; and when thou givest alms, let not thine eye be envious, neither turn on thy face from any poor, and the face of God shall not be turned away from thee.

The Old Testament Apocrypha
Tobit 4:7

The closed fist locks up heaven, but the open hand is the key of mercy.

Hindu Proverb

If I knew all things that are in the world and be not in charity, what should that help me before God who shall doom me according to my deeds?

THOMAS À KEMPIS (1380–1471)
The Imitation of Christ

Did universal charity prevail, earth would be a heaven, and hell a fable.

CHARLES CALEB COLTON (1780–1832)
Lacon

Give for the sake of God even to the unbeliever.   *Moroccan Proverb*

Give all thou canst; high Heaven rejects the lore
Of nicely calculated less or more.

WILLIAM WORDSWORTH (1770–1850)
Ecclesiastical Sonnets

A man's house should be open wide to the north, to the south, to the east, to the west—so that the poor should not be put to trouble in finding entrance.

Ethics of the Fathers

He that hath pity upon the poor lendeth unto the Lord.   *The Old Testament*
Proverbs 19:17

God sends the Poor to try us, as well as he tries them by being such: and he that refuses them a little out of the great deal that God has given him, lays up Poverty in Store for his own Posterity.

WILLIAM PENN (1644–1718)
Some Fruits of Solitude

Remember, Heaven has an avenging rod;
To smite the poor is treason against God.

WILLIAM COWPER (1731–1800)
Charity

It matters not whether a man gives little or much, if only his heart goes out with it to his Father in Heaven.   *The Gemarah*

Whosoever has compassion on the poor, the Holy One, blessed be He, has compassion on him.

JOSEPH BEN EPHRAIM KARO (1488–1575)
Shulhan Aruk

Whatever good you do for others, you send it before your own souls and shall find it with Allah who sees all you do.

The Koran

He that is gracious unto the poor lendeth unto the Lord, and his good deed will He repay unto him.   *The Old Testament*
Proverbs 19:17

When mankind languisheth in pain let no man say I shall return unto mine own household, eat and drink and be at peace! Nay, each man must be willing to suffer with his fellowmen. He who shares the afflictions of others will merit to behold the comforting of humanity.

The Talmud

Lose your silver for the sake of a brother or a friend, and do not let it rust under a stone and be lost. Lay up your treasure according to the commandments of the Most High, and it will profit you more than gold. *The Old Testament Apocrypha Ecclesiasticus 29:10–11*

If thou draw out thy soul to the hungry, and satisfy the afflicted soul; then shall thy light rise in obscurity, and thy darkness be as the noonday; and the Lord shall guide thee continually. *The Old Testament Isaiah 58:10–11*

The world is pushed forward by men to care; but it is lifted to companionship with the heart of God by men who share.

HENRY SLOANE COFFIN (1877–1954)
Joy in Believing

To love our neighbor in charity is so to love God in man, or man in God.

SAINT FRANCIS OF SALES (1567–1622)
Sermons

But whoso hath this world's goods, and seeth his brother hath need, and shutteth up his bowels of compassion from him, how dwelleth the love of God in him?

The New Testament 1 John 3:17

Charity is the unselfish love of friendship, by which we love God for his own sake, because his goodness is supremely loveable. It is a true friendship, for it is mutual: God has loved from all eternity anyone who has loved, is loving, or will love him in time. There is also mutual knowledge and expression of that love: God is not unaware of our love for him, since it is his gift to us; nor can we be unaware of his love for us, since he has proclaimed it so widely.

SAINT FRANCIS OF SALES (1567–1622)
The Love of God

The magnanimous know very well that they who give time, or money, or shelter, to the stranger—so be it done for love, and not for ostentation—do, as it were, put God under obligation to them, so perfect are the compensations of the universe.

RALPH WALDO EMERSON (1803–1882)
Heroism

Every good deed is charity, and it is a good deed that thou meet thy brother with a cheerful countenance and that thou pour water from thy bucket into the vessel of thy brother. MOHAMMED (570–632)
The Hadith

He that giveth to the poor, lendeth to the Lord: there is more rhetoric in that one sentence than in a library of sermons.

SIR THOMAS BROWNE (1605–1682)
Religio Medici

Charity is not something different from faith, but a form of faith, an amplification of one's trust in man.

MIGUEL DE UNAMUNO (1864–1936)
Faith

Let the lips of the poor be the trumpet of thy gift, lest in seeking applause thou lose thy reward. Nothing is more pleasing to God than an open hand and a closed mouth. FRANCIS QUARLES (1592–1644)
Emblems

One act of charity will teach us more of the love of God than a thousand sermons —one act of unselfishness, of real self-denial, the putting forth of one loving feeling to the outcast and "those who are of the way," will tell us more than whole volumes of the wisest writers on theology.

FREDERICK WILLIAM ROBERTSON
(1816–1853)
Sermons

You will say, "Charity is greater than justice." Yes, it is greater: it is the summit of justice—it is the temple of which justice is the foundation. But you can't have the top without the bottom; you cannot build upon charity. You must build upon justice, for this main reason, that you have not at first charity to build with. It is the last reward of good work.

JOHN RUSKIN (1819–1900)
Fors Clavigera

Seek Love in the pity of others' woe,
In the gentle relief of another's care,
In the darkness of night and the winter's
    snow,
In the naked and outcast, seek Love
    there.

WILLIAM BLAKE (1757–1827)
Where to Seek Love

To be reconciled to God, to be saved to him, to be in fellowship with him as sons with a Father, to be partakers of the divine nature, alive with his life, animated by his spirit, conformed to his character, is to share his loving purpose for his children, and to give ourselves, as our Father gives himself, to make them wholly his.

HENRY SLOANE COFFIN (1877–1954)
Sermons

Our love for God does not depend upon the emotions of the moment. If you fancy you do not love Him enough, above all when Satan tempts you to look inward, go immediately and minister to others; visit the sick, perform some act of self-sacrifice or thanksgiving.

CHARLES KINGSLEY (1819–1875)
Daily Thoughts

In faith and hope the world will disagree,
But all mankind's concern is charity:
All must be false that thwart this one
    great end;
And all of God, that bless mankind, or
    mend.

ALEXANDER POPE (1688–1744)
Essay on Man

VI · God's Golden Rule

To worship God and to leave every other
man free to worship Him in his own way;
to love one's neighbors, enlightening them
if one can and pitying those who remain
in error;—this is my religion, and it is
worth all your systems and symbols.

—VOLTAIRE

A FUNDAMENTAL LESSON the prophets and sages of every century have reiterated throughout this anthology is that all living beings are equally holy to God. Although it is a precept that God implants within our soul the exact moment that He creates us, somehow it has always been too challenging for all but a few to accept.

Why the vast majority of humankind push this nonpareil gift from God into the most inaccessible abyss of their souls is a quandary permeated with sadness. For every person who heeds the life of a Francis of Assisi or an Albert Schweitzer there seem to be ten thousand who have not risen above the fratricidal setting of the Bible's first two brothers, Cain and Abel. In this section we will find the God Seekers' thoughts on the fellowship of all people and the practice of God's golden rule.

It is not as if God had been remiss in sending us the messages of joyous survival. All the more cause then for sadness that we, his children, after the billions of years of evolving from primal matter to the present stage of God's timeless plan for us, have now become virtually an endangered species. Why have we persisted in paying ransom to our fears for so long in our irrational hatred of fellow humans who have different pigmentation, religious customs, or even philosophies of living?

In the most terrible defiance to the spirituality that God has implanted within us, we have for hundreds of years killed our fellow humans who worshiped him in a different mode from our own, invariably hiding our hideous acts under the banner of his name.

Dr. William Temple, one of the most eloquent of modern archbishops of Canterbury, called love of God the root, and love of our neighbor the fruit, of the Tree of Life. Clearly, neither can exist without the other, but love of God is the *cause* and love of neighbor the *effect*.

In a letter to a friend, Mohandas Gandhi wrote that he believed in the fundamental truth of all great religions of the world. Not only were they necessary for the people to whom these religions were revealed, but if we could only read the scriptures of the different faiths from the standpoint of the followers of these faiths we would find that at the core they were all one, and all were helpful to one

244

another. This anthology, it will be recognized, is essentially an attempt to amplify Gandhi's vision.

As another modern Indian, Sri Ramakrishna, observed, it serves no purpose to say "This man believes in a Personal God and that man believes in an Impersonal God, while that man over there worships a God without Form." That one person calls himself a Hindu, while another may call herself a Christian or a Muslim, should not be a cause for conflict, Ramakrishna pointed out, "because God had made different people understand Him in different ways."

God has sent us a golden rule through messengers who have stated it again and again throughout our history. There may be a slight variance in the manner it is related, but the message itself never varies: Do unto others as you would have them do unto you.

Whether in the words of Kabir, Confucius, Zoroaster, or Jesus of Nazareth the golden rule has served as a universal symbol appealing to the reason as well as to the heart of all peoples. To Rabbi Hillel not doing to another what is hateful to oneself was "the whole of the Torah and the remainder but commentary." John Stuart Mill said that the golden rule encompassed the complete spirit of utilitarian morality.

It also emerges in the proverbs of many countries, such as in the Jains of India, who extended its meaning to all the creatures of the world, not just humankind. There is a Hindu version that says we should not force on our neighbor a hat that hurts our own head.

Our refusal to do little more than mouth the words of God's golden rule, as if they were some neat little slogan that Madison Avenue turned out to sell the newest brand of toothpaste, may anticipate a time when we will not have even that option. It may soon be too late to stop humankind's collision course with an atomic holocaust.

In our deepest prayers we need to plead that God will enter the hearts of the cynical people who command worldly power and, at best, give a grudging lip service to his golden rule. To many among the world's power structure, sitting in their crisis security rooms in Bonn, Washington, Moscow, or Beijing pondering the dangers of a hostile atmosphere, the answer is a futuristic weapon system, perhaps the latest version of a laser beam designed to shoot down a planet-destroying bevy of nuclear intercontinental missiles from Armageddon. What a mockery of the golden rule that one hundred million children will go to sleep hungry tonight, while the vultures of power in every chancellery in the world argue which system of weapons is the most expeditious way to kill fifty or sixty million people in the "enemy's" country in the first preemptive attack.

Another dominant theme in this section is that to love our neighbors is the truest actualization of God's golden rule. But what if our neighbors act as if they were our enemies? Difficult as it may be to love our enemies, the God Seekers are in accord in enjoining us to do no less. Not only must we love them, we also must be able to forgive them. Truly forgive them. As Sir Thomas Browne wrote in *Urne-Burial:*

To forgive our enemies, yet hope that God will punish them is not to forgive enough. To forgive them ourselves, and not to pray to God to forgive them, is a partial act of charity. Forgive thine enemies totally, and without any reserve that, however, God will avenge thee.

The Talmud adds that you must forgive those "who transgress against you before you can look to forgiveness from Above."

To be sure, as Meister Eckhart observed, it is a tremendously difficult thing to practice this kind of universal love and "to love our neighbors as ourselves," but he noted, "if you will understand it rightly, there is a greater reward attached to this command than to any other."

We are not ever able to love our enemies, truly feel love toward them, unless we believe that God's love intends no evil for any man or woman. This means that we truly believe, indeed would stake our very lives on it, that God's love intends no evil for anyone. If this is mere rhetoric we are telling ourselves because it sounds good and thereby affords us some momentary surcease from fear and anxiety, it is not true belief.

Love your neighbor even if he or she appears to be an enemy! That is the message that God has been sending us throughout the centuries by the God Seekers. Seldom has it been stated more directly than by Sören Kierkegaard: "In love of your neighbor, God is the middle term; if you love God above all else, then you may also love your neighbor, and in your neighbor every man."

The God Seekers, throughout this section, urging, pleading, cajoling, enjoining us to realize and accept into the depths of our hearts the message of fellowship, seem to imply yet one thing more. They know that God, ruling this vast universe in all its inconceivable complexity with a plan they and we cannot ever presume to understand, is a patient and merciful Master. Were it not so, if indeed our Creator had thrown up his hands and dismissed us as a bad experiment, He could have provided Neanderthal humans with nuclear weapons rather than primitive spears.

The wisdom that the God Seekers have learned is that our Creator, who is not bound by time, to whom fifteen billion years may be only a pause in his infinite consciousness, does not judge us by our rules but rather by his. In the countless manifestations of himself throughout the universe, God has impressed his evolving plan everywhere. We cannot know if He has provided prophets and messengers on other planets where his creatures exist and strive to fulfill his plan, but we do know that He is trying to speak to us through these voices we call the God Seekers.

One more major theme is explored in this section of our anthology—what Dr. Albert Schweitzer termed "reverence for life." Reverence for every single creature that exists is what Schweitzer meant, for "the man who has consciously found his ground in the unconscious will-to-live feels a compulsion to give to every will-to-live the same reverence for life that he gives his own."

John Donne, in another of his sermons, remarked: "If every gnat that flies were an archangel, all that could but tell me that there is a God; and the poorest worm that creeps tells me that." Henry David Thoreau echoed Donne's words in the natural piety which emerged so effortlessly from his *Journals:* "Each natural object is an end to itself. A brave, undoubting life do they all live, and are content to be a part of the mystery which is God, and throw the responsibility on man of explaining them and himself too."

As Gerald Vann reminded us, Francis of Assisi preached to the birds because he knew that they sang the same song as he. There is no better way to summarize what the God Seekers tell us in this portion of our anthology than to quote Father Gerald Vann, who cautions that we must never forget that the song of Saint Francis' birds was no less than the *laudes creaturarum,* the song of the spheres. Would that the cynical God evaders who conjecture about the survival of the earth (or the few unfortunates who will survive their neutron bombs and laser artillery) could listen to Father Vann's words: "It is because we are all in the One, and if we forget our oneness we isolate and kill ourselves; it is because we are responsible for one another, and if we deny our responsibility we deny our destiny."

· HAVE WE NOT ALL ONE FATHER? ·

Religion is the relation of the soul to God, and therefore the progress of sectarianism marks the decline of religion. Religion is as effectually destroyed by bigotry as by indifference.

RALPH WALDO EMERSON (1803–1882)
Journals

Whoever hateth any man hateth Him who spoke and the world came into existence.
Hebrew Proverb

Knowledge—know each other. Goodness—love thy brother.
Hindu Proverb

Love one another, and with long-suffering hide ye one another's faults. For God
delighteth in the unity of brethren, and in
the purpose of a heart that taketh pleasure
in love.

The Testament of the Twelve Patriarchs

Gather us in: we worship only Thee;
In varied names we stretch a common
   hand;
In diverse forms a common soul we see;
In many ships we seek one spirit-land;
Gather us in.

GEORGE MATHESON (1842–1906)
Hymn

Into the bosom of the one great sea
Flow streams that come from hills on
   every side.
Their names are various as their springs,
And thus in every land do men bow down
To one great God, though known by
   many names.

South Indian Folk Song

You are all children of one Father; so be
like your Father, i.e., do not make distinctions between your own people and other
peoples; be the same with all of them. I
now understand that my welfare is only
possible if I acknowledge my unity with all
the people of the world without exception.

LEO TOLSTOY (1828–1910)
What I Believe

A vast similitude interlocks all,
All distances of time, all inanimate forms,
All souls, all living bodies though they be
   ever so different, or in different
   worlds,
All nations, colours, barbarisms,
   civilizations, languages,
All identities that have existed or may
   exist on this globe, or any globe,
All lives and deaths, all of the past,
   present, future,

This vast similitude spans them, and
   always has spann'd,
And shall forever span them and
   compactly hold and enclose them.

WALT WHITMAN (1819–1892)
On the Beach at Night Alone

I see everywhere the inevitable expression of the Infinite in our world: through
it the supernatural is at the bottom of
every heart. As long as the mystery of the
Infinite weighs on human thought, temples will be erected for the worship of the
Infinite, whether God is called Brahma,
Allah, Jehovah or Jesus, and on the pave-
ment of those temples men will be seen
kneeling, prostrated, annihilated in the
thought of the Infinite.

LOUIS PASTEUR (1822–1895)
Letters

Different creeds are but different paths
to reach the Almighty. As with one gold
various ornaments are made having different forms and names, so one God is
worshipped in different countries and
ages, and has different forms and names.

SRI RAMAKRISHNA (1834–1886)
Sayings

It is a travesty of true religion to consider one's own religion as superior and
others' as inferior. All religions enjoin the
worship of One God who is all-pervasive.
He is present even in a droplet of water or
in a tiny speck of dust. Even those who
worship idols, worship not the stone of
which it is made; they try to see God who
resides in it. Various religions are like the
leaves of a tree. No two leaves are alike,
yet there is no antagonism between them
or between the branches on which they
grow. Even so is there an underlying unity
in the variety which we see in God's creation.

MOHANDAS K. GANDHI (1869–1948)
Harijan

There must be more than one St. Peter; particular Churches and Sects usurp the gates of Heaven, and turn the key against each other; and thus we go to Heaven against each others' wills, conceits and opinions, and, with as much uncharity, as ignorance, do err, I fear, in points not only of our own, but one another's salvation.

SIR THOMAS BROWNE (1605–1682)
Religio Medici

Almost everything that goes beyond the worship of a supreme Being, and the submission of one's heart to his eternal commands, is superstition.

VOLTAIRE (1694–1778)
Philosophical Dictionary

Ethics and religion differ herein; that the one is the system of human duties commencing from man; the other, from God. Religion includes the personality of God; ethics does not.

RALPH WALDO EMERSON (1803–1882)
Nature

I speak not of men's creeds—they rest between
Man and his Maker.

GEORGE GORDON, LORD BYRON
(1788–1824)
Childe Harold's Pilgrimage

In the kingdom of God there is no invidious distinction, and therefore this dispensation gathers all men and nations, all races and tribes, the high and the low, and seeks to establish one vast brotherhood among the children of the great God, who hath made of one blood all nations of men.

KESHUB CHUNDER SEN (1838–1884)
Teachings

It is difficult to make a man miserable while he feels he is worthy of himself and claims kindred to the great God who made him.

ABRAHAM LINCOLN (1809–1865)
Address, August 14, 1862

Have we not all one father? Has not one God created us? Why then are we faithless to one another, profaning the covenant of our fathers? *The Old Testament Malachi 2:10*

The universe is but one great city, full of beloved ones, divine and human by nature, endeared to each other.

EPICTETUS (1st century)
Discourses

For My house shall be called a house of prayer for all peoples, saith the Lord God who gathereth the dispersed of Israel.

The Old Testament Isaiah 56:7

Lo, soul! seest thou not God's purpose from the first?
The earth to be spann'd, connected by network,
The people to become brothers and sisters,
The races, neighbors, to marry and be given in marriage,
The oceans to be cross'd, the distant brought near,
The lands to be welded together.

WALT WHITMAN (1819–1892)
Passage to India

Whatever forms or ceremonies spring
From custom's force, there lies the real thing:
Jew, Turk, or Christian, be the lover's name,
If same the love, religion is the same.

JOHN BYROM (1692–1763)
Divine Love

I will bring your offspring from the east, and from the west I will gather you; I will

say to the north, Give up, and to the south, Do not withhold; bring my sons from afar and my daughters from the end of the earth, every one who is called by my name, whom I created for my glory, whom I formed and made.   *The Old Testament*
Isaiah 43:5–8

Benares is to the East, Mecca to the West; but explore your own heart, for there are both Rama and Allah.

KABIR (1440–1518)
One Hundred Poems

Like the bee, gathering honey from different flowers, the wise man accepts the essence of different Scriptures and sees only good in all religions.

The Srimad Bhagavatra

My heart is capable of every form,
A cloister for the monk, a fane for idols,
A pasture for gazelles, the pilgrim's
    Ka'ba,
The Tables of the Torah, the Koran.
Love is the faith I hold: wherever turn
His camels, still the one true faith is mine.

IBN ARABI (1165–1240)

We shall never be able, I say, to rest in the bosom of the Father, till the fatherhood is fully revealed to us in the love of the brothers. For He cannot be our Father, save as He is their Father; and if we do not see Him and feel Him as their Father, we cannot know Him as ours.

GEORGE MACDONALD (1824–1905)
Unspoken Sermons

And among His signs are the creation of the Heavens and of the earth, and your variety of tongues and color. Herein, truly, are signs for all men.   *The Koran*

We are not bidden to love God with one love, and our neighbor with another; neither are we instructed to cleave to the Creator with part of our love, and to creation

with another part; but in one and the same undivided love should we embrace both God and our neighbor.

JOHANNES SCOTUS ERIGENA (815–877)
De Divisione Naturae

Try to love your neighbor with relentless, active, affective fervor. As your love grows, you will become more and more convinced of both the existence of God and the immortality of the soul.

FYODOR DOSTOEVSKY (1821–1881)
The Brothers Karamazov

Your brother needs your help, but you meanwhile mumble your little prayers to God, pretending not to see your brother's need.

DESIDERIUS ERASMUS (1466–1536)
Enchiridion

Does it never come to your mind to fear lest He should demand of you why you had not exercised towards your brother a little of that mercy which He, who is your Master, so abundantly bestows on you?

FRANÇOIS FÉNELON (1651–1715)
Letters and Reflections

No creed, no history, or Bible shall interpose a cloud betwixt man and God: reverence for Moses, Jesus, or Mohamet shall no more be a stone between our eyes and truth, but a glass telescope, a microscope to bring the thought of God yet nearer to our hearts.

THEODORE PARKER (1810–1860)
Theism, Atheism and the Popular Theology

To consider mankind otherwise than brethren, to think favors are peculiar to one nation and exclude others, plainly supposes a darkness in the understanding. For, as God's love is universal, so where the mind is sufficiently influenced by it, it begets a likeness of itself, and the heart is enlarged towards all men.

JOHN WOOLMAN (1720–1772)
Journal

Every unkindness to another is a little Death
In the Divine Image; nor can Man exist but by Brotherhood.

WILLIAM BLAKE (1757–1827)
Jerusalem

I cannot love God without devoting my whole heart as living for the sake of my fellow-men, without devoting my entire soul as responsive to all the spiritual trends in the world around me, without devoting all my force to this God in His correlation with man.

HERMANN COHEN (1842–1918)
The Concept of Religion in the System of Philosophy

The man who perceives in his own mind the Supreme Mind present in all creatures, acquires equanimity toward them all, and shall be absorbed at last in the highest essence, even the eternal One himself.   *The Code of Manu*

A wise man once cried from the depth of his heart: "Would I could love the best of men as tenderly as God loves the worst."
The Hasidic Anthology

He that saith he is in the light, and hateth his brother, is in darkness even until now. He that loveth his brother abideth in the light, and there is no occasion of stumbling in him. But he who hateth his brother is in darkness, and walketh in darkness, and knoweth not whither he goeth, because that darkness hath blinded his eyes.   *The New Testament*
1 John 2:9–11

The Christian is not to become a Hindu, or a Buddhist, nor a Hindu or Buddhist to become a Christian. But each must assimilate the spirit of the others and yet preserve his individuality and grow according to his own law of growth. If the Parliament of Religions has shown anything to the world it is this: it has proved to the world that holiness, purity, and charity are not the exclusive possessions of any church in the world and that every system has produced men and women of the most exalted character.

SWAMI VIVEKANANDA (1863–1902)
The Universal Gospel

Gratitude to God, who treats all men as equal!
Thou art our Universal Father. All are partners in Thee.
Thou disownest none.

GURU ARJAN (1563–1606)
Hymns

If we have sinned against the man who loves us,
Have ever wronged a brother, friend, or comrade,
The neighbor ever with us, or a stranger,
O Varuna, remove us from the trespass!
The Rig-Veda

This commandment have we from Him: that he who loveth God, loves his brother also.   *The New Testament*
1 John 4:21

Therefore if thou bring thy gift to the altar, and there rememberest that thy brother hath ought against thee; leave there thy gift before the altar, and go thy way; first be reconciled to thy brother, and then come and offer thy gift.

The New Testament
Matthew 5:23–24

The Lord looketh from Heaven; he be-
holdeth all the sons of men. He fashioneth
their hearts alike.   *The Old Testament*
Psalms 33:13–15

Regard all men as equal, since God's
light is contained in the heart of each.
GURU NANAK (1469–1539)
Hymns

O brother man, fold to thy heart thy
  brother!
Where pity dwells, the peace of God is
  there;
To worship rightly is to love each other,
Each smile a hymn, each kindly deed a
  prayer.
JOHN GREENLEAF WHITTIER (1807–1892)
Worship

Do you wish to receive mercy? Show
mercy to thy neighbor.
SAINT JOHN CHRYSOSTOM (345–407)
Homilies

He who prays for his neighbor will be
heard for himself.   *Hebrew Proverb*

And I know that the hand of God is the
  elder hand of my own,
And I know that the spirit of God is the
  eldest brother of my own,
And that all men ever born are also my
  brothers.
WALT WHITMAN (1819–1892)
Leaves of Grass

Truly I perceive that God shows no particularity, but in every nation, any one who
fears him and does what is right is acceptable to Him.   *The New Testament*
Acts 10:34–35

Whatever form one desires to worship
in faith and devotion, in that very form I
make that faith of his secure.
The Bhagavad Gita

I understand the origin of brotherhood
among men. Men were brothers in God.
One can be a brother only *in* something.
Where there is no tie that binds men, men
are not united but merely lined up. One
cannot be a brother to nobody.
ANTOINE DE SAINT-EXUPÉRY (1900–1945)
Flight to Arras

Although God is merciful and pardons
the sins of man against himself, he who
has wronged his neighbor must gain that
neighbor's forgiveness before he can claim
the mercy of the Lord.   *The Talmud*

This was the commandment, "Thou
shalt love thy neighbor as thyself," but
when the commandment is rightly understood, it also says the converse, "Thou
shalt love thyself in the right way."
SÖREN KIERKEGAARD (1813–1855)
Works of Love

The younger Samuel used to say, "Rejoice not when thine enemy falls and let
not thy heart be glad when he stumbles,
lest the Lord see it and it be evil in his
sight, and he turn his wrath from him."
The Talmud

Judge not thy neighbor till thou art in
his situation.   *The Mishnah*

It is impossible for man to stand alone.
He must be near to his fellow-men. One
should never say: What have I to do with
so-and-so; he is not worthy of being my
friend; he has sinned; he is wicked. Nay,
man should strive to bring others near
unto himself and not repel them.
JUDAH LOEW BEN BEZALEL (16th century)
The Path of Life

The rich and the poor meet face to face,
for the Lord is the creator of them both.
The Old Testament
Proverbs 22:2

When mankind languishes in pain let no man say I shall return unto my own household, eat and drink and be at peace! Nay, each man must be willing to suffer with his fellowmen. He who shares the afflictions of others will merit to behold the comforting of humanity. *The Talmud*

I believe in God, who made of one blood all nations that on earth do dwell. I believe that all men, black and brown and white are brothers, varying through time and opportunity, in form and gift and feature, but differing in no essential particular, and alike in soul and the possibility of infinite development.

W. E. B. DU BOIS (1868–1963)
Dark Water

And why beholdest thou the mote that is in thy brother's eye, but considerest not the beam that is in thy eye? Or how wilt thou say to thy brother, "Let me pull the mote out of thine eye"; and, behold, that is in thine own eye? Thou hypocrite, first cast the beam out of thine own eye; and then shalt thou see clearly to cast the mote out of thy brother's eye.

The New Testament
Matthew 7:3–5

Before God, there is neither Greek nor barbarian, neither rich nor poor, and the slave is as good as the master, for by birth all men are free; they are citizens of the universal commonwealth which embraces all the world, brethren of one family, and children of God.

JOHN EMERICH EDWARD DALBERG ACTON
(1834–1902)
The History of Freedom in Antiquity

The glory of Friendship is not the outstretched hand, nor the kindly smile, nor the joy of companionship; it is the spiritual inspiration that comes to one when he discovers that someone else believes in him and is willing to trust him with his friendship. My friends have come unsought. The great God gave them to me.

RALPH WALDO EMERSON (1803–1882)
Journal

And let none of you imagine evil in your hearts against his neighbor; and love no false oath: for all these are things that I hate, saith the Lord. *The Old Testament*
Zechariah 8:17

So that we need not strive about any thing, we have no cause of contention with each other. Let every one only exercise himself in learning how he may enter again into the Love of God and his Brother. JACOB BOEHME (1575–1624)
Regeneration

To pray together, in whatever tongue or ritual, is the most tender brotherhood of hope and sympathy that men can contact in this life.

MADAME DE STAËL (1766–1817)
Corinne

The most elementary ethical principle, when understood by the heart, means that out of reverence for the unfathomable, infinite, and living Reality we call God, we must never consider ourselves strangers toward any human being. Rather, we must bind ourselves to the task of sharing his experiences and try being of help to him.

ALBERT SCHWEITZER (1875–1965)
Reverence for Life

After long study and experience, I have come to the conclusion that (1) all religions are true; (2) all religions have some error in them; (3) all religions are almost as dear to me as my own Hinduism, in as much as all human beings should be as dear to one as one's own close relatives. My own veneration for other faiths is the same as that for my own faith; therefore no thought of conversion is possible. The aim of the Fellowship should be to help a Hindu to become a better Hindu, a Mussalman to become a better Mussalman, and a Christian a better Christian. Our prayer for others must be not "God, give him the light thou hast given me," but "Give him all the light and truth he needs for his development." Pray merely that your friends may become better men, whatever their form of religion.

> MOHANDAS K. GANDHI (1869–1948)
> *Selected Addresses*

Brotherly love brings to earth, through the heart of man, the fire of eternal life, which is the true peacemaker, and it must vitalize from within that natural virtue of friendship, disregarded by so many fools, which is the very soul of social communities.   JACQUES MARITAIN (1882–1973)
> *The Range of Reason*

Obedience to God consists solely in love for our neighbor—for whosoever loveth his neighbor, as a means of obeying God, hath, as St. Paul says (Romans 13:8), fulfilled the law.

> BENEDICT SPINOZA (1632–1677)
> *Theologico-Political Treatise*

For, brethren, ye have been called unto liberty; only use not liberty as an occasion for the flesh, but by love serve one another. For all the law is fulfilled in one word, even in this: Thou shalt love thy neighbor as thyself.   *The New Testament*
> *Galatians 5:13–14*

Regard all men as equal since God's light is contained in the heart of each.

> GURU NANAK (1469–1539)
> *The Adi Granth*

All Adam's sons are limbs of one another,
Each of the self-same substance as his
   brothers,

So, while one member suffers ache and
   grief,
The other members cannot win relief.
Thou, who art heedless of thy brother's
   pain,
It is not right at all to name thee man.
> SAADI (1184–1291)
> *Gulistan*

Let man ever be subtle in the fear of God, giving a soft answer that turneth away wrath. Let him increase the peace with his brothers, with his relatives, and with all men, that he may be loved above and desired below, and well-received by his fellow creatures.   *The Talmud*

He's true to God who's true to man;
   wherever wrong is done
To the humblest and the weakest, 'neath
   the all-beholding sun,
That wrong is also done to us. . . .
> JAMES RUSSELL LOWELL (1819–1891)
> *On the Capture of Certain Fugitive Slaves*

Intimacy with God means becoming filled with love towards everyone—love which means the desire to do what will be good for them and not what will be good or pleasant for us.

> WILLIAM TEMPLE (1881–1944)
> *Daily Readings*

Do not displease God by hating him whom he loves. A father's love for his child is only a drop in the ocean compared with God's love for man. How, then, can you slander your neighbor or raise your voice against him?   JACOB KRANZ (1740–1804)
> *Sefer ha-Middoth*

Remember that we should not call our brother a fool; for we ourselves do not know what we are. God alone can judge and know.   PARACELSUS (1493–1541)
> *Philosophia Sagax*

"If we love one another, God dwelleth in us." Where there is no recognition of the neighbor, there can be no recognition of God; and furthermore, where there is no recognition of the reality of the corporeal world, there can be no recognition either of the neighbor or of God, since it is in the world that I encounter my neighbor, and God through my neighbor, and my neighbor through God.

JOHN BAILLIE (1886–1960)
The Sense of the Presence of God

To the one Father God corresponds the unifying conception of the family of peoples. Just as the one origin in creation, so the one redemption and fulfilment as the goal of history gathers the destinies of nations into a comprehensive unity.

EMIL BRUNNER (1889–1966)
Eternal Hope

I understand, finally, why the love of God created men responsible for one another and gave them hope as a virtue. Since it made of each of them the ambassador of the same God, in the hands of each rested the salvation of all.

ANTOINE DE SAINT-EXUPÉRY (1900–1945)
Flight to Arras

So long as thou hast a whole and undivided love towards all men, a share of the virtues and divine influences which God intends to bestow on men will flow out through thee in this love of thine.

JOHANNES TAULER (1300–1361)
Sermons on the Inner Way

The Lord make you to increase and abound in love toward one another, and toward all men. *The New Testament*
1 Thessalonians 3:12

The family of God is meant to be a unity, but a unity of real living men and women, really bringing something—a unique creative gift—to the common life.

GERALD VANN (1906–1963)
The Divine Pity

It is true that we are all brothers; one God made us all, and we all have one plan, one purpose. This is the meaning and purpose of creation, for we all have one Creator who acknowledges that He is the rightful Husband of the most miserable and pitiful creature, of even the most detestable prostitute. This is an astonishing, incomprehensible, and heart-stirring truth: He makes no distinctions; all souls are His.

COUNT NIKOLAUS LUDWIG VON ZINZENDORF
(1700–1760)
Nine Public Lectures on Religion

Union is one of the most amiable things that pertains to human society; yea, it is one of the most beautiful and happy things on earth, which indeed makes earth most like heaven. God has made of one blood all nations of men, to dwell on all the face of the earth; hereby teaching us this moral lesson, that it becomes mankind all to be united as one family.

JONATHAN EDWARDS (1703–1758)
Sermons

In the last resort, a love of God without love of man is no love at all.

HANS KÜNG (1928–)
On Being a Christian

All men are brothers; all receive the blessings of the same heaven.

Shinto Proverb

To love our neighbor as ourself is such a fundamental truth for regulating human society, that by that alone one might determine all the cases in social morality.

JOHN LOCKE (1632–1704)
The Reasonableness of Christianity

Biology has long since confirmed Paul's discovery that God has made of one blood all the nations of the earth. Every civilization built on less than that has crashed or crumbled to ruin. Unless we can learn to practice brotherhood, our children's children must go back to the cave, perhaps to cannibalism.

HAROLD MARSHALL (1866–1932)
Sermons

To honour every man, absolutely every man, is the truth, and this is what it is to fear God and love one's "neighbor."

SÖREN KIERKEGAARD (1813–1855)
That Individual

Ah, yet, we cannot be kind to each other
    here for an hour;
We whisper, and hint, and chuckle, and
    grin at a brother's shame;
However we brave it out, we men are a
    little breed.

ALFRED LORD TENNYSON (1809–1892)
Maud

"Our Father" requires that we regard all men as brothers, for the "our" cannot be muted. Beyond race and rank, beyond learning and ignorance (if any man is learned), beyond goodness and badness (if any man is good), we accept our neighbors when we pray, as we ourselves are accepted of God. Perhaps prayer is the only bond of brotherhood.

GEORGE ARTHUR BUTTRICK (1892–1979)
Sermons Preached in a University Church

Since God, if we regard him only as Creator, is our common Father, we are all brothers as we are all his creatures, and this natural relationship should lead us all to love one another.

JEAN NICHOLAS GROU (1730–1803)
The School of Jesus Christ

God can show Himself as He really is only to real men. And that means not simply to men who are individually good, but to men who are united together in a body, loving one another, helping one another, showing Him to one another. For that is what God meant humanity to be like; like players in one band, or organs in one body.

C. S. LEWIS (1898–1963)
Beyond Personality

When you love men, the world quickly becomes yours: and yourself become a greater treasure than the world is. For all their persons are your treasures, and all the things in Heaven and Earth that serve them are yours.

THOMAS TRAHERNE (1637–1674)
Centuries of Meditations

Men who are partners in the redemptive task of God Himself have all the dignity of personal life that is required to lift them out of mediocrity, but their glorification does not come at the expense of others or by means of antagonism.

D. ELTON TRUEBLOOD (1900–)
Alternative to Futility

In the sphere of religion we cannot adopt the dualistic attitude that the plants in my garden are of God, while those in my neighbor's garden are planted by the devil which we should destroy at any cost.

SARVEPALLI RADHAKRISHNAN (1888–1975)
Addresses

I let men worship as they will, I reap
No revenue from the field of unbelief.
I call from every faith and race the best
And bravest soul for counsellor and
    friend.

ALFRED LORD TENNYSON (1809–1892)
Akbar's Dream

It is a shame for you to forget that men are brothers. Are not two who come out of the heart of God as closely related as if they had lain in the womb of one mother?

GEORGE MACDONALD (1824–1905)
Unspoken Sermons

Do justice to your brother (you can do that whether you love him or not), and you will come to love him. But do injustice to him because you don't love him, and you will come to hate him.

JOHN RUSKIN (1819–1900)
Unto This Last

Have Love. Not love alone for one,
  But man as man thy brother
call;
And scatter like the circling sun
  Thy charities on all.

JOHANN FRIEDRICH VON SCHILLER
(1759–1805)
Three Lessons

Everywhere I am hindered of meeting God in my brother, because he has shut his own temple doors, and recites fables mostly of his brother's or his brother's brother's God.

RALPH WALDO EMERSON (1803–1882)
Self-Reliance

If ye fulfill the royal law according to the scripture, "Thou shalt love thy neighbor as thyself," ye do well. *The New Testament James 2:8*

In order to receive the life of the World-Spirit, and have religion, man must first, in love, and through love, have found humanity. A longing for love, ever satisfied and ever again renewed, forthwith becomes religion.

FRIEDRICH SCHLEIERMACHER (1768–1834)
On Religion

"Love your neighbor as yourself"—as yourself without difference or distinction, without subterfuge and mental reservation, literally as yourself.

MOSES LUZZATTO (1707–1747)
The Way of the Upright

The love of our neighbor is the only door out of the dungeon of self, where we mope and mow, striking sparks, and rubbing phosphorescence out of the walls, and blowing our own breath in our own nostrils, instead of issuing to the fair sunlight of God, the sweet winds of the universe.

GEORGE MACDONALD (1824–1905)
Sermons

But as touching brotherly love ye need not that I write unto you: for ye yourselves are taught of God to love one another.

*The New Testament
1 Thessalonians 4:9*

Enthroned in the heart of Reality there is One whose demand it is that men shall lose themselves in mutual love. For us who walk our little day upon the surface of a second-rate satellite of a tenth-rate star to defy this decree of Him who transcends Time and Space, is suicidal folly.

BERNARD IDDINGS BELL (1886–1958)
Still Shine the Stars

The children of the world are all separated one from another because their hearts are in different places; but the children of God having their heart where their treasure is, and all having only one treasure which is the same God, are, consequently, always joined and united together.

SAINT FRANCIS OF SALES (1567–1622)
Sermons

If I hate or despise any one man in the world, I hate something that God cannot hate, and despise that which He loves.

WILLIAM LAW (1686–1761)
A Serious Call to a Devout and Holy Life

The saint is he who bears enmity to no
living creature.
There is but one Spirit: he has no enemy.

DADU (1554–1603)
The Bani

"Thy priests are clad in righteousness."
This verse of the Psalms refers to righteous men of all nations. They are priests
to the Holy One, blessed be He.

The Midrash

Humanity does not find the ideal of
brotherhood so easily realised as expected,
but finds more and more divisions of individuals, parties, and nations; the impulses, emotions, and passions of human
nature develop deeper and wider; the tyranny of the petty common life becomes
more and more brutal; and more and
more we are threatened with the death of
the Spiritual Life.

RUDOLF EUCKEN (1846–1926)
The Truth of Religion

We have heard it said that there is not a
Quaker or a Baptist, a Presbyterian or an
Episcopalian, a Catholic or a Protestant in
heaven; that on entering the gate, we leave
those badges of schism behind, and find
ourselves united in those principles only in
which God has united us all. Let us not be
uneasy then about the different roads we
may pursue, as believing them the shortest, to that our last abode; but, following
the guidance of a good conscience, let us
be happy in the hope that by these different paths we shall all meet in the end.

THOMAS JEFFERSON (1743–1826)
Letters to Miles King

In the presence of God with His dream
of order there is neither male nor female,
white nor black, Gentile nor Jew, Protestant nor Catholic, Hindu, Buddhist, nor
Moslem, but a human spirit stripped to the
literal substance of itself.

HOWARD THURMAN (1899–1981)
Sermons

All souls are brother-spirits, the offspring
of one womb;
Consider this truth. Who then is the
other, O foolish one?

DADU (1554–1603)
The Bani

So long as thou hast a whole and undivided love toward all men, a share of the
divine influences which God intends to bestow on all men will flow out through thee
in this love of thine. The moment thou
severest thyself from this spirit of universal love thou wilt miss this outflow of divine love, which otherwise would fill thy
vessel overbrimming full.

JOHANNES TAULER (1300–1361)
Sermons on the Inner Way

Consider to what a dignity he exalts
himself who esteems his brother's salvation as of great importance. Such a man is
imitating God as far as lies within the
power of man. Hear what God says speaking through His prophet: "He who separates the worthy from the vile shall be as
my mouth." What He says is that he who
is eager to save a brother who has fallen
into careless ways, that man imitates Me as
far as lies in human power.

SAINT JOHN CHRYSOSTOM (347–407)
Sermons

There is one, and only one, conception
of the world in which a man necessarily
assumes a right attitude and relationship
to his fellow-men. It is that conception
which thinks of the whole world as God's
Family.   PHILLIPS BROOKS (1835–1893)
The Mystery of Iniquity

The true meaning of love of one's
neighbor is not that it is a command from

God which we are to fulfill, but that through it and in it we meet God.

MARTIN BUBER (1878–1965)
At the Turning

The bidding, "Thou shalt love thy neighbor as thyself," has true value only when it springs from and is linked to the bidding "And thou shalt love the Lord thy God," and acquires endurance and significance only from this linkage.

SHOLEM ASCH (1880–1957)
What I Believe

It is not by driving away our brother that we can be alone with God.

GEORGE MACDONALD (1824–1905)
Alec Forbes

The Lord took dust from the four corners of the earth in equal measure. Some of the dust was red, some black, some white, and some as yellow as sand. These He mixed with water from all the oceans in the seas, to indicate that all races of mankind should be included in the first man and none be counted as superior to the other.   *The Midrash*

The Maker has linked together the whole race of man with a chain of love. I like to think that there is no man but has had kindly feelings for some other, and he for his neighbor, until we bind together the whole family of Adam.

WILLIAM MAKEPEACE THACKERAY
(1811–1863)
Cornhill to Grand Cairo

· THE GOLDEN RULE OF MANKIND ·

As thou conductest thyself towards others, so doth the Lord conduct Himself towards thee. If thou are kind and merciful, the Lord will be kind and merciful towards thee.

BAAL SHEM TOV (1700–1760)
Sayings

When God created man, He gave him his heart; in paradise He gave him knowledge of good and evil, and taught him not to do unto others what he would not have done unto himself. For such is the law, and such is the heart we received from the hand of God when He created us.

PARACELSUS (1493–1541)
On the Generation of Man

In joy and sorrow, in pleasure and pain, one should act towards others as one would have them act toward oneself.

The Mahabharata

In the name, then, and in the strength of God, let us resolve not to hurt one another; to do nothing unkind or unfriendly to each other, nothing which we would not have done to ourselves.

JOHN WESLEY (1703–1791)
A Letter to a Roman Catholic

The duty of man is not a wilderness of turnpike gates, through which he is to pass by tickets from one to another. It is plain and simple, and consists but of two points —his duty to God, which every man must feel; and with respect to his neighbor, to do as he would be done by.

THOMAS PAINE (1737–1809)
The Age of Reason

Wouldst thou then serve God? Do not that alone, which thou wouldst not that another should see thee do.

WILLIAM PENN (1644–1718)
Some Fruits of Solitude

Thou shalt love the Lord thy God, and thy neighbor as thyself. This means: you shall forgive others as you wish God to forgive you. You shall do to others what you ask may be done to you, so that the blood of love, through which alone forgiveness comes, may circulate full circle.

ROMANO GUARDINI (1885–1968)
The Lord's Prayer

To desire to communicate good to every creature, in the degree we can, and it is capable of receiving from us, is a divine temper; for thus God stands unchangeably disposed toward the whole creation.

WILLIAM LAW (1686–1761)
A Serious Call to a Devout and Holy Life

He conceived it his duty and much delighted in the obligation, that he was to treat every man in the whole world as the representative of mankind, and that he was to meet him, and to pay unto him all the love of God, Angels and Men.

THOMAS TRAHERNE (1637–1674)
Centuries of Meditations

Do with another, that it may be done with thee; for thou aboundest and thou lackest. Thou aboundest in things temporal; thou lackest things eternal. A beggar is at thy gate, thou art thyself a beggar at God's gate. As thou dealest with *thy* seeker, even God will deal with His. Thou art both empty and full. Fill thou the empty out of thy fulness, that out of the fulness of God thine emptiness may be filled.   SAINT AUGUSTINE (354–430)
Sermons

Is there a deed, Rahula, thou dost wish to do? Then bethink thee thus: "Is this deed conducive to my own harm, or to others' harm, or to that of both?" Then

this is a bad deed, entailing suffering. Such a deed must thou surely not do.

GAUTAMA BUDDHA (563–483 B.C.)
Majjhima Nikaya

This is the sum of true righteousness— treat others as thou would'st thyself be treated. Do nothing to thy neighbor which hereafter thou would'st not have thy neighbor do to thee, in causing pleasure or in giving pain, in doing good, or injury to others.   *The Mahabharata*

He who returns evil for good, shall not evil go forth from his abode? He who returns evil for evil acts wrongly. He should have patience and God will give him help on this account.   *The Zohar*

For the whole law is fulfilled in one word, "You shall love your neighbor as yourself."   *The New Testament*
Galatians 5:14

Deal not unjustly with others, and ye shall not be dealt with unjustly.

The Koran

Tzu Kung asked: "Is there any one word that can serve as a principle for the conduct of life?" Confucius said: "Perhaps the word 'reciprocity': Do not do to others what you would not want others to do to you."   CONFUCIUS (551–479 B.C.)
Analects

The correlation between man and God is predicated on the correlation between man and man. Only when we are aware of our neighbor as a fellow-man are we fit to enter into correlation with God.

HERMANN COHEN (1842–1918)
Rational Religion

That nature alone is good which refrains from doing unto another whatsoever is not good for itself.

Zoroastrian Golden Rule
Dadistan-i-dinik 94:5

Regard your neighbor's gain as your own gain, and your neighbor's loss as your own loss. *Taoist Golden Rule*
T'ai Shang Kan Ying P'ien

No one of you is a believer until he desires for his brother that which he desires for himself. *The Koran*

The Lord seeks out the heart that is full of love for God and neighbor. This is the throne upon which he likes to sit and where he appears in the plenitude of his heavenly glory. "Son, give me your heart," he says, "and everything else I shall add unto you," because the Kingdom of God is in the human heart.

SAINT SERAPHIM OF SAROV (1759–1833)
Sermons

He who wins honor through his neighbor's shame will never reach Paradise.
Hebrew Proverb

Skilful alike with tongue and pen,
He preached to all men everywhere
The Gospel of the Golden Rule,
The New Commandments given to men,
Thinking the deed, and not the creed,
Would help us in our utmost need.

HENRY WADSWORTH LONGFELLOW
(1807–1882)
Tales of a Wayside Inn

God's attitude toward us is regulated by our attitude toward our neighbor. That is why if we need something badly, the best way to pray for it is to give something away. If we have sinned and need forgiveness, then let us forgive our enemies. God will never be outdone by our love.

FULTON J. SHEEN (1895–1979)
The Electronic Christian

The man who fears the Lord keeps his friendships in repair, for he treats his neighbor as himself.

The Old Testament Apocrypha
Ecclesiasticus 6:17

Every man takes care that his neighbor does not cheat him. But a day comes when he begins to care that he do not cheat his neighbor. Then all goes well.

RALPH WALDO EMERSON (1803–1882)
Conduct of Life

In happiness and suffering, in joy and grief, we should regard all creatures as we regard our own self, and should therefore refrain from inflicting upon others such injury as would appear undesirable to us if inflicted upon ourselves.

Jain Golden Rule
Yogashastra 2:20

As thou deemest thyself so deem others. Then shalt thou become a partner in heaven. KABIR (1450–1518)
The Adi Granth

Be you to others kind and true,
As you'd have others be to you;
And neither do nor say to men
Whate'er you would not take again.

ISAAC WATTS (1674–1748)
Divine Songs for Children

Confucius has not yet gathered all his fame. When Socrates heard that the oracle declared that he was the wisest of men, he said, it must mean that other men held that they were wise, but that he knew that he knew nothing. Confucius had already affirmed this of himself: and what we call the Golden Rule of Jesus, Confucius had uttered in the same terms five hundred years before.

RALPH WALDO EMERSON (1803–1882)
Speech at Chinese Embassy, 1868

He that loves his neighbor has fulfilled the Law. *Hebrew Proverb*

I believe that the true welfare of man lies in the fulfillment of the Will of God; and that His will consists in men loving each other, and therefore behaving to-

ward others as they desire that others should behave with them. I believe that the meaning of the life of every man, therefore, lies only in the increase of love in himself; that this increase of love leads the individual man in this life toward greater and greater welfare; that after death it gives the greater welfare the more love there be in the man; and that, at the same time, more than anything else, it contributes to the establishment of the Kingdom of God on earth, i.e., to an order of life where the discord, deceit, and violence which now reign will be replaced by free agreement, truth, and brotherly love between men.   LEO TOLSTOY (1828–1910)
My Confession

Those that have loved themselves and not their neighbors will find themselves April fools when the great April opens the truth that neither selves nor neighbor-selves were anything more than vicinities.
CHARLES PEIRCE (1839–1914)
Collected Papers

Should anyone turn aside the right of the stranger, it is as though he were to turn aside the right of the most high God.
The Talmud

Your neighbor's right is God's right.
Turkish Proverb

The sufferings and miseries of men continue because of their neglect of the law of the Golden Rule given them two thousand years ago.   LEO TOLSTOY (1828–1910)
Emblems

As thou deemest thyself, so deem others; then shalt thou become a partner in heaven.   KABIR (1440–1518)
Hymns

He who loves best his fellow man is serving God in the holiest way he can.
CONFUCIUS (551–479 B.C.)
Analects

As to what God expects from man with relation to each other, everyone must know his duty who considers that the common parent of mankind has the whole species alike under his protection, and will equally punish him for injuring others, as he would others for injuring him; and consequently that it is his duty to deal with them, as he expects they should deal with him in the like circumstances.
MATTHEW TINDAL (1657–1733)
Christianity as Old as the Creation

The golden rule of conduct is mutual toleration, seeing that we will never all think alike and that we shall always see Truth in fragments and from different angles of vision.
MOHANDAS K. GANDHI (1869–1948)
Harijan

When evil is unpleasant to thee, do not do it thyself;
Say, after that, to thy neighbor: "Do not evil."

SAADI (1184–1291)
Bustan

Until we begin to learn that the only way to serve God in any real sense of the word is to serve our neighbor, we may have knocked at the wicket gate, but I doubt if we have got one foot across the threshold of the Kingdom.
GEORGE MACDONALD (1824–1905)
Unspoken Sermons

· To Love Your Neighbor ·

Who is mighty? He who turns an enemy into his friend.   *The Talmud*

Love your enemy not because he is your enemy but because beneath his enmity is the eternal fact of brotherhood. Because there is one God and Father of us all, no child of God can be outside the pale of human brotherhood.

HAROLD MARSHALL (1866–1932)
Sermons

Let a man believe that whatever occurs to him is from the Blessed One! For instance, when a wicked man meets him and abuses him, and puts him to shame, let him receive it with love, and say, "The Lord told him to curse, and he is the messenger of God on account of my Sin."

The Kabbalah

Everything has two handles, one by which it may be carried, the other by which it cannot. If your brother be unjust, do not take up the matter by that handle—the handle of his injustice—for that handle is the one by which it cannot be taken up; but rather by the handle that he is your brother and brought up with you; and then you will be taking it up as it can be carried.   EPICTETUS (1st century)
Enchiridion

If God's love is in us we cannot intend evil for any man. God's love intends no evil for any man and can wish evil for no one. He who does not will evil for any man, because of the quality and the power of the love of God, will not be deceived by any man nor led astray by word or deed.

JOHANN ARNDT (1555–1621)
True Christianity

Is it then reasonable to love our enemies? God does; therefore it must be the highest reason. But is it reasonable to expect that man should become capable of doing so? Yes; on one ground: that the divine energy is at work in man, to render at length man's doing divine as his nature is.   GEORGE MACDONALD (1824–1905)
Unspoken Sermons

If you think evil of men, it means that an evil spirit lives in you and inspires you with those thoughts. And if anyone does not repent and dies without forgiving his brother, his soul will go where the evil spirit who took possession of his soul resides. We live under this law: if you forgive people, it means that you are forgiven by God, but if you do not forgive your brother, your sin remains with you.

STARETZ SILOUAN (1866–1938)
Meditations

Show love to all creatures, and thou wilt be happy; for when thou lovest all things, thou lovest the Lord, for he is all in all.

TULSI DAS (1543–1623)
The Lake of Rama's Deeds

We cannot know whether we love God, although there may be strong reasons for thinking so, but there can be no doubt about whether we love our neighbor or no.

SAINT TERESA (1515–1582)
El Castillo Interior

"Love your neighbor as yourself" is the great principle of the Torah.

The Midrash

A love both just and balanced will be yours, if you deny not to your brother's need what you refuse to your own base desires. The love of God extended thus becomes benevolence.

SAINT BERNARD OF CLAIRVAUX (1091–1153)
On the Love of God

What saves me, that is, transfigures my nature, is not only love for God but also love for humanity. Love for my neighbor, for my brothers and sisters, matters of love enter into the way of my salvation, my transfiguration. Into the way of my salvation enters love for animals and plants, for each blade of grass, for stones, for rivers and seas, for mountains and fields. I am saved by this love and the whole world is saved as well; illumination is achieved.

NIKOLAI BERDYAEV (1874–1948)
Salvation and Creativity

Let us live happily, without enemies in a world of enmity; let us dwell without enmity among men who are filled with enmity.   *The Dhammapada*

The best principle whereby a man can steer his course in this world, is that which being well prosecuted will make his life at once honorable and happy: which is to love every man in the whole world as God does.

THOMAS TRAHERNE (1637–1674)
Christian Ethics

Lovest thou God as thou oughtest, then
   lovest thou likewise thy brethren;
One is the sun in heaven, and one, only
   one, is Love also.

HENRY WADSWORTH LONGFELLOW
(1807–1882)
The Children of the Lord's Supper

· LET EVERY CREATURE HAVE YOUR LOVE ·

Let every creature have your love. Love, with its fruits of meekness, patience, and humility, is all that we can wish for ourselves, and our fellow-creatures; for this is to live in God, united to him, both for time and eternity.

WILLIAM LAW (1686–1761)
A Serious Call to a Devout and Holy Life

Nothing could persuade me that "in the image of God" applied only to man. In fact it seemed to me that the high mountains, the rivers, lakes, trees, flowers, and animals far better exemplified the essence of God than men with their ridiculous clothes, their meanness, vanity, mendacity, and abhorrent egotism.

CARL JUNG (1875–1961)
Memories, Dreams, Reflections

There is no life so humble that, if it be true and genuinely human and obedient to God, it may not hope to shed some of His light. There is no life so meager that the greatest and wisest of us can afford to despise it. We cannot know at all what sudden moment it may flash forth with the life of God.   PHILLIPS BROOKS (1835–1893)
Sermons

To say we love God, and, at the same time exercise cruelty toward the least creatures, is a contradiction in itself.

JOHN WOOLMAN (1720–1772)
The Inward Life

God says to his prophets, "Think not that if you do not carry my messages my will cannot be made known in the world. I have many messengers—even such as a scorpion, a snake, a frog, or an insect."

The Midrash

In this light my spirit saw through all things and into all creatures and I recognized God in grass and plants.

JACOB BOEHME (1575–1624)
Aurora

All creatures desire to speak God in their works: they all speak him as well as they can, but they cannot really pronounce him. MEISTER ECKHART (1260–1327)
Sermons

A hundred thousand secrets are
  imbedded in an ant,
And in its heart an agitation arises out of
  love for Him!
Every particle is a lover filled with desire;
It is filled with a ray of the love of God!

SHARAFUDDIN MANERI (14th century)
The Hundred Letters

Whatever living beings there are, either feeble or strong, all either long or great, middle-sized, short, small or large, either seen or which are not seen, and which live far or near, either born or seeking birth, may all creatures be happy-minded.

GAUTAMA BUDDHA (563–483 B.C.)
Sutra of Mercy

The Holy One, blessed be He, declares no creature unworthy; rather He receives every one. The gates are opened at every hour, and whoever seeks to enter, will enter. *The Midrash*

Boundless compassion for all living beings is the surest and most certain guarantee of pure moral conduct, and needs no casuistry. Whoever is filled with it will assuredly injure no one, do harm to no one, encroach on no man's rights; he will rather have regard for everyone, forgive everyone, help everyone as far as he can, and all his actions will bear the stamp of justice and loving-kindness.

ARTHUR SCHOPENHAUER (1788–1860)
The Basis of Morality

The essence of God's omnipotence is, that while he can take the infinitely wide view of all created things, he can also take, I would fain believe, the infinitely just and minute point of view, and see the case from the standpoint of the smallest of his creatures!

ARTHUR CHRISTOPHER BENSON
(1862–1925)
The Thread of Gold

VII · Whatever Name They Give to God

O Thou Infinite Power, whom men call by varying names, but whose grandeur and whose love no name expresses and no words can tell; O Thou Creative Cause of all, Conserving Providence to each, we flee unto thee, and would seek for a moment to be conscious of the sunlight of thy presence, that we may lift up our souls unto thee, and fill ourselves with exceeding comfort and surpassing strength.

—THEODORE PARKER

FINALLY, in the last section of this collection, the God Seekers deal with a problem that has plagued humanity for thousands of years: our failure to realize that God does not favor any one of his creatures exclusively, and that any human being, regardless of his or her religious beliefs, is equally precious in God's eyes.

Even within our limited perception of God's ways, it is impossible to believe that He is other than One, the Master Architect of a universe in which his unity is indelibly imprinted in every single being that has or ever will exist.

The central theme of this final section is that whatever name we give to God is less important than the depth and reality with which we seek him. Do we really believe in the deepest recesses of our hearts that the Master of the Universe is concerned whether He is sought as the Tao, Brahman, Yahweh, Adonai, Father in Heaven, Amon, or any of the thousands of names men and women have addressed him as? As all true seekers are the same in his compassion, so all the mere symbols of language merge into the same word to God. Jacques Maritain wrote: "Under many names, names which are not that of God, in ways known only to God, the interior act of a soul's thought can be directed towards a reality which in fact may be God."

We find, then, that the God Seekers who have achieved their greatest spiritual joy in contemplating the Eternal Creator have never been excessively concerned with naming God. Like Saint Augustine they realized that the City of God is composed of men and women of every nation and every tongue. They also fully understood that the human experience in perceiving God often gets entangled in the symbols of language. As Harry Emerson Fosdick remarked, we can no more catch the essence of God in an abstract definition than a boy with a butterfly net can capture the sun at noon.

No matter by which name they sought their Creator, the God Seekers we have traveled with throughout this anthology believed that God has a personal and intimate concern with every single creature that has existed since the beginning of the universe.

Without question, many skeptics would say that such a thought is inconceivable, that it is a fantasy to believe that a tiny cricket chirping outside my open window is in rapport with the God who created it. How do they know that the cricket's song is not as welcome to God's ear as a magnificent choir chanting the *qui tolis* of Bach's Mass in B Minor?

Somehow it does not stretch the faith of our God Seekers to consider that the Master of the Universe can be concerned with every single one of his creations. Why? Because they do not conceive of God as some kind of ultimate superman or a gigantic, impersonal computer with an infinite number of terminals, and thus they do not limit God's power to the human equation. If, as William Paley perceived in the eighteenth century, even the most exquisitely designed and crafted of clocks could not describe or define the master clockmaker who had created it, how dare we presume we can limit the Illimitable Creator?

Does it make any difference to the Eternal Creator by which name we seek him? Only when we attribute human needs and practices to him are we compelled to speculate on such matters, as if the Master of the Universe were conducting some kind of cosmic Gallup Poll.

George Arthur Buttrick noted that humankind has always devised names for God, names that reflect what a particular people or culture visualized as the highest attribute of the Deity. Whether He is addressed by the Zoroastrians as Ahura Mazda, the Wise Creator, or as Allah, the Great Adored, by the followers of Mohammed, or by our Old English word *God,* which means the Ultimate Good, the Unknowable is always the Unnameable. If God is "the nameless of the hundred names," Buttrick said, it is equally true that we may find him in a hundred, a thousand names.

The essential message of the God Seekers is that the Master of the Universe hears the heartbeat of every single one of his creatures no matter by which name He is sought. As Martin Buber put it, "What does all mistaken talk about God's being and works matter in comparison with the one truth that all men who have addressed God had God himself in mind? For he who speaks the word God and has *Thou* in mind (whatever the illusion by which He is held), addresses the true *Thou* of his life."

Scientists tell us that the universe (or at least that part of it they can conceptualize) is fifteen billion years old. In the master plan of the Creator, our own special star, the sun, and the planets that revolved around it, came into being some ten billion years later. When the first single-cell species of life on earth evolved some three and a half billion years ago, was God any less present? In the nearly two and three-quarter billion years that passed before multicellular life manifested itself on earth, if God was not present, where was He?

Three or four million years ago the first humans appeared on earth, again fulfilling a plan that had been in God's mind before the existence of the entire universe. Finally, nearly three million years later, only five or six thousand years ago, humankind began to seek a name for the Creator of this incalculable vastness. Was God any less real for having been nameless during that long period of nearly three million years?

Too often we fail to realize that our efforts to name God are essentially a reflection of our search for him, and that all men and women in the world have an equal, God-given right to address him by any name that fulfills their search. When people forget this, as some have done throughout the thousands of years spent trying to stamp an exclusive name onto the Creator, they often end up defiling him in the most egregious way, by justifying the wholesale slaying of their fellows under the name *they* have given him!

Writing in *The Dial* in July 1842, Ralph Waldo Emerson captured the essence of this last section of our anthology; indeed, his words could serve as a theme for this volume as a whole:

Each nation has its bible more or less pure; none has yet been willing or able in a wise and devout spirit to collate its own with those of other nations, and sinking the civil-historical and ritual portions to bring together the grand expressions of the moral sentiment in different ages and races, the rules for the guidance of life, the bursts of piety and of abandonment to the Invisible and Eternal—a work inevitable sooner or later.

George MacDonald surmised that God has a different response for all who strive to find him: "With every man He has a secret—the secret of a new name. In every man there is a loneliness, an inner chamber of peculiar life which God only can enter."

And, surely, He did enter the lives of profound God Seekers as diverse as the Neoplatonic philosopher Plotinus, or Jalal-ud-din Rumi, the Sufi poet of poets, or the Catholic mystic Meister Eckhart, as well as the Hassidic saint the Baal Shem Tov, or the Quaker John Woolman—each of whom experienced a communion of their souls with a Creator who transcends all names.

The greatest of the God Seekers urge us to be faithful to our vision of God regardless of the religious creed of our birth. Just as many paths may lead to the top of a mountain, the paths we climb in our search for God lead us not only through cathedrals, synagogues, pagodas, and mosques, but perhaps through the forest in India where Gautama once achieved the peace that passeth understanding, or through meadows resplendent with flowers, or on an ocean shore where the great waves roll incessantly.

The message of salvation that the Master of the Universe had delegated to the God Seekers since the beginning of civilization is that we must now and forever live together peacefully. Jacques Maritain prayed for the day "when all the faithful could live with men of other creeds in perfect justice, love and understanding. If each person truly believed in the ethics of his or her respective religion, and if each kept that faith as purely as possible, said Maritain, strife between the peoples of the world would wither away.

Throughout this anthology we have turned again and again to the religious wisdom that emanated in all periods from India—India, where an exalted search for God preceded the Vedic literature at the beginning of humankind's religious sensibility; India, which gave birth to such profound God Seekers as Gautama Buddha, Guru Nanak, Kabir, Sri Ramakrishna, and Rabindranath Tagore. It seems appropriate that we turn yet once more to the eminent Indian scholar of comparative religion, the noted philosopher and statesman Sarvepalli Radhakrishnan. In *My Search for Truth,* Dr. Radhakrishnan drew together all the threads of this book:

My main contention has been to make out there is one perennial and universal philosophy which is found in all lands and cultures, in the seers of the Upanishads and the Buddha, Plato and Plotinus, in Hillel and Philo, Jesus and Paul and the medieval mystics of Islam. It is this spirit which binds continents and unites the ages that can save us from the meaninglessness of the present situation.

God in his grace and compassion has given humankind the need and the desire to seek communion with his eternal love. This yearning for an affirmation of our Creator has been expressed in various ways: in the paintings of Michelangelo or El Greco, the notes of a Bach cantata or a requiem mass by Mozart, or, as in this anthology, the words of some profound God Seekers. Together they have left an extraordinary spiritual legacy to all men and women who day by day seek the core of their existence; in their collective wisdom they have inspired us in the quest to find rapport with our Eternal Creator.

· WHATEVER NAME THEY GIVE ·

They call him Indra, Mitra, Varuna, Agni, and he is heavenly, nobly winged Garutman. To what is one, sages give many a name. They call it Agni, Yana, Matarisvam.   *The Rig-Veda*

Wherever I look, I see men quarrelling in the name of religion—Hindus, Mohammedans, Brahmans, Vaishnavas, and the rest. But they never reflect that He who is called Krishna is also called Siva, and bears the name of the Primal Energy, Jesus and Allah as well—the same Rama with a thousand names.

SRI RAMAKRISHNA (1834–1886)
Works

In the depth of every living religion there is a point at which the religion itself loses its importance, and that to which it points breaks through its particularity, elevating it to spiritual freedom and with it to a vision of the spiritual presence in other expressions of the ultimate meaning of man's existence.

PAUL TILLICH (1886–1965)
*Christianity and the Encounter
of the World's Religions*

May He Who is the Father in Heaven of the Christians, Holy One of the Jews, Allah of the Mohammedans, Buddha of the Buddhists, Tao of the Chinese, Ahura Mazda of the Zoroastrians and Brahman of the Hindus lead us from the unreal to the Real, from darkness to light, from disease and death to immortality. May the All-Loving Being manifest Himself unto us, and grant us abiding understanding and all-consuming divine love. Peace. Peace. Peace be unto all.

SWAMI AKHILANANDA (1894–1962)
Prayer of Religious Harmony

Call him, as thou pleasest, either Nature, or Fate, or Fortune—it makes no matter, because they are all the names of the self-same God, who diversely useth his divine providence. Even as Justice, Integrity, Prudence, Magnanimity, Temperance, and the goods and virtues of the soul of any of these, please thee, it is then the soul that pleaseth thee also.

LUCIUS ANNAEUS SENECA (4 B.C.–A.D. 65)
God in Nature

Children of men! the unseen Power,
  whose eye
Forever doth accompany mankind,
Hath look'd on no religion scornfully
  That men did ever find.

MATTHEW ARNOLD (1822–1888)
Progress

The world is waiting for a universal faith that can be believed. God's eternal presence and power, the God who is universal Love, is the truth we need as individuals, as people, and as the world.

NELS F. S. FERRE (1908–1971)
Know Your Faith

O thou who art! Ecclesiastes names Thee the Almighty; Maccabee names Thee Creator; the Epistle to the Ephesians names Thee Liberty; Baruch names Thee Immensity; the Psalms name Thee Wisdom and Truth; John names Thee Light; the Book of Kings names Thee Lord; Exodus calls Thee Providence; Leviticus, Holiness; Esdras, Justice; Creation calls Thee God; man names Thee Father; but Solomon names Thee Compassion, and that is the most beautiful of all Thy names.

VICTOR HUGO (1802–1885)
Les Misérables

A thousand creeds have come and gone
But what is that to you or me?
Creeds are but branches of a tree
The root of love lives on and on.

ELLA WHEELER WILCOX (1850–1919)
Creeds

I do not believe in a self-naming of God, a self-definition of God before men. The Word of revelation is *I am that I am.* That which reveals is that which reveals. The eternal source of strength streams, the eternal contact persists, the eternal voice sounds forth, and nothing more.

MARTIN BUBER (1878–1965)
I and Thou

There are as many ways to God as souls;
As many as the breaths of Adam's sons.

The Hadith

It has always struck me that to call the Unknowable "God" is a masterpiece of confused thinking: any other name would fit as well, and no name is really possible.

SIR HENRY JONES (1852–1922)
A Faith That Enquires

The symbol "God" may be used to denote all the gods of all the faiths taken together, not pantheistically, but as a free, federal union acknowledging, respecting, and conserving their individualities but orchestrating their functions in such wise that the faithful of any may feel assurance of help in need from the faithful of every other.

HORACE M. KALLEN (1882–1972)
This Is My Faith

We have in the Veda the invocations Dyas-pitar, the Greek Zeuspater, the Latin Jupiter; and that means in all three languages what it meant before these three languages were torn asunder—it means the Heaven-Father.

MAX MÜLLER (1823–1900)
Life and Letters

Men felt God long before they defined Him or described Him—a strange Reality deeper than the senses. The Pacific Islanders called it *Mana*. It is foolish to say, as did Reginald Heber in the hymn, that "the heathen in his blindness bows down to wood and stone." He does not. He never did. He bows down to the mysterious something, for him incarnate in the wood and stone.

BERNARD IDDINGS BELL (1886–1958)
Beyond Agnosticism

Like every other term that points to an enduring reality, the word God is in process of constant redefinition, and to this redefinition each man's life, and not least his life of prayer, has its contribution to make.

WILLIAM ADAMS BROWN (1865–1943)
The Life of Prayer in a World of Science

Truly, there probably is no greater miracle in man's entire intellectual history than that disclosed by this sentence. Here, a primeval language, emerging without

any philosophical concepts, stammers the most profound word of any philosophy. God's name, it says, is "I am that I am." God is the One Who Is. God is the I that signifies being as such.

HERMANN COHEN (1842–1918)
Jewish Writings

We are forced, in order some way to speak of God, to use a great number of names, saying that He is good, wise, omnipotent, true, just, holy, infinite, immortal, invisible—and certainly we speak truly; God is all this together, because he is more than all this.

SAINT FRANCIS OF SALES (1567–1622)
Treatise

We may call it spirituality, enthusiasm, spontaneity, outlook, insight,—many names will do,—but what we mean by all of them is essentially the same. It is the power to see the element of eternal principles in which things live,—to see the way in which each fact and act is a true wave on the great ocean of infinity, to see all life full of the life of God,—and so to lose the sense of hardness and separateness in the things which happen and things we do.

PHILLIPS BROOKS (1835–1893)
The More Abundant Life

There is no race so wild and untamed as to be ignorant of the existence of God.

MARCUS TULLIUS CICERO (106–43 B.C.)
De Natura Deorem

The creeds of the Churches have gradually to pass into the universal religion of reason, and so into a moral, that is, a Divine, community on earth.

IMMANUEL KANT (1724–1804)
Religion Within the Limits of Pure Reason

Heaven is large, and affords space for all modes of love and fortitude.

RALPH WALDO EMERSON (1803–1882)
Essays, First Series

Although the tongue of God is busy speaking through all things, yet in order to speak to the deaf ears of many among us, it is necessary for Him to speak through the lips of man. He has done this all through the history of man, every great teacher of the past having been this Guiding Spirit living the life of God in human guise. In other words, their human guise consists of various coats worn by the same person, who appeared to be different in each. Shiva, Buddha, Rama, Krishna on the one side, Abraham, Moses, Jesus, Mohammad on the other; and many more, known or unknown to history, always one and the same person.

HAZRAT INAYAT KHAN (died 1927)
The Sufi Message

While this City of God is in exile on earth, it enrolls its citizens from men of all nations and tongues. It does not worry about differences in culture, laws and ways of life.

SAINT AUGUSTINE (354–430)
The City of God

Beyond doubt, the worshipper of God shows ignorance when he criticizes others on account of their beliefs. If he understood the saying of Junayd, "The color of the water is the color of the vessel containing it," he would not interfere with the beliefs of others, but would perceive God in every form and in every belief.

IBN ARABI (1165–1240)
Gems of Philosophy

Whoever performs devotional exercises, in the belief that there is but one God, is bound to attain Him, no matter in what aspect, name or manner he is worshipped.

SRI RAMAKRISHNA (1834–1886)
Sayings

There is no expeditious road
To pack and label men for God,
And save them by the barrel-load.
Some may perchance, with strange
    surprise,
Have blundered into Paradise.

FRANCIS THOMPSON (1859–1907)
A Judgment in Heaven

Theist and Atheist: the fight between them is as to whether God shall be called God or shall have some other name.

SAMUEL BUTLER (1835–1902)
Note-Books

I call that mind free which sets no bounds to its love, which is not imprisoned in itself or in a sect, which recognizes in all human beings the image of God and the rights of his children, which delights in virtue and sympathizes with suffering wherever they are seen, which conquers pride, anger and sloth, and offers itself up a willing victim to the cause of mankind.

WILLIAM ELLERY CHANNING (1780–1842)
Sermons

Because He that is praised is, in fact, One,
In this respect all religions are one
    religion.

JALAL-UD-DIN RUMI (1207–1273)
The Masnawi

In the tablet of the universe there is no
    letter save thy Name,
By what name, then, shall we invoke
    thee?   JAMI (1414–1492)
The Beharistan

There is an eternal, most powerful and most knowing Being; which whether any one will please to call God, it matters not.

JOHN LOCKE (1632–1704)
Of Our Knowledge of the Existence of God

There is but one possible way for man to attain this salvation, of life of God in the soul. There is not one for the Jew, another for a Christian and a third for the heathen. No, God is one, human nature is

one, salvation is one, and the way to it is one; that is the desire of the soul turned to God.   WILLIAM LAW (1686–1761)
The Spirit of Prayer

It is certain that in one point all the nations of the earth, and all religions agree —all believe in a God; the things in which they disagree are the redundancies annexed to that belief; and therefore, if ever a universal religion should prevail, it will not be by believing anything new, but in getting rid of the redundancies, and believing as man believed at first. Adam, if ever there was such a man, was created a Deist; but in the meantime let every man follow, as he has a right to do, the religion and worship he prefers.

THOMAS PAINE (1737–1809)
The Age of Reason

The notion that God continually watches over the creation and all of its contents is one very dear to mankind. It appears in all forms of conscious religion. The worshipper of a fetish regards his bit of wood or amulet as a special providence working magically and exceptionally for his good alone. Polytheism is only the splitting up of the idea of God into a multitude of special providences, each one a sliver of deity. Thus man has parcelled out the glorious name! The Catholic invokes his patron saint, who is only a rude symbol and mint-mark of that Providence which is always at hand. Pantheism puts a Providence in every blade of grass, in each atom of matter. In virtue of the functions of providence ascribed to God, He is called by various names.

THEODORE PARKER (1810–1860)
Theism, Atheism and the Popular Theology

A study of comparative religion gives insight into the values of the various faiths, values which transcend their different symbols and creeds and in transcending penetrate to the depths of the spiritual consciousness where the symbols and formulas shrink into insignificance.

SARVEPALLI RADHAKRISHNAN (1888–1975)
East and West: Some Reflections

All religion, all life, all art, all expression come down to this: to the effort of the human soul to break through its barrier of loneliness, of intolerable loneliness, and make some contact with another seeking soul, or with what all souls seek, which is (by any name) God.

DON MARQUIS (1878–1937)
Chapters for the Orthodox

The Humble, Meek, Merciful, Just, Pious and Devout Souls, are everywhere of one Religion; and when Death has taken off the Mask, they will know one another, 'tho the divers Liveries they wear here make them Strangers.

WILLIAM PENN (1644–1718)
Some Fruits of Solitude

Ever since men have taken it into their heads to make the Deity speak, every people make him speak in their own way, and say what they like best. Had they listened only to what the Deity hath said to their hearts, there would have been but one religion on earth.

JEAN JACQUES ROUSSEAU (1712–1778)
Emile

To suppose that God Almighty has confined his goodness to this world to the exclusion of all others, is much to the idle fancies of some individuals, and that they, and those of their communion of faith, are the favorites of heaven, exclusively; but these are narrow and bigoted conceptions, which are degrading to a rational nature, and utterly unworthy of God of

whom we should form the most exalted ideas. ETHAN ALLEN (1738–1789)
Reason, the Only Oracle of Man

The charm of study is in finding the agreements, the identities in all religions of man.

RALPH WALDO EMERSON (1803–1882)
Speeches

I care not what terms you may use, be it Kindly Light, Providence, the Over-Soul, Omnipotence, or whatever term may be most convenient, so long as we are agreed in regard to the great central fact itself. God then fills the universe alone, so that all is from Him and in Him, and there is nothing that is outside.

WILLIAM JAMES (1842–1910)
The Varieties of Religious Experience

God will not seek thy race, nor will he ask thy birth; alone he will demand of thee what hast thou done on earth.

Persian Proverb

The church of the Lord is spread over the whole globe, and thus is universal; and all those are in it who have lived in the good of charity according to their religious belief.

EMANUEL SWEDENBORG (1688–1772)
Heaven and Hell

O God, in every temple I see people that
  see thee,
And in every longing I hear spoken,
  people praise thee.
ALFRED LORD TENNYSON (1809–1892)
Akbar's Dream

If someone wants to recite your Ten Commandments without servile fear, Lord God, but does not keep the one he is about to utter, this is not true love. Many may call you Father, but he who does not take me for a brother speaks the stern words with a weak spirit. We are all made of the same substance; if someone found naked bones from which worms had devoured the flesh, who could then discern the servant from the master? Not even having known them well in life would help. Christians, Jews, and heathens all serve Him who upholds every living wondrous thing.

WALTHER VON DER VOGELWEIDE (1170–1230)
Kreuzlied

There is a principle which is pure, placed in the human mind, which in different places and ages hath had different names; it is however pure and proceeds from God. It is deep and inward, confined to no forms of religion nor excluded from any, where the heart stands in perfect sincerity. In whomsoever this takes root and grows, of what nation soever, they become brethren, in the best sense of that expression. JOHN WOOLMAN (1720–1772)
Journal

The Supreme Critic on the errors of the past and the present, and the only prophet of that which must be, is that great nature in which we rest as the earth lies in the soft arms of the atmosphere; that Unity, that Over-Soul, within which every man's particular being is contained and made one with all other.

RALPH WALDO EMERSON (1803–1882)
The Over-Soul

There is a God who laughs at the
  damasked cloths
Of altars, at incense and at the large
  golden chalices,
Who during the lull of the hosannahs
  falls asleep
And awakens when mothers rise up
In anguish, weeping under their dark old
  bonnets
And give him the large penny tied in
  their kerchiefs.
ARTHUR RIMBAUD (1854–1891)
Evil

The One Reality the learned speak of in many ways.

The Rig-Veda

The Master said: Great indeed was Yao as sovereign!
How sublime was he! There is no greatness like that of Heaven,
And only Yao corresponded to it. How vast was this virtue!
The people could find no name for it.

CONFUCIUS (551–479 B.C.)
Analects

I am the same to all mankind. They who serve other gods with a firm belief, in doing so involuntarily worship me. I am he who partaketh of all worship, and I am their reward. I am in them, and they in me.

The Bhagavad Gita

What we have in the world is not religion, but *religions*. In its nature, religion is universal and one; yet everywhere it is local, partisan, plural. Followers of Moses, Confucius, Buddha, Jesus, Sankaracharya, Mohammed, find themselves for the most part in separate camps. Is this a normal situation, or an historical accident which now, in the interest of world order, requires a remedy?

WILLIAM ERNEST HOCKING (1873–1966)
Living Religions and a World Faith

Many religions have spread inspiring hope upon earth, but one Faith has been their tree, just as good will is the one roof of all truly beneficent activities. It has crossed my mind that religion may perhaps be man's despair in not finding God, while faith is hope—God's searching for man.

HELEN KELLER (1880–1968)
The Open Door

Who can sing Him, who appeareth to be far, but is known to be near. Who can sing Him, who is all-seeing and omnipresent?

In describing Him there would never be an end. Millions of men give millions upon millions of descriptions of Him, but they fail to describe Him.

GURU NANAK (1469–1539)
The Japji

As one can ascend to the top of a house by means of a ladder or a bamboo or a staircase or a rope, so divers are the ways and means to approach God, and every religion in the world shows one of these ways.

SRI RAMAKRISHNA (1834–1886)
Sayings

The less determinate the names are, and the more universal and absolute they are, the more properly are they applied to God. Hence Damascene says that, *He who is,* is the principal of all names applied to God; for comprehending all in itself, it contains existence itself as an infinite and indeterminate sea of substance. By any other name some mode of substance is determined, whereas this name, *He who is,* determines no mode of being but is determinate to all; and therefore it denominates the infinite ocean of substance.

SAINT THOMAS AQUINAS (1225–1274)
Summa Theologica

It seems that all men, free from prejudice, who know something of more than one religion, recognize, as does Sir Edwin Arnold, that the great faiths are "Sisters," or as Arthur Lillie says, that "Buddha and Christ taught much the same doctrine."

RICHARD M. BUCKE (1837–1902)
Cosmic Consciousness

Monism stands upon the principle that all the different truths are but so many different aspects of one and the same truth.

PAUL CARUS (1852–1919)
The Point of View

Every person, of whatever religious denomination he may be, is a Deist in the first

article of his Creed. Deism, from the Latin word *deus*, God, is the belief in a God, and this belief is the first article of every man's creed.
THOMAS PAINE (1737–1809)
Prospect Papers

The Word Om is the Imperishable; all this its manifestation. Past, present, future —everything is Om. Whatever transcends the three divisions of time, that too is Om.
The Upanishads

The Great Spirit, whom all the wild and untaught nations of the earth still seek after, and feel and adore. Even among the most savage tribes, how elevated does poetry and sentiment become through the all-pervading feeling of this infinite invisible Spirit!
JOHANN GOTTFRIED HERDER (1744–1803)
The Spirit of Hebrew Poetry

Because he has set his love upon Me, therefore I will deliver him; I will set him on high, because he has known My name.
The Old Testament
Psalms 91:14

The One Universal God does not require one universal church in which to be worshipped, but one universal devotion.
ABBA HILLEL SILVER (1893–1963)
Sermons

Moses conceived the Deity as a Being who has always existed, does exist, and always will exist, and he therefore called him Jehovah, which in Hebrew signifies these three phases.
BENEDICT SPINOZA (1632–1677)
Theologico-Political Treatise

There are innumerable definitions of God, because His manifestations are innumerable.
MOHANDAS K. GANDHI (1869–1948)
Autobiography

In the adorations and benedictions of righteous men
The praises of all the prophets are kneaded together.
All their praises are mingled into one stream,
All the vessels are emptied into one ewer.
Because He that is praised is, in fact, only One.
In this respect all religions are only one religion.
Because all praises are directed toward God's Light,
These varied forms and figures are borrowed from it.
JALUL-UD-DIN RUMI (1207–1273)
The Masnawi

I accept all the religions that were in the past and worship with them all; I worship God with every one of them, in whatever form they worship Him. . . . The Bible, the Vedas, the Koran, and all other sacred books are so many pages, and an infinite number of pages remain to be unfolded. I shall leave my heart open for all of them.
SWAMI VIVEKANANDA (1863–1902)
The Universal Gospel

Among the ideas which form the philosopher's stock in trade, that of God is one of the oldest and most persistent. "God" is the name he gives to the ultimate reality, however that reality may be defined. Whether conceived as spirit or as matter, or as a mysterious substance having the attributes of both, whether immanent reason, moral personality, or blind, unconscious will, God is the basic fact in the philosopher's universe of discourse, the ultimate boundary beyond which his thought cannot go.
WILLIAM ADAMS BROWN (1865–1943)
Beliefs That Matter

The Creator has many and diverse
    names.
Choose the name that comes to mind;
Thus do the saints practice remembrance.

DADU (1554–1603)
The Bani

    A sun but dimly seen
Here, till the mortal morning mists of
    earth
Fade in the noon of heaven, when creed
    and race
Shall bear false witness, each of each, no
    more,
But find their limits by that larger light,
And overstep them, moving easily
Thro' after-ages in the love of Truth,
The truth of Love.

ALFRED LORD TENNYSON (1809–1892)
Akbar's Dream

This life of the five senses, life in the
material world, is not all; it is only a small
portion, and merely superficial. Behind
and beyond is the Infinite; some people
call it God, some Allah, some Jehovah,
Jove, and so on. The Vedantist calls it
Brahman.

SWAMI VIVEKANANDA (1863–1902)
Jnana-Yoga

The object of all religions is alike. All
men seek their beloved; and all the world
is love's dwelling: why talk of a mosque or
a church? HAFIZ (14th century)
The Diwan

The communion of the soul with God
has found the same expression whether
the mystic is a Neoplatonic philosopher
like Plotinus, a Mohammedan Sufi, a Catholic monk, or a Quaker.

WILLIAM RALPH INGE (1860–1954)
Freedom, Love and Truth

Let men know what is divine; let them
know; that is all. If a Greek is stirred to the
remembrance of God by the art of Phidias,
an Egyptian by paying worship to animals,
another man by a river, another by fire—
I have no anger for their divergences; only
let them know, let them love, let them remember.

MAXIMUS OF TYRE (2nd century)
Discourses

The chief hurt of a sect is this, that it
takes itself to be necessary to the truth,
whereas the truth is only then found when
it is known to be of no sect but as free and
universal as the goodness of God and as
common to all names and nations as the
air and light of this world.

WILLIAM LAW (1686–1761)
The Way to Divine Knowledge

Lead Thou me God, Law, Reason, Duty,
    Life!
All names for Thee alike are vain and
    hollow—

JOHN ADDINGTON SYMONDS (1840–1893)
An Invocation

Some contemplate one name and some
another. Which of these is the best? All are
eminent clues to the transcendent, immortal, unembodied Brahman; these names
are to be contemplated, lauded and at last
denied. For by them one rises higher and
higher in these worlds; but when all comes
to the end, there he attains to the unity of
the Person. *The Upanishads*

Whether we continue to use the word of
three letters commencing with G is a matter of minor importance. The word is not
the reality under consideration. The only
point under consideration is whether that
something which we indicate by the word
"God," but which might be indicated by
another word, is essentially involved in

that order of value in which human life must find its fulfillment.

HENRY NELSON WIEMAN (1884–1975)
The Issues of Life

No matter!—so long as the world is the work of eternal goodness, and so long as conscience has not deceived us—to give happiness and to do good, there is our only law, our anchor of salvation, our beacon light, our reason for existing. All religions may crumble away; so long as this survives we have still an ideal, and life is worth living.

HENRI FRÉDÉRIC AMIEL (1821–1881)
Journal Intime

When the soul claims freedom, it is the freedom of its self-development, the self-development of the divine in man in all his being. When it claims equality, what it is claiming is that freedom equally for all and the recognition of the same soul, the same godhead in all human beings.

SRI AUROBINDO (1872–1950)
Works

Where might I find a word to describe the highest! If I took the purest, most sparkling concept from the inner treasure-chamber of the philosophers, I could only capture thereby an unbinding product of thought. I could not capture the presence of Him whom the generations of men have honored and degraded with their awesome living and dying.

MARTIN BUBER (1878–1965)
Eclipse of God

It is true that God is king of all the earth, yet may He be king of a peculiar and chosen nation? For there is no more incongruity therein than that he that hath the general command of the whole army should have withal a peculiar regiment or company of his own.

THOMAS HOBBES (1588–1679)
Leviathan

I used, at one time, to know by heart the thousand names of God which a booklet in Hinduism gives in verse form and which perhaps tens of thousands recite every morning. But nowadays nothing so completely describes my God as Truth.

MOHANDAS K. GANDHI (1869–1948)
Contemporary Indian Philosophy

Perhaps everything we say and do is an attempt, a groping question, to learn God's name. But since He is God and we are creatures of flesh, how can we ever know unless He tells us?

GEORGE ARTHUR BUTTRICK (1892–1979)
Sermons Preached in a University Church

As the fir-tree lifts up itself with a far different need from the need of the palm-tree, so does each man stand before God, and lift up a different humanity to the common Father.

GEORGE MACDONALD (1824–1905)
Unspoken Sermons

The word God is a theology in itself, indivisibly one, inexhaustibly various, from the vastness and simplicity of its meaning.

JOHN CARDINAL NEWMAN (1801–1890)
On the Scope and Nature of University Education

I give immortality to man, for I am
  Truth.
I include and impart all bliss, for I am
  Love.
I give life, without beginning and without
  end, for I am Life.
I am supreme and give all, for I am
  Mind.

I am the substance of all, because *I am that I am.*

MARY BAKER EDDY (1821–1910)
Science and Health

The Shadow cloaked from head to foot,
Who keeps the keys of all the creeds.

ALFRED LORD TENNYSON (1809–1892)
In Memoriam

To make even the slightest reference to God, we have no option but to resort to a large selection of names, saying that he is good, wise, almighty, true, just, holy, infinite, immortal, invisible. Most assuredly, we are speaking the truth: God is all that, but he is more than all that.

SAINT FRANCIS OF SALES (1567–1622)
The Love of God

From Sinai's cliffs it echoed, it breathed
     from Buddha's tree,
It charmed in Athens' market, it hallowed
     Galilee;
The hammerstroke of Luther, the Pilgrim
     seaside prayer,
The oracles of Concord, one holy word
     declare.

WILLIAM CHANNING GANNETT
(1840–1923)
It Sounds Along the Ages

The whole of religion is nothing but the sum of all relations of man to God, apprehended in all the possible ways in which any man can be immediately conscious in his life. In this sense there is but one religion, for it would be but a poverty-stricken and halting life, if all these relations did not exist wherever religion ought to be.

FRIEDRICH SCHLEIERMACHER (1768–1834)
On Religion

The religions of all nations are derived from each nation's different reception of

the Poetic Genius which is everywhere call'd the Spirit of Prophecy.

WILLIAM BLAKE (1757–1827)
All Religions Are One

God is one, as Humanity is one. There is but *one* religion, *one* truth, older than Man. But this is as eternal as God, and its variant revelations in Man and through Man constitute relative and progressive truth, corresponding with the varying phases of history. Holding this for our guiding clue in one hand—*the eternally progressive humanity;* and in the other, for our torch—*God eternally self-revealing and to be revealed by man;* it is no longer possible to stumble and lose one's way amid the history of mankind for that is *the history of God himself* in his relations to us.

F. R. DE LAMENNAIS (1782–1854)
Essai sur l'indifférence en matière de religion

The usual conception of God as one single being outside of the world and behind the world is not the beginning and the end of religion. It is only one manner of expressing God, seldom entirely pure and always inadequate.

FRIEDRICH SCHLEIERMACHER (1768–1834)
On Religion

God's never tied man's salvation to any pattern. Whatever possibilities inhere in any pattern of life inhere in all, because God has given it so and denied it to none. One good way does not conflict with another, for not all people may travel the same road.

MEISTER ECKHART (1260–1327)
Talks of Instruction

The only idea man can affix to the name of God is that of a first cause, the cause of all things. Incomprehensible and difficult as it is for a man to conceive what a first cause is, he arrives at the belief of it from

the tenfold greater difficulty of disbelieving it.　　THOMAS PAINE (1737–1809)
The Age of Reason

It would be completely wrong to ask: So God is nothing but a symbol? Because the next question has to be: a symbol for what? And then the answer would be: for God! God is symbol for God.
　　　　　PAUL TILLICH (1886–1965)
Dynamics of Faith

Let that vain struggle to read the mystery of the Infinite cease to harass us. It is a mystery which, through all ages, we shall only read here a line of, there another line of. Do we not already know that the name of the Infinite is Good, is God?
　　　　　THOMAS CARLYLE (1795–1881)
Characteristics

The great doctrine that God dwells in the human heart in a manner so intimate that it is because he there is present that we exist, so that a man is not so much an individual as a manifestation of the Eternal and Universal One, is no new or peculiar doctrine. It does not belong to any church but to a certain elevation of mind in all churches.
　　RALPH WALDO EMERSON (1803–1882)
Sermons

Followers of a merciful God, if you were cruel of heart; if, in worshipping him whose whole law consisted in loving one's neighbor as oneself, you had burdened this pure and holy law with sophistry and unintelligible disputes; if you had lit the fires of discord for the sake of a new word or a single letter of the alphabet; if you had attached eternal torment to the omission of a few words or ceremonies that other peoples could not know, I should say to you:
　　Transport yourselves with me to the day on which all men will be judged, when God will deal with each according to his works. I see all the dead of former ages and of our own stand in his presence. Are you sure that our Creator and Father will say to the wise and virtuous Confucius, to the lawgiver Solon, to Pythagoras, to Socrates, to Plato, to Epictetus, and to many other model men: "Go, monsters, go and submit to a chastisement infinite in its intensity and duration; your torment shall be as eternal as I."
　　You shrink with horror from such sentiments; and now that they have escaped me, I have no more to say to you.
　　　　　VOLTAIRE (1694–1778)
Philosophical Letters

If you have yourself come to God,
The others too are seeking Him;
However different be the ways
The destination is the same.
　　MOHAMMED TAQUI MIR (1723–1810)
First Diwan

Hatred of cant and doubt of human
　　creeds
May well be felt; the unpardonable sin
Is to deny the word of God within.
　　JOHN GREENLEAF WHITTIER (1807–1892)
The Word

There are various, nay, incredible faiths; why should we be alarmed at any of them? What man believes, God believes.
　　HENRY DAVID THOREAU (1817–1862)
A Week on the Concord and Merrimack Rivers

The lamps are different, but the Light is
　　the same; it comes from Beyond.
If thou keep looking at the lamp, thou art
　　lost: for thence arises the appearance of
　　number and plurality.
Fix thy gaze upon the Light, and thou art
　　delivered from the dualism inherent in
　　the finite body.

O thou who art the kernel of Existence,
   the disagreement between Moslem,
   Zoroastrian and Jew depends on the
   standpoint.

       JALAL-UD-DIN RUMI (1207–1273)
              The Masnawi

When God confused the speech of the builders of the Tower of Babel, He said, "In this world, by reason of the evil inclination, my creatures are at variance; they are divided into seventy tongues. But in the world to come they will all be equal. All with one accord will call upon my name and serve me, as it says, 'For then will I restore to the nations one pure tongue that they may call, all of them, upon the name of the Lord and serve Him unanimously.'"   *The Talmud*

Is not everything Brahman when the name and the form have been removed from it?   *The Vedanta*

Allah and Abhekh are the same; the Purans and the Koran are the same; they are all alike; it is the one God who created all.   GOBIND SINGH (1666–1708)
              Dasam Granth

Who dare express Him?
And who profess Him,
Saying: I believe in Him!
Who, feeling, seeing,
Deny His being,
Saying: I believe Him not!
The All-enfolding, the All-upholding,
Folds and upholds he not
Thee, me, Himself?
Arches not there the sky above us?
Lies not beneath us, firm, the earth?
And rise not, on us shining,
Friendly, the everlasting stars?
Vast as it is, fill with that force thy heart,
And when thou in the feeling wholly
   blessed art,
Call it, then, what thou wilt,—

Call it Bliss! Heart! Love! God!
I have no name to give it!
Feeling is all in all:
The Name is sound and smoke,
Obscuring Heaven's clear glow.

       JOHANN WOLFGANG VON GOETHE
                (1749–1832)
                   Faust

To the universal religion belong only such dogmas as are absolutely required in order to attain obedience to God, and without which such obedience would be impossible. As for the rest, each man—seeing that he is the best judge of his own character—should adopt whatever he thinks best adapted to strengthen his love of justice.

      BENEDICT SPINOZA (1632–1677)
       Theologico-Political Treatise

All the philosophers on earth who had a religion have said at all times: "There is a God, and men must be just." This, then, is the universal religion established in all times and for all men.

         VOLTAIRE (1694–1778)
        Philosophical Dictionary

There is but one God, there is but one true religious experience, but under a multitude of names, under veils and darknesses, God has in this manner come into countless lives.

        H. G. WELLS (1866–1946)
         God the Invisible King

In many forms we try
To utter God's infinity,
But the boundless hath no form,
And the Universal Friend
Doth as far transcend
An angel as a worm.

       RALPH WALDO EMERSON
             (1803–1882)
           The Bohemian Hymn

Thine is the name that is hidden from the wise, the strength that sustains the world over the void, the power to bring to light all that is hidden.

SOLOMON IBN GABIROL (1021–1058)
The Kingly Crown

Let none trouble about caste and creed: whoever calleth on God is called of God.
Hindu Proverb

My brother kneels, so saith Kabir,
To stone and brass in heathen wise,
But in my brother's voice I hear
My own unanswered agonies.
His God is as his fates assign,
His prayer is all the world's—and mine.

RUDYARD KIPLING (1865–1936)
The Prayer

For all people will walk every one in the name of his god, but we will walk in the name of the Lord our God for ever and ever.
The Old Testament
Micah 4:5

Heaven is such that all who have lived well, of whatever religion, have a place there.

EMANUEL SWEDENBORG (1688–1772)
Divine Providence

To the philosopher all sects, all nations, are alike. I like Brahma, Hari, Buddha, the Great Spirit, as well as God.

HENRY DAVID THOREAU (1817–1862)
Journals

Men have addressed their eternal Thou with many names. In singing of Him who was thus named they always had the Thou in mind: the first myths were hymns of praise. Then the names took refuge in the language of It; men were more and more strongly moved to think of and to address their eternal Thou as an It. But all God's names are hallowed, for in them He is not merely spoken about, but also spoken to.

MARTIN BUBER (1878–1965)
I and Thou

It has been my experience that I am always true from my point of view, and often wrong from the point of view of my honest critics. I know that we are both right from our respective points of view. The seven blind men who gave seven different descriptions of the elephant were all right from their respective points of view. I very much like this doctrine of the manyness of reality. It has taught me to judge a Mussulman from his own standpoint and a Christian from his. Formerly I used to resent the ignorance of my opponents. Today I can love them because I am gifted with the eye to see myself as others see me and vice versa.

MOHANDAS K. GANDHI (1869–1948)
Young India

God has granted to every people a prophet in its own tongue.   *The Koran*

Not only the tribe of Levi, but every single individual from among the world's inhabitants whose spirit moved him and whose intelligence gave him the understanding to withdraw from the world in order to stand before God—to serve and minister to Him, to know God—behold! this person has been totally consecrated and God will be his portion and inheritance forever and ever.

MAIMONIDES (1135–1204)
Laws of the Sabbatical Year

Creeds grow so thick along the way,
Their boughs hide God.

LIZETTE WOODWORTH REESE
(1856–1935)
Doubt

My atheism, like that of Spinoza, is true piety towards the universe and denies only gods fashioned by men in their own image, to be servants of their human interests.

GEORGE SANTAYANA (1863–1952)
Soliloquies in England

The builder of heaven has not so ill constructed his creature as that the religion, that is, the public nature, should fall out: the public and the private element, like north and south, like inside and outside, like centrifugal and centripetal, adhere to every soul, and cannot be subdued except the soul is dissipated. God builds his temple in the heart on the ruins of churches and religions.

RALPH WALDO EMERSON (1803–1882)
The Conduct of Life

If a person is united to God and has penetrated into him, it is wholly immaterial in which way he has arrived at this end; and it would be a very useless and perverse task perpetually to renew the memory of the way, instead of living in the thing itself.

JOHANN GOTTLIEB FICHTE (1762–1814)
The Vocation of Man

Pure anthropomorphism reaches its most dangerous form in our inward imaginations of God's character. How the pot has called the kettle black! Man has read his vanities into God, until he has supposed that singing anthems to God's praise might flatter him as it would flatter us. Man has read his cruelties into God, and what in moments of vindictiveness and wrath we would like to do to our enemies, we have supposed the Eternal God would do to his. Man has read religious partisanship into God; he who holds Orion and the Pleiades in his leash, the Almighty and Everlasting God, before whom in the beginning the morning stars sang together, has been conceived as though he were a Baptist or a Methodist, a Presbyterian or an Anglican. Man has read racial pride into God; nations have thought themselves his chosen people above all other children because they seemed so to themselves. The centuries are sick with a god made in man's image, and all the time the real God has been saying, "Thou thoughtest that I was altogether such a one as thyself."

HARRY EMERSON FOSDICK (1878–1969)
Christianity and Progress

Religions commit suicide when they find their inspirations in their dogmas.

ALFRED NORTH WHITEHEAD (1861–1947)
Religion in the Making

All creeds were shouted in my ears
As with the tongues of Babel.

JOHN GREENLEAF WHITTIER (1807–1892)
A Spiritual Manifestation

Very desirable it were since the gates of the East are now opening wide and giving the free commerce of mind with mind, to collect and compare the Bibles of the races for general circulation and careful reading.

BRONSON ALCOTT (1799–1888)
Tablets

The things in civilization we most prize are not of ourselves. They exist by grace of the doings and sufferings of the continuous human community in which we are a link. Ours is the responsibility of conserving, transmitting, rectifying and expanding the heritage of values we have received, that those who come after us may receive it more solid and secure, more widely accessible and more generously shared that we have received it. Here are all the elements for a religious faith that shall not be confined to sect, class or race.

Such a faith has always been implicitly the common faith of mankind.

JOHN DEWEY (1859–1952)
A Common Faith

How thrilling a noble sentiment in the oldest books—in Homer, the Zendavesta, or Confucius! It is a strain of music wafted down to us on the breeze of time, through the aisles of innumerable ages. By its very nobleness it is made near and audible to us.

RALPH WALDO EMERSON (1803–1882)
Journals

He made little of sacraments and priests, because God was so intensely real to him. What should he do with lenses who stood thus full in the torrent of the sunshine?

PHILLIPS BROOKS (1835–1893)
Sermons

Rituals, liturgies, credos, Sinai thunder: I know more or less the history of these; the rise, progress, decline and fall of these. Can thunder from all the thirty-two azimuths, repeated daily for centuries of years, make God's laws more godlike to me? Brother, no.

THOMAS CARLYLE (1795–1881)
Past and Present

If thinking men would have the courage to think for themselves, and to speak what they think, it would be found they do not differ in religious opinions as much as is supposed.

THOMAS JEFFERSON (1743–1826)
Letters

As for the necessity of coining new names for God, it is incomprehensible that philosophy and civilization can be enriched by ceasing to think of God as Life, Truth, Beauty, and Love, and beginning to think of Him as a blind and whirling space-time configuration dancing dizzily in an Einstein universe, plunging forward along a path of which He is ignorant, toward a goal of which He knows nothing whatever.

FULTON J. SHEEN (1895–1979)
The Electronic Christian

Wherever the concept of the world is complete without God, God has become an empty name that one utters for the sake of religion, but which can be dispensed with completely, since it is all the same whether the universe is called "matter" or "spirit."

PAUL TILLICH (1886–1965)
What Is Religion?

There is more than one path up the hill of the Lord. It is only from the top, we may say in a figure, that the paths meet and the view is the same. But true men are all engaged upon the same quest.

WILLIAM RALPH INGE (1860–1954)
Sermons

Forgive, O Lord, our severing ways,
The separate altars that we raise,
The varying tongues that mar Thy
praise!

Suffice it now. In time to be
Shall one great temple rise to Thee,
Thy church our broad humanity.

JOHN GREENLEAF WHITTIER (1807–1892)
Religious Poems

Sublime and Living Will, named by no name, compassed by no thought! I may well raise my soul to Thee, for Thou and I are not divided.

JOHANN GOTTLIEB FICHTE (1762–1814)
The Vocation of Man

Well, I dreamed
That stone by stone I rear'd a sacred
fane,
A temple, neither Pagoda, Mosque, nor
Church,
But loftier, simpler, always open-door'd

To every breath from heaven, and Truth
and Peace
And Love and Justice came and dwelt
therein.
ALFRED LORD TENNYSON (1809–1892)
Akbar's Dream

So long as the word God endures in a
language it will direct the eyes of men upward. It is with the Eternal, even as the
sun, which, if but its smallest part can
shine uneclipsed, prolongs the day and
gives its rounded image in the dark chamber. JEAN PAUL F. RICHTER (1763–1825)
Levana

Whatever form any worshipper wishes
to worship with faith, to that form I render
his faith steady. Possessed of that faith he
seeks to propitiate that form and obtains
from it those beneficial things which he
desires, really given by me.
The Bhagavad Gita

In the image of God there is no coercion, but rather free, eager service of love,
just as a limb of the body or a branch of
the tree gladly serves the other members.
JACOB BOEHME (1575–1624)
Aurora

Whatever creed be taught or land be
trod,
Man's conscience is the oracle of God.
GEORGE GORDON, LORD BYRON
(1788–1824)
The Island

The Old Men studied magic in the
flowers,
And human fortunes in astronomy,
And an omnipotence in chemistry,
Preferring things to names, for these
were men,
Were unitarians of the united world,
And, wheresoever their clear eye-beams
fell,

They caught the footprints of the *same*.
RALPH WALDO EMERSON (1803–1882)
Blight

He is one: there is no second.
Rama, Khuda, Sakti, Siva, are one:
Tell me, pray, how will you distinguish
them?
By the One name I hold fast.
KABIR (1440–1518)
Songs

Take tight hold of Allah's ropes all together. And do not part in sects.
The Koran

Let each one follow zealously his uncor-
rupted, unprejudiced love! Let each one
of you vie in competition to bring to the
daylight the power of the stone in his ring!
Assist that power by gentleness, by heart-
felt peaceability, by charity, by fervent devotion to God.
GOTTHOLD EPHRAIM LESSING (1729–1781)
Nathan the Wise

It is Thou who art sought in various
ways in the different religions and art
called by different names. Be merciful and
reveal Thy countenance, and salvation will
come to all peoples. When Thou doest so
by mercy, the sword and envious hatred
and all evil shall end, and all will see that
there is only one religion in the manifold
religious customs.
NICHOLAS OF CUSA (1401–1464)
Pace Seu Concordantia Fide

The word God is a theology in itself, indivisibly one, inexhaustibly various, from
the vastness and simplicity of its meaning.
Admit a God, and you introduce among
the subjects of your knowledge a fact encompassing, closing in upon, absorbing,
every other fact conceivable.
JOHN CARDINAL NEWMAN (1801–1890)
*On the Scope and Nature
of University Education*

I do not understand how people declare themselves to be believers in God, and at the same time think that God has handed over to a little body of men all truth, and that they are the guardians of the rest of humanity.

SWAMI VIVEKANANDA (1863–1902)
The Universal Gospel

Oh, be prepared my soul!
To read the inconceivable, to scan
The million forms of God those stars
  unroll
When, in turn, we show them to a Man.

ALICE MEYNELL (1847–1922)
Christ in the Universe

Of all human and long-existent beliefs concerning religion, that one seems to me to be most probable and most justifiable which recognises God as a power incomprehensible, source and preserver of all things; all goodness, all perfection, receiving and accepting in good part the honor and reverence which human beings render him under whatever form, under whatever name, and in whatever manner it may be.

MICHEL EYQUEM DE MONTAIGNE
(1533–1592)
Apology for Raimond Sebond

Index of Authors' Names and Titles

Index of Selected Subjects